ESSAYS ON
EDUCATION
AND
KINDRED SUBJECTS

ESSAYS ON EDUCATION AND KINDRED SUBJECTS

HERBERT SPENCER,
CHARLES WILLIAM ELIOT

ISBN: 978-93-89560-69-5

Published: 1911

LECTOR HOUSE LLP
E-MAIL: lectorpublishing@gmail.com

HERBERT SPENCER

Born at Derby in 1820, the son of a teacher, from whom he received most of his education. Obtained employment on the London and Birmingham Railway. After the strike of 1846 he devoted himself to journalism, and in 1848 was sub-editor of The Economist.

He died in 1903.

ESSAYS ON EDUCATION AND KINDRED SUBJECTS

BY

HERBERT SPENCER

INTRODUCTION BY CHARLES W. ELIOT

1911

INTRODUCTION

The four essays on education which Herbert Spencer published in a single volume in 1861 were all written and separately published between 1854 and 1859. Their tone was aggressive and their proposals revolutionary; although all the doctrines—with one important exception—had already been vigorously preached by earlier writers on education, as Spencer himself was at pains to point out. The doctrine which was comparatively new ran through all four essays; but was most amply stated in the essay first published in 1859 under the title "What Knowledge is of Most Worth?" In this essay Spencer divided the leading kinds of human activity into those which minister to self-preservation, those which secure the necessaries of life, those whose end is the care of offspring, those which make good citizens, and those which prepare adults to enjoy nature, literature, and the fine arts; and he then maintained that in each of these several classes, knowledge of science was worth more than any other knowledge. He argued that everywhere throughout creation faculties are developed through the performance of the appropriate functions; so that it would be contrary to the whole harmony of nature "if one kind of culture were needed for the gaining of information, and another kind were needed as a mental gymnastic." He then maintained that the sciences are superior in all respects to languages as educational material; they train the memory better, and a superior kind of memory; they cultivate the judgment, and they impart an admirable moral and religious discipline. He concluded that "for discipline, as well as for guidance, science is of chiefest value. In all its effects, learning the meaning of things is better than learning the meaning of words." He answered the question "what knowledge is of most worth?" with the one word—science.

This doctrine was extremely repulsive to the established profession of education in England, where Latin, Greek, and mathematics had been the staples of education for many generations, and were believed to afford the only suitable preparation for the learned professions, public life, and cultivated society. In proclaiming this doctrine with ample illustration, ingenious argument, and forcible reiteration, Spencer was a true educational pioneer, although some of his scientific contemporaries were really preaching similar doctrines, each in his own field.

The profession of teaching has long been characterised by certain habitual convictions, which Spencer undertook to shake rudely, and even to deride. The first of these convictions is that all education, physical, intellectual, and moral, must be authoritative, and need take no account of the natural wishes, tendencies, and motives of the ignorant and undeveloped child. The second dominating conviction is that to teach means to tell, or show, children what they ought to see, believe, and utter. Expositions by the teacher and books are therefore the true means of education. The third and supreme conviction is that the method of education which produced the teacher himself and the contemporary or earlier scholars, authors, and publicists, must be the righteous and sufficient method. Its fruits demonstrate its soundness, and make it sacred. Herbert Spencer, in the essays included in the present volume, assaulted all three of these firm convictions. Accordingly, the ideas on education which he put forth more than fifty years ago have penetrated educational practice very slowly—particularly in England; but they are now coming to prevail in most civilised countries, and they will prevail more and more. Through him, the thoughts on education of Comenius, Montaigne, Locke, Milton, Rousseau, Pestalozzi, and other noted writers on this neglected subject are at last winning their way into practice, with the modifications or adaptations which the immense gains of the human race in knowledge and power since the nineteenth century opened have shown to be wise.

For teachers and educational administrators it is interesting to observe the steps by which Spencer's doctrines—and especially his doctrine of the supreme value of science—have advanced towards acceptance in practice. In general, the advance has been brought about through the indirect effects of the enormous industrial, social, and political changes of the last fifty years. The first practical step was the introduction of laboratory teaching of one or more of the sciences into the secondary schools and colleges. Chemistry and physics were the commonest subjects selected. These two subjects had been taught from books even earlier; but memorising science out of books is far less useful as training than memorising grammars and vocabularies. The characteristic discipline of science can be imparted only through the laboratory method. The schoolmasters and college faculties who took this step by no means admitted Spencer's contention that science should be the universal staple at all stages of child development. On the contrary, they believed, as most people do to-day, that the mind of the young child cannot grasp the processes and generalisations of science, and that science is no more universally fitted to develop mental power than the classics or mathematics. Indeed, experience during the past fifty years seems to have proved that fewer minds are naturally inclined to scientific study than to linguistic or historical study; so that if some science is to be learnt by everybody, the amount of such study should be limited to acquiring in one or two sciences knowledge of the scientific method in general. So much scientific training is indeed universally desirable; because good training of the senses to observe accurately is universally desirable, and the collecting, comparing, and grouping of many facts teach orderliness in thinking, and lead up to something which Spencer valued highly in education—"a rational explanation of phenomena."

Science having obtained a foothold in secondary schools and colleges, an adequate development of science-teaching resulted from the introduction of options or elections for the pupils among numerous different courses, in place of a curriculum prescribed for all. The elaborate teaching of many sciences was thus introduced. The pupil or student saw and recorded for himself; used books only as helps and guides in seeing, recording, and generalising; proceeded from the known to the unknown; and in short, made numerous applications of the doctrines which pervade all Spencer's writings on education. In the United States these methods were introduced earlier and have been carried farther than in England; but within the last few years the changes made in education have been more extensive and rapid in England than in any other country;—witness the announcements of the new high schools and the re-organised grammar schools, of such colleges as South Kensington, Armstrong, King's, the University College (London), and Goldsmiths', and of the new municipal universities such as Victoria, Bristol, Sheffield, Birmingham, Liverpool, and Leeds. The new technical schools also illustrate the advent of instruction in applied science as an important element in advanced education. Such institutions as the Seafield Park Engineering College, the City Guilds of London Institute, the City of London College, and the Battersea Polytechnic are instances of the same development. Some endowed institutions for girls illustrate the same tendencies, as, for example, the Bedford College for Women and the Royal Holloway College. All these institutions teach sciences in considerable variety, and in the way that Spencer advocated,—not so much because they have distinctly accepted his views, as because modern industrial and social conditions compel the preparation in science of young people destined for various occupations and services indispensable to modern society. The method of the preparation is essentially that which he advocated.

Spencer's propositions to the effect that the study of science was desirable for artisans, artists, and, in general, for people who were to get their livings through various skills of hand and eye, were received with great incredulity, not to say derision—particularly when he maintained that some knowledge of the theory which underlies an art was desirable for manual practitioners of the art; but the changes of the last fifty years in the practice of the arts and trades may be said to have demonstrated that his views were thoroughly sound. The applications of science in the arts and trades have been so numerous and productive, that widespread training in science has become indispensable to any nation which means to excel in the manufacturing industries, whether of large scale or small scale. The extraordinary popularity of evening schools and correspondence schools in the United States rests on the need which young people employed in the various industries of the country feel of obtaining more theoretical knowledge about the physical or chemical processes through which they are earning a livelihood. The Young Men's Christian Associations in the American cities have become great centres of evening instruction for just such young persons. The correspondence schools are teaching hundreds of thousands of young people at work in machine-shops, mills, mines, and factories, who believe that they can advance themselves in their several occupations by supplementing their elementary education with correspondence courses, taken while they are at work earning a livelihood in industries that rest ultimately on applications of science.

Spencer's objection to the constant exercise of authority and compulsion in schools, families, and the State is felt to-day much more widely than it was in 1858, when he wrote his essay on moral education. His proposal that children should be allowed to suffer the natural consequences of their foolish or wrong acts does not seem to the present generation—any more than it did to him—to be applicable to very young children, who need protection from the undue severity of many natural penalties; but the soundness of his general doctrine that it is the true function of parents and teachers to see that children habitually experience the normal consequences of their conduct, without putting artificial consequences in place of them, now commands the assent of most persons whose minds have been freed from the theological dogmas of original sin and total depravity. Spencer did not expect the immediate adoption of this principle; because society as a whole was not yet humane enough. He admitted that the uncontrollable child of ill-controlled adults might sometimes have to be scolded or beaten, and that these barbarous methods might be "perhaps the best preparation such children can have for the barbarous society in which they are presently to play a part." He hoped, however, that the civilised members of society would by and by spontaneously use milder measures; and this hope has been realised in good degree, with the result that happiness in childhood is much commoner and more constant than it used to be. Parents and teachers are beginning to realise that self-control is a prime object in moral education, and that this self-control cannot be practised under a regime of constant supervision, unexplained commands, and painful punishments, but must be gained in freedom. Some large-scale experience with American secondary schools which prepare boys for admission to college has been edifying in this respect. The American colleges, as a rule, do not undertake to exercise much supervision over their students, but leave them free to regulate their own lives in regard to both work and play. Now it is the boys who come from the secondary schools where the closest supervision is maintained that are in most danger of falling into evil ways when they first go to college.

Spencer put very forcibly a valuable doctrine for which many earlier writers on the theory of education had failed to get a hearing—the doctrine, namely, that all instruction should be pleasurable and interesting. Fifty years ago almost all teachers believed that it was impossible to make school-work interesting, or life-work either; so that the child must be forced to grind without pleasure, in preparation for life's grind; and the forcing was to be done by experience of the teacher's displeasure and the infliction of pain. Through the slow effects of Spencer's teaching and of the experience of practical teachers who have demonstrated that instruction can be made pleasurable, and that the very hardest work is done by interested pupils because they are interested, it has gradually come to pass that his heresy has become the prevailing judgment among sensible and humane teachers. The experience of many adults, hard at work in the modern industrial, commercial, and financial world, has taught them that human beings can make their intensest application only to problems in which they are personally interested for one reason or another, and that freemen work much harder than slaves, because they feel within themselves strong motives for exertion which slaves cannot possibly feel. So, many intelligent adults, including many parents and teachers, have come to believe it possible that children will learn to do hard work, both in school and in after life, through the free play of interior motives which appeal to them, and prompt them to persistent exertion.

The justice of Spencer's views about training through pleasurable sensation and achievement in freedom rather than through uninterested work and pain inflicted by despotic government, is well illustrated by the recent improvements in the discipline of reformatories for boys and girls and young men and women. It has been demonstrated that the only useful reformatories are those which diminish the criminal's liberty of action as little as possible, require him to perform productive labour, educate him for a trade or other useful occupation, and offer him the reward of an abridgment of sentence in return for industry and self-control. Repression and compulsion under penalties however severe fail to reform, and often make bad moral conditions worse. Instruction, as much freedom as is consistent with the safety of society, and an appeal to the ordinary motives of emulation, satisfaction in achievement, and the desire to win credit, can, and do, reform.

Many schools, both public and private, have now adopted — in most cases unconsciously — many of Spencer's more detailed suggestions. The laboratory method of instruction, for example, now common for scientific subjects in good schools, is an application of his doctrines of concrete illustration, training in the accurate use of the senses, and subordination of book-work. Many schools realise, too, that learning by heart and, in general, memorising from books are not the only means of storing the mind of a child. They should make parts of a sound education, but should not be used to the exclusion of learning through eye, ear, and hand. Spencer pointed out with much elaboration that children acquire in their early years a vast amount of information exclusively through the incessant use of their senses. To-day teachers know this fact, and realise much better than the teachers of fifty years ago did, that all through the school and college period the pupils should be getting a large part of their new knowledge through the careful application of their own powers of observation, aided, indeed, by books and pictures which record the observations, old and new, of other people. The young human being, unlike the puppy or the kitten, is not confined to the use of his own senses as sources of information and discovery; but can enjoy the fruits of a prodigious width and depth of observation acquired by preceding generations and adult members of his own generation. A recent illustration of this extension of the method of observation in teaching to observations made by other people is the new method of giving moral instruction to school children through photographs of actual scenes which illustrate both good morals and bad, the exhibition of the photographs being accompanied by a running oral comment from the teacher. In this kind of moral instruction it seems to be possible to interest all kinds of children, both civilised and barbarous, both ill-bred and well-bred. The teaching comes through the eye, for the children themselves observe intently the pictures which the lantern throws on the screen; but the striking scenes thus put before them probably lie in most instances quite outside the region of their own experiences.

The essay on "What Knowledge is of Most Worth?" contains a hot denunciation of that kind of information which in most schools used to usurp the name of history. It is enough to say of this part of Spencer's educational doctrine that all the best historical writers since the middle of the nineteenth century seem to have adopted the principles which he declared should govern the writing of history. As a result, the teaching of history in schools and colleges has undergone a profound change. It now deals with the nature and action of government, central, local, and ecclesiastical, with social observances, industrial systems, and the customs which regulate popular life, out-of-doors and indoors. It depicts also the intellectual condition of the nation and the progress it has made in applied science, the fine arts, and legislation, and includes descriptions of the peoples' food, shelters, and amusements. To this result many authors and teachers have contributed; but Spencer's violent denunciation of history as it was taught in his time has greatly promoted this important reform.

Many twentieth-century teachers are sure to put in practice Spencer's exhortation to teach children to draw with pen and pencil, and to use paints and brush. He maintained that the common omission of drawing as an important element in the training of children was in contempt of some of the most obvious of nature's suggestions with regard to the natural development of human faculties; and the better recent practice in some English and American schools verifies his statement; nevertheless some of the best secondary schools in both countries still fail to recognise drawing and painting as important elements in liberal education.

Modern society as yet hardly approaches the putting into effective practice of the sound views which Spencer set forth with great detail in his essay on "Physical Education." The instruction given in schools and colleges on the care of the body and the laws of health is still very meagre; and in certain subjects of the utmost importance no instruction whatever is given, as, for example, in the normal methods of reproduction in plants and animals, in eugenics, and in the ruinous consequences of disregarding sexual purity and honour. In one respect his fundamental doctrine of freedom, carried into the domain of physical exercise, has been extensively adopted in England, on the Continent, and in America. He taught that although gymnastics, military drill, and formal exercises of the limbs are better than nothing, they can never serve in place of the plays prompted by nature. He maintained that "for girls as well as boys the sportive activities to which the instincts impel are essential to bodily welfare." This principle is now being carried into practice not only for school-children, but for operatives in factories, clerks, and other young persons whose occupations are sedentary and monotonous. For all such persons, free plays are vastly better than formal exercises of any sort.

The wide adoption of Spencer's educational ideas has had to await the advent of the new educational administration and the new public interest therein. It awaited the coming of the state university in the United States and of the city university in England, the establishment of numerous technical schools, the profound modifications made in grammar schools and academies, and the multiplication in both countries of the secondary schools called high schools. In other words, his ideas gradually gained admission to a vast number of new institutions of education, which were created and maintained because both the governments and the nations felt a new sense of responsibility for the training of the future generations. These new agencies have been created in great variety, and the introduction of Spencer's ideas has been much facilitated by this variety. These institutions were national, state, or municipal. They were tax-supported or endowed. They charged tuition fees, or were open to competent children or adults without fee. They undertook to meet alike the needs of the individual and the needs of the community; and this undertaking involved the introduction of many new subjects of instruction and many new methods. Through their variety they could be sympathetic with both individualism and collectivism. The variety of instruction offered is best illustrated in the strongest American universities, some of which are tax-supported and some endowed. These universities maintain a great variety of courses of instruction in subjects none of which was taught with the faintest approach to adequacy in American universities sixty years ago; but in making these extensions the universities have not found it necessary to reduce the instruction offered in the classics and mathematics. The traditional cultural studies are still provided; but they represent only one programme among many, and no one is compelled to follow it. The domination of the classics is at an end; but any student who prefers the traditional path to culture, or whose parents choose that path for him, will find in several American universities much richer provisions of classical instruction than any university in the country offered sixty years ago. The present proposals to widen the influence of Oxford University do not mean, therefore, that the classics, history, and philosophy are to be taught less there, but only that other subjects are to be taught more, and that a greater number and variety of young men will be prepared there for the service of the nation.

The new public interest in education as a necessary of modern industrial and political life has gradually brought about a great increase in the proportional number of young men and women whose education is prolonged beyond the period of primary or elementary instruction; and this multitude of young people is preparing for a great variety of callings, many of which are new within sixty years, having been brought into being by the extraordinary advances of applied science. The advent of these new callings has favoured the spread of Spencer's educational ideas. The recent agitation in favour of what is called vocational training is a vivid illustration of the wide acceptance of his arguments. Even the farmers, their farmhands, and their children must nowadays be offered free instruction in agriculture; because the public, and especially the urban public, believes that by disseminating better methods of tillage, better seed, and appropriate manures, the yield of the farms can be improved in quality and multiplied in quantity. In regard to all material interests, the free peoples are acting on the principle that science is the knowledge of most worth. Spencer's doctrine of natural consequences in place of artificial penalties, his view that all young people should be taught how to be wise parents and good citizens, and his advocacy of instruction in public and private hygiene, lie at the roots of many of the philanthropic and reformatory movements of the day.

On the whole, Herbert Spencer has been fortunate among educational philosophers. He has not had to wait so long for the acceptance of his teachings as Comenius, Montaigne, or Rousseau waited. His ideas have been floated on a prodigious tide of industrial and social change, which necessarily involved wide-spread and profound educational reform.

This introduction deals with Spencer's four essays on education; but in the present volume are included three other famous essays written by him during the same period (1854-59) which produced the essays on education. All three are germane to the educational essays, because they deal with the general law of human progress, with the genesis of that science which Spencer thought to be the knowledge of most worth, and with the origin and function of music, a subject which he maintained should play an important part in any scheme of education.

CHARLES W. ELIOT.

SELECT BIBLIOGRAPHY

WORKS. *The Proper Sphere of Government*, 1843; *Social Statics*, 1850; *Theory of Population (Westminster Review)*, April 1852; *The Development of Hypothesis (The Leader)*, 20th March 1852; *The Ultimate Laws of Physiology (National Review)*, April 1857; *Essays, Scientific, Political and Speculative*, 2 vols., 1858-63; *Education*, 1861; *A System of Synthetic Philosophy* (12 vols., 1862-96), made up as follows: *First Principles*, 1862; *Principles of Biology*, 2 vols., 1864-7; *Principles of Psychology*, 2 vols., 1870-2; *Principles of Sociology*, 3 vols., 1876-96; *Ceremonial Institutions*, 1879; *Principles of Morality*, 2 vols., 1879-93 (vol. i, part I published as *Data of Ethics*, 1879; part 4 as *Justice*, 1891); *Political Institutions*, 1882. Meanwhile the following works were also published: *The Classification of the Sciences*, 1864; *The Study of Sociology*, 1872; *Descriptive Sociology*, 1873; *The Man versus the State*, 1884; *The Factors of Organic Evolution*, 1887; *The Inadequacy of Natural Selection*, 1893. Spencer's *Autobiography* appeared posthumously, 2 vols., 1904.

COLLECTED EDITION. Nineteen volumes, 1861-1902.

BIOGRAPHY AND CRITICISM. T. Funk-Brentano, *Les Sophistes grecs et les Sophistes contemporains* (Mill and Spencer), 1879; F.H. Collins, *An Epitome of the Synthetic Philosophy*, 1889; H. Sidgwick, *Lectures on the Ethics of Green, Spencer and Martineau*, 1902; 'The Philosophy of Herbert Spencer' (in *The Philosophy of Kant and Other Lectures*, 1905); D. Duncan, *An Introduction to the Philosophy of Spencer*, 1904; *Life and Letters of Herbert Spencer*, 1908; J. Royce, *Herbert Spencer. An Estimate and a Review*, 1904; J.A. Thomson, *Herbert Spencer*, 1906; W.H. Hudson, *Herbert Spencer*, 1916; J. Rumney, *Herbert Spencer's Sociology*, 1934; R.C.K. Ensor, *Some Reflections on Herbert Spencer's Doctrine*, 1946.

ORIGINAL PREFACE

TO
EDUCATION: INTELLECTUAL, MORAL, AND PHYSICAL

The four chapters of which this work consists, originally appeared as four Review-articles: the first in the *Westminster Review* for July 1859; the second in the *North British Review* for May 1854; and the remaining two in the *British Quarterly Review* for April 1858 and for April 1859. Severally treating different divisions of the subject, but together forming a tolerably complete whole, I originally wrote them with a view to their republication in a united form; and they would some time since have thus been issued, had not a legal difficulty stood in the way. This difficulty being now removed, I hasten to fulfil the intention with which they were written.

That in their first shape these chapters were severally independent, is the reason to be assigned for some slight repetitions which occur in them: one leading idea, more especially, reappearing twice. As, however, this idea is on each occasion presented under a new form, and as it can scarcely be too much enforced, I have not thought well to omit any of the passages embodying it.

Some additions of importance will be found in the chapter on Intellectual Education; and in the one on Physical Education there are a few minor alterations. But the chief changes which have been made, are changes of expression: all of the essays having undergone a careful verbal revision.

H.S.

LONDON, *May 1861*

CONTENTS

PART I
ON EDUCATION: INTELLECTUAL, MORAL, AND PHYSICAL

SPENCER'S ESSAYS

WHAT KNOWLEDGE IS OF MOST WORTH?

It has been truly remarked that, in order of time, decoration precedes dress. Among people who submit to great physical suffering that they may have themselves handsomely tattooed, extremes of temperature are borne with but little attempt at mitigation. Humboldt tells us that an Orinoco Indian, though quite regardless of bodily comfort, will yet labour for a fortnight to purchase pigment wherewith to make himself admired; and that the same woman who would not hesitate to leave her hut without a fragment of clothing on, would not dare to commit such a breach of decorum as to go out unpainted. Voyagers find that coloured beads and trinkets are much more prized by wild tribes than are calicoes or broadcloths. And the anecdotes we have of the ways in which, when shirts and coats are given, savages turn them to some ludicrous display, show how completely the idea of ornament predominates over that of use. Nay, there are still more extreme illustrations: witness the fact narrated by Capt. Speke of his African attendants, who strutted about in their goat-skin mantles when the weather was fine, but when it was wet, took them off, folded them up, and went about naked, shivering in the rain! Indeed, the facts of aboriginal life seem to indicate that dress is developed out of decorations. And when we remember that even among ourselves most think more about the fineness of the fabric than its warmth, and more about the cut than the convenience—when we see that the function is still in great measure subordinated to the appearance—we have further reason for inferring such an origin.

It is curious that the like relations hold with the mind. Among mental as among bodily acquisitions, the ornamental comes before the useful. Not only in times past, but almost as much in our own era, that knowledge which conduces to personal well-being has been postponed to that which brings applause. In the Greek schools, music, poetry, rhetoric, and a philosophy which, until Socrates taught, had but little bearing upon action, were the dominant subjects; while knowledge aiding the arts of life had a very subordinate place. And in our own universities and schools at the present moment, the like antithesis holds. We are guilty of something like a platitude when we say that throughout his after-career, a boy, in nine cases out of ten, applies his Latin and Greek to no practical purposes. The remark is trite that in his shop, or his office, in managing his estate or his family, in playing his part as director of a bank or a railway, he is very little aided by this knowledge he took so many years to acquire—so little, that generally the greater part of it drops out of his memory; and if he occasionally vents a Latin quotation, or alludes to some Greek myth, it is less to throw light on the topic in hand than for the sake of effect. If we inquire what is the real motive for giving boys a classical education, we find it to be simply conformity to public opinion. Men dress their children's minds as they do their bodies, in the prevailing fashion. As the Orinoco Indian puts on paint before leaving his hut, not with a view to any direct benefit, but because he would be ashamed to be seen without it; so, a boy's drilling in Latin and Greek is insisted on, not because of their intrinsic value, but that he may not be disgraced by being found ignorant of them—that he may have "the education of a gentleman"—the badge marking a certain social position, and bringing a consequent respect.

This parallel is still more clearly displayed in the case of the other sex. In the treatment of both mind and body, the decorative element has continued to predominate in a greater degree among women than among men. Originally, personal adornment occupied the attention of both sexes equally. In these latter days of civilisation, however, we see that in the dress of men the regard for appearance has in a considerable degree yielded to the regard for comfort; while in their education the useful has of late been trenching on the ornamental. In neither direction has this change gone so far with women. The wearing of earrings, finger-rings, bracelets; the elaborate dressings of the hair; the still occasional use of paint; the immense labour bestowed in making habiliments sufficiently attractive; and the great discomfort that will be submitted to for the sake of conformity; show how greatly, in the attiring of women, the desire of approbation overrides the desire for warmth and convenience. And similarly in their education, the immense preponderance of "accomplishments" proves how here, too, use is subordinated to display. Dancing, deportment, the piano, singing, drawing—what a large space do these occupy! If you ask why Italian and German are learnt, you will find that, under all the sham reasons given, the real reason is, that a knowledge of those tongues is thought ladylike. It is not that the books written in them may be utilised, which they scarcely ever are; but that Italian and German songs may be sung, and that the extent of attainment may bring whispered admiration. The births, deaths, and marriages of kings, and other like historic trivialities, are committed to memory, not because of any direct benefits that can possibly result from knowing them: but because society considers them parts of a good education—because the absence of such knowledge may bring the contempt of others. When we have named reading, writing, spelling, grammar, arithmetic, and sewing, we have named about all the things a girl is taught with a view to their actual uses in life; and even some of these have more reference to the good opinion of others than to immediate personal welfare.

Thoroughly to realise the truth that with the mind as with the body the ornamental precedes the useful, it is requisite to glance at its rationale. This lies in the fact that, from the far past down even to the present, social needs have subordinated individual needs, and that the chief social need has been the control of individuals. It is not, as we commonly suppose, that there are no governments but those of monarchs, and parliaments, and constituted authorities. These acknowledged governments are supplemented by other unacknowledged ones, that grow up in all circles, in which every man or woman strives to be king or queen or lesser dignitary. To get above some and be reverenced by them, and to propitiate those who are above us, is the universal struggle in which the chief energies of life are expended. By the accumulation of wealth, by style of living, by beauty of dress, by display of knowledge or intellect, each tries to subjugate others; and so aids in weaving that ramified network of restraints by which society is kept in order. It is not the savage chief only, who, in formidable war-paint, with scalps at his belt, aims to strike awe into his inferiors; it is not only the belle who, by elaborate toilet, polished manners, and numerous accomplishments, strives to "make conquests;" but the scholar, the historian, the philosopher, use their acquirements to the same end. We are none of us content with quietly unfolding our own individualities to the full in all directions; but have a restless craving to impress our individualities upon others, and in some way subordinate them. And this it is which determines the character of our education. Not what knowledge is of most real worth, is the consideration; but what will bring most applause, honour, respect—what will most conduce to social position and influence—what will be most imposing. As, throughout life, not what we are, but what we shall be thought, is the question; so in education, the question is, not the intrinsic value of knowledge, so much as its extrinsic effects on others. And this being our dominant idea, direct utility is scarcely more regarded than by the barbarian when filing his teeth and staining his nails.

If there requires further evidence of the rude, undeveloped character of our education, we have it in the fact that the comparative worths of different kinds of knowledge have been as yet scarcely even discussed—much less discussed in a methodic way with definite results. Not only is it that no standard of relative values has yet been agreed upon; but the existence of any such standard has not been conceived in a clear manner. And not only is it that the existence of such a standard has not been clearly conceived; but the need for it seems to have been scarcely even felt. Men read books on this topic, and attend lectures on that; decide that their children shall be instructed in these branches of knowledge, and shall not be instructed in those; and all under the guidance of mere custom, or liking, or prejudice; without ever considering the enormous importance of determining in some rational way what things are really most worth learning. It is true that in all circles we hear occasional remarks on the importance of this or the other order of information. But whether the degree of its importance justifies the expenditure of the time needed to acquire it; and whether there are not things of more importance to which such time might be better devoted; are queries which, if raised at all, are disposed of quite summarily, according to personal predilections. It is true also, that now and then, we hear revived the standing controversy respecting the comparative merits of classics and mathematics. This controversy, however, is carried on in an empirical manner, with no reference to an ascertained criterion; and the question at issue is insignificant when compared with the general question of which it is part. To suppose that deciding whether a mathematical or a classical education is the best is deciding what is the proper *curriculum*, is much the same thing as to suppose that the whole of dietetics lies in ascertaining whether or not bread is more nutritive than potatoes!

The question which we contend is of such transcendent moment, is, not whether such or such knowledge is of worth but what is its *relative* worth? When they have named certain advantages which a given course of study has secured them, persons are apt to assume that they have justified themselves; quite forgetting that the adequateness of the advantages is the point to be judged. There is, perhaps, not a subject to which men devote attention that has not *some* value. A year diligently spent in getting up heraldry, would very possibly give a little further insight into ancient manners and morals. Any one who should learn the distances between all the towns in England, might, in the course of his life, find one or two of the thousand facts he had acquired of some slight service when arranging a journey. Gathering together all the small gossip of a county, profitless occupation as it would be, might yet occasionally help to establish some useful fact—say, a good example of hereditary transmission. But in these cases, every one would admit that there was no proportion between the required labour and the probable benefit. No one would tolerate the proposal to devote some years of a boy's time to getting such information, at the cost of much more valuable information which he might else have got. And if here the test of relative value is appealed to and held conclusive, then should it be appealed to and held conclusive throughout. Had we time to master all subjects we need not be particular. To quote the old song:—

> Could a man be secure
> That his day would endure
> As of old, for a thousand long years,
> What things might he know!
> What deeds might he do!
> And all without hurry or care.

"But we that have but span-long lives" must ever bear in mind our limited time for acquisition. And remembering how narrowly this time is limited, not only by the shortness of life, but also still more by the business of life, we ought to be especially solicitous to employ what time we have to the greatest advantage. Before devoting years to some subject which fashion or fancy suggests, it is surely wise to weigh with great care the worth of the results, as compared with the worth of various alternative results which the same years might bring if otherwise applied.

In education, then, this is the question of questions, which it is high time we discussed in some methodic way. The first in importance, though the last to be considered, is the problem—how to decide among the conflicting claims of various subjects on our attention. Before there can be a rational *curriculum*, we must settle which things it most concerns us to know; or, to use a word of Bacon's, now unfortunately obsolete—we must determine the relative values of knowledges.

To this end, a measure of value is the first requisite. And happily, respecting the true measure of value, as expressed in general terms, there can be no dispute. Every one in contending for the worth of any particular order of information, does so by showing its bearing upon some part of life. In reply to the question—"Of what use is it?" the mathematician, linguist, naturalist, or philosopher, explains the way in which his learning beneficially influences action—saves from evil or secures good—conduces to happiness. When the teacher of writing has pointed out how great an aid writing is to success in business—that is, to the obtainment of sustenance—that is, to satisfactory living; he is held to have proved his case. And when the collector of dead facts (say a numismatist) fails to make clear any appreciable effects which these facts can produce on human welfare, he is obliged to admit that they are comparatively valueless. All then, either directly or by implication, appeal to this as the ultimate test.

How to live?—that is the essential question for us. Not how to live in the mere material sense only, but in the widest sense. The general problem which comprehends every special problem is—the right ruling of conduct in all directions under all circumstances. In what way to treat the body; in what way to treat the mind; in what way to manage our affairs; in what way to bring up a family; in what way to behave as a citizen; in what way to utilise those sources of happiness which nature supplies—how to use all our faculties to the greatest advantage of ourselves and others—how to live completely? And this being the great thing needful for us to learn, is, by consequence, the great thing which education has to teach. To prepare us for complete living is the function which education has to discharge; and the only rational mode of judging of an educational course is, to judge in what degree it discharges such function.

This test, never used in its entirety, but rarely even partially used, and used then in a vague, half conscious way, has to be applied consciously, methodically, and throughout all cases. It behoves us to set before ourselves, and ever to keep clearly in view, complete living as the end to be achieved; so that in bringing up our children we may choose subjects and methods of instruction, with deliberate reference to this end. Not only ought we to cease from the mere unthinking adoption of the current fashion in education, which has no better warrant than any other fashion; but we must also rise above that rude, empirical style of judging displayed by those more intelligent people who do bestow some care in overseeing the cultivation of their children's minds. It must not suffice simply to *think* that such or such information will be useful in after life, or that this kind of knowledge is of more practical value than that; but we must seek out some process of estimating their respective values, so that as far as possible we may positively *know* which are most deserving of attention.

Doubtless the task is difficult—perhaps never to be more than approximately achieved. But, considering the vastness of the interests at stake, its difficulty is no reason for pusillanimously passing it by; but rather for devoting every energy to its mastery. And if we only proceed systematically, we may very soon get at results of no small moment.

Our first step must obviously be to classify, in the order of their importance, the leading kinds of activity which constitute human life. They may be naturally arranged into:—1. those activities which directly minister to self-preservation; 2. those activities which, by securing the necessaries of life, indirectly minister to self-preservation; 3. those activities which have for their end the rearing and discipline of offspring; 4. those activities which are involved in the maintenance of proper social and political relations; 5. those miscellaneous activities which fill up the leisure part of life, devoted to the gratification of the tastes and feelings.

That these stand in something like their true order of subordination, it needs no long consideration to show. The actions and precautions by which, from moment to moment, we secure personal safety, must clearly take precedence of all others. Could there be a man, ignorant as an infant of surrounding objects and movements, or how to guide himself among them, he would pretty certainly lose his life the first time he went into the street; notwithstanding any amount of learning he might have on other matters. And as entire ignorance in all other directions would be less promptly fatal than entire ignorance in this direction, it must be admitted that knowledge immediately conducive to self-preservation is of primary importance.

That next after direct self-preservation comes the indirect self-preservation which consists in acquiring the means of living, none will question. That a man's industrial functions must be considered before his parental ones, is manifest from the fact that, speaking generally, the discharge of the parental functions is made possible only by the previous discharge of the industrial ones. The power of self-maintenance necessarily preceding the power of maintaining offspring, it follows that knowledge needful for self-maintenance has stronger claims than knowledge needful for family welfare—is second in value to none save knowledge needful for immediate self-preservation.

As the family comes before the State in order of time—as the bringing up of children is possible before the State exists, or when it has ceased to be, whereas the State is rendered possible only by the bringing up of children; it follows that the duties of the parent demand closer attention than those of the citizen. Or, to use a further argument—since the goodness of a society ultimately depends on the nature of its citizens; and since the nature of its citizens is more modifiable by early training than by anything else; we must conclude that the welfare of the family underlies the welfare of society. And hence knowledge directly conducing to the first, must take precedence of knowledge directly conducing to the last.

Those various forms of pleasurable occupation which fill up the leisure left by graver occupations—the enjoyments of music, poetry, painting, etc.—manifestly imply a pre-existing society. Not only is a considerable development of them impossible without a long-established social union; but their very subject-matter consists in great part of social sentiments and sympathies. Not only does society supply the conditions to their growth; but also the ideas and sentiments they express. And, consequently, that part of human conduct which constitutes good citizenship, is of more moment than that which goes out in accomplishments or exercise of the tastes; and, in education, preparation for the one must rank before preparation for the other.

Such then, we repeat, is something like the rational order of subordination:— That education which prepares for direct self-preservation; that which prepares for indirect self-preservation; that which prepares for parenthood; that which prepares for citizenship; that which prepares for the miscellaneous refinements of life. We do not mean to say that these divisions are definitely separable. We do not deny that they are intricately entangled with each other, in such way that there can be no training for any that is not in some measure a training for all. Nor do we question that of each division there are portions more important than certain portions of the preceding divisions: that, for instance, a man of much skill in business but little other faculty, may fall further below the standard of complete living than one of but moderate ability in money-getting but great judgment as a parent; or that exhaustive information bearing on right social action, joined with entire want of general culture in literature and the fine arts, is less desirable than a more moderate share of the one joined with some of the other. But, after making due qualifications, there still remain these broadly-marked divisions; and it still continues substantially true that these divisions subordinate one another in the foregoing order, because the corresponding divisions of life make one another *possible* in that order.

Of course the ideal of education is—complete preparation in all these divisions. But failing this ideal, as in our phase of civilisation every one must do more or less, the aim should be to maintain *a due proportion* between the degrees of preparation in each. Not exhaustive cultivation in any one, supremely important though it may be—not even an exclusive attention to the two, three, or four divisions of greatest importance; but an attention to all:—greatest where the value is greatest; less where the value is less; least where the value is least. For the average man (not to forget the cases in which peculiar aptitude for some one department of knowledge, rightly makes pursuit of that one the bread-winning occupation)—for the average man, we say, the desideratum is, a training that approaches nearest to perfection in the things which most subserve complete living, and falls more and more below perfection in the things that have more and more remote bearings on complete living.

In regulating education by this standard, there are some general considerations that should be ever present to us. The worth of any kind of culture, as aiding complete living, may be either necessary or more or less contingent. There is knowledge of intrinsic value; knowledge of quasi-intrinsic value; and knowledge of conventional value. Such facts as that sensations of numbness and tingling commonly precede paralysis, that the resistance of water to a body moving through it varies as the square of the velocity, that chlorine is a disinfectant,—these, and the truths of Science in general, are of intrinsic value: they will bear on human conduct ten thousand years hence as they do now. The extra knowledge of our own language, which is given by an acquaintance with Latin and Greek, may be considered to have a value that is quasi-intrinsic: it must exist for us and for other races whose languages owe much to these sources; but will last only as long as our languages last. While that kind of information which, in our schools, usurps the name History—the mere tissue of names and dates and dead unmeaning events— has a conventional value only: it has not the remotest bearing on any of our actions; and is of use only for the avoidance of those unpleasant criticisms which current opinion passes upon its absence. Of course, as those facts which concern all mankind throughout all time must be held of greater moment than those which concern only a portion of them during a limited era, and of far greater moment than those which concern only a portion of them during the continuance of a fashion; it follows that in a rational estimate, knowledge of intrinsic worth must, other things equal, take precedence of knowledge that is of quasi-intrinsic or conventional worth.

One further preliminary. Acquirement of every kind has two values—value as *knowledge* and value as *discipline*. Besides its use for guiding conduct, the acquisition of each order of facts has also its use as mental exercise; and its effects as a preparative for complete living have to be considered under both these heads.

These, then, are the general ideas with which we must set out in discussing a *curriculum*:—Life as divided into several kinds of activity of successively decreasing importance; the worth of each order of facts as regulating these several kinds of activity, intrinsically, quasi-intrinsically, and conventionally; and their regulative influences estimated both as knowledge and discipline.

Happily, that all-important part of education which goes to secure direct self-preservation, is in great part already provided for. Too momentous to be left to our blundering, Nature takes it into her own hands. While yet in its nurse's arms, the infant, by hiding its face and crying at the sight of a stranger, shows the dawning instinct to attain safety by flying from that which is unknown and may be dangerous; and when it can walk, the terror it manifests if an unfamiliar dog comes near, or the screams with which it runs to its mother after any startling sight or sound, shows this instinct further developed. Moreover, knowledge subserving direct self-preservation is that which it is chiefly busied in acquiring from hour to hour. How to balance its body; how to control its movements so as to avoid collisions; what objects are hard, and will hurt if struck; what objects are heavy, and injure if they fall on the limbs; which things will bear the weight of the body, and which not; the pains inflicted by fire, by missiles, by sharp instruments—these, and various other pieces of information needful for the avoidance of death or accident, it is ever learning. And when, a few years later, the energies go out in running, climbing, and jumping, in games of strength and games of skill, we see in all these actions by which the muscles are developed, the perceptions sharpened, and the judgment quickened, a preparation for the safe conduct of the body among surrounding objects and movements; and for meeting those greater dangers that occasionally occur in the lives of all. Being thus, as we say, so well cared for by Nature, this fundamental education needs comparatively little care from us. What we are chiefly called upon to see, is, that there shall be free scope for gaining this experience and receiving this discipline—that there shall be no such thwarting of Nature as that by which stupid schoolmistresses commonly prevent the girls in their charge from the spontaneous physical activities they would indulge in; and so render them comparatively incapable of taking care of themselves in circumstances of peril.

This, however, is by no means all that is comprehended in the education that prepares for direct self-preservation. Besides guarding the body against mechanical damage or destruction, it has to be guarded against injury from other causes—against the disease and death that follow breaches of physiologic law. For complete living it is necessary, not only that sudden annihilations of life shall be warded off; but also that there shall be escaped the incapacities and the slow annihilation which unwise habits entail. As, without health and energy, the industrial, the parental, the social, and all other activities become more or less impossible; it is clear that this secondary kind of direct self-preservation is only less important than the primary kind; and that knowledge tending to secure it should rank very high.

It is true that here, too, guidance is in some measure ready supplied. By our various physical sensations and desires, Nature has insured a tolerable conformity to the chief requirements. Fortunately for us, want of food, great heat, extreme cold, produce promptings too peremptory to be disregarded. And would men habitually obey these and all like promptings when less strong, comparatively few evils would arise. If fatigue of body or brain were in every case followed by desistance; if the oppression produced by a close atmosphere always led to ventilation; if there were no eating without hunger, or drinking without thirst; then would the system be but seldom out of working order. But so profound an ignorance is there of the laws of life, that men do not even know that their sensations are their natural guides, and (when not rendered morbid by long—continued disobedience) their trustworthy guides. So that though, to speak teleologically, Nature has provided efficient safeguards to health, lack of knowledge makes them in a great measure useless.

If any one doubts the importance of an acquaintance with the principles of physiology, as a means to complete living, let him look around and see how many men and women he can find in middle or later life who are thoroughly well. Only occasionally do we meet with an example of vigorous health continued to old age; hourly do we meet with examples of acute disorder, chronic ailment, general debility, premature decrepitude. Scarcely is there one to whom you put the question, who has not, in the course of his life, brought upon himself illnesses which a little information would have saved him from. Here is a case of heart-disease consequent on a rheumatic fever that followed reckless exposure. There is a case of eyes spoiled for life by over-study. Yesterday the account was of one whose long-enduring lameness was brought on by continuing, spite of the pain, to use a knee after it had been slightly injured. And to-day we are told of another who has had to lie by for years, because he did not know that the palpitation he suffered under resulted from overtaxed brain. Now we hear of an irremediable injury which followed some silly feat of strength; and, again, of a constitution that has never recovered from the effects of excessive work needlessly undertaken. While on every side we see the perpetual minor ailments which accompany feebleness. Not to dwell on the pain, the weariness, the gloom, the waste of time and money thus entailed, only consider how greatly ill-health hinders the discharge of all duties—makes business often impossible, and always more difficult; produces an irritability fatal to the right management of children; puts the functions of citizenship out of the question; and makes amusement a bore. Is it not clear that the physical sins—partly our forefathers' and partly our own—which produce this ill-health, deduct more from complete living than anything else? and to a great extent make life a failure and a burden instead of a benefaction and a pleasure?

Nor is this all. Life, besides being thus immensely deteriorated, is also cut short. It is not true, as we commonly suppose, that after a disorder or disease from which we have recovered, we are as before. No disturbance of the normal course of the functions can pass away and leave things exactly as they were. A permanent damage is done—not immediately appreciable, it may be, but still there; and along with other such items which Nature in her strict account-keeping never drops, it will tell against us to the inevitable shortening of our days. Through the accumulation of small injuries it is that constitutions are commonly undermined, and break down, long before their time. And if we call to mind how far the average duration of life falls below the possible duration, we see how immense is the loss. When, to the numerous partial deductions which bad health entails, we add this great final deduction, it results that ordinarily one-half of life is thrown away.

Hence, knowledge which subserves direct self-preservation by preventing this loss of health, is of primary importance. We do not contend that possession of such knowledge would by any means wholly remedy the evil. It is clear that in our present phase of civilisation, men's necessities often compel them to transgress. And it is further clear that, even in the absence of such compulsion, their inclinations would frequently lead them, spite of their convictions, to sacrifice future good to present gratification. But we *do* contend that the right knowledge impressed in the right way would effect much; and we further contend that as the laws of health must be recognised before they can be fully conformed to, the imparting of such knowledge must precede a more rational living—come when that may. We infer that as vigorous health and its accompanying high spirits are larger elements of happiness than any other things whatever, the teaching how to maintain them is a teaching that yields in moment to no other whatever. And therefore we assert that such a course of physiology as is needful for the comprehension of its general truths, and their bearings on daily conduct, is an all-essential part of a rational education.

Strange that the assertion should need making! Stranger still that it should need defending! Yet are there not a few by whom such a proposition will be received with something approaching to derision. Men who would blush if caught saying Iphigénia instead of Iphigenía, or would resent as an insult any imputation of ignorance respecting the fabled labours of a fabled demi-god, show not the slightest shame in confessing that they do not know where the Eustachian tubes are, what are the actions of the spinal cord, what is the normal rate of pulsation, or how the lungs are inflated. While anxious that their sons should be well up in the superstitions of two thousand years ago, they care not that they should be taught anything about the structure and functions of their own bodies—nay, even wish them not to be so taught. So overwhelming is the influence of established routine! So terribly in our education does the ornamental over-ride the useful!

We need not insist on the value of that knowledge which aids indirect self-preservation by facilitating the gaining of a livelihood. This is admitted by all; and, indeed, by the mass is perhaps too exclusively regarded as the end of education. But while every one is ready to endorse the abstract proposition that instruction fitting youths for the business of life is of high importance, or even to consider it of supreme importance; yet scarcely any inquire what instruction will so fit them. It is true that reading, writing, and arithmetic are taught with an intelligent appreciation of their uses. But when we have said this we have said nearly all. While the great bulk of what else is acquired has no bearing on the industrial activities, an immensity of information that has a direct bearing on the industrial activities is entirely passed over.

For, leaving out only some very small classes, what are all men employed in? They are employed in the production, preparation, and distribution of commodities. And on what does efficiency in the production, preparation, and distribution of commodities depend? It depends on the use of methods fitted to the respective natures of these commodities; it depends on an adequate acquaintance with their physical, chemical, or vital properties, as the case may be; that is, it depends on Science. This order of knowledge which is in great part ignored in our school-courses, is the order of knowledge underlying the right performance of those processes by which civilised life is made possible. Undeniable as is this truth, there seems to be no living consciousness of it: its very familiarity makes it unregarded. To give due weight to our argument, we must, therefore, realise this truth to the reader by a rapid review of the facts.

Passing over the most abstract science, Logic, on the due guidance by which, however, the large producer or distributor depends, knowingly or unknowingly, for success in his business-forecasts, we come first to Mathematics. Of this, the most general division, dealing with number, guides all industrial activities; be they those by which processes are adjusted, or estimates framed, or commodities bought and sold, or accounts kept. No one needs to have the value of this division of abstract science insisted upon.

For the higher arts of construction, some acquaintance with the more special division of Mathematics is indispensable. The village carpenter, who lays out his work by empirical rules, equally with the builder of a Britannia Bridge, makes hourly reference to the laws of space-relations. The surveyor who measures the land purchased; the architect in designing a mansion to be built on it; the builder when laying out the foundations; the masons in cutting the stones; and the various artizans who put up the fittings; are all guided by geometrical truths. Railway-making is regulated from beginning to end by geometry: alike in the preparation of plans and sections; in staking out the line; in the mensuration of cuttings and embankments; in the designing and building of bridges, culverts, viaducts, tunnels, stations. Similarly with the harbours, docks, piers, and various engineering and architectural works that fringe the coasts and overspread the country, as well as the mines that run underneath it. And now-a-days, even the farmer, for the correct laying-out of his drains, has recourse to the level—that is, to geometrical principles.

Turn next to the Abstract-Concrete sciences. On the application of the simplest of these, Mechanics, depends the success of modern manufactures. The properties of the lever, the wheel-and-axle, etc., are recognised in every machine, and to machinery in these times we owe all production. Trace the history of the breakfast-roll. The soil out of which it came was drained with machine-made tiles; the surface was turned over by a machine; the wheat was reaped, thrashed, and winnowed by machines; by machinery it was ground and bolted; and had the flour been sent to Gosport, it might have been made into biscuits by a machine. Look round the room in which you sit. If modern, probably the bricks in its walls were machine-made; and by machinery the flooring was sawn and planed, the mantel-shelf sawn and polished, the paper-hangings made and printed. The veneer on the table, the turned legs of the chairs, the carpet, the curtains, are all products of machinery. Your clothing—plain, figured, or printed—is it not wholly woven, nay, perhaps even sewed, by machinery? And the volume you are reading—are not its leaves fabricated by one machine and covered with these words by another? Add to which that for the means of distribution over both land and sea, we are similarly indebted. And then observe that according as knowledge of mechanics is well or ill applied to these ends, comes success or failure. The engineer who miscalculates the strength of materials, builds a bridge that breaks down. The manufacturer who uses a bad machine cannot compete with another whose machine wastes less in friction and inertia. The ship-builder adhering to the old model is out-sailed by one who builds on the mechanically-justified wave-line principle. And as the ability of a nation to hold its own against other nations, depends on the skilled activity of its units, we see that on mechanical knowledge may turn the national fate.

On ascending from the divisions of Abstract-Concrete science dealing with molar forces, to those divisions of it which deal with molecular forces, we come to another vast series of applications. To this group of sciences joined with the preceding groups we owe the steam-engine, which does the work of millions of labourers. That section of physics which formulates the laws of heat, has taught us how to economise fuel in various industries; how to increase the produce of smelting furnaces by substituting the hot for the cold blast; how to ventilate mines; how to prevent explosions by using the safety-lamp; and, through the thermometer, how to regulate innumerable processes. That section which has the phenomena of light for its subject, gives eyes to the old and the myopic; aids through the microscope in detecting diseases and adulterations; and, by improved lighthouses, prevents shipwrecks. Researches in electricity and magnetism have saved innumerable lives and incalculable property through the compass; have subserved many arts by the electrotype; and now, in the telegraph, have supplied us with an agency by which for the future, mercantile transactions will be regulated and political intercourse carried on. While in the details of in-door life, from the improved kitchen-range up to the stereoscope on the drawing-room table, the applications of advanced physics underlie our comforts and gratifications.

Still more numerous are the applications of Chemistry. The bleacher, the dyer, the calico-printer, are severally occupied in processes that are well or ill done according as they do or do not conform to chemical laws. Smelting of copper, tin, zinc, lead, silver, iron, must be guided by chemistry. Sugar-refining, gas-making, soap-boiling, gunpowder-manufacture, are operations all partly chemical; as are likewise those which produce glass and porcelain. Whether the distiller's wort stops at the alcoholic fermentation or passes into the acetous, is a chemical question on which hangs his profit or loss; and the brewer, if his business is extensive, finds it pay to keep a chemist on his premises. Indeed, there is now scarcely any manufacture over some part of which chemistry does not preside. Nay, in these times even agriculture, to be profitably carried on, must have like guidance. The analysis of manures and soils; the disclosure of their respective adaptations; the use of gypsum or other substance for fixing ammonia; the utilisation of coprolites; the production of artificial manures—all these are boons of chemistry which it behoves the farmer to acquaint himself with. Be it in the lucifer match, or in disinfected sewage, or in photographs—in bread made without fermentation, or perfumes extracted from refuse, we may perceive that chemistry affects all our industries; and that, therefore, knowledge of it concerns every one who is directly or indirectly connected with our industries.

Of the Concrete sciences, we come first to Astronomy. Out of this has grown that art of navigation which has made possible the enormous foreign commerce that supports a large part of our population, while supplying us with many necessaries and most of our luxuries.

Geology, again, is a science knowledge of which greatly aids industrial success. Now that iron ores are so large a source of wealth; now that the duration of our coal-supply has become a question of great interest; now that we have a College of Mines and a Geological Survey; it is scarcely needful to enlarge on the truth that the study of the Earth's crust is important to our material welfare.

And then the science of life—Biology: does not this, too, bear fundamentally on these processes of indirect self-preservation? With what we ordinarily call manufactures, it has, indeed, little connection; but with the all-essential manufacture—that of food—it is inseparably connected. As agriculture must conform its methods to the phenomena of vegetal and animal life, it follows that the science of these phenomena is the rational basis of agriculture. Various biological truths have indeed been empirically established and acted upon by farmers, while yet there has been no conception of them as science; such as that particular manures are suited to particular plants; that crops of certain kinds unfit the soil for other crops; that horses cannot do good work on poor food; that such and such diseases of cattle and sheep are caused by such and such conditions. These, and the every-day knowledge which the agriculturist gains by experience respecting the management of plants and animals, constitute his stock of biological facts; on the largeness of which greatly depends his success. And as these biological facts, scanty, indefinite, rudimentary, though they are, aid him so essentially; judge what must be the value to him of such facts when they become positive, definite, and exhaustive. Indeed, even now we may see the benefits that rational biology is conferring on him. The truth that the production of animal heat implies waste of substance, and that, therefore, preventing loss of heat prevents the need for extra food—a purely theoretical conclusion—now guides the fattening of cattle: it is found that by keeping cattle warm, fodder is saved. Similarly with respect to variety of food. The experiments of physiologists have shown that not only is change of diet beneficial, but that digestion is facilitated by a mixture of ingredients in each meal. The discovery that a disorder known as "the staggers," of which many thousands of sheep have died annually, is caused by an entozoon which presses on the brain, and that if the creature is extracted through the softened place in the skull which marks its position, the sheep usually recovers, is another debt which agriculture owes to biology.

Yet one more science have we to note as bearing directly on industrial success—the Science of Society. Men who daily look at the state of the money-market glance over prices current; discuss the probable crops of corn, cotton, sugar, wool, silk; weigh the chances of war; and from these data decide on their mercantile operations; are students of social science: empirical and blundering students it may be; but still, students who gain the prizes or are plucked of their profits, according as they do or do not reach the right conclusion. Not only the manufacturer and the merchant must guide their transactions by calculations of supply and demand, based on numerous facts, and tacitly recognising sundry general principles of social action; but even the retailer must do the like: his prosperity very greatly depending upon the correctness of his judgments respecting the future wholesale prices and the future rates of consumption. Manifestly, whoever takes part in the entangled commercial activities of a community, is vitally interested in understanding the laws according to which those activities vary.

Thus, to all such as are occupied in the production, exchange, or distribution of commodities, acquaintance with Science in some of its departments, is of fundamental importance. Each man who is immediately or remotely implicated in any form of industry (and few are not) has in some way to deal with the mathematical, physical, and chemical properties of things; perhaps, also, has a direct interest in biology; and certainly has in sociology. Whether he does or does not succeed well in that indirect self-preservation which we call getting a good livelihood, depends in a great degree on his knowledge of one or more of these sciences: not, it may be, a rational knowledge; but still a knowledge, though empirical. For what we call learning a business, really implies learning the science involved in it; though not perhaps under the name of science. And hence a grounding in science is of great importance, both because it prepares for all this, and because rational knowledge has an immense superiority over empirical knowledge. Moreover, not only is scientific culture requisite for each, that he may understand the *how* and the *why* of the things and processes with which he is concerned as maker or distributor; but it is often of much moment that he should understand the *how* and the *why* of various other things and processes. In this age of joint-stock undertakings, nearly every man above the labourer is interested as capitalist in some other occupation than his own; and, as thus interested, his profit or loss often depends on his knowledge of the sciences bearing on this other occupation. Here is a mine, in the sinking of which many shareholders ruined themselves, from not knowing that a certain fossil belonged to the old red sandstone, below which no coal is found. Numerous attempts have been made to construct electromagnetic engines, in the hope of superseding steam; but had those who supplied the money understood the general law of the correlation and equivalence of forces, they might have had better balances at their bankers. Daily are men induced to aid in carrying out inventions which a mere tyro in science could show to be futile. Scarcely a locality but has its history of fortunes thrown away over some impossible project.

And if already the loss from want of science is so frequent and so great, still greater and more frequent will it be to those who hereafter lack science. Just as fast as productive processes become more scientific, which competition will inevitably make them do; and just as fast as joint-stock undertakings spread, which they certainly will; so fast must scientific knowledge grow necessary to every one.

That which our school-courses leave almost entirely out, we thus find to be that which most nearly concerns the business of life. Our industries would cease, were it not for the information which men begin to acquire, as they best may, after their education is said to be finished. And were it not for this information, from age to age accumulated and spread by unofficial means, these industries would never have existed. Had there been no teaching but such as goes on in our public schools, England would now be what it was in feudal times. That increasing acquaintance with the laws of phenomena, which has through successive ages enabled us to subjugate Nature to our needs, and in these days gives the common labourer comforts which a few centuries ago kings could not purchase, is scarcely in any degree owed to the appointed means of instructing our youth. The vital knowledge—that by which we have grown as a nation to what we are, and which now underlies our whole existence, is a knowledge that has got itself taught in nooks and corners; while the ordained agencies for teaching have been mumbling little else but dead formulas.

We come now to the third great division of human activities—a division for which no preparation whatever is made. If by some strange chance not a vestige of us descended to the remote future save a pile of our school-books or some college examination papers, we may imagine how puzzled an antiquary of the period would be on finding in them no sign that the learners were ever likely to be parents. "This must have been the *curriculum* for their celibates," we may fancy him concluding. "I perceive here an elaborate preparation for many things; especially for reading the books of extinct nations and of co-existing nations (from which indeed it seems clear that these people had very little worth reading in their own tongue); but I find no reference whatever to the bringing up of children. They could not have been so absurd as to omit all training for this gravest of responsibilities. Evidently then, this was the school-course of one of their monastic orders."

Seriously, is it not an astonishing fact, that though on the treatment of offspring depend their lives or deaths, and their moral welfare or ruin; yet not one word of instruction on the treatment of offspring is ever given to those who will by and by be parents? Is it not monstrous that the fate of a new generation should be left to the chances of unreasoning custom, impulse, fancy—joined with the suggestions of ignorant nurses and the prejudiced counsel of grandmothers? If a merchant commenced business without any knowledge of arithmetic and book-keeping, we should exclaim at his folly, and look for disastrous consequences. Or if, before studying anatomy, a man set up as a surgical operator, we should wonder at his audacity and pity his patients. But that parents should begin the difficult task of rearing children, without ever having given a thought to the principles—physical, moral, or intellectual—which ought to guide them, excites neither surprise at the actors nor pity for their victims.

To tens of thousands that are killed, add hundreds of thousand that survive with feeble constitutions, and millions that grow up with constitutions not so strong as they should be; and you will have some idea of the curse inflicted on their offspring by parents ignorant of the laws of life. Do but consider for a moment that the regimen to which children are subject, is hourly telling upon them to their life-long injury or benefit; and that there are twenty ways of going wrong to one way of going right; and you will get some idea of the enormous mischief that is almost everywhere inflicted by the thoughtless, haphazard system in common use. Is it decided that a boy shall be clothed in some flimsy short dress, and be allowed to go playing about with limbs reddened by cold? The decision will tell on his whole future existence—either in illnesses; or in stunted growth; or in deficient energy; or in a maturity less vigorous than it ought to have been, and in consequent hindrances to success and happiness. Are children doomed to a monotonous dietary, or a dietary that is deficient in nutritiveness? Their ultimate physical power, and their efficiency as men and women, will inevitably be more or less diminished by it. Are they forbidden vociferous play, or (being too ill-clothed to bear exposure) are they kept indoors in cold weather? They are certain to fall below that measure of health and strength to which they would else have attained. When sons and daughters grow up sickly and feeble, parents commonly regard the event as a misfortune—as a visitation of Providence. Thinking after the prevalent chaotic fashion, they assume that these evils come without causes; or that the causes are supernatural. Nothing of the kind. In some cases the causes are doubtless inherited; but in most cases foolish regulations are the causes. Very generally, parents themselves are responsible for all this pain, this debility, this depression, this misery. They have undertaken to control the lives of their offspring from hour to hour; with cruel carelessness they have neglected to learn anything about these vital processes which they are unceasingly affecting by their commands and prohibitions; in utter ignorance of the simplest physiologic laws, they have been year by year undermining the constitutions of their children; and have so inflicted disease and premature death, not only on them but on their descendants.

Equally great are the ignorance and the consequent injury, when we turn from physical training to moral training. Consider the young mother and her nursery-legislation. But a few years ago she was at school, where her memory was crammed with words, and names, and dates, and her reflective faculties scarcely in the slightest degree exercised—where not one idea was given her respecting the methods of dealing with the opening mind of childhood; and where her discipline did not in the least fit her for thinking out methods of her own. The intervening years have been passed in practising music, in fancy-work, in novel-reading, and in party-going: no thought having yet been given to the grave responsibilities of maternity; and scarcely any of that solid intellectual culture obtained which would be some preparation for such responsibilities. And now see her with an unfolding human character committed to her charge—see her profoundly ignorant of the phenomena with which she has to deal, undertaking to do that which can be done but imperfectly even with the aid of the profoundest knowledge. She knows nothing about the nature of the emotions, their order of evolution, their functions, or where use ends and abuse begins. She is under the impression that some of the feelings are wholly bad, which is not true of any one of them; and that others are good however far they may be carried, which is also not true of any one of them. And then, ignorant as she is of the structure she has to deal with, she is equally ignorant of the effects produced on it by this or that treatment. What can be more inevitable than the disastrous results we see hourly arising? Lacking knowledge of mental phenomena, with their cause and consequences, her interference is frequently more mischievous than absolute passivity would have been. This and that kind of action, which are quite normal and beneficial, she perpetually thwarts; and so diminishes the child's happiness and profit, injures its temper and her own, and produces estrangement. Deeds which she thinks it desirable to encourage, she gets performed by threats and bribes, or by exciting a desire for applause: considering little what the inward motive may be, so long as the outward conduct conforms; and thus cultivating hypocrisy, and fear, and selfishness, in place of good feeling. While insisting on truthfulness, she constantly sets an example of untruth by threatening penalties which she does not inflict. While inculcating self-control, she hourly visits on her little ones angry scoldings for acts undeserving of them. She has not the remotest idea that in the nursery, as in the world, that alone is the truly salutary discipline which visits on all conduct, good and bad, the natural consequences—the consequences, pleasurable or painful, which in the nature of things such conduct tends to bring. Being thus without theoretic guidance, and quite incapable of guiding herself by tracing the mental processes going on in her children, her rule is impulsive, inconsistent, mischievous; and would indeed be generally ruinous were it not that the overwhelming tendency of the growing mind to assume the moral type of the race usually subordinates all minor influences.

And then the culture of the intellect—is not this, too, mismanaged in a similar manner? Grant that the phenomena of intelligence conform to laws; grant that the evolution of intelligence in a child also conforms to laws; and it follows inevitably that education cannot be rightly guided without a knowledge of these laws. To suppose that you can properly regulate this process of forming and accumulating ideas, without understanding the nature of the process, is absurd. How widely, then, must teaching as it is differ from teaching as it should be; when hardly any parents, and but few tutors, know anything about psychology. As might be expected, the established system is grievously at fault, alike in matter and in manner. While the right class of facts is withheld, the wrong class is forcibly administered in the wrong way and in the wrong order. Under that common limited idea of education which confines it to knowledge gained from books, parents thrust primers into the hands of their little ones years too soon, to their great injury. Not recognising the truth that the function of books is supplementary—that they form an indirect means to knowledge when direct means fail—a means of seeing through other men what you cannot see for yourself; teachers are eager to give second-hand facts in place of first-hand facts. Not perceiving the enormous value of that spontaneous education which goes on in early years—not perceiving that a child's restless observation, instead of being ignored or checked, should be diligently ministered to, and made as accurate and complete as possible; they insist on occupying its eyes and thoughts with things that are, for the time being, incomprehensible and repugnant. Possessed by a superstition which worships the symbols of knowledge instead of the knowledge itself, they do not see that only when his acquaintance with the objects and processes of the household, the streets, and the fields, is becoming tolerably exhaustive—only then should a child be introduced to the new sources of information which books supply: and this, not only because immediate cognition is of far greater value than mediate cognition; but also, because the words contained in books can be rightly interpreted into ideas, only in proportion to the antecedent experience of things. Observe next, that this formal instruction, far too soon commenced, is carried on with but little reference to the laws of mental development. Intellectual progress is of necessity from the concrete to the abstract. But regardless of this, highly abstract studies, such as grammar, which should come quite late, are begun quite early. Political geography, dead and uninteresting to a child, and which should be an appendage of sociological studies, is commenced betimes; while physical geography, comprehensible and comparatively attractive to a child, is in great part passed over. Nearly every subject dealt with is arranged in abnormal order: definitions and rules and principles being put first, instead of being disclosed, as they are in the order of nature, through the study of cases. And then, pervading the whole, is the vicious system of rote learning—a system of sacrificing the spirit to the letter. See the results. What with perceptions unnaturally dulled by early thwarting, and a coerced attention to books—what with the mental confusion produced by teaching subjects before they can be understood, and in each of them giving generalisations before the facts of which they are the generalisations—what with making the pupil a mere passive recipient of other's ideas, and not in the least leading him to be an active inquirer or self-instructor—and what with taxing the faculties to excess; there are very few minds that become as efficient as they might be. Examinations being once passed, books are laid aside; the greater part of what has been acquired, being unorganised, soon drops out of recollection; what remains is mostly inert—the art of applying knowledge not having been cultivated; and there is but little power either of accurate observation or independent thinking. To all which add, that while much of the information gained is of relatively small value, an immense mass of information of transcendent value is entirely passed over.

Thus we find the facts to be such as might have been inferred *à priori*. The training of children—physical, moral, and intellectual—is dreadfully defective. And in great measure it is so because parents are devoid of that knowledge by which this training can alone be rightly guided. What is to be expected when one of the most intricate of problems is undertaken by those who have given scarcely a thought to the principles on which its solution depends? For shoe-making or house-building, for the management of a ship or a locomotive engine, a long apprenticeship is needful. Is it, then, that the unfolding of a human being in body and mind is so comparatively simple a process that any one may superintend and regulate it with no preparation whatever? If not—if the process is, with one exception, more complex than any in Nature, and the task of ministering to it one of surpassing difficulty; is it not madness to make no provision for such a task? Better sacrifice accomplishments than omit this all-essential instruction. When a father, acting on false dogmas adopted without examination, has alienated his sons, driven them into rebellion by his harsh treatment, ruined them, and made himself miserable; he might reflect that the study of Ethology would have been worth pursuing, even at the cost of knowing nothing about Æschylus. When a mother is mourning over a first-born that has sunk under the sequelæ of scarlet-fever — when perhaps a candid medical man has confirmed her suspicion that her child would have recovered had not its system been enfeebled by over-study — when she is prostrate under the pangs of combined grief and remorse; it is but a small consolation that she can read Dante in the original.

Thus we see that for regulating the third great division of human activities, a knowledge of the laws of life is the one thing needful. Some acquaintance with the first principles of physiology and the elementary truths of psychology, is indispensable for the right bringing up of children. We doubt not that many will read this assertion with a smile. That parents in general should be expected to acquire a knowledge of subjects so abstruse will seem to them an absurdity. And if we proposed that an exhaustive knowledge of these subjects should be obtained by all fathers and mothers, the absurdity would indeed be glaring enough. But we do not. General principles only, accompanied by such illustrations as may be needed to make them understood, would suffice. And these might be readily taught — if not rationally, then dogmatically. Be this as it may, however, here are the indisputable facts: — that the development of children in mind and body follows certain laws; that unless these laws are in some degree conformed to by parents, death is inevitable; that unless they are in a great degree conformed to, there must result serious physical and mental defects; and that only when they are completely conformed to, can a perfect maturity be reached. Judge, then, whether all who may one day be parents, should not strive with some anxiety to learn what these laws are.

From the parental functions let us pass now to the functions of the citizen. We have here to inquire what knowledge fits a man for the discharge of these functions. It cannot be alleged that the need for knowledge fitting him for these functions is wholly overlooked; for our school-courses contain certain studies, which, nominally at least, bear upon political and social duties. Of these the only one that occupies a prominent place is History.

But, as already hinted, the information commonly given under this head, is almost valueless for purposes of guidance. Scarcely any of the facts set down in our school-histories, and very few of those contained in the more elaborate works written for adults, illustrate the right principles of political action. The biographies of monarchs (and our children learn little else) throw scarcely any light upon the science of society. Familiarity with court intrigues, plots, usurpations, or the like, and with all the personalities accompanying them, aids very little in elucidating the causes of national progress. We read of some squabble for power, that it led to a pitched battle; that such and such were the names of the generals and their leading subordinates; that they had each so many thousand infantry and cavalry, and so many cannon; that they arranged their forces in this and that order; that they manœuvred, attacked, and fell back in certain ways; that at this part of the day such disasters were sustained, and at that such advantages gained; that in one particular movement some leading officer fell, while in another a certain regiment was decimated; that after all the changing fortunes of the fight, the victory was gained by this or that army; and that so many were killed and wounded on each side, and so many captured by the conquerors. And now, out of the accumulated details making up the narrative, say which it is that helps you in deciding on your conduct as a citizen. Supposing even that you had diligently read, not only *The Fifteen Decisive Battles of the World,* but accounts of all other battles that history mentions; how much more judicious would your vote be at the next election? "But these are facts—interesting facts," you say. Without doubt they are facts (such, at least, as are not wholly or partially fictions); and to many they may be interesting facts. But this by no means implies that they are valuable. Factitious or morbid opinion often gives seeming value to things that have scarcely any. A tulipomaniac will not part with a choice bulb for its weight in gold. To another man an ugly piece of cracked old china seems his most desirable possession. And there are those who give high prices for the relics of celebrated murderers. Will it be contended that these tastes are any measures of value in the things that gratify them? If not, then it must be admitted that the liking felt for certain classes of historical facts is no proof of their worth; and that we must test their worth, as we test the worth of other facts, by asking to what uses they are applicable. Were some one to tell you that your neighbour's cat kittened yesterday, you would say the information was valueless. Fact though it might be, you would call it an utterly useless fact—a fact that could in no way influence your actions in life—a fact that would not help you in learning how to live completely. Well, apply the same test to the great mass of historical facts, and you will get the same result. They are facts from which no conclusions can be drawn—*unorganisable* facts; and therefore facts of no service in establishing principles of conduct, which is the chief use of facts. Read them, if you like, for amusement; but do not flatter your self they are instructive.

That which constitutes History, properly so called, is in great part omitted from works on the subject. Only of late years have historians commenced giving us, in any considerable quantity, the truly valuable information. As in past ages the king was everything and the people nothing; so, in past histories the doings of the king fill the entire picture, to which the national life forms but an obscure background. While only now, when the welfare of nations rather than of rulers is becoming the dominant idea, are historians beginning to occupy themselves with the phenomena of social progress. The thing it really concerns us to know is the natural history of society. We want all facts which help us to understand how a nation has grown and organised itself. Among these, let us of course have an account of its government; with as little as may be of gossip about the men who officered it, and as much as possible about the structure, principles, methods, prejudices, corruptions, etc., which it exhibited: and let this account include not only the nature and actions of the central government, but also those of local governments, down to their minutest ramifications. Let us of course also have a parallel description of the ecclesiastical government—its organisation, its conduct, its power, its relations to the State; and accompanying this, the ceremonial, creed, and religious ideas—not only those nominally believed, but those really believed and acted upon. Let us at the same time be informed of the control exercised by class over class, as displayed in social observances—in titles, salutations, and forms of address. Let us know, too, what were all the other customs which regulated the popular life out of doors and in-doors: including those concerning the relations of the sexes, and the relations of parents to children. The superstitions, also, from the more important myths down to the charms in common use, should be indicated. Next should come a delineation of the industrial system: showing to what extent the division of labour was carried; how trades were regulated, whether by caste, guilds, or otherwise; what was the connection between employers and employed; what were the agencies for distributing commodities; what were the means of communication; what was the circulating medium. Accompanying all which should be given an account of the industrial arts technically considered: stating the processes in use, and the quality of the products. Further, the intellectual condition of the nation in its various grades should be depicted; not only with respect to the kind and amount of education, but with respect to the progress made in science, and the prevailing manner of thinking. The degree of æsthetic culture, as displayed in architecture, sculpture, painting, dress, music, poetry, and fiction, should be described. Nor should there be omitted a sketch of the daily lives of the people—their food, their homes, and their amusements. And lastly, to connect the whole, should be exhibited the morals, theoretical and practical, of all classes: as indicated in their laws, habits, proverbs, deeds. These facts, given with as much brevity as consists with clearness and accuracy, should be so grouped and arranged that they may be comprehended in their *ensemble*, and contemplated as mutually-dependent parts of one great whole. The aim should be so to present them that men may readily trace the *consensus* subsisting among them; with the view of learning what social phenomena co-exist with what other. And then the corresponding delineations of succeeding ages should be so managed as to show how each belief, institution, custom, and arrangement was modified; and how the *consensus* of preceding structures and functions was developed into the *consensus* of succeeding ones. Such alone is the kind of information respecting past times which can be of service to the citizen for the regulation of his conduct. The only history that is of practical value is what may be called Descriptive Sociology. And the highest office which the historian can discharge, is that of so narrating the lives of nations, as to furnish materials for a Comparative Sociology; and for the subsequent determination of the ultimate laws to which social phenomena conform.

But now mark, that even supposing an adequate stock of this truly valuable historical knowledge has been acquired, it is of comparatively little use without the key. And the key is to be found only in Science. In the absence of the generalisations of biology and psychology, rational interpretation of social phenomena is impossible. Only in proportion as men draw certain rude, empirical inferences respecting human nature, are they enabled to understand even the simplest facts of social life: as, for instance, the relation between supply and demand. And if the most elementary truths of sociology cannot be reached until some knowledge is obtained of how men generally think, feel, and act under given circumstances; then it is manifest that there can be nothing like a wide comprehension of sociology, unless through a competent acquaintance with man in all his faculties, bodily, and mental. Consider the matter in the abstract, and this conclusion is self-evident. Thus:—Society is made up of individuals; all that is done in society is done by the combined actions of individuals; and therefore, in individual actions only can be found the solutions of social phenomena. But the actions of individuals depend on the laws of their natures; and their actions cannot be understood until these laws are understood. These laws, however, when reduced to their simplest expressions, prove to be corollaries from the laws of body and mind in general. Hence it follows, that biology and psychology are indispensable as interpreters of sociology. Or, to state the conclusions still more simply:—all social phenomena are phenomena of life—are the most complex manifestations of life—must conform to the laws of life—and can be understood only when the laws of life are understood. Thus, then, for the regulation of this fourth division of human activities, we are, as before, dependent on Science. Of the knowledge commonly imparted in educational courses, very little is of service for guiding a man in his conduct as a citizen. Only a small part of the history he reads is of practical value; and of this small part he is not prepared to make proper use. He lacks not only the materials for, but the very conception of, descriptive sociology; and he also lacks those generalisations of the organic sciences, without which even descriptive sociology can give him but small aid.

And now we come to that remaining division of human life which includes the relaxations and amusements filling leisure hours. After considering what training best fits for self-preservation, for the obtainment of sustenance, for the discharge of parental duties, and for the regulation of social and political conduct; we have now to consider what training best fits for the miscellaneous ends not included in these—for the enjoyment of Nature, of Literature, and of the Fine Arts, in all their forms. Postponing them as we do to things that bear more vitally upon human welfare; and bringing everything, as we have, to the test of actual value; it will perhaps be inferred that we are inclined to slight these less essential things. No greater mistake could be made, however. We yield to none in the value we attach to aesthetic culture and its pleasures. Without painting, sculpture, music, poetry, and the emotions produced by natural beauty of every kind, life would lose half its charm. So far from regarding the training and gratification of the tastes as unimportant, we believe that in time to come they will occupy a much larger share of human life than now. When the forces of Nature have been fully conquered to man's use—when the means of production have been brought to perfection—when labour has been economised to the highest degree—when education has been so systematised that a preparation for the more essential activities may be made with comparative rapidity—and when, consequently, there is a great increase of spare time; then will the beautiful, both in Art and Nature, rightly fill a large space in the minds of all.

But it is one thing to approve of æsthetic culture as largely conducive to human happiness; and another thing to admit that it is a fundamental requisite to human happiness. However important it may be, it must yield precedence to those kinds of culture which bear directly upon daily duties. As before hinted, literature and the fine arts are made possible by those activities which make individual and social life possible; and manifestly, that which is made possible, must be postponed to that which makes it possible. A florist cultivates a plant for the sake of its flower; and regards the roots and leaves as of value, chiefly because they are instrumental in producing the flower. But while, as an ultimate product, the flower is the thing to which everything else is subordinate, the florist has learnt that the root and leaves are intrinsically of greater importance; because on them the evolution of the flower depends. He bestows every care in rearing a healthy plant; and knows it would be folly if, in his anxiety to obtain the flower, he were to neglect the plant. Similarly in the case before us. Architecture, sculpture, painting, music, and poetry, may truly be called the efflorescence of civilised life. But even supposing they are of such transcendent worth as to subordinate the civilised life out of which they grow (which can hardly be asserted), it will still be admitted that the production of a healthy civilised life must be the first consideration; and that culture subserving this must occupy the highest place.

And here we see most distinctly the vice of our educational system. It neglects the plant for the sake of the flower. In anxiety for elegance, it forgets substance. While it gives no knowledge conducive to self-preservation—while of knowledge that facilitates gaining a livelihood it gives but the rudiments, and leaves the greater part to be picked up any how in after life—while for the discharge of parental functions it makes not the slightest provision—and while for the duties of citizenship it prepares by imparting a mass of facts, most of which are irrelevant, and the rest without a key; it is diligent in teaching whatever adds to refinement, polish, éclat. Fully as we may admit that extensive acquaintance with modern languages is a valuable accomplishment, which, through reading, conversation, and travel, aids in giving a certain finish; it by no means follows that this result is rightly purchased at the cost of the vitally important knowledge sacrificed to it. Supposing it true that classical education conduces to elegance and correctness of style; it cannot be said that elegance and correctness of style are comparable in importance to a familiarity with the principles that should guide the rearing of children. Grant that the taste may be improved by reading the poetry written in extinct languages; yet it is not to be inferred that such improvement of taste is equivalent in value to an acquaintance with the laws of health. Accomplishments, the fine arts, *belles-lettres*, and all those things which, as we say, constitute the efflorescence of civilisation, should be wholly subordinate to that instruction and discipline in which civilisation rests. *As they occupy the leisure part of life, so should they occupy the leisure part of education.*

Recognising thus the true position of aesthetics, and holding that while the cultivation of them should form a part of education from its commencement, such cultivation should be subsidiary; we have now to inquire what knowledge is of most use to this end—what knowledge best fits for this remaining sphere of activity? To this question the answer is still the same as heretofore. Unexpected though the assertion may be, it is nevertheless true, that the highest Art of every kind is based on Science—that without Science there can be neither perfect production nor full appreciation. Science, in that limited acceptation current in society, may not have been possessed by various artists of high repute; but acute observers as such artists have been, they have always possessed a stock of those empirical generalisations which constitute science in its lowest phase; and they have habitually fallen far below perfection, partly because their generalisations were comparatively few and inaccurate. That science necessarily underlies the fine arts, becomes manifest, *à priori*, when we remember that art-products are all more or less representative of objective or subjective phenomena; that they can be good only in proportion as they conform to the laws of these phenomena; and that before they can thus conform, the artist must know what these laws are. That this *à priori* conclusion tallies with experience, we shall soon see.

Youths preparing for the practice of sculpture have to acquaint themselves with the bones and muscles of the human frame in their distribution, attachments, and movements. This is a portion of science; and it has been found needful to impart it for the prevention of those many errors which sculptors who do not possess it commit. A knowledge of mechanical principles is also requisite; and such knowledge not being usually possessed, grave mechanical mistakes are frequently made. Take an instance. For the stability of a figure it is needful that the perpendicular from the centre of gravity—"the line of direction," as it is called—should fall within the base of support; and hence it happens, that when a man assumes the attitude known as "standing at ease," in which one leg is straightened and the other relaxed, the line of direction falls within the foot of the straightened leg. But sculptors unfamiliar with the theory of equilibrium, not uncommonly so represent this attitude, that the line of direction falls midway between the feet. Ignorance of the law of momentum leads to analogous blunders: as witness the admired Discobolus, which, as it is posed, must inevitably fall forward the moment the quoit is delivered.

In painting, the necessity for scientific information, empirical if not rational, is still more conspicuous. What gives the grotesqueness of Chinese pictures, unless their utter disregard of the laws of appearances—their absurd linear perspective, and their want of aerial perspective? In what are the drawings of a child so faulty, if not in a similar absence of truth—an absence arising, in great part, from ignorance of the way in which the aspects of things vary with the conditions? Do but remember the books and lectures by which students are instructed; or consider the criticisms of Ruskin; or look at the doings of the Pre-Raffaelites; and you will see that progress in painting implies increasing knowledge of how effects in Nature are produced. The most diligent observation, if unaided by science, fails to preserve from error. Every painter will endorse the assertion that unless it is known what appearances must exist under given circumstances, they often will not be perceived; and to know what appearances must exist, is, in so far, to understand the science of appearances. From want of science Mr. J. Lewis, careful painter as he is, casts the shadow of a lattice-window in sharply-defined lines upon an opposite wall; which he would not have done, had he been familiar with the phenomena of penumbræ. From want of science, Mr. Rosetti, catching sight of a peculiar iridescence displayed by certain hairy surfaces under particular lights (an iridescence caused by the diffraction of light in passing the hairs), commits the error of showing this iridescence on surfaces and in positions where it could not occur.

To say that music, too, has need of scientific aid will cause still more surprise.

Yet it may be shown that music is but an idealisation of the natural language of emotion; and that consequently, music must be good or bad according as it conforms to the laws of this natural language. The various inflections of voice which accompany feelings of different kinds and intensities, are the germs out of which music is developed. It is demonstrable that these inflections and cadences are not accidental or arbitrary; but that they are determined by certain general principles of vital action; and that their expressiveness depends on this. Whence it follows that musical phrases and the melodies built of them, can be effective only when they are in harmony with these general principles. It is difficult here properly to illustrate this position. But perhaps it will suffice to instance the swarms of worthless ballads that infest drawing-rooms, as compositions which science would forbid. They sin against science by setting to music ideas that are not emotional enough to prompt musical expression; and they also sin against science by using musical phrases that have no natural relations to the ideas expressed: even where these are emotional. They are bad because they are untrue. And to say they are untrue, is to say they are unscientific.

Even in poetry the same thing holds. Like music, poetry has its root in those natural modes of expression which accompany deep feeling. Its rhythm, its strong and numerous metaphors, its hyperboles, its violent inversions, are simply exaggerations of the traits of excited speech. To be good, therefore, poetry must pay attention to those laws of nervous action which excited speech obeys. In intensifying and combining the traits of excited speech, it must have due regard to proportion—must not use its appliances without restriction; but, where the ideas are least emotional, must use the forms of poetical expression sparingly; must use them more freely as the emotion rises; and must carry them to their greatest extent, only where the emotion reaches a climax. The entire contravention of these principles results in bombast or doggerel. The insufficient respect for them is seen in didactic poetry. And it is because they are rarely fully obeyed, that so much poetry is inartistic.

Not only is it that the artist, of whatever kind, cannot produce a truthful work without he understands the laws of the phenomena he represents; but it is that he must also understand how the minds of spectators or listeners will be affected by the several peculiarities of his work—a question in psychology. What impression any art-product generates, manifestly depends upon the mental natures of those to whom it is presented; and as all mental natures have certain characteristics in common, there must result certain corresponding general principles on which alone art-products can be successfully framed. These general principles cannot be fully understood and applied, unless the artist sees how they follow from the laws of mind. To ask whether the composition of a picture is good is really to ask how the perceptions and feelings of observers will be affected by it. To ask whether a drama is well constructed, is to ask whether its situations are so arranged as duly to consult the power of attention of an audience, and duly to avoid overtaxing any one class of feelings. Equally in arranging the leading divisions of a poem or fiction, and in combining the words of a single sentence, the goodness of the effect depends upon the skill with which the mental energies and susceptibilities of the reader are economised. Every artist, in the course of his education and after-life, accumulates a stock of maxims by which his practice is regulated. Trace such maxims to their roots, and they inevitably lead you down to psychological principles. And only when the artist understands these psychological principles and their various corollaries can he work in harmony with them.

We do not for a moment believe that science will make an artist. While we contend that the leading laws both of objective and subjective phenomena must be understood by him, we by no means contend that knowledge of such laws will serve in place of natural perception. Not the poet only, but the artist of every type, is born, not made. What we assert is, that innate faculty cannot dispense with the aid of organised knowledge. Intuition will do much, but it will not do all. Only when Genius is married to Science can the highest results be produced.

As we have above asserted, Science is necessary not only for the most successful production, but also for the full appreciation, of the fine arts. In what consists the greater ability of a man than of a child to perceive the beauties of a picture; unless it is in his more extended knowledge of those truths in nature or life which the picture renders? How happens the cultivated gentleman to enjoy a fine poem so much more than a boor does; if it is not because his wider acquaintance with objects and actions enables him to see in the poem much that the boor cannot see? And if, as is here so obvious, there must be some familiarity with the things represented, before the representation can be appreciated, then, the representation can be completely appreciated only when the things represented are completely understood. The fact is, that every additional truth which a word of art expresses, gives an additional pleasure to the percipient mind—a pleasure that is missed by those ignorant of this truth. The more realities an artist indicates in any given amount of work, the more faculties does he appeal to; the more numerous ideas does he suggest; the more gratification does he afford. But to receive this gratification the spectator, listener, or reader, must know the realities which the artist has indicated; and to know these realities is to have that much science.

And now let us not overlook the further great fact, that not only does science underlie sculpture, painting, music, poetry, but that science is itself poetic. The current opinion that science and poetry are opposed, is a delusion. It is doubtless true that as states of consciousness, cognition and emotion tend to exclude each other. And it is doubtless also true that an extreme activity of the reflective powers tends to deaden the feelings; while an extreme activity of the feelings tends to deaden the reflective powers: in which sense, indeed, all orders of activity are antagonistic to each other. But it is not true that the facts of science are unpoetical; or that the cultivation of science is necessarily unfriendly to the exercise of imagination and the love of the beautiful. On the contrary, science opens up realms of poetry where to the unscientific all is a blank. Those engaged in scientific researches constantly show us that they realise not less vividly, but more vividly, than others, the poetry of their subjects. Whoso will dip into Hugh Miller's works of geology, or read Mr. Lewes's *Sea-side Studies*, will perceive that science excites poetry rather than extinguishes it. And he who contemplates the life of Goethe, must see that the poet and the man of science can co-exist in equal activity. Is it not, indeed, an absurd and almost a sacrilegious belief, that the more a man studies Nature the less he reveres it? Think you that a drop of water, which to the vulgar eye is but a drop of water, loses anything in the eye of the physicist who knows that its elements are held together by a force which, if suddenly liberated, would produce a flash of lightning? Think you that what is carelessly looked upon by the uninitiated as a mere snow-flake, does not suggest higher associations to one who had seen through a microscope the wondrously-varied and elegant forms of snow-crystals? Think you that the rounded rock marked with parallel scratches, calls up as much poetry in an ignorant mind as in the mind of a geologist, who knows that over this rock a glacier slid a million years ago? The truth is, that those who have never entered upon scientific pursuits are blind to most of the poetry by which they are surrounded. Whoever has not in youth collected plants and insects, knows not half the halo of interest which lanes and hedge-rows can assume. Whoever has not sought for fossils, has little idea of the poetical associations that surround the places where imbedded treasures were found. Whoever at the sea-side has not had a microscope and aquarium, has yet to learn what the highest pleasures of the sea-side are. Sad, indeed, is it to see how men occupy themselves with trivialities, and are indifferent to the grandest phenomena—care not to understand the architecture of the Heavens, but are deeply interested in some contemptible controversy about the intrigues of Mary Queen of Scots!—are learnedly critical over a Greek ode, and pass by without a glance that grand epic written by the finger of God upon the strata of the Earth!

We find, then, that even for this remaining division of human activities, scientific culture is the proper preparation. We find that aesthetics in general are necessarily based upon scientific principles; and can be pursued with complete success only through an acquaintance with these principles. We find that for the criticism and due appreciation of works of art, a knowledge of the constitution of things, or in other words, a knowledge of science, is requisite. And we not only find that science is the handmaid to all forms of art and poetry, but that, rightly regarded, science is itself poetic.

Thus far our question has been, the worth of knowledge of this or that kind for purposes of guidance. We have now to judge the relative value of different kinds of knowledge for purposes of discipline. This division of our subject we are obliged to treat with comparative brevity; and happily, no very lengthened treatment of it is needed. Having found what is best for the one end, we have by implication found what is best for the other. We may be quite sure that the acquirement of those classes of facts which are most useful for regulating conduct, involves a mental exercise best fitted for strengthening the faculties. It would be utterly contrary to the beautiful economy of Nature, if one kind of culture were needed for the gaining of information and another kind were needed as a mental gymnastic. Everywhere throughout creation we find faculties developed through the performance of those functions which it is their office to perform; not through the performance of artificial exercises devised to fit them for those functions. The Red Indian acquires the swiftness and agility which make him a successful hunter, by the actual pursuit of animals; and through the miscellaneous activities of his life, he gains a better balance of physical powers than gymnastics ever give. That skill in tracking enemies and prey which he had reached after long practice, implies a subtlety of perception far exceeding anything produced by artificial training. And similarly in all cases. From the Bushman whose eye, habitually employed in identifying distant objects that are to be pursued or fled from, has acquired a telescopic range, to the accountant whose daily practice enables him to add up several columns of figures simultaneously; we find that the highest power of a faculty results from the discharge of those duties which the conditions of life require it to discharge. And we may be certain, *à priori*, that the same law holds throughout education. The education of most value for guidance, must at the same time be the education of most value for discipline. Let us consider the evidence.

One advantage claimed for that devotion to language-learning which forms so prominent a feature in the ordinary *curriculum*, is, that the memory is thereby strengthened. This is assumed to be an advantage peculiar to the study of words. But the truth is, that the sciences afford far wider fields for the exercise of memory. It is no slight task to remember everything about our solar system; much more to remember all that is known concerning the structure of our galaxy. The number of compound substances, to which chemistry daily adds, is so great that few, save professors, can enumerate them; and to recollect the atomic constitutions and affinities of all these compounds, is scarcely possible without making chemistry the occupation of life. In the enormous mass of phenomena presented by the Earth's crust, and in the still more enormous mass of phenomena presented by the fossils it contains, there is matter which it takes the geological student years of application to master. Each leading division of physics—sound, heat, light, electricity— includes facts numerous enough to alarm any one proposing to learn them all. And when we pass to the organic sciences, the effort of memory required becomes still greater. In human anatomy alone, the quantity of detail is so great, that the young surgeon has commonly to get it up half-a-dozen times before he can permanently retain it. The number of species of plants which botanists distinguish, amounts to some 320,000; while the varied forms of animal life with which the zoologist deals, are estimated at some 2,000,000. So vast is the accumulation of facts which men of science have before them, that only by dividing and subdividing their labours can they deal with it. To a detailed knowledge of his own division, each adds but a general knowledge of the allied ones; joined perhaps to a rudimentary acquaintance with some others. Surely, then, science, cultivated even to a very moderate extent, affords adequate exercise for memory. To say the very least, it involves quite as good a discipline for this faculty as language does.

But now mark that while, for the training of mere memory, science is as good as, if not better than, language; it has an immense superiority in the kind of memory it trains. In the acquirement of a language, the connections of ideas to be established in the mind correspond to facts that are in great measure accidental; whereas, in the acquirement of science, the connections of ideas to be established in the mind correspond to facts that are mostly necessary. It is true that the relations of words to their meanings are in one sense natural; that the genesis of these relations may be traced back a certain distance, though rarely to the beginning; and that the laws of this genesis form a branch of mental science—the science of philology. But since it will not be contended that in the acquisition of languages, as ordinarily carried on, these natural relations between words and their meanings are habitually traced, and their laws explained; it must be admitted that they are commonly learned as fortuitous relations. On the other hand, the relations which science presents are causal relations; and, when properly taught, are understood as such. While language familiarises with non-rational relations, science familiarises with rational relations. While the one exercises memory only, the other exercises both memory and understanding.

Observe next, that a great superiority of science over language as a means of discipline, is, that it cultivates the judgment. As, in a lecture on mental education delivered at the Royal Institution, Professor Faraday well remarks, the most common intellectual fault is deficiency of judgment. "Society, speaking generally," he says, "is not only ignorant as respects education of the judgment, but it is also ignorant of its ignorance." And the cause to which he ascribes this state, is want of scientific culture. The truth of his conclusion is obvious. Correct judgment with regard to surrounding objects, events, and consequences, becomes possible only through knowledge of the way in which surrounding phenomena depend on each other. No extent of acquaintance with the meanings of words, will guarantee correct inferences respecting causes and effects. The habit of drawing conclusions from data, and then of verifying those conclusions by observation and experiment, can alone give the power of judging correctly. And that it necessitates this habit is one of the immense advantages of science.

Not only, however, for intellectual discipline is science the best; but also for *moral* discipline. The learning of languages tends, if anything, further to increase the already undue respect for authority. Such and such are the meanings of these words, says the teacher of the dictionary. So and so is the rule in this case, says the grammar. By the pupil these dicta are received as unquestionable. His constant attitude of mind is that of submission to dogmatic teaching. And a necessary result is a tendency to accept without inquiry whatever is established. Quite opposite is the mental tone generated by the cultivation of science. Science makes constant appeal to individual reason. Its truths are not accepted on authority alone; but all are at liberty to test them—nay, in many cases, the pupil is required to think out his own conclusions. Every step in a scientific investigation is submitted to his judgment. He is not asked to admit it without seeing it to be true. And the trust in his own powers thus produced is further increased by the uniformity with which Nature justifies his inferences when they are correctly drawn. From all which there flows that independence which is a most valuable element in character. Nor is this the only moral benefit bequeathed by scientific culture. When carried on, as it should always be, as much as possible under the form of original research, it exercises perseverance and sincerity. As says Professor Tyndall of inductive inquiry, "It requires patient industry, and an humble and conscientious acceptance of what Nature reveals. The first condition of success is an honest receptivity and a willingness to abandon all preconceived notions, however cherished, if they be found to contradict the truth. Believe me, a self-renunciation which has something noble in it, and of which the world never hears, is often enacted in the private experience of the true votary of science."

Lastly we have to assert—and the assertion will, we doubt not, cause extreme surprise—that the discipline of science is superior to that of our ordinary education, because of the *religious* culture that it gives. Of course we do not here use the words scientific and religious in their ordinary limited acceptations; but in their widest and highest acceptations. Doubtless, to the superstitions that pass under the name of religion, science is antagonistic; but not to the essential religion which these superstitions merely hide. Doubtless, too, in much of the science that is current, there is a pervading spirit of irreligion; but not in that true science which had passed beyond the superficial into the profound.

> "True science and true religion," says Professor Huxley at the close of a recent course of lectures, "are twin-sisters, and the separation of either from the other is sure to prove the death of both. Science prospers exactly in proportion as it is religious; and religion flourishes in exact proportion to the scientific depth and firmness of its basis. The great deeds of philosophers have been less the fruit of their intellect than of the direction of that intellect by an eminently religious tone of mind. Truth has yielded herself rather to their patience, their love, their single-heartedness, and their self-denial, than to their logical acumen."

So far from science being irreligious, as many think, it is the neglect of science that is irreligious—it is the refusal to study the surrounding creation that is irreligious. Take a humble simile. Suppose a writer were daily saluted with praises couched in superlative language. Suppose the wisdom, the grandeur, the beauty of his works, were the constant topics of the eulogies addressed to him. Suppose those who unceasingly uttered these eulogies on his works were content with looking at the outsides of them; and had never opened them, much less tried to understand them. What value should we put upon their praises? What should we think of their sincerity? Yet, comparing small things to great, such is the conduct of mankind in general, in reference to the Universe and its Cause. Nay, it is worse. Not only do they pass by without study, these things which they daily proclaim to be so wonderful; but very frequently they condemn as mere triflers those who give time to the observation of Nature—they actually scorn those who show any active interest in these marvels. We repeat, then, that not science, but the neglect of science, is irreligious. Devotion to science, is a tacit worship—a tacit recognition of worth in the things studied; and by implication in their Cause. It is not a mere lip-homage, but a homage expressed in actions—not a mere professed respect, but a respect proved by the sacrifice of time, thought, and labour.

Nor is it thus only that true science is essentially religious. It is religious, too, inasmuch as it generates a profound respect for, and an implicit faith in, those uniformities of action which all things disclose. By accumulated experiences the man of science acquires a thorough belief in the unchanging relations of phenomena—in the invariable connection of cause and consequence—in the necessity of good or evil results. Instead of the rewards and punishments of traditional belief, which people vaguely hope they may gain, or escape, spite of their disobedience; he finds that there are rewards and punishments in the ordained constitution of things; and that the evil results of disobedience are inevitable. He sees that the laws to which we must submit are both inexorable and beneficent. He sees that in conforming to them, the process of things is ever towards a greater perfection and a higher happiness. Hence he is led constantly to insist on them, and is indignant when they are disregarded. And thus does he, by asserting the eternal principles of things and the necessity of obeying them, prove himself intrinsically religious.

Add lastly the further religious aspect of science, that it alone can give us true conceptions of ourselves and our relation to the mysteries of existence. At the same time that it shows us all which can be known, it shows us the limits beyond which we can know nothing. Not by dogmatic assertion, does it teach the impossibility of comprehending the Ultimate Cause of things; but it leads us clearly to recognise this impossibility by bringing us in every direction to boundaries we cannot cross. It realises to us in a way which nothing else can, the littleness of human intelligence in the face of that which transcends human intelligence. While towards the traditions and authorities of men its attitude may be proud, before the impenetrable veil which hides the Absolute its attitude is humble—a true pride and a true humility. Only the sincere man of science (and by this title we do not mean the mere calculator of distances, or analyser of compounds, or labeller of species; but him who through lower truths seeks higher, and eventually the highest)—only the genuine man of science, we say, can truly know how utterly beyond, not only human knowledge but human conception, is the Universal Power of which Nature, and Life, and Thought are manifestations.

We conclude, then, that for discipline, as well as for guidance, science is of chiefest value. In all its effects, learning the meanings of things, is better than learning the meanings of words. Whether for intellectual, moral, or religious training, the study of surrounding phenomena is immensely superior to the study of grammars and lexicons.

Thus to the question we set out with—What knowledge is of most worth?—the uniform reply is—Science. This is the verdict on all the counts. For direct self-preservation, or the maintenance of life and health, the all-important knowledge is—Science. For that indirect self-preservation which we call gaining a livelihood, the knowledge of greatest value is—Science. For the due discharge of parental functions, the proper guidance is to be found only in—Science. For that interpretation of national life, past and present, without which the citizen cannot rightly regulate his conduct, the indispensable key is—Science. Alike for the most perfect production and highest enjoyment of art in all its forms, the needful preparation is still—Science. And for purposes of discipline—intellectual, moral, religious—the most efficient study is, once more—Science. The question which at first seemed so perplexed, has become, in the course of our inquiry, comparatively simple. We have not to estimate the degrees of importance of different orders of human activity, and different studies as severally fitting us for them; since we find that the study of Science, in its most comprehensive meaning, is the best preparation for all these orders of activity. We have not to decide between the claims of knowledge of great though conventional value, and knowledge of less though intrinsic value; seeing that the knowledge which proves to be of most value in all other respects, is intrinsically most valuable: its worth is not dependent upon opinion, but is as fixed as is the relation of man to the surrounding world. Necessary and eternal as are its truths, all Science concerns all mankind for all time. Equally at present and in the remotest future, must it be of incalculable importance for the regulation of their conduct, that men should understand the science of life, physical, mental, and social; and that they should understand all other science as a key to the science of life.

And yet this study, immensely transcending all other in importance, is that which, in an age of boasted education, receives the least attention. While what we call civilisation could never have arisen had it not been for science, science forms scarcely an appreciable element in our so-called civilised training. Though to the progress of science we owe it, that millions find support where once there was food only for thousands; yet of these millions but a few thousands pay any respect to that which has made their existence possible. Though increasing knowledge of the properties and relations of things has not only enabled wandering tribes to grow into populous nations, but has given to the countless members of these populous nations, comforts and pleasures which their few naked ancestors never even conceived, or could have believed, yet is this kind of knowledge only now receiving a grudging recognition in our highest educational institutions. To the slowly growing acquaintance with the uniform co-existences and sequences of phenomena—to the establishment of invariable laws, we owe our emancipation from the grossest superstitions. But for science we should be still worshipping fetishes; or, with hecatombs of victims, propitiating diabolical deities. And yet this science, which, in place of the most degrading conceptions of things, has given us some insight into the grandeurs of creation, is written against in our theologies and frowned upon from our pulpits.

Paraphrasing an Eastern fable, we may say that in the family of knowledges, Science is the household drudge, who, in obscurity, hides unrecognised perfections. To her has been committed all the works; by her skill, intelligence, and devotion, have all conveniences and gratifications been obtained; and while ceaselessly ministering to the rest, she has been kept in the background, that her haughty sisters might flaunt their fripperies in the eyes of the world. The parallel holds yet further. For we are fast coming to the *dénouement*, when the positions will be changed; and while these haughty sisters sink into merited neglect, Science, proclaimed as highest alike in worth and beauty, will reign supreme.

INTELLECTUAL EDUCATION

There cannot fail to be a relationship between the successive systems of education, and the successive social states with which they have co-existed. Having a common origin in the national mind, the institutions of each epoch, whatever be their special functions, must have a family likeness. When men received their creed and its interpretations from an infallible authority deigning no explanations, it was natural that the teaching of children should be purely dogmatic. While "believe and ask no questions" was the maxim of the Church, it was fitly the maxim of the school. Conversely, now that Protestantism has gained for adults a right of private judgment and established the practice of appealing to reason, there is harmony in the change that has made juvenile instruction a process of exposition addressed to the understanding. Along with political despotism, stern in its commands, ruling by force of terror, visiting trifling crimes with death, and implacable in its vengeance on the disloyal, there necessarily grew up an academic discipline similarly harsh—a discipline of multiplied injunctions and blows for every breach of them—a discipline of unlimited autocracy upheld by rods, and ferules, and the black-hole. On the other hand, the increase of political liberty, the abolition of laws restricting individual action, and the amelioration of the criminal code, have been accompanied by a kindred progress towards non-coercive education: the pupil is hampered by fewer restraints, and other means than punishments are used to govern him. In those ascetic days when men, acting on the greatest-misery principle, held that the more gratifications they denied themselves the more virtuous they were, they, as a matter of course, considered that the best education which most thwarted the wishes of their children, and cut short all spontaneous activity with—"You mustn't do so." While, on the contrary, now that happiness is coming to be regarded as a legitimate aim—now that hours of labour are being shortened and popular recreations provided—parents and teachers are beginning to see that most childish desires may rightly be gratified, that childish sports should be encouraged, and that the tendencies of the growing mind are not altogether so diabolical as was supposed. The age in which all believed that trades must be established by bounties and prohibitions; that manufacturers needed their materials and qualities and prices to be prescribed; and that the value of money could be determined by law; was an age which unavoidably cherished the notions that a child's mind could be made to order; that its powers were to be imparted by the schoolmaster; that it was a receptacle into which knowledge was to be put, and there built up after the teacher's ideal. In this free-trade era, however, when we are learning that there is much more self-regulation in things than was supposed; that labour, and commerce, and agriculture, and navigation, can do better without management than with it; that political governments, to be efficient, must grow up from within and not be imposed from without; we are also being taught that there is a natural process of mental evolution which is not to be disturbed without injury; that we may not force on the unfolding mind our artificial forms; but that psychology, also, discloses to us a law of supply and demand to which, if we would not do harm, we must conform. Thus, alike in its oracular dogmatism, in its harsh discipline, in its multiplied restrictions, in its professed asceticism, and in its faith in the devices of men, the old educational regime was akin to the social systems with which it was contemporaneous; and similarly, in the reverse of these characteristics, our modern modes of culture correspond to our more liberal religious and political institutions.

But there remain further parallelisms to which we have not yet adverted: that, namely, between the processes by which these respective changes have been wrought out; and that between the several states of heterogeneous opinion to which they have led. Some centuries ago there was uniformity of belief—religious, political, and educational. All men were Romanists, all were Monarchists, all were disciples of Aristotle; and no one thought of calling in question that grammar-school routine under which all were brought up. The same agency has in each case replaced this uniformity by a constantly-increasing diversity. That tendency towards assertion of the individuality, which, after contributing to produce the great Protestant movement, has since gone on to produce an ever-increasing number of sects—that tendency which initiated political parties, and out of the two primary ones has, in these modern days, evolved a multiplicity to which every year adds—that tendency which led to the Baconian rebellion against the schools, and has since originated here and abroad, sundry new systems of thought—is a tendency which, in education also, has caused divisions and the accumulation of methods. As external consequences of the same internal change, these processes have necessarily been more or less simultaneous. The decline of authority, whether papal, philosophic, kingly, or tutorial, is essentially one phenomenon; in each of its aspects a leaning towards free action is seen alike in the working out of the change itself, and in the new forms of theory and practice to which the change has given birth.

While many will regret this multiplication of schemes of juvenile culture, the catholic observer will discern in it a means of ensuring the final establishment of a rational system. Whatever may be thought of theological dissent, it is clear that dissent in education results in facilitating inquiry by the division in labour. Were we in possession of the true method, divergence from it would, of course, be prejudicial; but the true method having to be found, the efforts of numerous independent seekers carrying out their researches in different directions, constitute a better agency for finding it than any that could be devised. Each of them struck by some new thought which probably contains more or less of basis in facts—each of them zealous on behalf of his plan, fertile in expedients to test its correctness, and untiring in his efforts to make known its success—each of them merciless in his criticism on the rest; there cannot fail, by composition of forces, to be a gradual approximation of all towards the right course. Whatever portion of the normal method any one has discovered, must, by the constant exhibition of its results, force itself into adoption; whatever wrong practices he has joined with it must, by repeated experiment and failure, be exploded. And by this aggregation of truths and elimination of errors, there must eventually be developed a correct and complete body of doctrine. Of the three phases through which human opinion passes—the unanimity of the ignorant, the disagreement of the inquiring, and the unanimity of the wise—it is manifest that the second is the parent of the third. They are not sequences in time only, they are sequences in causation. However impatiently, therefore, we may witness the present conflict of educational systems, and however much we may regret its accompanying evils, we must recognise it as a transition stage needful to be passed through, and beneficent in its ultimate effects.

Meanwhile, may we not advantageously take stock of our progress? After fifty years of discussion, experiment, and comparison of results, may we not expect a few steps towards the goal to be already made good? Some old methods must by this time have fallen out of use; some new ones must have become established; and many others must be in process of general abandonment or adoption. Probably we may see in these various changes, when put side by side, similar characteristics— may find in them a common tendency; and so, by inference, may get a clue to the direction in which experience is leading us, and gather hints how we may achieve yet further improvements. Let us then, as a preliminary to a deeper consideration of the matter, glance at the leading contrasts between the education of the past and that of the present.

The suppression of every error is commonly followed by a temporary ascendency of the contrary one; and so it happened, that after the ages when physical development alone was aimed at, there came an age when culture of the mind was the sole solicitude—when children had lesson-books put before them at between two and three years old, and the getting of knowledge was thought the one thing needful. As, further, it usually happens that after one of these reactions the next advance is achieved by co-ordinating the antagonist errors, and perceiving that they are opposite sides of one truth; so, we are now coming to the conviction that body and mind must both be cared for, and the whole thing being unfolded. The forcing-system has been, by many, given up; and precocity is discouraged. People are beginning to see that the first requisite to success in life, is to be a good animal. The best brain is found of little service, if there be not enough vital energy to work it; and hence to obtain the one by sacrificing the source of the other, is now considered a folly—a folly which the eventual failure of juvenile prodigies constantly illustrates. Thus we are discovering the wisdom of the saying, that one secret in education is "to know how wisely to lose time."

The once universal practice of learning by rote, is daily falling more into discredit. All modern authorities condemn the old mechanical way of teaching the alphabet. The multiplication table is now frequently taught experimentally. In the acquirement of languages, the grammar-school plan is being superseded by plans based on the spontaneous process followed by the child in gaining its mother tongue. Describing the methods there used, the "Reports on the Training School at

Battersea" say:—"The instruction in the whole preparatory course is chiefly oral, and is illustrated as much as possible by appeals to nature." And so throughout. The rote-system, like ether systems of its age, made more of the forms and symbols than of the things symbolised. To repeat the words correctly was everything; to understand their meaning nothing; and thus the spirit was sacrificed to the letter. It is at length perceived that, in this case as in others, such a result is not accidental but necessary—that in proportion as there is attention to the signs, there must be inattention to the things signified; or that, as Montaigne long ago said—*Sçavoir par cœur n'est pas sçavoir*.

Along with rote-teaching, is declining also the nearly-allied teaching by rules. The particulars first, and then the generalisation, is the new method—a method, as the Battersea School Reports remarks, which, though "the reverse of the method usually followed, which consists in giving the pupil the rule first," is yet proved by experience to be the right one. Rule-teaching is now condemned as imparting a merely empirical knowledge—as producing an appearance of understanding without the reality. To give the net product of inquiry, without the inquiry that leads to it, is found to be both enervating and inefficient. General truths to be of due and permanent use, must be earned. "Easy come easy go," is a saying as applicable to knowledge as to wealth. While rules, lying isolated in the mind—not joined to its other contents as out-growths from them—are continually forgotten; the principles which those rules express piecemeal, become, when once reached by the understanding, enduring possessions. While the rule-taught youth is at sea when beyond his rules, the youth instructed in principles solves a new case as readily as an old one. Between a mind of rules and a mind of principles, there exists a difference such as that between a confused heap of materials, and the same materials organised into a complete whole, with all its parts bound together. Of which types this last has not only the advantage that its constituent parts are better retained, but the much greater advantage that it forms an efficient agent for inquiry, for independent thought, for discovery—ends for which the first is useless. Nor let it be supposed that this is a simile only: it is the literal truth. The union of facts into generalisations *is* the organisation of knowledge, whether considered as an objective phenomenon or a subjective one; and the mental grasp may be measured by the extent to which this organisation is carried.

From the substitution of principles for rules, and the necessarily co-ordinate practice of leaving abstractions untaught till the mind has been familiarised with the facts from which they are abstracted, has resulted the postponement of some once early studies to a late period. This is exemplified in the abandonment of that intensely stupid custom, the teaching of grammar to children. As M. Marcel says:—"It may without hesitation be affirmed that grammar is not the stepping-stone, but the finishing instrument." As Mr. Wyse argues:—"Grammar and Syntax are a collection of laws and rules. Rules are gathered from practice; they are the results of induction to which we come by long observation and comparison of facts. It is, in fine, the science, the philosophy of language. In following the process of nature, neither individuals nor nations ever arrive at the science *first*. A language is spoken, and poetry written, many years before either a grammar or prosody is even thought of. Men did not wait till Aristotle had constructed his logic, to reason." In short, as grammar was made after language, so ought it to be taught after language: an inference which all who recognise the relationship between the evolution of the race and that of the individual, will see to be unavoidable.

Of new practices that have grown up during the decline of these old ones, the most important is the systematic culture of the powers of observation. After long ages of blindness, men are at last seeing that the spontaneous activity of the observing faculties in children has a meaning and a use. What was once thought mere purposeless action, or play, or mischief, as the case might be, is now recognised as the process of acquiring a knowledge on which all after-knowledge is based. Hence the well-conceived but ill-conducted system of *object-lessons*. The saying of Bacon, that physics is the mother of the sciences, has come to have a meaning in education. Without an accurate acquaintance with the visible and tangible properties of things, our conceptions must be erroneous, our inferences fallacious, and our operations unsuccessful. "The education of the senses neglected, all after education partakes of a drowsiness, a haziness, an insufficiency, which it is impossible to cure." Indeed, if we consider it, we shall find that exhaustive observation is an element in all great success. It is not to artists, naturalists, and men of science only, that it is needful; it is not only that the physician depends on it for the correctness of his diagnosis, and that to the engineer it is so important that some years in the workshop are prescribed for him; but we may see that the philosopher, also, is fundamentally one who *observes* relationships of things which others had overlooked, and that the poet, too, is one who *sees* the fine facts in nature which all recognise when pointed out, but did not before remark. Nothing requires more to be insisted on than that vivid and complete impressions are all-essential. No sound fabric of wisdom can be woven out of a rotten raw-material.

While the old method of presenting truths in the abstract has been falling out of use, there has been a corresponding adoption of the new method of presenting them in the concrete. The rudimentary facts of exact science are now being learnt by direct intuition, as textures, and tastes, and colours are learnt. Employing the ball-frame for first lessons in arithmetic exemplifies this. It is well illustrated, too, in Professor De Morgan's mode of explaining the decimal notation. M. Marcel, rightly repudiating the old system of tables, teaches weights and measures by referring to the actual yard and foot, pound and ounce, gallon and quart; and lets the discovery of their relationships be experimental. The use of geographical models and models of the regular bodies, etc., as introductory to geography and geometry respectively, are facts of the same class. Manifestly, a common trait of these methods is, that they carry each child's mind through a process like that which the mind of humanity at large has gone through. The truths of number, of form, of relationship in position, were all originally drawn from objects; and to present these truths to the child in the concrete is to let him learn them as the race learnt them. By and by, perhaps, it will be seen that he cannot possibly learn them in any other way; for that if he is made to repeat them as abstractions, the abstractions can have no meaning for him, until he finds that they are simply statements of what he intuitively discerns.

But of all the changes taking place, the most significant is the growing desire to make the acquirement of knowledge pleasurable rather than painful—a desire based on the more or less distinct perception, that at each age the intellectual action which a child likes is a healthful one for it; and conversely. There is a spreading opinion that the rise of an appetite for any kind of information implies that the unfolding mind has become fit to assimilate it, and needs it for purposes of growth; and that, on the other hand, the disgust felt towards such information is a sign either that it is prematurely presented, or that it is presented in an indigestible form. Hence the efforts to make early education amusing, and all education interesting. Hence the lectures on the value of play. Hence the defence of nursery rhymes and fairy tales. Daily we more and more conform our plans to juvenile opinion. Does the child like this or that kind of teaching?—does he take to it? we constantly ask. "His natural desire of variety should be indulged," says M. Marcel; "and the gratification of his curiosity should be combined with his improvement." "Lessons," he again remarks, "should cease before the child evinces symptoms of weariness." And so with later education. Short breaks during school-hours, excursions into the country, amusing lectures, choral songs—in these and many like traits the change may be discerned. Asceticism is disappearing out of education as out of life; and the usual test of political legislation—its tendency to promote happiness—is beginning to be, in a great degree, the test of legislation for the school and the nursery.

What now is the common characteristic of these several changes? Is it not an increasing conformity to the methods of Nature? The relinquishment of early forcing, against which Nature rebels, and the leaving of the first years for exercise of the limbs and senses, show this. The superseding of rote-learnt lessons by lessons orally and experimentally given, like those of the field and play-ground, shows this. The disuse of rule-teaching, and the adoption of teaching by principles—that is, the leaving of generalisations until there are particulars to base them on—show this. The system of object-lessons shows this. The teaching of the rudiments of science in the concrete instead of the abstract, shows this. And above all, this tendency is shown in the variously-directed efforts to present knowledge in attractive forms, and so to make the acquirement of it pleasurable. For, as it is the order of Nature in all creatures that the gratification accompanying the fulfilment of needful functions serves as a stimulus to their fulfilment—as, during the self-education of the young child, the delight taken in the biting of corals and the pulling to pieces of toys, becomes the prompter to actions which teach it the properties of matter; it follows that, in choosing the succession of subjects and the modes of instruction which most interest the pupil, we are fulfilling Nature's behests, and adjusting our proceedings to the laws of life.

Thus, then, we are on the highway towards the doctrine long ago enunciated by Pestalozzi, that alike in its order and its methods, education must conform to the natural process of mental evolution—that there is a certain sequence in which the faculties spontaneously develop, and a certain kind of knowledge which each requires during its development; and that it is for us to ascertain this sequence, and supply this knowledge. All the improvements above alluded to are partial applications of this general principle. A nebulous perception of it now prevails among teachers; and it is daily more insisted on in educational works. "The method of nature is the archetype of all methods," says M. Marcel. "The vital principle in the pursuit is to enable the pupil rightly to instruct himself," writes Mr. Wyse. The more science familiarises us with the constitution of things, the more do we see in them an inherent self-sufficingness. A higher knowledge tends continually to limit our interference with the processes of life. As in medicine the old "heroic treatment" has given place to mild treatment, and often no treatment save a normal regimen—as we have found that it is not needful to mould the bodies of babes by bandaging them in papoose-fashion or otherwise—as in gaols it is being discovered that no cunningly-devised discipline of ours is so efficient in producing reformation as the natural discipline of self-maintenance by productive labour; so in education, we are finding that success is to be achieved only by making our measures subservient to that spontaneous unfolding which all minds go through in their progress to maturity.

Of course, this fundamental principle of tuition, that the arrangement of matter and method must correspond with the order of evolution and mode of activity of the faculties—a principle so obviously true, that once stated it seems almost self-evident—has never been wholly disregarded. Teachers have unavoidably made their school-courses coincide with it in some degree, for the simple reason that education is possible only on that condition. Boys were never taught the rule-of-three until after they had learnt addition. They were not set to write exercises before they had got into their copybooks. Conic sections have always been preceded by Euclid. But the error of the old methods consists in this, that they do not recognise in detail what they are obliged to recognise in general. Yet the principle applies throughout. If from the time when a child is able to conceive two things as related in position, years must elapse before it can form a true concept of the Earth, as a sphere made up of land and sea, covered with mountains, forests, rivers, and cities, revolving on its axis, and sweeping round the Sun—if it gets from the one concept to the other by degrees—if the intermediate concepts which it forms are consecutively larger and more complicated; is it not manifest that there is a general succession through which alone it can pass; that each larger concept is made by the combination of smaller ones, and presupposes them; and that to present any of these compound concepts before the child is in possession of its constituent ones, is only less absurd than to present the final concept of the series before the initial one? In the mastering of every subject some course of increasingly complex ideas has to be gone through. The evolution of the corresponding faculties consists in the assimilation of these; which, in any true sense, is impossible without they are put into the mind in the normal order. And when this order is not followed, the result is, that they are received with apathy or disgust; and that unless the pupil is intelligent enough eventually to fill up the gaps himself, they lie in his memory as dead facts, capable of being turned to little or no use.

"But why trouble ourselves about any *curriculum* at all?" it may be asked. "If it be true that the mind like the body has a predetermined course of evolution—if it unfolds spontaneously—if its successive desires for this or that kind of information arise when these are severally required for its nutrition—if there thus exists in itself a prompter to the right species of activity at the right time; why interfere in any way? Why not leave children *wholly* to the discipline of nature?—why not remain quite passive and let them get knowledge as they best can?—why not be consistent throughout?" This is an awkward-looking question. Plausibly implying as it does, that a system of complete *laissez-faire* is the logical outcome of the doctrines set forth, it seems to furnish a disproof of them by *reductio ad absurdum*. In truth, however, they do not, when rightly understood, commit us to any such untenable position. A glance at the physical analogies will clearly show this. It is a general law of life that the more complex the organism to be produced, the longer the period during which it is dependent on a parent organism for food and protection. The difference between the minute, rapidly-formed, and self-moving spore of a conferva, and the slowly-developed seed of a tree, with its multiplied envelopes and large stock of nutriment laid by to nourish the germ during its first stages of growth, illustrates this law in its application to the vegetal world. Among animals we may trace it in a series of contrasts from the monad whose spontaneously-divided halves are as self-sufficing the moment after their separation as was the original whole; up to man, whose offspring not only passes through a protracted gestation, and subsequently long depends on the breast for sustenance; but after that must have its food artificially administered; must, when it has learned to feed itself, continue to have bread, clothing, and shelter provided; and does not acquire the power of complete self-support until a time varying from fifteen to twenty years after its birth. Now this law applies to the mind as to the body. For mental pabulum also, every higher creature, and especially man, is at first dependent on adult aid. Lacking the ability to move about, the babe is almost as powerless to get materials on which to exercise its perceptions as it is to get supplies for its stomach. Unable to prepare its own food, it is in like manner unable to reduce many kinds of knowledge to a fit form for assimilation. The language through which all higher truths are to be gained, it wholly derives from those surrounding it. And we see in such an example as the Wild Boy of Aveyron, the arrest of development that results when no help is received from parents and nurses. Thus, in providing from day to day the right kind of facts, prepared in the right manner, and giving them in due abundance at appropriate intervals, there is as much scope for active ministration to a child's mind as to its body. In either case, it is the chief function of parents to see that the *conditions* requisite to growth are maintained. And as, in supplying aliment, and clothing, and shelter, they may fulfil this function without at all interfering with the spontaneous development of the limbs and viscera, either in their order or mode; so, they may supply sounds for imitation, objects for examination, books for reading, problems for solution, and, if they use neither direct nor indirect coercion, may do this without in any way disturbing the normal process of mental evolution; or rather, may greatly facilitate that process. Hence the admission of the doctrines enunciated does not, as some might argue, involve the abandonment of teaching; but leaves ample room for an active and elaborate course of culture.

Passing from generalities to special considerations, it is to be remarked that in practice the Pestalozzian system seems scarcely to have fulfilled the promise of its theory. We hear of children not at all interested in its lessons,—disgusted with them rather; and, so far as we can gather, the Pestalozzian school have not turned out any unusual proportion of distinguished men: if even they have reached the average. We are not surprised at this. The success of every appliance depends mainly upon the intelligence with which it is used. It is a trite remark that, having the choicest tools, an unskilful artisan will botch his work; and bad teachers will fail even with the best methods. Indeed, the goodness of the method becomes in such case a cause of failure; as, to continue the simile, the perfection of the tool becomes in undisciplined hands a source of imperfection in results. A simple, un-changing, almost mechanical routine of tuition, may be carried out by the com-monest intellects, with such small beneficial effect as it is capable of producing; but a complete system—a system as heterogeneous in its appliances as the mind in its faculties—a system proposing a special means for each special end, demands for its right employment powers such as few teachers possess. The mistress of a dame-school can hear spelling-lessons; and any hedge-schoolmaster can drill boys in the multiplication-table. But to teach spelling rightly by using the powers of the letters instead of their names, or to instruct in numerical combinations by experimental synthesis, a modicum of understanding is needful; and to pursue a like rational course throughout the entire range of studies, asks an amount of judg-ment, of invention, of intellectual sympathy, of analytical faculty, which we shall never see applied to it while the tutorial official is held in such small esteem. True education is practicable only by a true philosopher. Judge, then, what prospect a philosophical method now has of being acted out! Knowing so little as we yet do of psychology, and ignorant as our teachers are of that little, what chance has a system which requires psychology for its basis?

Further hindrance and discouragement has arisen from confounding the Pestalozzian principle with the forms in which it has been embodied. Because particular plans have not answered expectation, discredit has been cast upon the doctrine associated with them: no inquiry being made whether these plans truly conform to the doctrine. Judging as usual by the concrete rather than the abstract, men have blamed the theory for the bunglings of the practice. It is as though the first futile attempt to construct a steam-engine had been held to prove that steam could not be used as a motive power. Let it be constantly borne in mind that while right in his fundamental ideas, Pestalozzi was not therefore right in all his appli-cations of them. As described even by his admirers, Pestalozzi was a man of par-tial intuitions—a man who had occasional flashes of insight rather than a man of systematic thought. His first great success at Stantz was achieved when he had no books or appliances of ordinary teaching, and when "the only object of his atten-tion was to find out at each moment what instruction his children stood peculiarly in need of, and what was the best manner of connecting it with the knowledge they already possessed." Much of his power was due, not to calmly reasoned-out plans of culture, but to his profound sympathy, which gave him a quick percep-tion of childish needs and difficulties. He lacked the ability logically to co-ordinate and develop the truths which he thus from time to time laid hold of; and had in great measure to leave this to his assistants, Kruesi, Tobler, Buss, Niederer, and Schmid. The result is, that in their details his own plans, and those vicariously devised, contain numerous crudities and inconsistencies. His nursery-method, described in *The Mother's Manual*, beginning as it does with a nomenclature of the different parts of the body, and proceeding next to specify their relative positions, and next their connections, may be proved not at all in accordance with the initial stages of mental evolution. His process of teaching the mother-tongue by formal exercises in the meanings of words and in the construction of sentences, is quite needless, and must entail on the pupil loss of time, labour, and happiness. His proposed lessons in geography are utterly unpestalozzian. And often where his plans are essentially sound, they are either incomplete or vitiated by some remnant of the old regime. While, therefore, we would defend in its entire extent the general doctrine which Pestalozzi inaugurated, we think great evil likely to result from an uncritical reception of his specific methods. That tendency, constantly exhibited by mankind, to canonise the forms and practices along with which any great truth has been bequeathed to them—their liability to prostrate their intellects before the prophet, and swear by his every word—their proneness to mistake the clothing of the idea for the idea itself; renders it needful to insist strongly upon the distinction between the fundamental principle of the Pestalozzian system, and the set of expedients devised for its practice; and to suggest that while the one may be considered as established, the other is probably nothing but an adumbration of the normal course. Indeed, on looking at the state of our knowledge, we may be quite sure that is the case. Before educational methods can be made to harmonise in character and arrangement with the faculties in their mode and order of unfolding, it is first needful that we ascertain with some completeness how the faculties *do* unfold. At present we have acquired, on this point, only a few general notions. These general notions must be developed in detail—must be transformed into a multitude of specific propositions, before we can be said to possess that *science* on which the *art* of education must be based. And then, when we have definitely made out in what succession and in what combinations the mental powers become active, it remains to choose out of the many possible ways of exercising each of them, that which best conforms to its natural mode of action. Evidently, therefore, it is not to be supposed that even our most advanced modes of teaching are the right ones, or nearly the right ones.

Bearing in mind then this distinction between the principle and the practice of Pestalozzi, and inferring from the grounds assigned that the last must necessarily be very defective, the reader will rate at its true worth the dissatisfaction with the system which some have expressed; and will see that the realisation of the Pestalozzian idea remains to be achieved. Should he argue, however, from what has just been said, that no such realisation is at present practicable, and that all effort ought to be devoted to the preliminary inquiry; we reply, that though it is not possible for a scheme of culture to be perfected either in matter or form until a rational psychology has been established, it is possible, with the aid of certain guiding principles, to make empirical approximations towards a perfect scheme. To prepare the way for further research we will now specify these principles. Some of them have been more or less distinctly implied in the foregoing pages; but it will be well here to state them all in logical order.

1. That in education we should proceed from the simple to the complex, is a truth which has always been to some extent acted upon: not professedly, indeed, nor by any means consistently. The mind develops. Like all things that develop it progresses from the homogeneous to the heterogeneous; and a normal training system, being an objective counterpart of this subjective process, must exhibit a like progression. Moreover, thus interpreting it, we may see that this formula has much wider application than at first appears. For its *rationale* involves, not only that we should proceed from the single to the combined in the teaching of each branch of knowledge; but that we should do the like with knowledge as a whole. As the mind, consisting at first of but few active faculties, has its later-completed faculties successively brought into play, and ultimately comes to have all its faculties in simultaneous action; it follows that our teaching should begin with but few subjects at once, and successively adding to these, should finally carry on all subjects abreast. Not only in its details should education proceed from the simple to the complex, but in its *ensemble* also.

2. The development of the mind, as all other development, is an advance from the indefinite to the definite. In common with the rest of the organism, the brain reaches its finished structure only at maturity; and in proportion as its structure is unfinished, its actions are wanting in precision. Hence like the first movements and the first attempts at speech, the first perceptions and thoughts are extremely vague. As from a rudimentary eye, discerning only the difference between light and darkness, the progress is to an eye that distinguishes kinds and gradations of colour, and details of form, with the greatest exactness; so, the intellect as a whole and in each faculty, beginning with the rudest discriminations among objects and actions, advances towards discriminations of increasing nicety and distinctness. To this general law our educational course and methods must conform. It is not practicable, nor would it be desirable if practicable, to put precise ideas into the undeveloped mind. We may indeed at an early age communicate the verbal forms in which such ideas are wrapped up; and teachers, who habitually do this, suppose that when the verbal forms have been correctly learnt, the ideas which should fill them have been acquired. But a brief cross-examination of the pupil proves the contrary. It turns out either that the words have been committed to memory with little or no thought about their meaning, or else that the perception of their meaning which has been gained is a very cloudy one. Only as the multiplication of experiences gives materials for definite conceptions—only as observation year by year discloses the less conspicuous attributes which distinguish things and processes previously confounded together—only as each class of co-existences and sequences becomes familiar through the recurrence of cases coming under it—only as the various classes of relations get accurately marked off from each other by mutual limitation, can the exact definitions of advanced knowledge become truly comprehensible. Thus in education we must be content to set out with crude notions. These we must aim to make gradually clearer by facilitating the acquisition of experiences such as will correct, first their greatest errors, and afterwards their successively less marked errors. And the scientific formulæ must be given only as fast as the conceptions are perfected.

3. To say that our lessons ought to start from the concrete and end in the abstract, may be considered as in part a repetition of the first of the foregoing principles. Nevertheless it is a maxim that must be stated: if with no other view, then with the view of showing in certain cases what are truly the simple and the complex. For unfortunately there has been much misunderstanding on this point. General formulas which men have devised to express groups of details, and which have severally simplified their conceptions by uniting many facts into one fact, they have supposed must simplify the conceptions of a child also. They have forgotten that a generalisation is simple only in comparison with the whole mass of particular truths it comprehends—that it is more complex than any one of these truths taken singly—that only after many of these single truths have been acquired does the generalisation ease the memory and help the reason—and that to a mind not possessing these single truths it is necessarily a mystery. Thus confounding two kinds of simplification, teachers have constantly erred by setting out with "first principles": a proceeding essentially, though not apparently, at variance with the primary rule; which implies that the mind should be introduced to principles through the medium of examples, and so should be led from the particular to the general—from the concrete to the abstract.

4. The education of the child must accord both in mode and arrangement with the education of mankind, considered historically. In other words, the genesis of knowledge in the individual must follow the same course as the genesis of knowledge in the race. In strictness, this principle may be considered as already expressed by implication; since both, being processes of evolution, must conform to those same general laws of evolution above insisted on, and must therefore agree with each other. Nevertheless this particular parallelism is of value for the specific guidance it affords. To M. Comte we believe society owes the enunciation of it; and we may accept this item of his philosophy without at all committing ourselves to the rest. This doctrine may be upheld by two reasons, quite independent of any abstract theory; and either of them sufficient to establish it. One is deducible from the law of hereditary transmission as considered in its wider consequences. For if it be true that men exhibit likeness to ancestry, both in aspect and character—if it be true that certain mental manifestations, as insanity, occur in successive members of the same family at the same age—if, passing from individual cases in which the traits of many dead ancestors mixing with those of a few living ones greatly obscure the law, we turn to national types, and remark how the contrasts between them are persistent from age to age—if we remember that these respective types came from a common stock, and that hence the present marked differences between them must have arisen from the action of modifying circumstances upon successive generations who severally transmitted the accumulated effects to their descendants—if we find the differences to be now organic, so that a French child grows into a French man even when brought up among strangers—and if the general fact thus illustrated is true of the whole nature, intellect inclusive; then it follows that if there be an order in which the human race has mastered its various kinds of knowledge, there will arise in every child an aptitude to acquire these kinds of knowledge in the same order. So that even were the order intrinsically indifferent, it would facilitate education to lead the individual mind through the

steps traversed by the general mind. But the order is *not* intrinsically indifferent; and hence the fundamental reason why education should be a repetition of civilisation in little. It is provable both that the historical sequence was, in its main outlines, a necessary one; and that the causes which determined it apply to the child as to the race. Not to specify these causes in detail, it will suffice here to point out that as the mind of humanity placed in the midst of phenomena and striving to comprehend them, has, after endless comparisons, speculations, experiments, and theories, reached its present knowledge of each subject by a specific route; it may rationally be inferred that the relationship between mind and phenomena is such as to prevent this knowledge from being reached by any other route; and that as each child's mind stands in this same relationship to phenomena, they can be accessible to it only through the same route. Hence in deciding upon the right method of education, an inquiry into the method of civilisation will help to guide us.

5. One of the conclusions to which such an inquiry leads, is, that in each branch of instruction we should proceed from the empirical to the rational. During human progress, every science is evolved out of its corresponding art. It results from the necessity we are under, both individually and as a race, of reaching the abstract by way of the concrete, that there must be practice and an accruing experience with its empirical generalisation, before there can be science. Science is organised knowledge; and before knowledge can be organised, some of it must be possessed. Every study, therefore, should have a purely experimental introduction; and only after an ample fund of observations has been accumulated, should reasoning begin. As illustrative applications of this rule, we may instance the modern course of placing grammar, not before language, but after it; or the ordinary custom of prefacing perspective by practical drawing. By and by further applications of it will be indicated.

6. A second corollary from the foregoing general principle, and one which cannot be too strenuously insisted on, is, that in education the process of self-development should be encouraged to the uttermost. Children should be led to make their own investigations, and to draw their own inferences. They should be *told* as little as possible, and induced to *discover* as much as possible. Humanity has progressed solely by self-instruction; and that to achieve the best results, each mind must progress somewhat after the same fashion, is continually proved by the marked success of self-made men. Those who have been brought up under the ordinary school-drill, and have carried away with them the idea that education is practicable only in that style, will think it hopeless to make children their own teachers. If, however, they will consider that the all-important knowledge of surrounding objects which a child gets in its early years is got without help — if they will remember that the child is self-taught in the use of its mother tongue — if they will estimate the amount of that experience of life, that out-of-school wisdom, which every boy gathers for himself — if they will mark the unusual intelligence of the uncared-for London *gamin*, as shown in whatever directions his faculties have been tasked — if, further, they will think how many minds have struggled up unaided, not only through the mysteries of our irrationally-planned *curriculum*, but through hosts of other obstacles besides; they will find it a not unreasonable conclusion that if

the subjects be put before him in right order and right form, any pupil of ordinary capacity will surmount his successive difficulties with but little assistance. Who indeed can watch the ceaseless observation, and inquiry, and inference going on in a child's mind, or listen to its acute remarks on matters within the range of its faculties, without perceiving that these powers it manifests, if brought to bear systematically upon studies *within the same range*, would readily master them without help? This need for perpetual telling results from our stupidity, not from the child's. We drag it away from the facts in which it is interested, and which it is actively assimilating of itself. We put before it facts far too complex for it to understand; and therefore distasteful to it. Finding that it will not voluntarily acquire these facts, we thrust them into its mind by force of threats and punishment. By thus denying the knowledge it craves, and cramming it with knowledge it cannot digest, we produce a morbid state of its faculties; and a consequent disgust for knowledge in general. And when, as a result partly of the stolid indolence we have brought on, and partly of still-continued unfitness in its studies, the child can understand nothing without explanation, and becomes a mere passive recipient of our instruction, we infer that education must necessarily be carried on thus. Having by our method induced helplessness, we make the helplessness a reason for our method. Clearly then, the experience of pedagogues cannot rationally be quoted against the system we are advocating. And whoever sees this, will see that we may safely follow the discipline of Nature throughout—may, by a skilful ministration, make the mind as self-developing in its later stages as it is in its earlier ones; and that only by doing this can we produce the highest power and activity.

7. As a final test by which to judge any plan of culture, should come the question,—Does it create a pleasurable excitement in the pupils? When in doubt whether a particular mode or arrangement is or is not more in harmony with the foregoing principles than some other, we may safely abide by this criterion. Even when, as considered theoretically, the proposed course seems the best, yet if it produces no interest, or less interest than some other course, we should relinquish it; for a child's intellectual instincts are more trustworthy than our reasonings. In respect to the knowing-faculties, we may confidently trust in the general law, that under normal conditions, healthful action is pleasurable, while action which gives pain is not healthful. Though at present very incompletely conformed to by the emotional nature, yet by the intellectual nature, or at least by those parts of it which the child exhibits, this law is almost wholly conformed to. The repugnances to this and that study which vex the ordinary teacher, are not innate, but result from his unwise system. Fellenberg says, "Experience has taught me that *indolence* in young persons is so directly opposite to their natural disposition to activity, that unless it is the consequence of bad education, it is almost invariably connected with some constitutional defect." And the spontaneous activity to which children are thus prone, is simply the pursuit of those pleasures which the healthful exercise of the faculties gives. It is true that some of the higher mental powers, as yet but little developed in the race, and congenitally possessed in any considerable degree only by the most advanced, are indisposed to the amount of exertion required of them. But these, in virtue of their very complexity, will, in a normal course of culture, come last into exercise; and will therefore have no demands made on them until

the pupil has arrived at an age when ulterior motives can be brought into play, and an indirect pleasure made to counterbalance a direct displeasure. With all faculties lower than these, however, the immediate gratification consequent on activity, is the normal stimulus; and under good management the only needful stimulus. When we have to fall back on some other, we must take the fact as evidence that we are on the wrong track. Experience is daily showing with greater clearness, that there is always a method to be found productive of interest—even of delight; and it ever turns out that this is the method proved by all other tests to be the right one.

With most, these guiding principles will weigh but little if left in this abstract form. Partly, therefore, to exemplify their application, and partly with a view of making sundry specific suggestions, we propose now to pass from the theory of education to the practice of it.

It was the opinion of Pestalozzi, and one which has ever since his day been gaining ground, that education of some kind should begin from the cradle. Whoever has watched, with any discernment, the wide-eyed gaze of the infant at surrounding objects knows very well that education *does* begin thus early, whether we intend it or not; and that these fingerings and suckings of everything it can lay hold of, these open-mouthed listenings to every sound, are first steps in the series which ends in the discovery of unseen planets, the invention of calculating engines, the production of great paintings, or the composition of symphonies and operas. This activity of the faculties from the very first, being spontaneous and inevitable, the question is whether we shall supply in due variety the materials on which they may exercise themselves; and to the question so put, none but an affirmative answer can be given. As before said, however, agreement with Pestalozzi's theory does not involve agreement with his practice; and here occurs a case in point. Treating of instruction in spelling he says:—

> "The spelling-book ought, therefore, to contain all the sounds of the language, and these ought to be taught in every family from the earliest infancy. The child who learns his spelling book ought to repeat them to the infant in the cradle, before it is able to pronounce even one of them, so that they may be deeply impressed upon its mind by frequent repetition."

Joining this with the suggestions for "a nursery method," set down in his *Mother's Manual*, in which he makes the names, positions, connections, numbers, properties, and uses of the limbs and body his first lessons, it becomes clear that Pestalozzi's notions on early mental development were too crude to enable him to devise judicious plans. Let us consider the course which Psychology dictates.

The earliest impressions which the mind can assimilate are the undecomposable sensations produced by resistance, light, sound, etc. Manifestly, decomposable states of consciousness cannot exist before the states of consciousness out of which they are composed. There can be no idea of form until some familiarity with light in its gradations and qualities, or resistance in its different intensities, has been acquired; for, as has been long known, we recognise visible form by means of varieties of light, and tangible form by means of varieties of resistance. Similarly, no articulate sound is cognisable until the inarticulate sounds which go to make it up have been learned. And thus must it be in every other case. Following, therefore, the necessary law of progression from the simple to the complex, we should provide for the infant a sufficiency of objects presenting different degrees and kinds of resistance, a sufficiency of objects reflecting different amounts and qualities of light, and a sufficiency of sounds contrasted in their loudness, their pitch and their *timbre*. How fully this *à priori* conclusion is confirmed by infantile instincts, all will see on being reminded of the delight which every young child has in biting its toys, in feeling its brother's bright jacket-buttons, and pulling papa's whiskers—how absorbed it becomes in gazing at any gaudily-painted object, to which it applies the word "pretty," when it can pronounce it, wholly because of the bright colours—and how its face broadens into a laugh at the tattlings of its nurse, the snapping of a visitor's fingers, or any sound which it has not before heard. Fortunately, the ordinary practices of the nursery fulfil these early requirements of education to a considerable degree. Much, however, remains to be done; and it is of more importance that it should be done than at first appears. Every faculty during that spontaneous activity which accompanies its evolution is capable of receiving more vivid impressions than at any other period. Moreover, as these simplest elements have to be mastered, and as the mastery of them whenever achieved must take time, it becomes an economy of time to occupy this first stage of childhood, during which no other intellectual action is possible, in gaining a complete familiarity with them in all their modifications. Nor let us omit the fact, that both temper and health will be improved by the continual gratification resulting from a due supply of these impressions which every child so greedily assimilates. Space, could it be spared, might here be well filled by some suggestions towards a more systematic ministration to these simplest of the perceptions. But it must suffice to point out that any such ministration, recognising the general law of evolution from the indefinite to the definite, should proceed upon the corollary that in the development of every faculty, markedly contrasted impressions are the first to be distinguished; that hence sounds greatly differing in loudness and pitch, colours very remote from each other, and substances widely unlike in hardness or texture, should be the first supplied; and that in each case the progression must be by slow degrees to impressions more nearly allied.

Passing on to object-lessons, which manifestly form a natural continuation of this primary culture of the senses, it is to be remarked, that the system commonly pursued is wholly at variance with the method of Nature, as exhibited alike in infancy, in adult life, and in the course of civilisation. "The child," says M. Marcel, "must be *shown* how all the parts of an object are connected, etc.;" and the various manuals of these object-lessons severally contain lists of the facts which the child is to be *told* respecting each of the things put before it. Now it needs but a glance at the daily life of the infant to see that all the knowledge of things which is gained before the acquirement of speech, is self-gained—that the qualities of hardness and weight associated with certain appearances, the possession of particular forms and colours by particular persons, the production of special sounds by animals of special aspects, are phenomena which it observes for itself. In manhood too, when there are no longer teachers at hand, the observations and inferences hourly required for guidance must be made unhelped; and success in life depends upon the accuracy and completeness with which they are made. Is it probable, then, that while the process displayed in the evolution of humanity at large is repeated alike by the infant and the man, a reverse process must be followed during the period between infancy and manhood? and that too, even in so simple a thing as learning the properties of objects? Is it not obvious, on the contrary, that one method must be pursued throughout? And is not Nature perpetually thrusting this method upon us, if we had but the wit to see it, and the humility to adopt it? What can be more manifest than the desire of children for intellectual sympathy? Mark how the infant sitting on your knee thrusts into your face the toy it holds, that you too may look at it. See when it makes a creak with its wet finger on the table, how it turns and looks at you; does it again, and again looks at you; thus saying as clearly as it can—"Hear this new sound." Watch the elder children coming into the room exclaiming—"Mamma, see what a curious thing," "Mamma, look at this," "Mamma, look at that:" a habit which they would continue, did not the silly mamma tell them not to tease her. Observe that, when out with the nurse-maid, each little one runs up to her with the new flower it has gathered, to show her how pretty it is, and to get her also to say it is pretty. Listen to the eager volubility with which every urchin describes any novelty he has been to see, if only he can find some one who will attend with any interest. Does not the induction lie on the surface? Is it not clear that we must conform our course to these intellectual instincts—that we must just systematise the natural process—that we must listen to all the child has to tell us about each object; must induce it to say everything it can think of about such object; must occasionally draw its attention to facts it has not yet observed, with the view of leading it to notice them itself whenever they recur; and must go on by and by to indicate or supply new series of things for a like exhaustive examination? Note the way in which, on this method, the intelligent mother conducts her lessons. Step by step she familiarises her little boy with the names of the simpler attributes, hardness, softness, colour, taste, size: in doing which she finds him eagerly help by bringing this to show her that it is red, and the other to make her feel that it is hard, as fast as she gives him words for these properties. Each additional property, as she draws his attention to it in some fresh thing which he brings her, she takes care to mention in connection with those he already knows; so that by the natural tendency to imitate, he may get into the habit of repeating them one after another. Gradually as there occur cases in which he omits to name one or more of the properties he has become acquainted with, she introduces the practice of asking him whether there is not something more that he can tell her about the thing he has got. Probably he does not understand. After letting him puzzle awhile she tells him; perhaps laughing at him a little for his failure. A few recurrences of this and he perceives what is to be done. When next she says she knows something more about the object than he has told her, his pride is roused; he looks at it intently; he thinks over all that he has heard; and the problem being easy, presently finds it out. He is full of glee at his success, and she sympathises with him. In common with every child, he delights in the discovery of his powers. He wishes for more victories, and goes in quest of more things about which to tell her. As his faculties unfold she adds quality after quality to his list: progressing from hardness and softness to roughness and smoothness, from colour to polish, from simple bodies to composite ones—thus constantly complicating the problem as he gains competence, constantly taxing his attention and memory to a greater extent, constantly maintaining his interest by supplying him with new impressions such as his mind can assimilate, and constantly gratifying him by conquests over such small difficulties as he can master. In doing this she is manifestly but following out that spontaneous process which was going on during a still earlier period—simply aiding self-evolution; and is aiding it in the mode suggested by the boy's instinctive behaviour to her. Manifestly, too, the course she is adopting is the one best calculated to establish a habit of exhaustive observation; which is the professed aim of these lessons. To *tell* a child this and to *show* it the other, is not to teach it how to observe, but to make it a mere recipient of another's observations: a proceeding which weakens rather than strengthens its powers of self-instruction—which deprives it of the pleasures resulting from successful activity—which presents this all-attractive knowledge under the aspect of formal tuition—and which thus generates that indifference and even disgust not unfrequently felt towards these object-lessons. On the other hand, to pursue the course above described is simply to guide the intellect to its appropriate food; to join with the intellectual appetites their natural adjuncts—*amour propre* and the desire for sympathy; to induce by the union of all these an intensity of attention which insures perceptions both vivid and complete; and to habituate the mind from the beginning to that practice of self-help which it must ultimately follow.

Object-lessons should not only be carried on after quite a different fashion from that commonly pursued, but should be extended to a range of things far wider, and continued to a period far later, than now. They should not be limited to the contents of the house; but should include those of the fields and the hedges, the quarry and the sea-shore. They should not cease with early childhood; but should be so kept up during youth, as insensibly to merge into the investigations of the naturalist and the man of science. Here again we have but to follow Nature's leadings. Where can be seen an intenser delight than that of children picking up new flowers and watching new insects; or hoarding pebbles and shells? And who is there but perceives that by sympathising with them they may be led on to any extent of inquiry into the qualities and structures of these things? Every botanist who has had children with him in the woods and lanes must have noticed how eagerly they joined in his pursuits, how keenly they searched out plants for him, how intently they watched while he examined them, how they overwhelmed him with questions. The consistent follower of Bacon—the "servant and interpreter of nature," will see that we ought modestly to adopt the course of culture thus indicated. Having become familiar with the simpler properties of inorganic objects, the child should by the same process be led on to an exhaustive examination of the things it picks up in its daily walks—the less complex facts they present being alone noticed at first: in plants, the colours, numbers, and forms of the petals, and shapes of the stalks and leaves; in insects, the numbers of the wings, legs, and antennæ, and their colours. As these become fully appreciated and invariably observed, further facts may be successively introduced: in the one case, the numbers of stamens and pistils, the forms of the flowers, whether radial or bilateral in symmetry, the arrangement and character of the leaves, whether opposite or alternate, stalked or sessile, smooth or hairy, serrated, toothed, or crenate; in the other, the divisions of the body, the segments of the abdomen, the markings of the wings, the number of joints in the legs, and the forms of the smaller organs—the system pursued throughout being that of making it the child's ambition to say respecting everything it finds all that can be said. Then when a fit age has been reached, the means of preserving these plants, which have become so interesting in virtue of the knowledge obtained of them, may as a great favour be supplied; and eventually, as a still greater favour, may also be supplied the apparatus needful for keeping the larvæ of our common butterflies and moths through their transformations—a practice which, as we can personally testify, yields the highest gratification; is continued with ardour for years; when joined with the formation of an entomological collection, adds immense interest to Saturday-afternoon rambles; and forms an admirable introduction to the study of physiology.

We are quite prepared to hear from many that all this is throwing away time and energy; and that children would be much better occupied in writing their copies or learning their pence-tables, and so fitting themselves for the business of life. We regret that such crude ideas of what constitutes education, and such a narrow conception of utility, should still be prevalent. Saying nothing on the need for a systematic culture of the perceptions and the value of the practices above inculcated as subserving that need, we are prepared to defend them even on the score of the knowledge gained. If men are to be mere cits, mere porers over ledgers, with no ideas beyond their trades—if it is well that they should be as the cockney whose conception of rural pleasures extends no further than sitting in a tea-garden smoking pipes and drinking porter; or as the squire who thinks of woods as places for shooting in, of uncultivated plants as nothing but weeds, and who classifies animals into game, vermin, and stock—then indeed it is needless to learn anything that does not directly help to replenish the till and fill the larder. But if there is a more worthy aim for us than to be drudges—if there are other uses in the things around than their power to bring money—if there are higher faculties to be exercised than acquisitive and sensual ones—if the pleasures which poetry and art and science and philosophy can bring are of any moment; then is it desirable that the instinctive inclination which every child shows to observe natural beauties and investigate natural phenomena, should be encouraged. But this gross utilitarianism which is content to come into the world and quit it again without knowing what kind of a world it is or what it contains, may be met on its own ground. It will by and by be found that a knowledge of the laws of life is more important than any other knowledge whatever—that the laws of life underlie not only all bodily and mental processes, but by implication all the transactions of the house and the street, all commerce, all politics, all morals—and that therefore without a comprehension of them, neither personal nor social conduct can be rightly regulated. It will eventually be seen too, that the laws of life are essentially the same throughout the whole organic creation; and further, that they cannot be properly understood in their complex manifestations until they have been studied in their simpler ones. And when this is seen, it will be also seen that in aiding the child to acquire the out-of-door information for which it shows so great an avidity, and in encouraging the acquisition of such information throughout youth, we are simply inducing it to store up the raw material for future organisation—the facts that will one day bring home to it with due force, those great generalisations of science by which actions may be rightly guided.

The spreading recognition of drawing as an element of education is one among many signs of the more rational views on mental culture now beginning to prevail. Once more it may be remarked that teachers are at length adopting the course which Nature has perpetually been pressing on their notice. The spontaneous attempts made by children to represent the men, houses, trees, and animals around them—on a slate if they can get nothing better, or with lead-pencil on paper if they can beg them—are familiar to all. To be shown through a picture-book is one of their highest gratifications; and as usual, their strong imitative tendency presently generates in them the ambition to make pictures themselves also. This effort to depict the striking things they see is a further instinctive exercise of the perceptions—a means whereby still greater accuracy and completeness of observation are induced. And alike by trying to interest us in their discoveries of the sensible properties of things, and by their endeavours to draw, they solicit from us just that kind of culture which they most need.

Had teachers been guided by Nature's hints, not only in making drawing a part of education but in choosing modes of teaching it, they would have done still better than they have done. What is that the child first tries to represent? Things that are large, things that are attractive in colour, things round which its pleasurable associations most cluster—human beings from whom it has received so many emotions; cows and dogs which interest by the many phenomena they present; houses that are hourly visible and strike by their size and contrast of parts. And which of the processes of representation gives it most delight? Colouring. Paper and pencil are good in default of something better; but a box of paints and a brush—these are the treasures. The drawing of outlines immediately becomes secondary to colouring—is gone through mainly with a view to the colouring; and if leave can be got to colour a book of prints, how great is the favour! Now, ridiculous as such a position will seem to drawing-masters who postpone colouring and who teach form by a dreary discipline of copying lines, we believe that the course of culture thus indicated is the right one. The priority of colour to form, which, as already pointed out, has a psychological basis, should be recognised from the beginning; and from the beginning also, the things imitated should be real. That greater delight in colour which is not only conspicuous in children but persists in most persons throughout life, should be continuously employed as the natural stimulus to the mastery of the comparatively difficult and unattractive form: the pleasure of the subsequent tinting should be the prospective reward for the labour of delineation. And these efforts to represent interesting actualities should be encouraged; in the conviction that as, by a widening experience, simpler and more practicable objects become interesting, they too will be attempted; and that so a gradual approximation will be made towards imitations having some resemblance to the realities. The extreme indefiniteness which, in conformity with the law of evolution, these first attempts exhibit, is anything but a reason for ignoring them. No matter how grotesque the shapes produced; no matter how daubed and glaring the colours. The question is not whether the child is producing good drawings. The question is, whether it is developing its faculties. It has first to gain some command over its fingers, some crude notions of likeness; and this practice is better than any other for these ends, since it is the spontaneous and interesting one. During early childhood no formal drawing-lessons are possible. Shall we therefore repress, or neglect to aid, these efforts at self-culture? or shall we encourage and guide them as normal exercises of the perceptions and the powers of manipulation? If by furnishing cheap woodcuts to be painted, and simple contour-maps to have their boundary lines tinted, we can not only pleasurably draw out the faculty of colour, but can incidentally produce some familiarity with the outlines of things and countries, and some ability to move the brush steadily; and if by the supply of tempting objects we can keep up the instinctive practice of making representations, however rough; it must happen that when the age for lessons in drawing is reached, there will exist a facility that would else have been absent. Time will have been gained; and trouble, both to teacher and pupil, saved.

From what has been said, it may be readily inferred that we condemn the practice of drawing from copies; and still more so that formal discipline in making straight lines and curved lines and compound lines, with which it is the fashion of some teachers to begin. We regret that the Society of Arts has recently, in its series of manuals on "Rudimentary Art Instruction," given its countenance to an elementary drawing-book, which is the most vicious in principle that we have seen. We refer to the *Outline from Outline, or from the Flat*, by John Bell, sculptor. As explained in the prefatory note, this publication proposes "to place before the student a simple, yet logical mode of instruction;" and to this end sets out with a number of definitions thus:—

"A simple line in drawing is a thin mark drawn from one point to another.

"Lines may be divided, as to their nature in drawing, into two classes:—

"1. *Straight*, which are marks that go the shortest road between two points, as A B.

"2. Or *Curved*, which are marks which do not go the shortest road between two points, as C D."

And so the introduction progresses to horizontal lines, perpendicular lines, oblique lines, angles of the several kinds, and the various figures which lines and angles make up. The work is, in short, a grammar of form, with exercises. And thus the system of commencing with a dry analysis of elements, which, in the teaching of language, has been exploded, is to be re-instituted in the teaching of drawing. We are to set out with the definite, instead of with the indefinite. The abstract is to be preliminary to the concrete. Scientific conceptions are to precede empirical experiences. That this is an inversion of the normal order, we need scarcely repeat. It has been well said concerning the custom of prefacing the art of speaking any tongue by a drilling in the parts of speech and their functions, that it is about as reasonable as prefacing the art of walking by a course of lessons on the bones, muscles, and nerves of the legs; and much the same thing may be said of the proposal to preface the art of representing objects, by a nomenclature and definitions of the lines which they yield on analysis. These technicalities are alike repulsive and needless. They render the study distasteful at the very outset; and all with the view of teaching that which, in the course of practice, will be learnt unconsciously. Just as the child incidentally gathers the meanings of ordinary words from the conversations going on around it, without the help of dictionaries; so, from the remarks on objects, pictures, and its own drawings, will it presently acquire, not only without effort but even pleasurably, those same scientific terms which, when taught at first, are a mystery and a weariness.

If any dependence is to be placed on the general principles of education that have been laid down, the process of learning to draw should be throughout continuous with those efforts of early childhood, described above as so worthy of encouragement. By the time that the voluntary practice thus initiated has given some steadiness of hand, and some tolerable ideas of proportion, there will have arisen a vague notion of body as presenting its three dimensions in perspective. And when, after sundry abortive, Chinese-like attempts to render this appearance on paper, there has grown up a pretty clear perception of the thing to be done, and a desire to do it, a first lesson in empirical perspective may be given by means of the apparatus occasionally used in explaining perspective as a science. This sounds alarming; but the experiment is both comprehensible and interesting to any boy or girl of ordinary intelligence. A plate of glass so framed as to stand vertically on the table, being placed before the pupil, and a book or like simple object laid on the other side of it, he is requested, while keeping the eye in one position, to make ink-dots on the glass so that they may coincide with, or hide, the corners of this object. He is next told to join these dots by lines; on doing which he perceives that the lines he makes hide, or coincide with, the outlines of the object. And then by putting a sheet of paper on the other side of the glass, it is made manifest to him that the lines he has thus drawn represent the object as he saw it. They not only look like it, but he perceives that they must be like it, because he made them agree with its outlines; and by removing the paper he can convince himself that they do agree with its outlines. The fact is new and striking; and serves him as an experimental demonstration, that lines of certain lengths, placed in certain directions on a plane, can represent lines of other lengths, and having other directions, in space. By gradually changing the position of the object, he may be led to observe how some lines shorten and disappear, while others come into sight and lengthen. The convergence of parallel lines, and, indeed, all the leading facts of perspective, may, from time to time, be similarly illustrated to him. If he has been duly accustomed to self-help, he will gladly, when it is suggested, attempt to draw one of these outlines on paper, by the eye only; and it may soon be made an exciting aim to produce, unassisted, a representation as like as he can to one subsequently sketched on the glass. Thus, without the unintelligent, mechanical practice of copying other drawings, but by a method at once simple and attractive—rational, yet not abstract—a familiarity with the linear appearances of things, and a faculty of rendering them, may be step by step acquired. To which advantages add these:—that even thus early the pupil learns, almost unconsciously, the true theory of a picture (namely, that it is a delineation of objects as they appear when projected on a plane placed between them and the eye); and that when he reaches a fit age for commencing scientific perspective, he is already thoroughly acquainted with the facts which form its logical basis.

As exhibiting a rational mode of conveying primary conceptions in geometry, we cannot do better than quote the following passage from Mr. Wyse:—

"A child has been in the habit of using cubes for arithmetic; let him use them also for the elements of geometry. I would begin with solids, the reverse of the usual plan. It saves all the difficulty of absurd definitions, and bad explanations on points, lines, and surfaces, which are nothing but abstractions.... A cube presents many of the principal elements of geometry; it at once exhibits points, straight lines, parallel lines, angles, parallelograms, etc., etc. These cubes are divisible into various parts. The pupil has already been familiarised with such divisions in numeration, and he now proceeds to a comparison of their several parts, and of the relation of these parts to each other.... From thence he advances to globes, which furnish him with elementary notions of the circle, of curves generally, etc., etc.

"Being tolerably familiar with solids, he may now substitute planes. The transition may be made very easy. Let the cube, for instance, be cut into thin divisions, and placed on paper; he will then see as many plane rectangles as he has divisions; so with all the others. Globes may be treated in the same manner; he will thus see how surfaces really are generated, and be enabled to abstract them with facility in every solid.

"He has thus acquired the alphabet and reading of geometry. He now proceeds to write it.

"The simplest operation, and therefore the first, is merely to place these planes on a piece of paper, and pass the pencil round them. When this has been frequently done, the plane may be put at a little distance, and the child required to copy it, and so on."

A stock of geometrical conceptions having been obtained, in some such manner as this recommended by Mr. Wyse, a further step may be taken, by introducing the practice of testing the correctness of figures drawn by eye: thus both exciting an ambition to make them exact, and continually illustrating the difficulty of fulfilling that ambition. There can be little doubt that geometry had its origin (as, indeed, the word implies) in the methods discovered by artizans and others, of making accurate measurements for the foundations of buildings, areas of inclosures, and the like; and that its truths came to be treasured up, merely with a view to their immediate utility. They would be introduced to the pupil under analogous relationships. In cutting out pieces for his card-houses, in drawing ornamental diagrams for colouring, and in those various instructive occupations which an inventive teacher will lead him into, he may for a length of time be advantageously left, like the primitive builder, to tentative processes; and so will learn through experience the difficulty of achieving his aims by the unaided senses. When, having meanwhile undergone a valuable discipline of the perceptions, he has reached a fit age for using a pair of compasses, he will, while duly appreciating these as enabling him to verify his ocular guesses, be still hindered by the imperfections of the approximative method. In this stage he may be left for a further period: partly as being yet too young for anything higher; partly because it is desirable that he should be made to feel still more strongly the want of systematic contrivances. If the acquisition of knowledge is to be made continuously interesting; and if, in the early civilisation of the child, as in the early civilisation of the race, science is valued only as ministering to art; it is manifest that the proper preliminary to geometry, is a long practice in those constructive processes which geometry will facilitate. Observe that here, too, Nature points the way. Children show a strong propensity to cut out things in paper, to make, to build—a propensity which, if encouraged and directed, will not only prepare the way for scientific conceptions, but will develop those powers of manipulation in which most people are so deficient.

When the observing and inventive faculties have attained the requisite power, the pupil may be introduced to empirical geometry; that is—geometry dealing with methodical solutions, but not with the demonstrations of them. Like all other transitions in education, this should be made not formally but incidentally; and the relationship to constructive art should still be maintained. To make, out of cardboard, a tetrahedron like one given to him, is a problem which will interest the pupil and serve as a convenient starting-point. In attempting this, he finds it needful to draw four equilateral triangles arranged in special positions. Being unable in the absence of an exact method to do this accurately, he discovers on putting the triangles into their respective positions, that he cannot make their sides fit; and that their angles do not meet at the apex. He may now be shown how, by describing a couple of circles, each of these triangles may be drawn with perfect correctness and without guessing; and after his failure he will value the information. Having thus helped him to the solution of his first problem, with the view of illustrating the nature of geometrical methods, he is in future to be left to solve the questions put to him as best he can. To bisect a line, to erect a perpendicular, to describe a square, to bisect an angle, to draw a line parallel to a given line, to describe a hexagon, are problems which a little patience will enable him to find out. And from these he may be led on step by step to more complex questions: all of which, under judicious management, he will puzzle through unhelped. Doubtless, many of those brought up under the old regime, will look upon this assertion sceptically. We speak from facts, however; and those neither few nor special. We have seen a class of boys become so interested in making out solutions to such problems, as to look forward to their geometry-lesson as a chief event of the week. Within the last month, we have heard of one girl's school, in which some of the young ladies voluntarily occupy themselves with geometrical questions out of school-hours; and of another, where they not only do this, but where one of them is begging for problems to find out during the holidays: both which facts we state on the authority of the teacher. Strong proofs, these, of the practicability and the immense advantage of self-development! A branch of knowledge which, as commonly taught, is dry and even repulsive, is thus, by following the method of Nature, made extremely interesting and profoundly beneficial. We say profoundly beneficial, because the effects are not confined to the gaining of geometrical facts, but often revolutionise the whole state of mind. It has repeatedly occurred that those who have been stupefied by the ordinary school-drill—by its abstract formulas, its wearisome tasks, its cramming—have suddenly had their intellects roused by thus ceasing to make them passive recipients, and inducing them to become active discoverers. The discouragement caused by bad teaching having been diminished by a little sympathy, and sufficient perseverance excited to achieve a first success, there arises a revulsion of feeling affecting the whole nature. They no longer find themselves incompetent; they, too, can do something. And gradually as success follows success, the incubus of despair disappears, and they attack the difficulties of their other studies with a courage insuring conquest.

A few weeks after the foregoing remarks were originally published, Professor Tyndall in a lecture at the Royal Institution "On the Importance of the Study of Physics as a Branch of Education," gave some conclusive evidence to the same effect. His testimony, based on personal observation, is of such great value that we cannot refrain from quoting it. Here it is.

> "One of the duties which fell to my share, during the period to which I have referred, was the instruction of a class in mathematics, and I usually found that Euclid and the ancient geometry generally, when addressed to the understanding, formed a very attractive study for youth. But it was my habitual practice to withdraw the boys from the routine of the book, and to appeal to their self-power in the treatment of questions not comprehended in that routine. At first, the change from the beaten track usually excited a little aversion: the youth felt like a child amid strangers; but in no single instance have I found this aversion to continue. When utterly disheartened, I have encouraged the boy by that anecdote of Newton, where he attributes the difference between him and other men, mainly to his own patience; or of Mirabeau, when he ordered his servant, who had stated something to be impossible, never to use that stupid word again. Thus cheered, he has returned to his task with a smile, which perhaps had something of doubt in it, but which, nevertheless, evinced a resolution to try again. I have seen the boy's eye brighten, and at length, with a pleasure of which the ecstasy of Archimedes was but a simple expansion, heard him exclaim, 'I have it, sir.' The consciousness of self-power, thus awakened, was of immense value; and animated by it, the progress of the class was truly astonishing. It was often my custom to give the boys their choice of pursuing their propositions in the book, or of trying their strength at others not to be found there. Never in a single instance have I known the book to

be chosen. I was ever ready to assist when I deemed help needful, but my offers of assistance were habitually declined. The boys had tasted the sweets of intellectual conquest and demanded victories of their own. I have seen their diagrams scratched on the walls, cut into the beams upon the play ground, and numberless other illustrations of the living interest they took in the subject. For my own part, as far as experience in teaching goes, I was a mere fledgling: I knew nothing of the rules of pedagogics, as the Germans name it; but I adhered to the spirit indicated at the commencement of this discourse, and endeavoured to make geometry a *means* and not a *branch* of education. The experiment was successful, and some of the most delightful hours of my existence have been spent in marking the vigorous and cheerful expansion of mental power, when appealed to in the manner I have described."

This empirical geometry which presents an endless series of problems, should be continued along with other studies for years; and may throughout be advantageously accompanied by those concrete applications of its principles which serve as its preliminary. After the cube, the octahedron, and the various forms of pyramid and prism have been mastered, may come the more complex regular bodies—the dodecahedron and icosahedron—to construct which out of single pieces of cardboard, requires considerable ingenuity. From these, the transition may naturally be made to such modified forms of the regular bodies as are met with in crystals—the truncated cube, the cube with its dihedral as well as its solid angles truncated, the octahedron and the various prisms as similarly modified: in imitating which numerous forms assumed by different metals and salts, an acquaintance with the leading facts of mineralogy will be incidentally gained.[1]

After long continuance in exercises of this kind, rational geometry, as may be supposed, presents no obstacles. Habituated to contemplate relationships of form and quantity, and vaguely perceiving from time to time the necessity of certain results as reached by certain means, the pupil comes to regard the demonstrations of Euclid as the missing supplements to his familiar problems. His well-disciplined faculties enable him easily to master its successive propositions, and to appreciate their value; and he has the occasional gratification of finding some of his own methods proved to be true. Thus he enjoys what is to the unprepared a dreary task. It only remains to add, that his mind will presently arrive at a fit condition for that most valuable of all exercises for the reflective faculties—the making of original demonstrations. Such theorems as those appended to the successive books of the Messrs. Chambers's Euclid, will soon become practicable to him; and in proving them, the process of self-development will be not intellectual only, but moral.

To continue these suggestions much further, would be to write a detailed treatise on education, which we do not purpose. The foregoing outlines of plans for exercising the perceptions in early childhood, for conducting object-lessons,

---

[1] Those who seek aid in carrying out the system of culture above described, will find it in a little work entitled *Inventional Geometry*; published by J. and C. Mozley, Paternoster Row, London.

for teaching drawing and geometry, must be considered simply as illustrations of the method dictated by the general principles previously specified. We believe that on examination they will be found not only to progress from the simple to the complex, from the indefinite to the definite, from the concrete to the abstract, from the empirical to the rational; but to satisfy the further requirements, that education shall be a repetition of civilisation in little, that it shall be as much as possible a process of self-evolution, and that it shall be pleasurable. The fulfilment of all these conditions by one type of method, tends alike to verify the conditions, and to prove that type of the method the right one. Mark too, that this method is the logical outcome of the tendency characterising all modern improvements in tuition—that it is but an adoption in full of the natural system which they adopt partially—that it displays this complete adoption of the natural system, both by conforming to the above principles, and by following the suggestions which the unfolding mind itself gives: facilitating its spontaneous activities, and so aiding the developments which Nature is busy with. Thus there seems abundant reason to conclude, that the mode of procedure above exemplified, closely approximates to the true one.

A few paragraphs must be added in further inculcation of the two general principles, that are alike the most important and the least attended to; namely, the principle that throughout youth, as in early childhood and in maturity, the process shall be one of self-instruction; and the obverse principle, that the mental action induced shall be throughout intrinsically grateful. If progression from simple to complex, from indefinite to definite, and from concrete to abstract, be considered the essential requirements as dictated by abstract psychology; then do the requirements that knowledge shall be self-mastered, and pleasurably mastered, become tests by which we may judge whether the dictates of abstract psychology are being obeyed. If the first embody the leading generalisations of the *science* of mental growth, the last are the chief canons of the *art* of fostering mental growth. For manifestly, if the steps in our *curriculum* are so arranged that they can be successively ascended by the pupil himself with little or no help, they must correspond with the stages of evolution in his faculties; and manifestly, if the successive achievements of these steps are intrinsically gratifying to him, it follows that they require no more than a normal exercise of his powers.

But making education a process of self-evolution, has other advantages than this of keeping our lessons in the right order. In the first place, it guarantees a vividness and permanency of impression which the usual methods can never produce. Any piece of knowledge which the pupil has himself acquired—any problem which he has himself solved, becomes, by virtue of the conquest, much more thoroughly his than it could else be. The preliminary activity of mind which his success implies, the concentration of thought necessary to it, and the excitement consequent on his triumph, conspire to register the facts in his memory in a way that no mere information heard from a teacher, or read in a school-book, can be registered. Even if he fails, the tension to which his faculties have been wound up, insures his remembrance of the solution when given to him, better than half-a-dozen repetitions would. Observe, again, that this discipline necessitates a continuous organisation of the knowledge he acquires. It is in the very nature of facts and inferences assimilated in this normal manner, that they successively become the premises of further conclusions—the means of solving further questions. The solution of yesterday's problem helps the pupil in mastering to-day's. Thus the knowledge is turned into faculty as soon as it is taken in, and forthwith aids in the general function of thinking—does not lie merely written on the pages of an internal library, as when rote-learnt. Mark further, the moral culture which this constant self-help involves. Courage in attacking difficulties, patient concentration of the attention, perseverance through failures—these are characteristics which after-life specially requires; and these are characteristics which this system of making the mind work for its food specially produces. That it is thoroughly practicable to carry out instruction after this fashion, we can ourselves testify; having been in youth thus led to solve the comparatively complex problems of perspective. And that leading teachers have been tending in this direction, is indicated alike in the saying of Fellenberg, that "the individual, independent activity of the pupil is of much greater importance than the ordinary busy officiousness of many who assume the office of educators;" in the opinion of Horace Mann, that "unfortunately education amongst us at present consists too much in *telling*, not in *training*;" and in the remark of M. Marcel, that "what the learner discovers by mental exertion is better known than what is told to him."

Similarly with the correlative requirement, that the method of culture pursued shall be one productive of an intrinsically happy activity,—an activity not happy because of extrinsic rewards to be obtained, but because of its own healthfulness. Conformity to this requirement, besides preventing us from thwarting the normal process of evolution, incidentally secures positive benefits of importance. Unless we are to return to an ascetic morality (or rather *im*-morality) the maintenance of youthful happiness must be considered as in itself a worthy aim. Not to dwell upon this, however, we go on to remark that a pleasurable state of feeling is far more favourable to intellectual action than a state of indifference or disgust. Every one knows that things read, heard, or seen with interest, are better remembered than things read, heard, or seen with apathy. In the one case the faculties appealed to are actively occupied with the subject presented; in the other they are inactively occupied with it, and the attention is continually drawn away by more attractive thoughts. Hence the impressions are respectively strong and weak. Moreover, to the intellectual listlessness which a pupil's lack of interest in any study involves, must be added the paralysing fear of consequences. This, by distracting his attention, increases the difficulty he finds in bringing his faculties to bear upon facts that are repugnant to them. Clearly, therefore, the efficiency of tuition will, other things equal, be proportionate to the gratification with which tasks are performed.

It should be considered also, that grave moral consequences depend upon the habitual pleasure or pain which daily lessons produce. No one can compare the faces and manners of two boys—the one made happy by mastering interesting subjects, and the other made miserable by disgust with his studies, by consequent inability, by cold looks, by threats, by punishment—without seeing that the disposition of the one is being benefited and that of the other injured. Whoever has marked the effects of success and failure upon the mind, and the power of the mind over the body, will see that in the one case both temper and health are favourably affected, while in the other there is danger of permanent moroseness, or permanent timidity, and even of permanent constitutional depression. There remains yet another indirect result of no small moment. The relationship between teachers and their pupils is, other things equal, rendered friendly and influential, or antagonistic and powerless, according as the system of culture produces happiness or misery. Human beings are at the mercy of their associated ideas. A daily minister of pain cannot fail to be regarded with secret dislike; and if he causes no emotions but painful ones, will inevitably be hated. Conversely, he who constantly aids children to their ends, hourly provides them with the satisfactions of conquest, hourly encourages them through their difficulties and sympathises in their successes, will be liked; nay, if his behaviour is consistent throughout, must be loved. And when we remember how efficient and benign is the control of a master who is felt to be a friend, when compared with the control of one who is looked upon with aversion, or at best indifference, we may infer that the indirect advantages of conducting education on the happiness principle do not fall far short of the direct ones. To all who question the possibility of acting out the system here advocated, we reply as before, that not only does theory point to it, but experience commends it. To the many verdicts of distinguished teachers who since Pestalozzi's time have testified this, may be here added that of Professor Pillans, who asserts that "where young people are taught as they ought to be, they are quite as happy in school as at play, seldom less delighted, nay, often more, with the well-directed exercise of their mental energies than with that of their muscular powers."

As suggesting a final reason for making education a process of self-instruction, and by consequence a process of pleasurable instruction, we may advert to the fact that, in proportion as it is made so, is there a probability that it will not cease when schooldays end. As long as the acquisition of knowledge is rendered habitually repugnant, so long will there be a prevailing tendency to discontinue it when free from the coercion of parents and masters. And when the acquisition of knowledge has been rendered habitually gratifying, then will there be as prevailing a tendency to continue, without superintendence, that self-culture previously carried on under superintendence. These results are inevitable. While the laws of mental association remain true—while men dislike the things and places that suggest painful recollections, and delight in those which call to mind by-gone pleasures—painful lessons will make knowledge repulsive, and pleasurable lessons will make it attractive. The men to whom in boyhood information came in dreary tasks along with threats of punishment, and who were never led into habits of independent inquiry, are unlikely to be students in after years; while those to whom it came in the natural forms, at the proper times, and who remember its facts as not only interesting in themselves, but as the occasions of a long series of gratifying successes, are likely to continue through life that self-instruction commenced in youth.

MORAL EDUCATION

The greatest defect in our programmes of education is entirely overlooked. While much is being done in the detailed improvement of our systems in respect both of matter and manner, the most pressing desideratum has not yet been even recognised as a desideratum. To prepare the young for the duties of life is tacitly admitted to be the end which parents and schoolmasters should have in view; and happily, the value of the things taught, and the goodness of the methods followed in teaching them, are now ostensibly judged by their fitness to this end. The propriety of substituting for an exclusively classical training, a training in which the modern languages shall have a share, is argued on this ground. The necessity of increasing the amount of science is urged for like reasons. But though some care is taken to fit youth of both sexes for society and citizenship, no care whatever is taken to fit them for the position of parents. While it is seen that for the purpose of gaining a livelihood, an elaborate preparation is needed, it appears to be thought that for the bringing up of children, no preparation whatever is needed. While many years are spent by a boy in gaining knowledge of which the chief value is that it constitutes "the education of a gentleman;" and while many years are spent by a girl in those decorative acquirements which fit her for evening parties; not an hour is spent by either in preparation for that gravest of all responsibilities—the management of a family. Is it that this responsibility is but a remote contingency? On the contrary, it is sure to devolve on nine out of ten. Is it that the discharge of it is easy? Certainly not: of all functions which the adult has to fulfil, this is the most difficult. Is it that each may be trusted by self-instruction to fit himself, or herself, for the office of parent? No: not only is the need for such self-instruction unrecognised, but the complexity of the subject renders it the one of all others in which self-instruction is least likely to succeed. No rational plea can be put forward for leaving the Art of Education out of our *curriculum*. Whether as bearing on the happiness of parents themselves, or whether as affecting the characters and lives of their children and remote descendants, we must admit that a knowledge of the right methods of juvenile culture, physical, intellectual, and moral, is a knowledge of extreme importance. This topic should be the final one in the course of instruction passed through by each man and woman. As physical maturity is marked by the ability to produce offspring, so mental maturity is marked by the ability to train those offspring. *The subject which involves all other subjects, and therefore the subject in which education should culminate, is the Theory and Practice of Education.*

In the absence of this preparation, the management of children, and more especially the moral management, is lamentably bad. Parents either never think about the matter at all, or else their conclusions are crude and inconsistent. In most cases, and especially on the part of mothers, the treatment adopted on every occasion is that which the impulse of the moment prompts: it springs not from any reasoned-out conviction as to what will most benefit the child, but merely expresses the dominant parental feelings, whether good or ill; and varies from hour to hour as these feelings vary. Or if the dictates of passion are supplemented by any definite doctrines and methods, they are those handed down from the past, or those suggested by the remembrances of childhood, or those adopted from nurses and servants—methods devised not by the enlightenment, but by the ignorance, of the time. Commenting on the chaotic state of opinion and practice relative to family government, Richter writes:—

> "If the secret variances of a large class of ordinary fathers were brought to light, and laid down as a plan of studies and reading, catalogued for a moral education, they would run somewhat after this fashion:—In the first hour 'pure morality must be read to the child, either by myself or the tutor;' in the second, 'mixed morality, or that which may be applied to one's own advantage;' in the third, 'do you not see that your father does so and so?' in the fourth, 'you are little, and this is only fit for grown-up people;' in the fifth, 'the chief matter is that you should succeed in the world, and become something in the state;' in the sixth, 'not the temporary, but the eternal, determines the worth of a man;' in the seventh, 'therefore rather suffer injustice, and be kind;' in the eighth, 'but defend yourself bravely if any one attack you;' in the ninth, 'do not make a noise, dear child;' in the tenth, 'a boy must not sit so quiet;' in the eleventh, 'you must obey your parents better;' in the twelfth, 'and educate yourself.' So by the hourly change of his principles, the father conceals their untenableness and onesidedness. As for his wife, she is neither like him, nor yet like that harlequin who came on to the stage with a bundle of papers under each arm, and answered to the inquiry, what he had under his right arm, 'orders,' and to what he had under his left arm, 'counter-orders.' But the mother might be much better compared to a giant Briareus, who had a hundred arms, and a bundle of papers under each."

This state of things is not to be readily changed. Generations must pass before a great amelioration of it can be expected. Like political constitutions, educational systems are not made, but grow; and within brief periods growth is insensible. Slow, however, as must be any improvement, even that improvement implies the use of means; and among the means is discussion.

We are not among those who believe in Lord Palmerston's dogma, that "all children are born good." On the whole, the opposite dogma, untenable as it is, seems to us less wide of the truth. Nor do we agree with those who think that, by skilful discipline, children may be made altogether what they should be. Contrariwise, we are satisfied that though imperfections of nature may be diminished by wise management, they cannot be removed by it. The notion that an ideal humanity might be forthwith produced by a perfect system of education, is near akin to that implied in the poems of Shelley, that would mankind give up their old institutions and prejudices, all the evils in the world would at once disappear: neither notion being acceptable to such as have dispassionately studied human affairs.

Nevertheless, we may fitly sympathise with those who entertain these too sanguine hopes. Enthusiasm, pushed even to fanaticism, is a useful motive-power—perhaps an indispensable one. It is clear that the ardent politician would never undergo the labours and make the sacrifices he does, did he not believe that the reform he fights for is the one thing needful. But for his conviction that drunkenness is the root of all social evils, the teetotaler would agitate far less energetically. In philanthropy, as in other things, great advantage results from division of labour; and that there may be division of labour, each class of philanthropists must be more or less subordinated to its function—must have an exaggerated faith in its work. Hence, of those who regard education, intellectual or moral, as the panacea, we may say that their undue expectations are not without use; and that perhaps it is part of the beneficent order of things that their confidence cannot be shaken.

Even were it true, however, that by some possible system of moral control, children could be moulded into the desired form; and even could every parent be indoctrinated with this system, we should still be far from achieving the object in view. It is forgotten that the carrying out of any such system presupposes, on the part of adults, a degree of intelligence, of goodness, of self-control, possessed by no one. The error made by those who discuss questions of domestic discipline, lies in ascribing all the faults and difficulties to the children, and none to the parents. The current assumption respecting family government, as respecting national government, is, that the virtues are with the rulers and the vices with the ruled. Judging by educational theories, men and women are entirely transfigured in their relations to offspring. The citizens we do business with, the people we meet in the world, we know to be very imperfect creatures. In the daily scandals, in the quarrels of friends, in bankruptcy disclosures, in lawsuits, in police reports, we have constantly thrust before us the pervading selfishness, dishonesty, brutality. Yet when we criticise nursery-management and canvass the misbehaviour of juveniles, we habitually take for granted that these culpable persons are free from moral delinquency in the treatment of their boys and girls! So far is this from the truth, that we do not hesitate to blame parental misconduct for a great part of the domestic disorder commonly ascribed to the perversity of children. We do not assert this of the more sympathetic and self-restrained, among whom we hope most of our readers may be classed; but we assert it of the mass. What kind of moral culture is to be expected from a mother who, time after time, angrily shakes her infant because it will not suck; which we once saw a mother do? How much sense of justice is likely to be instilled by a father who, on having his attention drawn by a scream to the fact that his child's finger is jammed between the window-sash and sill, begins to beat the child instead of releasing it? Yet that there are such fathers is testified to us by an eye-witness. Or, to take a still stronger case, also vouched for by direct testimony—what are the educational prospects of the boy who, on being taken home with a dislocated thigh, is saluted with a castigation? It is true that these are extreme instances—instances exhibiting in human beings that blind instinct which impels brutes to destroy the weakly and injured of their own race. But extreme though they are, they typify feelings and conduct daily observable in many families. Who has not repeatedly seen a child slapped by nurse or parent for a fretfulness probably resulting from bodily derangement? Who, when watching a mother snatch up a fallen little one, has not often traced, both in the rough manner and in the sharply-uttered exclamation—"You stupid little thing!"—an irascibility foretelling endless future squabbles? Is there not in the harsh tones in which a father bids his children be quiet, evidence of a deficient fellow-feeling with them? Are not the constant, and often quite needless, thwartings that the young experience—the injunctions to sit still, which an active child cannot obey without suffering great nervous irritation, the commands not to look out of the window when travelling by railway, which on a child of any intelligence entails serious deprivation—are not these thwartings, we ask, signs of a terrible lack of sympathy? The truth is, that the difficulties of moral education are necessarily of dual origin—necessarily result from the combined faults of parents and children. If hereditary transmission is a law of nature, as every naturalist knows it to be, and as our daily remarks and current proverbs admit it to be; then, on the average of cases, the defects of children mirror the defects of their parents;—on the average of cases, we say, because, complicated as the results are by the transmitted traits of remoter ancestors, the correspondence is not special but only general. And if, on the average of cases, this inheritance of defects exists, then the evil passions which parents have to check in their children, imply like evil passions in themselves: hidden, it may be, from the public eye, or perhaps obscured by other feelings, but still there. Evidently, therefore, the general practice of any ideal system of discipline is hopeless: parents are not good enough.

Moreover, even were there methods by which the desired end could be at once effected; and even had fathers and mothers sufficient insight, sympathy, and self-command to employ these methods consistently; it might still be contended that it would be of no use to reform family-government faster than other things are reformed. What is it that we aim to do? Is it not that education of whatever kind has for its proximate end to prepare a child for the business of life—to produce a citizen who, while he is well conducted, is also able to make his way in the world? And does not making his way in the world (by which we mean, not the acquirement of wealth, but of the funds requisite for bringing up a family)—does not this imply a certain fitness for the world as it now is? And if by any system of culture an ideal human being could be produced, is it not doubtful whether he would be fit for the world as it now is? May we not, on the contrary, suspect that his too keen sense of rectitude, and too elevated standard of conduct, would make life intolerable or even impossible? And however admirable the result might be, considered individually, would it not be self-defeating in so far as society and posterity are concerned? There is much reason for thinking that as in a nation so in a family, the kind of government is, on the whole, about as good as the general state of human nature permits it to be. We may argue that in the one case, as in the other, the average character of the people determines the quality of the control exercised. In both cases it may be inferred that amelioration of the average character leads to an amelioration of system; and further, that were it possible to ameliorate the system without the average character being first ameliorated, evil rather than good would follow. Such degree of harshness as children now experience from their parents and teachers, may be regarded as but a preparation for that greater harshness which they will meet on entering the world. And it may be urged that were it possible for parents and teachers to treat them with perfect equity and entire sympathy, it would but intensify the sufferings which the selfishness of men must, in after life, inflict on them.[2]

"But does not this prove too much?" some one will ask. "If no system of moral training can forthwith make children what they should be; if, even were there a system that would do this, existing parents are too imperfect to carry it out; and if even could such a system be successfully carried out, its results would be disastrously incongruous with the present state of society; does it not follow that to reform the system now in use is neither practicable nor desirable?" No. It merely follows that reform in domestic government must go on, *pari passu*, with other reforms. It merely follows that methods of discipline neither can be nor should be ameliorated, except by instalments. It merely follows that the dictates of abstract rectitude will, in practice, inevitably be subordinated by the present state of human nature—by the imperfections alike of children, of parents, and of society; and can only be better fulfilled as the general character becomes better.

"At any rate, then," may rejoin our critic, "it is clearly useless to set up any ideal standard of family discipline. There can be no advantage in elaborating and recommending methods that are in advance of the time." Again we contend for the contrary. Just as in the case of political government, though pure rectitude may be at present impracticable, it is requisite to know where the right lies, in order that the changes we make may be *towards* the right instead of *away* from it; so, in the case of domestic government, an ideal must be upheld, that there may be gradual approximations to it. We need fear no evil consequences from the maintenance of such an ideal. On the average the constitutional conservatism of mankind is strong enough to prevent too rapid a change. Things are so organised that until men have grown up to the level of a higher belief, they cannot receive it: nominally, they may hold it, but not virtually. And even when the truth gets recognised, the obstacles to conformity with it are so persistent as to outlive the patience of philanthropists and even of philosophers. We may be sure, therefore, that the difficulties in the

---

[2] Of this nature is the plea put in by some for the rough treatment experienced by boys at our public schools; where, as it is said, they are introduced to a miniature world whose hardships prepare them for those of the real world. It must be admitted that the plea has some force; but it is a very insufficient plea. For whereas domestic and school discipline, though they should not be much better than the discipline of adult life, should be somewhat better; the discipline which boys meet with at Eton, Winchester, Harrow, etc., is worse than that of adult life—more unjust and cruel. Instead of being an aid to human progress, which all culture should be, the culture of our public schools, by accustoming boys to a despotic form of government and an intercourse regulated by brute force, tends to fit them for a lower state of society than that which exists. And chiefly recruited as our legislature is from among those who are brought up at such schools, this barbarising influence becomes a hindrance to national progress.

way of a normal government of children, will always put an adequate check upon the efforts to realise it.

With these preliminary explanations, let us go on to consider the true aims and methods of moral education. After a few pages devoted to the settlement of general principles, during the perusal of which we bespeak the reader's patience, we shall aim by illustrations to make clear the right methods of parental behaviour in the hourly occurring difficulties of family government.

When a child falls, or runs its head against the table, it suffers a pain, the remembrance of which tends to make it more careful; and by repetition of such experiences, it is eventually disciplined into proper guidance of its movements. If it lays hold of the fire-bars, thrusts its hand into a candle-flame, or spills boiling water on any part of its skin, the resulting burn or scald is a lesson not easily forgotten. So deep an impression is produced by one or two events of this kind, that no persuasion will afterwards induce it thus to disregard the laws of its constitution.

Now in these cases, Nature illustrates to us in the simplest way, the true theory and practice of moral discipline — a theory and practice which, however much they may seem to the superficial like those commonly received, we shall find on examination to differ from them very widely.

Observe, first, that in bodily injuries and their penalties we have misconduct and its consequences reduced to their simplest forms. Though, according to their popular acceptations, *right* and *wrong* are words scarcely applicable to actions that have none but direct bodily effects; yet whoever considers the matter will see that such actions must be as much classifiable under these heads as any other actions. From whatever assumption they start, all theories of morality agree that conduct whose total results, immediate and remote, are beneficial, is good conduct; while conduct whose total results, immediate and remote, are injurious, is bad conduct. The *ultimate* standards by which all men judge of behaviour, are the resulting happiness or misery. We consider drunkenness wrong because of the physical degeneracy and accompanying moral evils entailed on the drunkard and his dependents. Did theft give pleasure both to taker and loser, we should not find it in our catalogue of sins. Were it conceivable that kind actions multiplied human sufferings, we should condemn them — should not consider them kind. It needs but to read the first newspaper-leader, or listen to any conversation on social affairs, to see that acts of parliament, political movements, philanthropic agitations, in common with the doings of individuals are judged by their anticipated results in augmenting the pleasures or pains of men. And if on analysing all secondary superinduced ideas, we find these to be our final tests of right and wrong, we cannot refuse to class bodily conduct as right or wrong according to the beneficial or detrimental results produced.

Note, in the second place, the character of the punishments by which these physical transgressions are prevented. Punishments, we call them, in the absence of a better word; for they are not punishments in the literal sense. They are not artificial and unnecessary inflictions of pain; but are simply the beneficent checks to actions that are essentially at variance with bodily welfare — checks in the absence of which life would be quickly destroyed by bodily injuries. It is the peculiarity of these penalties, if we must so call them, that they are simply the *unavoidable consequences* of the deeds which they follow: they are nothing more than the *inevitable reactions* entailed by the child's actions.

Let it be further borne in mind that these painful reactions are proportionate to the transgressions. A slight accident brings a slight pain; a more serious one, a severer pain. It is not ordained that an urchin who tumbles over the doorstep, shall suffer in excess of the amount necessary; with the view of making it still more cautious than the necessary suffering will make it. But from its daily experience it is left to learn the greater or less penalties of greater or less errors; and to behave accordingly.

And then mark, lastly, that these natural reactions which follow the child's wrong actions, are constant, direct, unhesitating, and not to be escaped. No threats; but a silent, rigorous performance. If a child runs a pin into its finger, pain follows. If it does it again, there is again the same result: and so on perpetually. In all its dealing with inorganic Nature it finds this unswerving persistence, which listens to no excuse, and from which there is no appeal; and very soon recognising this stern though beneficent discipline, it becomes extremely careful not to transgress.

Still more significant will these general truths appear, when we remember that they hold throughout adult life as well as throughout infantine life. It is by an experimentally-gained knowledge of the natural consequences, that men and women are checked when they go wrong. After home-education has ceased, and when there are no longer parents and teachers to forbid this or that kind of conduct, there comes into play a discipline like that by which the young child is trained to self-guidance. If the youth entering on the business of life idles away his time and fulfils slowly or unskilfully the duties entrusted to him, there by and by follows the natural penalty: he is discharged, and left to suffer for awhile the evils of a relative poverty. On the unpunctual man, ever missing his appointments of business and pleasure, there continually fall the consequent inconveniences, losses, and deprivations. The tradesmen who charges too high a rate of profit, loses his customers, and so is checked in his greediness. Diminishing practice teaches the inattentive doctor to bestow more trouble on his patients. The too credulous creditor and the over-sanguine speculator, alike learn by the difficulties which rashness entails on them, the necessity of being more cautious in their engagements. And so throughout the life of every citizen. In the quotation so often made *apropos* of such cases—"The burnt child dreads the fire"—we see not only that the analogy between this social discipline and Nature's early discipline of infants is universally recognised; but we also see an implied conviction that this discipline is of the most efficient kind. Nay indeed, this conviction is more than implied; it is distinctly stated. Every one has heard others confess that only by "dearly bought experience" had they been induced to give up some bad or foolish course of conduct formerly pursued. Every one has heard, in the criticism passed on the doings of this spendthrift or the other schemer, the remark that advice was useless, and that nothing but "bitter experience" would produce any effect: nothing, that is, but suffering the unavoidable consequences. And if further proof be needed that the natural reaction is not only the most efficient penalty, but that no humanly-devised penalty can replace it, we have such further proof in the notorious ill-success of our various penal systems. Out of the many methods of criminal discipline that have been proposed and legally enforced, none have answered the expectations of their advocates. Artificial punishments have failed to produce reformation; and have in many cases increased the criminality. The only successful reformatories are those privately-established ones which approximate their regime to the method of Nature—which do little more than administer the natural consequences of criminal conduct: diminishing the criminal's liberty of action as much as is needful for the safety of society, and requiring him to maintain himself while living under this restraint. Thus we see, both that the discipline by which the young child is taught to regulate its movements is the discipline by which the great mass of adults are kept in order, and more or less improved; and that the discipline humanly-devised for the worst adults, fails when it diverges from this divinely-ordained discipline, and begins to succeed on approximating to it.

Have we not here, then, the guiding principle of moral education? Must we not infer that the system so beneficent in its effects during infancy and maturity, will be equally beneficent throughout youth? Can any one believe that the method which answers so well in the first and the last divisions of life, will not answer in the intermediate division? Is it not manifest that as "ministers and interpreters of Nature" it is the function of parents to see that their children habitually experience the true consequences of their conduct—the natural reactions: neither warding them off, nor intensifying them, nor putting artificial consequences in place of them? No unprejudiced reader will hesitate in his assent.

Probably, however, not a few will contend that already most parents do this—that the punishments they inflict are, in the majority of cases, the true consequences of ill-conduct—that parental anger, venting itself in harsh words and deeds, is the result of a child's transgression—and that, in the suffering, physical or moral, which the child is subject to, it experiences the natural reaction of its misbehaviour. Along with much error this assertion contains some truth. It is unquestionable that the displeasure of fathers and mothers is a true consequence of juvenile delinquency; and that the manifestation of it is a normal check upon such delinquency. The scoldings, and threats, and blows, which a passionate parent visits on offending little ones, are doubtless effects actually drawn from such a parent by their offences; and so are, in some sort, to be considered as among the natural reactions of their wrong actions. Nor are we prepared to say that these modes of treatment are not relatively right—right, that is, in relation to the uncontrollable children of ill-controlled adults; and right in relation to a state of society in which such ill-controlled adults make up the mass of the people. As already suggested, educational systems, like political and other institutions, are generally as good as the state of human nature permits. The barbarous children of barbarous parents are probably only to be restrained by the barbarous methods which such parents spontaneously employ; while submission to these barbarous methods is perhaps the best preparation such children can have for the barbarous society in which they are presently to play a part. Conversely, the civilised members of a civilised society will spontaneously manifest their displeasure in less violent ways—will spontaneously use milder measures—measures strong enough for their better-natured children. Thus it is true that, in so far as the expression of parental feeling is concerned, the principle of the natural reaction is always more or less followed. The system of domestic government ever gravitates towards its right form.

But now observe two important facts. The first fact is that, in states of rapid transition like ours, which witness a continuous battle between old and new theories and old and new practices, the educational methods in use are apt to be considerably out of harmony with the times. In deference to dogmas fit only for the ages that uttered them, many parents inflict punishments that do violence to their own feelings, and so visit on their children *un*natural reactions; while other parents, enthusiastic in their hopes of immediate perfection, rush to the opposite extreme. The second fact is, that the discipline of chief value is not the experience of parental approbation or disapprobation; but it is the experience of those results which would ultimately flow from the conduct in the absence of parental opinion or interference. The truly instructive and salutary consequences are not those inflicted by parents when they take upon themselves to be Nature's proxies; but they are those inflicted by Nature herself. We will endeavour to make this distinction clear by a few illustrations, which, while they show what we mean by natural reactions as contrasted with artificial ones, will afford some practical suggestions.

In every family where there are young children there daily occur cases of what mothers and servants call "making a litter." A child has had out its box of toys, and leaves them scattered about the floor. Or a handful of flowers, brought in from a morning walk, is presently seen dispersed over tables and chairs. Or a little girl, making doll's-clothes, disfigures the room with shreds. In most cases the trouble of rectifying this disorder falls anywhere but where it should. Occurring in the nursery, the nurse herself, with many grumblings about "tiresome little things," undertakes the task; if below-stairs, the task usually devolves either on one of the elder children or on the housemaid: the transgressor being visited with nothing more than a scolding. In this very simple case, however, there are many parents wise enough to follow out, more or less consistently, the normal course—that of making the child itself collect the toys or shreds. The labour of putting things in order is the true consequence of having put them in disorder. Every trader in his office, every wife in her household, has daily experience of this fact. And if education be a preparation for the business of life, then every child should also, from the beginning, have daily experience of this fact. If the natural penalty be met by refractory behaviour (which it may perhaps be where the system of moral discipline previously pursued has been bad), then the proper course is to let the child feel the ulterior reaction caused by its disobedience. Having refused or neglected to pick up and put away the things it has scattered about, and having thereby entailed the trouble of doing this on some one else, the child should, on subsequent occasions, be denied the means of giving this trouble. When next it petitions for its toy-box, the reply of its mamma should be—"The last time you had your toys you left them lying on the floor, and Jane had to pick them up. Jane is too busy to pick up every day the things you leave about; and I cannot do it myself. So that, as you will not

put away your toys when you have done with them, I cannot let you have them."
This is obviously a natural consequence, neither increased nor lessened; and must
be so recognised by a child. The penalty comes, too, at the moment when it is most
keenly felt. A new-born desire is balked at the moment of anticipated gratification;
and the strong impression so produced can scarcely fail to have an effect on the
future conduct: an effect which, by consistent repetition, will do whatever can be
done in curing the fault. Add to which, that, by this method, a child is early taught
the lesson which cannot be learnt too soon, that in this world of ours pleasures are
rightly to be obtained only by labour.

Take another case. Not long since we had frequently to hear the reprimands
visited on a little girl who was scarcely ever ready in time for the daily walk. Of
eager disposition, and apt to become absorbed in the occupation of the moment,
Constance never thought of putting on her things till the rest were ready. The governess and the other children had almost invariably to wait; and from the mamma
there almost invariably came the same scolding. Utterly as this system failed, it
never occurred to the mamma to let Constance experience the natural penalty.
Nor, indeed, would she try it when it was suggested to her. In the world, unread-
iness entails the loss of some advantage that would else have been gained: the
train is gone; or the steam-boat is just leaving its moorings; or the best things in
the market are sold; or all the good seats in the concert-room are filled. And every
one, in cases perpetually occurring, may see that it is the prospective deprivations
which prevent people from being too late. Is not the inference obvious? Should
not the prospective deprivations control a child's conduct also? If Constance is
not ready at the appointed time, the natural result is that of being left behind, and
losing her walk. And after having once or twice remained at home while the rest
were enjoying themselves in the fields—after having felt that this loss of a much-
prized gratification was solely due to want of promptitude; amendment would in
all probability take place. At any rate, the measure would be more effective than
that perpetual scolding which ends only in producing callousness.

Again, when children, with more than usual carelessness, break or lose the
things given to them, the natural penalty—the penalty which makes grown-up
persons more careful—is the consequent inconvenience. The lack of the lost or
damaged article, and the cost of replacing it, are the experiences by which men and
women are disciplined in these matters; and the experiences of children should be
as much as possible assimilated to theirs. We do not refer to that early period at
which toys are pulled to pieces in the process of learning their physical properties,
and at which the results of carelessness cannot be understood; but to a later period, when the meaning and advantages of property are perceived. When a boy, old
enough to possess a penknife, uses it so roughly as to snap the blade, or leaves it
in the grass by some hedge-side where he was cutting a stick, a thoughtless parent, or some indulgent relative, will commonly forthwith buy him another, not
seeing that, by doing this, a valuable lesson is prevented. In such a case, a father
may properly explain that penknives cost money, and that to get money requires
labour; that he cannot afford to purchase new penknives for one who loses or
breaks them; and that until he sees evidence of greater carefulness he must decline

to make good the loss. A parallel discipline will serve to check extravagance.

These few familiar instances, here chosen because of the simplicity with which they illustrate our point, will make clear to every one the distinction between those natural penalties which we contend are the truly efficient ones, and those artificial penalties commonly substituted for them. Before going on to exhibit the higher and subtler applications of the principle exemplified, let us note its many and great superiorities over the principle, or rather the empirical practice, which prevails in most families.

One superiority is that the pursuance of it generates right conceptions of cause and effect; which by frequent and consistent experience are eventually rendered definite and complete. Proper conduct in life is much better guaranteed when the good and evil consequences of actions are understood, than when they are merely believed on authority. A child who finds that disorderliness entails the trouble of putting things in order, or who misses a gratification from dilatoriness, or whose carelessness is followed by the want of some much-prized possession, not only suffers a keenly-felt consequence, but gains a knowledge of causation: both the one and the other being just like those which adult life will bring. Whereas a child who in such cases receives a reprimand, or some factitious penalty, not only experiences a consequence for which it often cares very little, but misses that instruction respecting the essential natures of good and evil conduct, which it would else have gathered. It is a vice of the common system of artificial rewards and punishments, long since noticed by the clear-sighted, that by substituting for the natural results of misbehaviour certain tasks or castigations, it produces a radically wrong moral standard. Having throughout infancy and boyhood always regarded parental or tutorial displeasure as the chief result of a forbidden action, the youth has gained an established association of ideas between such action and such displeasure, as cause and effect. Hence when parents and tutors have abdicated, and their displeasure is not to be feared, the restraints on forbidden actions are in great measure removed: the true restraints, the natural reactions, having yet to be learnt by sad experience. As writes one who has had personal knowledge of this short-sighted system:—"Young men let loose from school, particularly those whose parents have neglected to exert their influence, plunge into every description of extravagance; they know no rule of action—they are ignorant of the reasons for moral conduct—they have no foundation to rest upon—and until they have been severely disciplined by the world are extremely dangerous members of society."

Another great advantage of this natural discipline is, that it is a discipline of pure justice; and will be recognised as such by every child. Whoso suffers nothing more than the evil which in the order of nature results from his own misbehaviour, is much less likely to think himself wrongly treated than if he suffers an artificially inflicted evil; and this will hold of children as of men. Take the case of a boy who is habitually reckless of his clothes—scrambles through hedges without caution, or is utterly regardless of mud. If he is beaten, or sent to bed, he is apt to consider himself ill-used; and is more likely to brood over his injuries than to repent of his transgressions. But suppose he is required to rectify as far as possible the harm he has done—to clean off the mud with which he has covered himself, or to mend the tear as well as he can. Will he not feel that the evil is one of his own producing? Will he not while paying this penalty be continuously conscious of the connection between it and its cause? And will he not, spite his irritation, recognise more or less clearly the justice of the arrangement? If several lessons of this kind fail to produce amendment—if suits of clothes are prematurely spoiled—if the father, pursuing this same system of discipline, declines to spend money for new ones until the ordinary time has elapsed—and if meanwhile, there occur occasions on which, having no decent clothes to go in, the boy is debarred from joining the rest of the family on holiday excursions and *fête* days, it is manifest that while he will keenly feel the punishment, he can scarcely fail to trace the chain of causation, and to perceive that his own carelessness is the origin of it. And seeing this, he will not have any such sense of injustice as if there were no obvious connection between the transgression and its penalty.

Again, the tempers both of parents and children are much less liable to be ruffled under this system than under the ordinary system. When instead of letting children experience the painful results which naturally follow from wrong conduct, parents themselves inflict certain other painful results, they produce double mischief. Making, as they do, multiplied family laws; and identifying their own supremacy and dignity with the maintenance of these laws; every transgression is regarded as an offence against themselves, and a cause of anger on their part. And then come the further vexations which result from taking upon themselves, in the shape of extra labour or cost, those evil consequences which should have been allowed to fall on the wrong-doers. Similarly with the children. Penalties which the necessary reaction of things brings round upon them—penalties which are inflicted by impersonal agency, produce an irritation that is comparatively slight and transient; whereas, penalties voluntarily inflicted by a parent, and afterwards thought of as caused by him or her, produce an irritation both greater and more continued. Just consider how disastrous would be the result if this empirical method were pursued from the beginning. Suppose it were possible for parents to take upon themselves the physical sufferings entailed on their children by ignorance and awkwardness; and that while bearing these evil consequences they visited on their children certain other evil consequences, with the view of teaching them the impropriety of their conduct. Suppose that when a child, who had been forbidden to meddle with the kettle, spilt boiling water on its foot, the mother vicariously assumed the scald and gave a blow in place of it; and similarly in all other cases. Would not the daily mishaps be sources of far more anger than now? Would there not be chronic ill-temper on both sides? Yet an exactly parallel policy is pursued in after-years. A father who beats his boy for carelessly or wilfully breaking a sister's toy, and then himself pays for a new toy, does substantially this same thing—inflicts an artificial penalty on the transgressor, and takes the natural penalty on himself: his own feelings and those of the transgressor being alike needlessly irritated. Did he simply require restitution to be made, he would produce far less heart-burning. If he told the boy that a new toy must be bought at his, the boy's, cost; and that his supply of pocket-money must be withheld to the needful extent; there would be much less disturbance of temper on either side: while in the deprivation afterwards felt, the boy would experience the equitable and salutary consequence. In brief, the system of discipline by natural reactions is less injurious to temper, both because it is perceived to be nothing more than pure justice, and because it in great part substitutes the impersonal agency of Nature for the personal agency of parents.

Whence also follows the manifest corollary, that under this system the parental and filial relation, being a more friendly, will be a more influential one. Whether in parent or child, anger, however caused, and to whomsoever directed, is detrimental. But anger in a parent towards a child, and in a child towards a parent, is especially detrimental; because it weakens that bond of sympathy which is essential to beneficent control. From the law of association of ideas, it inevitably results, both in young and old, that dislike is contracted towards things which in experience are habitually connected with disagreeable feelings. Or where attachment originally existed, it is diminished, or turned into repugnance, according to the quantity of painful impressions received. Parental wrath, venting itself in reprimands and castigations, cannot fail, if often repeated, to produce filial alienation; while the resentment and sulkiness of children cannot fail to weaken the affection felt for them, and may even end in destroying it. Hence the numerous cases in which parents (and especially fathers, who are commonly deputed to inflict the punishment) are regarded with indifference, if not with aversion; and hence the equally numerous cases in which children are looked upon as inflictions. Seeing then, as all must do, that estrangement of this kind is fatal to a salutary moral culture, it follows that parents cannot be too solicitous in avoiding occasions of direct antagonism with their children. And therefore they cannot too anxiously avail themselves of this discipline of natural consequences; which, by relieving them from penal functions, prevents mutual exasperations and estrangements.

The method of moral culture by experience of the normal reactions, which is the divinely-ordained method alike for infancy and for adult life, we thus find to be equally applicable during the intermediate childhood and youth. Among the advantages of this method we see:—First: that it gives that rational knowledge of right and wrong conduct which results from personal experience of their good and bad consequences. Second: that the child, suffering nothing more than the painful effects of its own wrong actions, must recognise more or less clearly the justice of the penalties. Third: that recognising the justice of the penalties, and receiving them through the working of things rather than at the hands of an individual, its temper is less disturbed; while the parent fulfilling the comparatively passive duty of letting the natural penalties be felt, preserves a comparative equanimity. Fourth: that mutual exasperations being thus prevented, a much happier, and a more influential relation, will exist between parent and child.

"But what is to be done in cases of more serious misconduct?" some will ask. "How is this plan to be carried out when a petty theft has been committed? or when a lie has been told? or when some younger brother or sister has been ill-used?"

Before replying to these questions, let us consider the bearings of a few illustrative facts.

Living in the family of his brother-in-law, a friend of ours had undertaken the education of his little nephew and niece. This he had conducted, more perhaps from natural sympathy than from reasoned-out conclusions, in the spirit of the method above set forth. The two children were in doors his pupils and out of doors his companions. They daily joined him in walks and botanising excursions, eagerly sought plants for him, looked on while he examined and identified them, and in this and other ways were ever gaining pleasure and instruction in his society. In short, morally considered, he stood to them much more in the position of parent than either their father or mother did. Describing to us the results of this policy, he gave, among other instances, the following. One evening, having need for some article lying in another part of the house, he asked his nephew to fetch it. Interested as the boy was in some amusement of the moment, he, contrary to his wont, either exhibited great reluctance or refused, we forget which. His uncle, disapproving of a coercive course, went himself for that which he wanted: merely exhibiting by his manner the annoyance this ill-behaviour gave him. And when, later in the evening, the boy made overtures for the usual play, they were gravely repelled—the uncle manifested just that coldness naturally produced in him; and so let the boy feel the necessary consequences of his conduct. Next morning at the usual time for rising, our friend heard a new voice outside the door, and in walked his little nephew with the hot water. Peering about the room to see what else could be done, the boy then exclaimed, "Oh! you want your boots;" and forthwith rushed downstairs to fetch them. In this and other ways he showed a true penitence for his misconduct. He endeavoured by unusual services to make up for the service he had refused. His better feelings had made a real conquest over his lower ones; and acquired strength by the victory. And having felt what it was to be without it, he valued more than before the friendship he thus regained.

This gentleman is now himself a father; acts on the same system; and finds it answer completely. He makes himself thoroughly his children's friend. The evening is longed for by them because he will be at home; and they especially enjoy Sunday because he is with them all day. Thus possessing their perfect confidence and affection, he finds that the simple display of his approbation or disapprobation gives him abundant power of control. If, on his return home, he hears that one of his boys has been naughty, he behaves towards him with that coolness which the consciousness of the boy's misconduct naturally produces; and he finds this a most efficient punishment. The mere withholding of the usual caresses, is a source of much distress—produces a more prolonged fit of crying than a beating would do. And the dread of this purely moral penalty is, he says, ever present during his absence: so much so, that frequently during the day his children ask their mamma how they have behaved, and whether the report will be good. Recently, the eldest, an active urchin of five, in one of those bursts of animal spirits common in healthy children, committed sundry extravagances during his mamma's absence—cut off part of his brother's hair and wounded himself with a razor taken from his father's dressing-case. Hearing of these occurrences on his return, the father did not speak to the boy either that night or next morning. Besides the immediate tribulation the effect was, that when, a few days after, the mamma was about to go out, she was entreated by the boy not to do so; and on inquiry, it appeared his fear was that he might again transgress in her absence.

We have introduced these facts before replying to the question—"What is to be done with the graver offences?" for the purpose of first exhibiting the relation that may and ought to be established between parents and children; for on the existence of this relation depends the successful treatment of these graver offences. And as a further preliminary, we must now point out that the establishment of this relation will result from adopting the system here advocated. Already we have shown that by simply letting a child experience the painful reactions of its own wrong actions, a parent avoids antagonism and escapes being regarded as an enemy; but it remains to be shown that where this course has been consistently pursued from the beginning, a feeling of active friendship will be generated.

At present, mothers and fathers are mostly considered by their offspring as friend enemies. Determined as the impressions of children inevitably are by the treatment they receive; and oscillating as that treatment does between bribery and thwarting, between petting and scolding, between gentleness and castigation; they necessarily acquire conflicting beliefs respecting the parental character. A mother commonly thinks it sufficient to tell her little boy that she is his best friend; and assuming that he ought to believe her, concludes that he will do so. "It is all for your good;" "I know what is proper for you better than you do yourself;" "You are not old enough to understand it now, but when you grow up you will thank me for doing what I do;"—these, and like assertions, are daily reiterated. Meanwhile the boy is daily suffering positive penalties; and is hourly forbidden to do this, that, and the other, which he wishes to do. By words he hears that his happiness is the end in view; but from the accompanying deeds he habitually receives more or less pain. Incompetent as he is to understand that future which his mother has in view, or how this treatment conduces to the happiness of that future, he judges by the results he feels; and finding such results anything but pleasurable, he becomes sceptical respecting her professions of friendship. And is it not folly to expect any other issue? Must not the child reason from the evidence he has got? and does not this evidence seem to warrant his conclusion? The mother would reason in just the same way if similarly placed. If, among her acquaintance, she found some one who was constantly thwarting her wishes, uttering sharp reprimands, and occasionally inflicting actual penalties on her, she would pay small attention to any professions of anxiety for her welfare which accompanied these acts. Why, then, does she suppose that her boy will do otherwise?

But now observe how different will be the results if the system we contend for be consistently pursued—if the mother not only avoids becoming the instrument of punishment, but plays the part of a friend, by warning her boy of the punishments which Nature will inflict. Take a case; and that it may illustrate the mode in which this policy is to be early initiated, let it be one of the simplest cases. Suppose that, prompted by the experimental spirit so conspicuous in children, whose proceedings instinctively conform to the inductive method of inquiry—suppose that so prompted, the boy is amusing himself by lighting pieces of paper in the candle and watching them burn. A mother of the ordinary unreflective stamp, will either, on the plea of keeping him "out of mischief," or from fear that he will burn himself, command him to desist; and in case of non-compliance will snatch the paper from him. But, should he be fortunate enough to have a mother of some rationality, who knows that this interest with which he is watching the paper burn, results from a healthy inquisitiveness, and who has also the wisdom to consider the results of interference, she will reason thus:—"If I put a stop to this I shall prevent the acquirement of a certain amount of knowledge. It is true that I may save the child from a burn; but what then? He is sure to burn himself sometime; and it is quite essential to his safety in life that he should learn by experience the properties of flame. If I forbid him from running this present risk, he will certainly hereafter run the same or a greater risk when no one is present to prevent him; whereas, should he have an accident now that I am by, I can save him from any great injury. Moreover, were I to make him desist, I should thwart him in the pursuit of what is in itself a purely harmless, and indeed, instructive gratification; and he would regard me with more or less ill-feeling. Ignorant as he is of the pain from which I would save him, and feeling only the pain of a balked desire, he could not fail to look on me as the cause of that pain. To save him from a hurt which he cannot conceive, and which has therefore no existence for him, I hurt him in a way which he feels keenly enough; and so become, from his point of view, a minister of evil. My best course then, is simply to warn him of the danger, and to be ready to prevent any serious damage." And following out this conclusion, she says to the child—"I fear you will hurt yourself if you do that." Suppose, now, that the boy, persevering as he will probably do, ends by burning his hand. What are the results? In the first place he has gained an experience which he must gain eventually, and which, for his own safety, he cannot gain too soon. And in the second place, he has found that his mother's disapproval or warning was meant for his welfare: he has a further positive experience of her benevolence—a further reason for placing confidence in her judgment and kindness—a further reason for loving her.

Of course, in those occasional hazards where there is a risk of broken limbs or other serious injury, forcible prevention is called for. But leaving out extreme cases, the system pursued should be, not that of guarding a child from the small risks which it daily runs, but that of advising and warning it against them. And by pursuing this course, a much stronger filial affection will be generated than commonly exists. If here, as elsewhere, the discipline of the natural reactions is allowed to come into play—if in those out-door scramblings and in-door experiments, by which children are liable to injure themselves, they are allowed to persist, subject only to dissuasion more or less earnest according to the danger, there cannot fail to arise an ever-increasing faith in the parental friendship and guidance. Not only, as before shown, does the adoption of this course enable fathers and mothers to avoid the odium which attaches to the infliction of positive punishment; but, as we here see, it enables them to avoid the odium which attaches to constant thwartings; and even to turn those incidents that commonly cause squabbles, into a means of strengthening the mutual good feeling. Instead of being told in words, which deeds seem to contradict, that their parents are their best friends, children will learn this truth by a consistent daily experience; and so learning it, will acquire a degree of trust and attachment which nothing else can give.

And now, having indicated the more sympathetic relation which must result from the habitual use of this method, let us return to the question above put— How is this method to be applied to the graver offences?

Note, in the first place, that these graver offences are likely to be both less frequent and less grave under the régime we have described than under the ordinary régime. The ill-behaviour of many children is itself a consequence of that chronic irritation in which they are kept by bad management. The state of isolation and antagonism produced by frequent punishment, necessarily deadens the sympathies; necessarily, therefore, opens the way to those transgressions which the sympathies check. That harsh treatment which children of the same family inflict on each other, is often, in great measure, a reflex of the harsh treatment they receive from adults—partly suggested by direct example, and partly generated by the ill-temper and the tendency to vicarious retaliation, which follow chastisements and scoldings. It cannot be questioned that the greater activity of the affections and happier state of feeling, maintained in children by the discipline we have described, must prevent them from sinning against each other so gravely and so frequently. The still more reprehensible offences, as lies and petty thefts, will, by the same causes, be diminished. Domestic estrangement is a fruitful source of such transgressions. It is a law of human nature, visible enough to all who observe, that those who are debarred the higher gratifications fall back upon the lower; those who have no sympathetic pleasures seek selfish ones; and hence, conversely, the maintenance of happier relations between parents and children is calculated to diminish the number of those offences of which selfishness is the origin.

When, however, such offences are committed, as they will occasionally be even under the best system, the discipline of consequences may still be resorted to; and if there exists that bond of confidence and affection above described, this discipline will be efficient. For what are the natural consequences, say, of a theft? They are of two kinds—direct and indirect. The direct consequence, as dictated by pure equity, is that of making restitution. A just ruler (and every parent should aim to be one) will demand that, when possible, a wrong act shall be undone by a right one; and in the case of theft this implies either the restoration of the thing stolen, or, if it is consumed, the giving of an equivalent: which, in the case of a child, may be effected out of its pocket-money. The indirect and more serious consequence is the grave displeasure of parents—a consequence which inevitably follows among all peoples civilised enough to regard theft as a crime. "But," it will be said, "the manifestation of parental displeasure, either in words or blows, is the ordinary course in these cases: the method leads here to nothing new." Very true. Already we have admitted that, in some directions, this method is spontaneously pursued. Already we have shown that there is a tendency for educational systems to gravitate towards the true system. And here we may remark, as before, that the intensity of this natural reaction will, in the beneficent order of things, adjust itself to the requirements—that this parental displeasure will vent itself in violent measures during comparatively barbarous times, when children are also comparatively barbarous; and will express itself less cruelly in those more advanced social states in which, by implication, the children are amenable to milder treatment.

But what it chiefly concerns us here to observe is, that the manifestation of strong parental displeasure, produced by one of these graver offences, will be potent for good, just in proportion to the warmth of the attachment existing between parent and child. Just in proportion as the discipline of natural consequences has been consistently pursued in other cases, will it be efficient in this case. Proof is within the experience of all, if they will look for it.

For does not every one know that when he has offended another, the amount of regret he feels (of course, leaving worldly considerations out of the question) varies with the degree of sympathy he has for that other? Is he not conscious that when the person offended is an enemy, the having given him annoyance is apt to be a source rather of secret satisfaction than of sorrow? Does he not remember that where umbrage has been taken by some total stranger, he has felt much less concern than he would have done had such umbrage been taken by one with whom he was intimate? While, conversely, has not the anger of an admired and cherished friend been regarded by him as a serious misfortune, long and keenly regretted? Well, the effects of parental displeasure on children must similarly vary with the pre-existing relationship. Where there is an established alienation, the feeling of a child who has transgressed is a purely selfish fear of the impending physical penalties or deprivations; and after these have been inflicted, the injurious antagonism and dislike which result, add to the alienation. On the contrary, where there exists a warm filial affection produced by a consistent parental friendship, the state of mind caused by parental displeasure is not only a salutary check to future misconduct of like kind, but is intrinsically salutary. The moral pain consequent on having, for the time being, lost so loved a friend, stands in place of the physical pain usually inflicted; and proves equally, if not more, efficient. While instead of the fear and vindictiveness excited by the one course, there are excited by the other a sympathy with parental sorrow, a genuine regret for having caused it, and a desire, by some atonement, to reestablish the friendly relationship. Instead of bringing into play those egotistic feelings whose predominance is the cause of criminal acts, there are brought into play those altruistic feelings which check criminal acts. Thus the discipline of natural consequences is applicable to grave as well as trivial faults; and the practice of it conduces not simply to the repression, but to the eradication of such faults.

In brief, the truth is that savageness begets savageness, and gentleness begets gentleness. Children who are unsympathetically treated become unsympathetic; whereas treating them with due fellow-feeling is a means of cultivating their fellow-feeling. With family governments as with political ones, a harsh despotism itself generates a great part of the crimes it has to repress; while on the other hand a mild and liberal rule both avoids many causes of dissension, and so ameliorates the tone of feeling as to diminish the tendency to transgression. As John Locke long since remarked, "Great severity of punishment does but very little good, nay, great harm, in education; and I believe it will be found that, *cæteris paribus*, those children who have been most chastised seldom make the best men." In confirmation of which opinion we may cite the fact not long since made public by Mr. Rogers, Chaplain of the Pentonville Prison, that those juvenile criminals who have been whipped are those who most frequently return to prison. Conversely, the beneficial effects of a kinder treatment are well illustrated in a fact stated to us by a French lady, in whose house we recently stayed in Paris. Apologising for the disturbance daily caused by a little boy who was unmanageable both at home and at school, she expressed her fear that there was no remedy save that which had succeeded in the case of an elder brother; namely, sending him to an English school. She explained that at various schools in Paris this elder brother had proved utterly untractable; that in despair they had followed the advice to send him to England; and that on his return home he was as good as he had before been bad. This remarkable change she ascribed entirely to the comparative mildness of the English discipline.

After the foregoing exposition of principles, our remaining space may best be occupied by a few of the chief maxims and rules deducible from them; and with a view to brevity we will put these in a hortatory form.

Do not expect from a child any great amount of moral goodness. During early years every civilised man passes through that phase of character exhibited by the barbarous race from which he is descended. As the child's features—flat nose, forward-opening nostrils, large lips, wide-apart eyes, absent frontal sinus, etc.—resemble for a time those of the savage, so, too, do his instincts. Hence the tendencies to cruelty, to thieving, to lying, so general among children—tendencies which, even without the aid of discipline, will become more or less modified just as the features do. The popular idea that children are "innocent," while it is true with respect to evil *knowledge*, is totally false with respect to evil *impulses*; as half an hour's observation in the nursery will prove to any one. Boys when left to themselves, as at public schools, treat each other more brutally than men do; and were they left to themselves at an earlier age their brutality would be still more conspicuous.

Not only is it unwise to set up a high standard of good conduct for children, but it is even unwise to use very urgent incitements to good conduct. Already most people recognise the detrimental results of intellectual precocity; but there remains to be recognised the fact that *moral precocity* also has detrimental results. Our higher moral faculties, like our higher intellectual ones, are comparatively complex. By consequence, both are comparatively late in their evolution. And with the one as with the other, an early activity produced by stimulation will be at the expense of the future character. Hence the not uncommon anomaly that those who during childhood were models of juvenile goodness, by and by undergo a seemingly inexplicable change for the worse, and end by being not above but below par; while relatively exemplary men are often the issue of a childhood by no means promising.

Be content, therefore, with moderate measures and moderate results. Bear in mind that a higher morality, like a higher intelligence, must be reached by slow growth; and you will then have patience with those imperfections which your child hourly displays. You will be less prone to that constant scolding, and threatening, and forbidding, by which many parents induce a chronic domestic irritation, in the foolish hope that they will thus make their children what they should be.

This liberal form of domestic government, which does not seek despotically to regulate all the details of a child's conduct, necessarily results from the system we advocate. Satisfy yourself with seeing that your child always suffers the natural consequences of his actions, and you will avoid that excess of control in which so many parents err. Leave him wherever you can to the discipline of experience, and you will save him from that hot-house virtue which over-regulation produces in yielding natures, or that demoralising antagonism which it produces in independent ones.

By aiming in all cases to insure the natural reactions to your child's actions, you will put an advantageous check on your own temper. The method of moral education pursued by many, we fear by most, parents, is little else than that of venting their anger in the way that first suggests itself. The slaps, and rough shakings and sharp words, with which a mother commonly visits her offspring's small offences (many of them not offences considered intrinsically), are generally but the manifestations of her ill-controlled feelings—result much more from the promptings of those feelings than from a wish to benefit the offenders. But by pausing in each case of transgression to consider what is the normal consequence, and how it may best be brought home to the transgressor, some little time is obtained for the mastery of yourself; the mere blind anger first aroused settles down into a less vehement feeling, and one not so likely to mislead you.

Do not, however, seek to behave as a passionless instrument. Remember that besides the natural reactions to your child's actions which the working of things tends to bring round on him, your own approbation or disapprobation is also a natural reaction, and one of the ordained agencies for guiding him. The error we have been combating is that of *substituting* parental displeasure and its artificial penalties, for the penalties which Nature has established. But while it should not be *substituted* for these natural penalties, we by no means argue that it should not, in some form, *accompany* them. Though the *secondary* kind of punishment should not usurp the place of the *primary* kind; it may, in moderation, rightly supplement the primary kind. Such amount of sorrow or indignation as you feel, should be expressed in words or manner; subject, of course, to the approval of your judgment. The kind and degree of feeling produced in you will necessarily depend on your own character; and it is therefore useless to say it should be this or that. Nevertheless, you may endeavour to modify the feeling into that which you believe ought to be entertained. Beware, however, of the two extremes; not only in respect of the intensity, but in respect of the duration, of your displeasure. On the one hand, avoid that weak impulsiveness, so general among mothers, which scolds and forgives almost in the same breath. On the other hand, do not unduly continue to show estrangement of feeling, lest you accustom your child to do without your friendship, and so lose your influence over him. The moral reactions called forth from you by your child's actions, you should as much as possible assimilate to those which you conceive would be called forth from a parent of perfect nature.

Be sparing of commands. Command only when other means are inapplicable, or have failed. "In frequent orders the parents' advantage is more considered than the child's," says Richter. As in primitive societies a breach of law is punished, not so much because it is intrinsically wrong as because it is a disregard of the king's authority—a rebellion against him; so in many families, the penalty visited on a transgressor is prompted less by reprobation of the offence than by anger at the disobedience. Listen to the ordinary speeches—"How *dare* you disobey me?" "I tell you I'll *make* you do it, sir." "I'll soon teach you who is *master*"—and then consider what the words, the tone, and the manner imply. A determination to subjugate is far more conspicuous in them, than anxiety for the child's welfare. For the time being the attitude of mind differs but little from that of a despot bent on punishing a recalcitrant subject. The right-feeling parent, however, like the philanthropic legislator, will rejoice not in coercion, but in dispensing with coercion. He will do without law wherever other modes of regulating conduct can be successfully employed; and he will regret the having recourse to law when law is necessary. As Richter remarks—"The best rule in politics is said to be '*pas trop gouverner*:' it is also true in education." And in spontaneous conformity with this maxim, parents whose lust of dominion is restrained by a true sense of duty, will aim to make their children control themselves as much as possible, and will fall back upon absolutism only as a last resort.

But whenever you *do* command, command with decision and consistency. If the case is one which really cannot be otherwise dealt with, then issue your fiat, and having issued it, never afterwards swerve from it. Consider well what you are going to do; weigh all the consequences; think whether you have adequate firmness of purpose; and then, if you finally make the law, enforce obedience at whatever cost. Let your penalties be like the penalties inflicted by inanimate Nature—inevitable. The hot cinder burns a child the first time he seizes it; it burns him the second time; it burns him the third time; it burns him every time; and he very soon learns not to touch the hot cinder. If you are equally consistent—if the consequences which you tell your child will follow specified acts, follow with like uniformity, he will soon come to respect your laws as he does those of Nature. And this respect once established, will prevent endless domestic evils. Of errors in education one of the worst is inconsistency. As in a community, crimes multiply when there is no certain administration of justice; so in a family, an immense increase of transgressions results from a hesitating or irregular infliction of punishments. A weak mother, who perpetually threatens and rarely performs—who makes rules in haste and repents of them at leisure—who treats the same offence now with severity and now with leniency, as the passing humour dictates, is laying up miseries for herself and her children. She is making herself contemptible in their eyes; she is setting them an example of uncontrolled feelings; she is encouraging them to transgress by the prospect of probable impunity: she is entailing endless squabbles and accompanying damage to her own temper and the tempers of her little ones; she is reducing their minds to a moral chaos, which after years of bitter experience will with difficulty bring into order. Better even a barbarous form of domestic government carried out consistently, than a humane one inconsistently carried out. Again we say, avoid coercive measures whenever it is possible to do so; but when you find despotism really necessary, be despotic in good earnest.

Remember that the aim of your discipline should be to produce a *self-governing* being; not to produce a being to be *governed by others*. Were your children fated to pass their lives as slaves, you could not too much accustom them to slavery during their childhood; but as they are by and by to be free men, with no one to control their daily conduct, you cannot too much accustom them to self-control while they are still under your eye. This it is which makes the system of discipline by natural consequences so especially appropriate to the social state which we in England have now reached. In feudal times, when one of the chief evils the citizen had to fear was the anger of his superiors, it was well that during childhood, parental vengeance should be a chief means of government. But now that the citizen has little to fear from any one—now that the good or evil which he experiences is mainly that which in the order of things results from his own conduct, he should from his first years begin to learn, experimentally, the good or evil consequences which naturally follow this or that conduct. Aim, therefore, to diminish the parental government, as fast as you can substitute for it in your child's mind that self-government arising from a foresight of results. During infancy a considerable amount of absolutism is necessary. A three-year old urchin playing with an open razor, cannot be allowed to learn by this discipline of consequences; for the consequences may be too serious. But as intelligence increases, the number of peremptory interferences may be, and should be, diminished, with the view of gradually ending them as maturity is approached. All transitions are dangerous; and the most dangerous is the transition from the restraint of the family circle to the non-restraint of the world. Hence the importance of pursuing the policy we advocate; which, by cultivating a boy's faculty of self-restraint, by continually increasing the degree in which he is left to his self-restraint, and by so bringing him, step by step, to a state of unaided self-restraint, obliterates the ordinary sudden and hazardous change from externally-governed youth to internally-governed maturity. Let the history of your domestic rule typify, in little, the history of our political rule: at the outset, autocratic control, where control is really needful; by and by an incipient constitutionalism, in which the liberty of the subject gains some express recognition; successive extensions of this liberty of the subject; gradually ending in parental abdication.

Do not regret the display of considerable self-will on the part of your children. It is the correlative of that diminished coerciveness so conspicuous in modern education. The greater tendency to assert freedom of action on the one side, corresponds to the smaller tendency to tyrannise on the other. They both indicate an approach to the system of discipline we contend for, under which children will be more and more led to rule themselves by the experience of natural consequences; and they are both accompaniments of our more advanced social state. The independent English boy is the father of the independent English man; and you cannot have the last without the first. German teachers say that they had rather manage a dozen German boys than one English one. Shall we, therefore, wish that our boys had the manageableness of German ones, and with it the submissiveness and political serfdom of adult Germans? Or shall we not rather tolerate in our boys those feelings which make them free men, and modify our methods accordingly?

Lastly, always recollect that to educate rightly is not a simple and easy thing, but a complex and extremely difficult thing, the hardest task which devolves on adult life. The rough-and-ready style of domestic government is indeed practicable by the meanest and most uncultivated intellects. Slaps and sharp words are penalties that suggest themselves alike to the least reclaimed barbarian and the stolidest peasant. Even brutes can use this method of discipline; as you may see in the growl and half-bite with which a bitch will check a too-exigeant puppy. But if you would carry out with success a rational and civilised system, you must be prepared for considerable mental exertion—for some study, some ingenuity, some patience, some self-control. You will have habitually to consider what are the results which in adult life follow certain kinds of acts; and you must then devise methods by which parallel results shall be entailed on the parallel acts of your children. It will daily be needful to analyse the motives of juvenile conduct—to distinguish between acts that are really good and those which, though simulating them, proceed from inferior impulses; while you will have to be ever on your guard against the cruel mistake not unfrequently made, of translating neutral acts into transgressions, or ascribing worse feelings than were entertained. You must more or less modify your method to suit the disposition of each child; and must be prepared to make further modifications as each child's disposition enters on a new phase. Your faith will often be taxed to maintain the requisite perseverance in a course which seems to produce little or no effect. Especially if you are dealing with children who have been wrongly treated, you must be prepared for a lengthened trial of patience before succeeding with better methods; since that which is not easy even where a right state of feeling has been established from the beginning, becomes doubly difficult when a wrong state of feeling has to be set right. Not only will you have constantly to analyse the motives of your children, but you will have to analyse your own motives—to discriminate between those internal suggestions springing from a true parental solicitude and those which spring from your own selfishness, your love of ease, your lust of dominion. And then, more trying still, you will have not only to detect, but to curb these baser impulses. In brief, you will have to carry on your own higher education at the same time that you are educating your children. Intellectually you must cultivate to good purpose that most complex of subjects—human nature and its laws, as exhibited in your children, in yourself, and in the world. Morally, you must keep in constant exercise your higher feelings, and restrain your lower. It is a truth yet remaining to be recognised, that the last stage in the mental development of each man and woman is to be reached only through a proper discharge of the parental duties. And when this truth is recognised, it will be seen how admirable is the arrangement through which human beings are led by their strongest affections to subject themselves to a discipline that they would else elude.

While some will regard this conception of education as it should be with doubt and discouragement, others will, we think, perceive in the exalted ideal which it involves, evidence of its truth. That it cannot be realised by the impulsive, the unsympathetic, and the short-sighted, but demands the higher attributes of human nature, they will see to be evidence of its fitness for the more advanced states of humanity. Though it calls for much labour and self-sacrifice, they will see that it promises an abundant return of happiness, immediate and remote. They will see that while in its injurious effects on both parent and child a bad system is twice cursed, a good system is twice blessed—it blesses him that trains and him that's trained.

PHYSICAL EDUCATION

Equally at the squire's table after the withdrawal of the ladies, at the farmers' market-ordinary, and at the village ale-house, the topic which, after the political question of the day, excites the most general interest, is the management of animals. Riding home from hunting, the conversation usually gravitates towards horse-breeding, and pedigrees, and comments on this or that "good point;" while a day on the moors is very unlikely to end without something being said on the treatment of dogs. When crossing the fields together from church, the tenants of adjacent farms are apt to pass from criticisms on the sermon to criticisms on the weather, the crops, and the stock; and thence to slide into discussions on the various kinds of fodder and their feeding qualities. Hodge and Giles, after comparing notes over their respective pig-styes, show by their remarks that they have been observant of their masters' beasts and sheep; and of the effects produced on them by this or that kind of treatment. Nor is it only among the rural population that the regulations of the kennel, the stable, the cow-shed, and the sheep-pen, are favourite subjects. In towns, too, the numerous artisans who keep dogs, the young men who are rich enough to now and then indulge their sporting tendencies, and their more staid seniors who talk over agricultural progress or read Mr. Mechi's annual reports and Mr. Caird's letters to the *Times*, form, when added together, a large portion of the inhabitants. Take the adult males throughout the kingdom, and a great majority will be found to show some interest in the breeding, rearing, or training of animals, of one kind or other.

But, during after-dinner conversations, or at other times of like intercourse, who hears anything said about the rearing of children? When the country gentleman has paid his daily visit to the stable, and personally inspected the condition and treatment of his horses; when he has glanced at his minor live stock, and given directions about them; how often does he go up to the nursery and examine into its dietary, its hours, its ventilation? On his library-shelves may be found White's *Farriery*, Stephens's *Book of the Farm*, Nimrod *on the Condition of Hunters*; and with the contents of these he is more or less familiar; but how many books has he read on the management of infancy and childhood? The fattening properties of oil-cake, the relative values of hay and chopped straw, the dangers of unlimited clover, are points on which every landlord, farmer, and peasant has some knowledge; but what percentage of them inquire whether the food they give their children is adapted to the constitutional needs of growing boys and girls? Perhaps the business-interests of these classes will be assigned as accounting for this anomaly. The explanation is inadequate, however; seeing that the same contrast holds among other classes. Of a score of townspeople, few, if any, would prove ignorant of the fact that it is undesirable to work a horse soon after it has eaten; and yet, of this same score, supposing them all to be fathers, probably not one would be found who had considered whether the time elapsing between his children's dinner and their resumption of lessons was sufficient. Indeed, on cross-examination, nearly every man would disclose the latent opinion that the regimen of the nursery was no concern of his. "Oh, I leave all those things to the women," would probably be the reply. And in most cases the tone of this reply would convey the implication, that such cares are not consistent with masculine dignity.

Regarded from any but a conventional point of view, the fact seems strange that while the raising of first-rate bullocks is an occupation on which educated men willingly bestow much time and thought, the bringing up of fine human beings is an occupation tacitly voted unworthy of their attention. Mammas who have been taught little but languages, music, and accomplishments, aided by nurses full of antiquated prejudices, are held competent regulators of the food, clothing, and exercise of children. Meanwhile the fathers read books and periodicals, attend agricultural meetings, try experiments, and engage in discussions, all with the view of discovering how to fatten prize pigs! We see infinite pains taken to produce a racer that shall win the Derby: none to produce a modern athlete. Had Gulliver narrated of the Laputans that the men vied with each other in learning how best to rear the offspring of other creatures, and were careless of learning how best to rear their own offspring, he would have paralleled any of the other absurdities he ascribes to them.

The matter is a serious one, however. Ludicrous as is the antithesis, the fact it expresses is not less disastrous. As remarks a suggestive writer, the first requisite to success in life is "to be a good animal;" and to be a nation of good animals is the first condition to national prosperity. Not only is it that the event of a war often turns on the strength and hardiness of soldiers; but it is that the contests of commerce are in part determined by the bodily endurance of producers. Thus far we have found no reason to fear trials of strength with other races in either of these fields. But there are not wanting signs that our powers will presently be taxed to the uttermost. The competition of modern life is so keen, that few can bear the required application without injury. Already thousands break down under the high pressure they are subject to. If this pressure continues to increase, as it seems likely to do, it will try severely even the soundest constitutions. Hence it is becoming of especial importance that the training of children should be so carried on, as not only to fit them mentally for the struggle before them, but also to make them physically fit to bear its excessive wear and tear.

Happily the matter is beginning to attract attention. The writings of Mr. Kingsley indicate a reaction against over-culture; carried perhaps, as reactions usually are, somewhat too far. Occasional letters and leaders in the newspapers have shown an awakening interest in physical training. And the formation of a school, significantly nicknamed that of "muscular Christianity," implies a growing opinion that our present methods of bringing up children do not sufficiently regard the welfare of the body. The topic is evidently ripe for discussion.

To conform the regimen of the nursery and the school to the established truths of modern science—this is the desideratum. It is time that the benefits which our sheep and oxen are deriving from the investigations of the laboratory, should be participated in by our children. Without calling in question the great importance of horse-training and pig-feeding, we would suggest that, as the rearing of well-grown men and women is also of some moment, these conclusions which theory indicates and practice indorses, ought to be acted on in the last case as in the first. Probably not a few will be startled—perhaps offended—by this collocation of ideas. But it is a fact not to be disputed, and to which we must reconcile ourselves, that man is subject to the same organic laws as inferior creatures. No anatomist, no physiologist, no chemist, will for a moment hesitate to assert, that the general principles which are true of the vital processes in animals are equally true of the vital processes in man. And a candid admission of this fact is not without its reward: namely, that the generalisations established by observation and experiment on brutes, become available for human guidance. Rudimentary as is the Science of Life, it has already attained to certain fundamental principles underlying the development of all organisms, the human included. That which has now to be done, and that which we shall endeavour in some measure to do, is to trace the bearings of these fundamental principles on the physical training of childhood and youth.

The rhythmical tendency which is traceable in all departments of social life—which is illustrated in the access of despotism after revolution, or, among ourselves, in the alternation of reforming epochs and conservative epochs—which, after a dissolute age, brings an age of asceticism, and conversely,—which, in commerce, produces the recurring inflations and panics—which carries the devotees of fashion from one absurd extreme to the opposite one;—this rhythmical tendency affects also our table-habits, and by implication, the dietary of the young. After a period distinguished by hard drinking and hard eating, has come a period of comparative sobriety, which, in teetotalism and vegetarianism, exhibits extreme forms of protest against the riotous living of the past. And along with this change in the regimen of adults, has come a parallel change in the regimen for boys and girls. In past generations the belief was, that the more a child could be induced to eat, the better; and even now, among farmers and in remote districts, where traditional ideas most linger, parents may be found who tempt their children into repletion. But among the educated classes, who chiefly display this reaction towards abstemiousness, there may be seen a decided leaning to the under-feeding, rather than the over-feeding, of children. Indeed their disgust for by-gone animalism, is more clearly shown in the treatment of their offspring than in the treatment of themselves; for while their disguised asceticism is, in so far as their personal conduct is concerned, kept in check by their appetites, it has full play in legislating for juveniles.

That over-feeding and under-feeding are both bad, is a truism. Of the two, however, the last is the wourst. As writes a high authority, "the effects of casual repletion are less prejudicial, and more easily corrected, than those of inanition."[3] Besides, where there has been no injudicious interference, repletion seldom occurs. "Excess is the vice rather of adults than of the young, who are rarely either

---

[3] *Cyclopædia of Practical Medicine.*

gourmands or epicures, unless through the fault of those who rear them."[4] This system of restriction which many parents think so necessary, is based upon inadequate observation, and erroneous reasoning. There is an over-legislation in the nursery, as well as an over-legislation in the State; and one of the most injurious forms of it is this limitation in the quantity of food.

"But are children to be allowed to surfeit themselves? Shall they be suffered to take their fill of dainties and make themselves ill, as they certainly will do?" As thus put, the question admits of but one reply. But as thus put, it assumes the point at issue. We contend that, as appetite is a good guide to all the lower creation—as it is a good guide to the infant—as it is a good guide to the invalid—as it is a good guide to the differently-placed races of men—and as it is a good guide for every adult who leads a healthful life; it may safely be inferred that it is a good guide for childhood. It would be strange indeed were it here alone untrustworthy.

Perhaps some will read this reply with impatience; being able, as they think, to cite facts totally at variance with it. It may appear absurd if we deny the relevancy of these facts. And yet the paradox is quite defensible. The truth is, that the instances of excess which such persons have in mind, are usually the *consequences* of the restrictive system they seem to justify. They are the sensual reactions caused by an ascetic regimen. They illustrate on a small scale that commonly-remarked truth, that those who during youth have been subject to the most rigorous discipline, are apt afterwards to rush into the wildest extravagances. They are analogous to those frightful phenomena, once not uncommon in convents, where nuns suddenly lapsed from the extremest austerities into an almost demoniac wickedness. They simply exhibit the uncontrollable vehemence of long-denied desires. Consider the ordinary tastes and the ordinary treatment of children. The love of sweets is conspicuous and almost universal among them. Probably ninety-nine people in a hundred presume that there is nothing more in this than gratification of the palate; and that, in common with other sensual desires, it should be discouraged. The physiologist, however, whose discoveries lead him to an ever-increasing reverence for the arrangements of things, suspects something more in this love of sweets than is currently supposed; and inquiry confirms the suspicion. He finds that sugar plays an important part in the vital processes. Both saccharine and fatty matters are eventually oxidised in the body; and there is an accompanying evolution of heat. Sugar is the form to which sundry other compounds have to be reduced before they are available as heat-making food; and this *formation* of sugar is carried on in the body. Not only is starch changed into sugar in the course of digestion, but it has been proved by M. Claude Bernard that the liver is a factory in which other constituents of food are transformed into sugar: the need for sugar being so imperative that it is even thus produced from nitrogenous substances when no others are given. Now, when to the fact that children have a marked desire for this valuable heat-food, we join the fact that they have usually a marked dislike to that food which gives out the greatest amount of heat during oxidation (namely, fat), we have reason for thinking that excess of the one compensates for defect of the other—that the organism demands more sugar because it cannot deal with

---

[4] *Cyclopædia of Practical Medicine.*

much fat. Again, children are fond of vegetable acids. Fruits of all kinds are their delight; and, in the absence of anything better, they will devour unripe gooseberries and the sourest of crabs. Now not only are vegetable acids, in common with mineral ones, very good tonics, and beneficial as such when taken in moderation; but they have, when administered in their natural forms, other advantages. "Ripe fruit," says Dr. Andrew Combe, "is more freely given on the Continent than in this country; and, particularly when the bowels act imperfectly, it is often very useful." See, then, the discord between the instinctive wants of children and their habitual treatment. Here are two dominant desires, which in all probability express certain needs of the child's constitution; and not only are they ignored in the nursery-regimen, but there is a general tendency to forbid the gratification of them. Bread-and-milk in the morning, tea and bread-and-butter at night, or some dietary equally insipid, is rigidly adhered to; and any ministration to the palate is thought needless, or rather, wrong. What is the consequence? When, on fête-days, there is unlimited access to good things—when a gift of pocket-money brings the contents of the confectioner's window within reach, or when by some accident the free run of a fruit-garden is obtained; then the long-denied, and therefore intense, desires lead to great excesses. There is an impromptu carnival, due partly to release from past restraints, and partly to the consciousness that a long Lent will begin on the morrow. And then, when the evils of repletion display themselves, it is argued that children must not be left to the guidance of their appetites! These disastrous results of artificial restrictions, are themselves cited as proving the need for further restrictions! We contend, therefore, that the reasoning used to justify this system of interference is vicious. We contend that, were children allowed daily to partake of these more sapid edibles, for which there is a physiological requirement, they would rarely exceed, as they now mostly do when they have the opportunity: were fruit, as Dr. Combe recommends, "to constitute a part of the regular food" (given, as he advises, not between meals, but along with them), there would be none of that craving which prompts the devouring of crabs and sloes. And similarly in other cases.

Not only is it that the *à priori* reasons for trusting the appetites of children are strong; and that the reasons assigned for distrusting them are invalid; but it is that no other guidance is worthy of confidence. What is the value of this parental judgment, set up as an alternative regulator? When to "Oliver asking for more," the mamma or governess says "No," on what data does she proceed? She *thinks* he has had enough. But where are her grounds for so thinking? Has she some secret understanding with the boy's stomach—some *clairvoyant* power enabling her to discern the needs of his body? If not, how can she safely decide? Does she not know that the demand of the system for food is determined by numerous and involved causes—varies with the temperature, with the hygrometric state of the air, with the electric state of the air—varies also according to the exercise taken, according to the kind and quantity of food eaten at the last meal, and according to the rapidity with which the last meal was digested? How can she calculate the result of such a combination of causes? As we heard said by the father of a five-years-old boy, who stands a head taller than most of his age, and is proportionately robust, rosy, and active:—"I can see no artificial standard by which to mete out his food.

If I say, 'this much is enough,' it is a mere guess; and the guess is as likely to be wrong as right. Consequently, having no faith in guesses, I let him eat his fill." And certainly, any one judging of his policy by its effects, would be constrained to admit its wisdom. In truth, this confidence, with which most parents legislate for the stomachs of their children, proves their unacquaintance with physiology: if they knew more, they would be more modest. "The pride of science is humble when compared with the pride of ignorance." If any one would learn how little faith is to be placed in human judgments, and how much in the pre-established arrangements of things, let him compare the rashness of the inexperienced physician with the caution of the most advanced; or let him dip into Sir John Forbes's work, *On Nature and Art in the Cure of Disease*; and he will see that, in proportion as men gain knowledge of the laws of life, they come to have less confidence in themselves, and more in Nature.

Turning from the question of *quantity* of food to that of *quality*, we may discern the same ascetic tendency. Not simply a restricted diet, but a comparatively low diet, is thought proper for children. The current opinion is, that they should have but little animal food. Among the less wealthy classes, economy seems to have dictated this opinion—the wish has been father to the thought. Parents not affording to buy much meat, answer the petitions of juveniles with—"Meat is not good for little boys and girls;" and this, at first probably nothing but a convenient excuse, has by repetition grown into an article of faith. While the classes with whom cost is no consideration, have been swayed partly by the example of the majority, partly by the influence of nurses drawn from the lower classes, and in some measure by the reaction against past animalism.

If, however, we inquire for the basis of this opinion, we find little or none. It is a dogma repeated and received without proof, like that which, for thousands of years, insisted on swaddling-clothes. Very probably for the infant's stomach, not yet endowed with much muscular power, meat, which requires considerable trituration before it can be made into chyme, is an unfit aliment. But this objection does not tell against animal food from which the fibrous part has been extracted; nor does it apply when, after the lapse of two or three years, considerable muscular vigour has been acquired. And while the evidence in support of this dogma, partially valid in the case of very young children, is not valid in the case of older children, who are, nevertheless, ordinarily treated in conformity with it, the adverse evidence is abundant and conclusive. The verdict of science is exactly opposite to the popular opinion. We have put the question to two of our leading physicians, and to several of the most distinguished physiologists, and they uniformly agree in the conclusion, that children should have a diet not *less* nutritive, but, if anything, *more* nutritive than that of adults.

The grounds for this conclusion are obvious, and the reasoning simple. It needs but to compare the vital processes of a man with those of a boy, to see that the demand for sustenance is relatively greater in the boy than in the man. What are the ends for which a man requires food? Each day his body undergoes more or less wear—wear through muscular exertion, wear of the nervous system through mental actions, wear of the viscera in carrying on the functions of life; and the tissue thus wasted has to be renewed. Each day, too, by radiation, his body loses a large amount of heat; and as, for the continuance of the vital actions, the temperature of the body must be maintained, this loss has to be compensated by a constant production of heat: to which end certain constituents of the body are ever undergoing oxidation. To make up for the day's waste, and to supply fuel for the day's expenditure of heat, are, then, the sole purposes for which the adult requires food. Consider now the case of the boy. He, too, wastes the substance of his body by action; and it needs but to note his restless activity to see that, in proportion to his bulk, he probably wastes as much as a man. He, too, loses heat by radiation; and, as his body exposes a greater surface in proportion to its mass than does that of a man, and therefore loses heat more rapidly, the quantity of heat-food he requires is, bulk for bulk, greater than that required by a man. So that even had the boy no other vital processes to carry on than the man has, he would need, relatively to his size, a somewhat larger supply of nutriment. But, besides repairing his body and maintaining its heat, the boy has to make new tissue—to grow. After waste and thermal loss have been provided for, such surplus of nutriment as remains goes to the further building up of the frame; and only in virtue of this surplus is normal growth possible; the growth that sometimes takes place in the absence of it, causing a manifest prostration consequent upon defective repair. It is true that because of a certain mechanical law which cannot be here explained, a small organism has an advantage over a large one in the ratio between the sustaining and destroying forces—an advantage, indeed, to which the very possibility of growth is owing. But this admission only makes it the more obvious that though much adverse treatment may be borne without this excess of vitality being quite out-balanced; yet any adverse treatment, by diminishing it, must diminish the size or structural perfection reached. How peremptory is the demand of the unfolding organism for materials, is seen alike in that "schoolboy hunger," which after-life rarely parallels in intensity, and in the comparatively quick return of appetite. And if there needs further evidence of this extra necessity for nutriment, we have it in the fact that, during the famines following shipwrecks and other disasters, the children are the first to die.

This relatively greater need for nutriment being admitted, as it must be, the question that remains is—shall we meet it by giving an excessive quantity of what may be called dilute food, or a more moderate quantity of concentrated food? The nutriment obtainable from a given weight of meat is obtainable only from a larger weight of bread, or from a still larger weight of potatoes, and so on. To fulfil the requirement, the quantity must be increased as the nutritiveness is diminished. Shall, we, then, respond to the extra wants of the growing child by giving an adequate quantity of food as good as that of adults? Or, regardless of the fact that its stomach has to dispose of a relatively larger quantity even of this good food, shall we further tax it by giving an inferior food in still greater quantity?

The answer is tolerably obvious. The more the labour of digestion is economised, the more energy is left for the purposes of growth and action. The functions of the stomach and intestines cannot be performed without a large supply of blood and nervous power; and in the comparative lassitude that follows a hearty meal, every adult has proof that this supply of blood and nervous power is at the expense of the system at large. If the requisite nutriment is obtained from a great quantity of innutritious food, more work is entailed on the viscera than when it is obtained from a moderate quantity of nutritious food. This extra work is so much loss—a loss which in children shows itself either in diminished energy, or in smaller growth, or in both. The inference is, then, that they should have a diet which combines, as much as possible, nutritiveness and digestibility.

It is doubtless true that boys and girls may be reared upon an exclusively, or almost exclusively, vegetable diet. Among the upper classes are to be found children to whom comparatively little meat is given; and who, nevertheless, grow and appear in good health. Animal food is scarcely tasted by the offspring of labouring people; and yet they reach a healthy maturity. But these seemingly adverse facts have by no means the weight commonly supposed. In the first place, it does not follow that those who in early years flourish on bread and potatoes, will eventually reach a fine development; and a comparison between the agricultural labourers and the gentry, in England, or between the middle and lower classes in France is by no means in favour of vegetable feeders. In the second place, the question is not simply a question of *bulk*, but also a question of *quality*. A soft, flabby flesh makes as good a show as a firm one; but though to the careless eye, a child of full, flaccid tissue may appear the equal of one whose fibres are well toned, a trial of strength will prove the difference. Obesity in adults is often a sign of feebleness. Men lose weight in training. Hence the appearance of these low-fed children is far from conclusive. In the third place, besides *size*, we have to consider *energy*. Between children of the meat-eating classes and those of the bread-and-potato-eating classes, there is a marked contrast in this respect. Both in mental and physical vivacity the peasant-boy is greatly inferior to the son of a gentleman.

If we compare different kinds of animals, or different races of men, or the same animals or men when differently fed, we find still more distinct proof that *the degree of energy essentially depends on the nutritiveness of the food*.

In a cow, subsisting on so innutritive a food as grass, we see that the immense quantity required necessitates an enormous digestive system; that the limbs, small in comparison with the body, are burdened by its weight; that in carrying about this heavy body and digesting this excessive quantity of food, much force is expended; and that, having but little remaining, the creature is sluggish. Compare with the cow a horse—an animal of nearly allied structure, but habituated to a more concentrated diet. Here the body, and more especially its abdominal region, bears a smaller ratio to the limbs; the powers are not taxed by the support of such massive viscera, nor the digestion of so bulky a food; and, as a consequence, there is greater locomotive energy and considerable vivacity. If, again, we contrast the stolid inactivity of the graminivorous sheep with the liveliness of the dog, subsisting on flesh or farinaceous matters, or a mixture of the two, we see a difference similar in kind, but still greater in degree. And after walking through the Zoological Gardens, and noting the restlessness with which the carnivorous animals pace up and down their cages, it needs but to remember that none of the herbivorous animals habitually display this superfluous energy, to see how clear is the relation between concentration of food and degree of activity.

That these differences are not directly consequent on differences of constitution, as some may argue; but are directly consequent on differences in the food which the creatures are constituted to subsist on; is proved by the fact, that they are observable between different divisions of the same species. The varieties of the horse furnish an illustration. Compare the big-bellied, inactive, spiritless cart-horse with a racer or hunter, small in the flanks and full of energy; and then call to mind how much less nutritive is the diet of the one than that of the other. Or take the case of mankind. Australians, Bushmen, and others of the lowest savages who live on roots and berries, varied by larvae of insects and the like meagre fare, are comparatively puny in stature, have large abdomens, soft and undeveloped muscles, and are quite unable to cope with Europeans, either in a struggle or in prolonged exertion. Count up the wild races who are well grown, strong and active, as the Kaffirs, North-American Indians, and Patagonians, and you find them large consumers of flesh. The ill-fed Hindoo goes down before the Englishman fed on more nutritive food; to whom he is as inferior in mental as in physical energy. And generally, we think, the history of the world shows that the well-fed races have been the energetic and dominant races.

Still stronger, however, becomes the argument, when we find that the same individual animal is capable of more or less exertion according as its food is more or less nutritious. This has been demonstrated in the case of the horse. Though flesh may be gained by a grazing horse, strength is lost; as putting him to hard work proves. "The consequence of turning horses out to grass is relaxation of the muscular system." "Grass is a very good preparation for a bullock for Smithfield market, but a very bad one for a hunter." It was well known of old that, after passing the summer in the fields, hunters required some months of stable-feeding before becoming able to follow the hounds; and that they did not get into good condition till the beginning of the next spring. And the modern practice is that insisted on by Mr. Apperley—"Never to give a hunter what is called 'a summer's run at grass,' and, except under particular and very favourable circumstances, never to turn him out at all." That is to say, never give him poor food: great energy and endurance are to be obtained only by the continued use of nutritive food. So true is this that, as proved by Mr. Apperley, prolonged high-feeding enables a middling horse to equal, in his performances, a first-rate horse fed in the ordinary way. To which various evidences add the familiar fact that, when a horse is required to do double duty, it is the practice to give him beans—a food containing a larger proportion of nitrogenous, or flesh-making material, than his habitual oats.

Once more, in the case of individual men the truth has been illustrated with equal, or still greater, clearness. We do not refer to men in training for feats of strength, whose regimen, however, thoroughly conforms to the doctrine. We refer to the experience of railway-contractors and their labourers. It has been for years a well-established fact that an English navvy, eating largely of flesh, is far more efficient than a Continental navvy living on farinaceous food: so much more efficient, that English contractors for Continental railways found it pay to take their labourers with them. That difference of diet and not difference of race caused this superiority, has been of late distinctly shown. For it has turned out, that when the Continental navvies live in the same style as their English competitors, they presently rise, more or less nearly, to a par with them in efficiency. And to this fact let us here add the converse one, to which we can give personal testimony based upon six months' experience of vegetarianism, that abstinence from meat entails diminished energy of both body and mind.

Do not these various evidences endorse our argument respecting the feeding of children? Do they not imply that, even supposing the same stature and bulk to be attained on an innutritive as on a nutritive diet, the quality of tissue is greatly inferior? Do they not establish the position that, where energy as well as growth has to be maintained, it can only be done by high feeding? Do they not confirm the *à priori* conclusion that, though a child of whom little is expected in the way of bodily or mental activity, may thrive tolerably well on farinaceous substances, a child who is daily required, not only to form the due amount of new tissue, but to supply the waste consequent on great muscular action, and the further waste consequent on hard exercise of brain, must live on substances containing a larger ratio of nutritive matter? And is it not an obvious corollary, that denial of this better food will be at the expense either of growth, or of bodily activity, or of mental activity; as constitution and circumstances determine? We believe no logical intellect will question it. To think otherwise is to entertain in a disguised form the old fallacy of the perpetual-motion schemers—that it is possible to get power out of nothing.

Before leaving the question of food, a few words must be said on another requisite—*variety*. In this respect the dietary of the young is very faulty. If not, like our soldiers, condemned to "twenty years of boiled beef," our children have mostly to bear a monotony which, though less extreme and less lasting, is quite as clearly at variance with the laws of health. At dinner, it is true, they usually have food that is more or less mixed, and that is changed day by day. But week after week, month after month, year after year, comes the same breakfast of bread-and-milk, or, it may be, oatmeal-porridge. And with like persistence the day is closed, perhaps with a second edition of the bread-and-milk, perhaps with tea and bread-and-butter.

This practice is opposed to the dictates of physiology. The satiety produced by an often-repeated dish, and the gratification caused by one long a stranger to the palate, are *not* meaningless, as people carelessly assume; but they are the incentives to a wholesome diversity of diet. It is a fact, established by numerous experiments, that there is scarcely any one food, however good, which supplies in due proportions or right forms all the elements required for carrying on the vital processes in a normal manner: whence it follows that frequent change of food is desirable to balance the supplies of all the elements. It is a further fact, known to physiologists, that the enjoyment given by a much-liked food is a nervous stimulus, which, by increasing the action of the heart and so propelling the blood with increased vigour, aids in the subsequent digestion. And these truths are in harmony with the maxims of modern cattle-feeding, which dictate a rotation of diet.

Not only, however, is periodic change of food very desirable; but, for the same reasons, it is very desirable that a mixture of food should be taken at each meal. The better balance of ingredients, and the greater nervous stimulation, are advantages which hold here as before. If facts are asked for, we may name as one, the comparative ease with which the stomach disposes of a French dinner, enormous in quantity but extremely varied in materials. Few will contend that an equal weight of one kind of food, however well cooked, could be digested with as much facility. If any desire further facts, they may find them in every modern book on the management of animals. Animals thrive best when each meal is made up of several things. The experiments of Goss and Stark "afford the most decisive proof of the advantage, or rather the necessity, of a mixture of substances, in order to produce the compound which is the best adapted for the action of the stomach."[5]

Should any object, as probably many will, that a rotating dietary for children, and one which also requires a mixture of food at each meal, would entail too much trouble; we reply, that no trouble is thought too great which conduces to the mental development of children, and that for their future welfare, good bodily development is of still higher importance. Moreover, it seems alike sad and strange that a trouble which is cheerfully taken in the fattening of pigs, should be thought too great in the rearing of children.

One more paragraph, with the view of warning those who may propose to adopt the regimen indicated. The change must not be made suddenly; for continued low-feeding so enfeebles the system, as to disable it from at once dealing with a high diet. Deficient nutrition is itself a cause of dyspepsia. This is true even of animals. "When calves are fed with skimmed milk, or whey, or other poor food, they are liable to indigestion."[6] Hence, therefore, where the energies are low, the transition to a generous diet must be gradual: each increment of strength gained, justifying a fresh addition of nutriment. Further, it should be borne in mind that the concentration of nutriment may be carried too far. A bulk sufficient to fill the stomach is one requisite of a proper meal; and this requisite negatives a diet deficient in those matters which give adequate mass. Though the size of the digestive organs is less in the well-fed civilised races than in the ill-fed savage ones, and though their size may eventually diminish still further, yet, for the time being, the bulk of the ingesta must be determined by the existing capacity. But, paying due regard to these two qualifications, our conclusions are—that the food of children should be highly nutritive; that it should be varied at each meal and at successive meals; and that it should be abundant.

With clothing as with food, the usual tendency is towards an improper scantiness. Here, too, asceticism peeps out. There is a current theory, vaguely entertained if not put into a definite formula, that the sensations are to be disregarded. They do not exist for our guidance, but to mislead us, seems to be the prevalent belief reduced to its naked form. It is a grave error: we are much more beneficently constituted. It is not obedience to the sensations, but disobedience to them, which is the habitual cause of bodily evils. It is not the eating when hungry, but the eating in the absence of hunger, which is bad. It is not drinking when thirsty, but

[5] *Cyclopædia of Anatomy and Physiology.*
[6] Morton's *Cyclopædia of Agriculture.*

continuing to drink when thirst has ceased, that is the vice. Harm does not result from breathing that fresh air which every healthy person enjoys; but from breathing foul air, spite of the protest of the lungs. Harm does not result from taking that active exercise which, as every child shows us, Nature strongly prompts; but from a persistent disregard of Nature's promptings. Not that mental activity which is spontaneous and enjoyable does the mischief; but that which is persevered in after a hot or aching head commands desistance. Not that bodily exertion which is pleasant or indifferent, does injury; but that which is continued when exhaustion forbids. It is true that, in those who have long led unhealthy lives, the sensations are not trustworthy guides. People who have for years been almost constantly indoors, who have exercised their brains very much and their bodies scarcely at all, who in eating have obeyed their clocks without consulting their stomachs, may very likely be misled by their vitiated feelings. But their abnormal state is itself the result of transgressing their feelings. Had they from childhood never disobeyed what we may term the physical conscience, it would not have been seared, but would have remained a faithful monitor.

Among the sensations serving for our guidance are those of heat and cold; and a clothing for children which does not carefully consult these sensations, is to be condemned. The common notion about "hardening" is a grievous delusion. Not a few children are "hardened" out of the world; and those who survive, permanently suffer either in growth or constitution. "Their delicate appearance furnishes ample indication of the mischief thus produced, and their frequent attacks of illness might prove a warning even to unreflecting parents," says Dr. Combe. The reasoning on which this hardening-theory rests is extremely superficial. Wealthy parents, seeing little peasant boys and girls playing about in the open air only half-clothed, and joining with this fact the general healthiness of labouring people, draw the unwarrantable conclusion that the healthiness is the result of the exposure, and resolve to keep their own offspring scantily covered! It is forgotten that these urchins who gambol upon village-greens are in many respects favourably circumstanced — that their lives are spent in almost perpetual play; that they are all day breathing fresh air; and that their systems are not disturbed by over-taxed brains. For aught that appears to the contrary, their good health may be maintained, not in consequence of, but in spite of, their deficient clothing. This alternative conclusion we believe to be the true one; and that an inevitable detriment results from the loss of animal heat to which they are subject.

For when, the constitution being sound enough to bear it, exposure does produce hardness, it does so at the expense of growth. This truth is displayed alike in animals and in man. Shetland ponies bear greater inclemencies than the horses of the south, but are dwarfed. Highland sheep and cattle, living in a colder climate, are stunted in comparison with English breeds. In both the arctic and antarctic regions the human race falls much below its ordinary height: the Laplander and Esquimaux are very short; and the Terra del Fuegians, who go naked in a wintry land, are described by Darwin as so stunted and hideous, that "one can hardly make one's-self believe they are fellow-creatures."

Science explains this dwarfishness produced by great abstraction of heat;

showing that, food and other things being equal, it unavoidably results. For, as before pointed out, to make up for that cooling by radiation which the body is ever undergoing, there must be a constant oxidation of certain matters forming part of the food. And in proportion as the thermal loss is great, must the quantity of these matters required for oxidation be great. But the power of the digestive organs is limited. Consequently, when they have to prepare a large quantity of this material needful for maintaining the temperature, they can prepare but a small quantity of the material which goes to build up the frame. Excessive expenditure for fuel entails diminished means for other purposes. Wherefore there necessarily results a body small in size, or inferior in texture, or both.

Hence the great importance of clothing. As Liebig says:—"Our clothing is, in reference to the temperature of the body, merely an equivalent for a certain amount of food." By diminishing the loss of heat, it diminishes the amount of fuel needful for maintaining the heat; and when the stomach has less to do in preparing fuel, it can do more in preparing other materials. This deduction is confirmed by the experience of those who manage animals. Cold can be borne by animals only at an expense of fat, or muscle, or growth, as the case may be. "If fattening cattle are exposed to a low temperature, either their progress must be retarded, or a great additional expenditure of food incurred."[7] Mr. Apperley insists strongly that, to bring hunters into good condition, it is necessary that the stable should be kept warm. And among those who rear racers, it is an established doctrine that exposure is to be avoided.

The scientific truth thus illustrated by ethnology, and recognised by agriculturists and sportsmen, applies with double force to children. In proportion to their smallness and the rapidity of their growth is the injury from cold great. In France, new-born infants often die in winter from being carried to the office of the *maire* for registration. "M. Quetelet has pointed out, that in Belgium two infants die in January for one that dies in July." And in Russia the infant mortality is something enormous. Even when near maturity, the undeveloped frame is comparatively unable to bear exposure: as witness the quickness with which young soldiers succumb in a trying campaign. The *rationale* is obvious. We have already adverted to the fact that, in consequence of the varying relation between surface and bulk, a child loses a relatively larger amount of heat than an adult; and here we must point out that the disadvantage under which the child thus labours is very great. Lehmann says:—"If the carbonic acid excreted by children or young animals is calculated for an equal bodily weight, it results that children produce nearly twice as much acid as adults." Now the quantity of carbonic acid given off varies with tolerable accuracy as the quantity of heat produced. And thus we see that in children the system, even when not placed at a disadvantage, is called upon to provide nearly double the proportion of material for generating heat.

See, then, the extreme folly of clothing the young scantily. What father, full-grown though he is, losing heat less rapidly as he does, and having no physiological necessity but to supply the waste of each day—what father, we ask, would think it salutary to go about with bare legs, bare arms, and bare neck? Yet this

[7] Morton's *Cyclopædia of Agriculture*.

tax on the system, from which he would shrink, he inflicts on his little ones, who are so much less able to bear it! or, if he does not inflict it, sees it inflicted without protest. Let him remember that every ounce of nutriment needlessly expended for the maintenance of temperature, is so much deducted from the nutriment going to build up the frame; and that even when colds, congestions, or other consequent disorders are escaped, diminished growth or less perfect structure is inevitable.

"The rule is, therefore, not to dress in an invariable way in all cases, but to put on clothing in kind and quantity *sufficient in the individual case to protect the body effectually from an abiding sensation of cold, however slight.*" This rule, the importance of which Dr. Combe indicates by the italics, is one in which men of science and practitioners agree. We have met with none competent to form a judgment on the matter, who do not strongly condemn the exposure of children's limbs. If there is one point above others in which "pestilent custom" should be ignored, it is this.

Lamentable, indeed, is it to see mothers seriously damaging the constitutions of their children out of compliance with an irrational fashion. It is bad enough that they should themselves conform to every folly which our Gallic neighbours please to initiate; but that they should clothe their children in any mountebank dress which *Le petit Courrier des Dames* indicates, regardless of its insufficiency and unfitness, is monstrous. Discomfort, more or less great, is inflicted; frequent disorders are entailed; growth is checked or stamina undermined; premature death not uncommonly caused; and all because it is thought needful to make frocks of a size and material dictated by French caprice. Not only is it that for the sake of conformity, mothers thus punish and injure their little ones by scantiness of covering; but it is that from an allied motive they impose a style of dress which forbids healthful activity. To please the eye, colours and fabrics are chosen totally unfit to bear that rough usage which unrestrained play involves; and then to prevent damage the unrestrained play is interdicted. "Get up this moment: you will soil your clean frock," is the mandate issued to some urchin creeping about on the floor. "Come back: you will dirty your stockings," calls out the governess to one of her charges, who has left the footpath to scramble up a bank. Thus is the evil doubled. That they may come up to their mamma's standard of prettiness, and be admired by her visitors, children must have habiliments deficient in quantity and unfit in texture; and that these easily-damaged habiliments may be kept clean and uninjured, the restless activity so natural and needful for the young is restrained. The exercise which becomes doubly requisite when the clothing is insufficient, is cut short, lest it should deface the clothing. Would that the terrible cruelty of this system could be seen by those who maintain it! We do not hesitate to say that, through enfeebled health, defective energies, and consequent non-success in life, thousands are annually doomed to unhappiness by this unscrupulous regard for appearances: even when they are not, by early death, literally sacrificed to the Moloch of maternal vanity. We are reluctant to counsel strong measures, but really the evils are so great as to justify, or even to demand, a peremptory interference on the part of fathers.

Our conclusions are, then—that, while the clothing of children should never be in such excess as to create oppressive warmth, it should always be sufficient to prevent any general feeling of cold;[8] that, instead of the flimsy cotton, linen, or mixed fabrics commonly used, it should be made of some good non-conductor, such as coarse woollen cloth; that it should be so strong as to receive little damage from the hard wear and tear which childish sports will give it; and that its colours should be such as will not soon suffer from use and exposure.

To the importance of bodily exercise most people are in some degree awake. Perhaps less needs saying on this requisite of physical education than on most others: at any rate, in so far as boys are concerned. Public schools and private schools alike furnish tolerably adequate play-grounds; and there is usually a fair share of time for out-door games, and a recognition of them as needful. In this, if in no other direction, it seems admitted that the promptings of boyish instinct may advantageously be followed; and, indeed, in the modern practice of breaking the prolonged morning's and afternoon's lessons by a few minutes' open-air recreation, we see an increasing tendency to conform school-regulations to the bodily sensations of the pupils. Here, then, little needs be said in the way of expostulation or suggestion.

But we have been obliged to qualify this admission by inserting the clause "in so far as boys are concerned." Unfortunately the fact is quite otherwise with girls. It chances, somewhat strangely, that we have daily opportunity of drawing a comparison. We have both a boys' school and a girls' school within view; and the contrast between them is remarkable. In the one case, nearly the whole of a large garden is turned into an open, gravelled space, affording ample scope for games, and supplied with poles and horizontal bars for gymnastic exercises. Every day before breakfast, again towards eleven o'clock, again at mid-day, again in the afternoon, and once more after school is over, the neighbourhood is awakened by a chorus of shouts and laughter as the boys rush out to play; and for as long as they remain, both eyes and ears give proof that they are absorbed in that enjoyable activity which makes the pulse bound and ensures the healthful activity of every organ. How unlike is the picture offered by the "Establishment for Young Ladies!" Until the fact was pointed out, we actually did not know that we had a girl's school as close to us as the school for boys. The garden, equally large with the other, affords no sign whatever of any provision for juvenile recreation; but is entirely laid out with prim grass-plots, gravel-walks, shrubs, and flowers, after the usual suburban style. During five months we have not once had our attention drawn to the premises by a shout or a laugh. Occasionally girls may be observed sauntering along the paths with lesson-books in their hands, or else walking arm-in-arm. Once indeed, we saw one chase another round the garden; but, with this exception, nothing like vigorous exertion has been visible.

Why this astounding difference? Is it that the constitution of a girl differs so entirely from that of a boy as not to need these active exercises? Is it that a girl

[8] It is needful to remark that children whose legs and arms have been from the beginning habitually without covering, cease to be conscious that the exposed surfaces are cold; just as by use we have all ceased to be conscious that our faces are cold, even when out of doors. But though in such children the sensations no longer protest, it does not follow that the system escapes injury, any more than it follows that the Fuegian is undamaged by exposure, because he bears with indifference the melting of the falling snow on his naked body.

has none of the promptings to vociferous play by which boys are impelled? Or is it that, while in boys these promptings are to be regarded as stimuli to a bodily activity without which there cannot be adequate development, to their sisters, Nature has given them for no purpose whatever—unless it be for the vexation of school-mistresses? Perhaps, however, we mistake the aim of those who train the gentler sex. We have a vague suspicion that to produce a robust *physique* is thought undesirable; that rude health and abundant vigour are considered somewhat plebeian; that a certain delicacy, a strength not competent to more than a mile or two's walk, an appetite fastidious and easily satisfied, joined with that timidity which commonly accompanies feebleness, are held more lady-like. We do not expect that any would distinctly avow this; but we fancy the governess-mind is haunted by an ideal young lady bearing not a little resemblance to this type. If so, it must be admitted that the established system is admirably calculated to realise this ideal. But to suppose that such is the ideal of the opposite sex is a profound mistake. That men are not commonly drawn towards masculine women, is doubtless true. That such relative weakness as asks the protection of superior strength, is an element of attraction, we quite admit. But the difference thus responded to by the feelings of men, is the natural, pre-established difference, which will assert itself without artificial appliances. And when, by artificial appliances, the degree of this difference is increased, it becomes an element of repulsion rather than of attraction.

"Then girls should be allowed to run wild—to become as rude as boys, and grow up into romps and hoydens!" exclaims some defender of the proprieties. This, we presume, is the ever-present dread of school-mistresses. It appears, on inquiry, that at "Establishments for Young Ladies" noisy play like that daily indulged in by boys, is a punishable offence; and we infer that it is forbidden, lest unlady-like habits should be formed. The fear is quite groundless, however. For if the sportive activity allowed to boys does not prevent them from growing up into gentlemen; why should a like sportive activity prevent girls from growing up into ladies? Rough as may have been their play-ground frolics, youths who have left school do not indulge in leap-frog in the street, or marbles in the drawing-room. Abandoning their jackets, they abandon at the same time boyish games; and display an anxiety—often a ludicrous anxiety—to avoid whatever is not manly. If now, on arriving at the due age, this feeling of masculine dignity puts so efficient a restraint on the sports of boyhood, will not the feeling of feminine modesty, gradually strengthening as maturity is approached, put an efficient restraint on the like sports of girlhood? Have not women even a greater regard for appearances than men? and will there not consequently arise in them even a stronger check to whatever is rough or boisterous? How absurd is the supposition that the womanly instincts would not assert themselves but for the rigorous discipline of school-mistresses!

In this, as in other cases, to remedy the evils of one artificiality, another artificiality has been introduced. The natural, spontaneous exercise having been forbidden, and the bad consequences of no exercise having become conspicuous, there has been adopted a system of factitious exercise—gymnastics. That this is better than nothing we admit; but that it is an adequate substitute for play we deny. The defects are both positive and negative. In the first place, these formal, muscular motions, necessarily less varied than those accompanying juvenile sports, do not secure so equable a distribution of action to all parts of the body; whence it results that the exertion, falling on special parts, produces fatigue sooner than it would else have done: to which, in passing, let us add, that, if constantly repeated, this exertion of special parts leads to a disproportionate development. Again, the quantity of exercise thus taken will be deficient, not only in consequence of uneven distribution; but there will be a further deficiency in consequence of lack of interest. Even when not made repulsive, as they sometimes are by assuming the shape of appointed lessons, these monotonous movements are sure to become wearisome from the absence of amusement. Competition, it is true, serves as a stimulus; but it is not a lasting stimulus, like that enjoyment which accompanies varied play. The weightiest objection, however, still remains. Besides being inferior in respect of the *quantity* of muscular exertion which they secure, gymnastics are still more inferior in respect of the *quality*. This comparative want of enjoyment which we have named as a cause of early desistance from artificial exercises, is also a cause of inferiority in the effects they produce on the system. The common assumption that, so long as the amount of bodily action is the same, it matters not whether it be pleasurable or otherwise, is a grave mistake. An agreeable mental excitement has a highly invigorating influence. See the effect produced upon an invalid by good news, or by the visit of an old friend. Mark how careful medical men are to recommend lively society to debilitated patients. Remember how beneficial to health is the gratification produced by change of scene. The truth is that happiness is the most powerful of tonics. By accelerating the circulation of the blood, it facilitates the performance of every function; and so tends alike to increase health when it exists, and to restore it when it has been lost. Hence the intrinsic superiority of play to gymnastics. The extreme interest felt by children in their games, and the riotous glee with which they carry on their rougher frolics, are of as much importance as the accompanying exertion. And as not supplying these mental stimuli, gymnastics must be radically defective.

Granting then, as we do, that formal exercises of the limbs are better than nothing—granting, further, that they may be used with advantage as supplementary aids; we yet contend that they can never serve in place of the exercises prompted by Nature. For girls, as well as boys, the sportive activities to which the instincts impel, are essential to bodily welfare. Whoever forbids them, forbids the divinely-appointed means to physical development.

A topic still remains—one perhaps more urgently demanding consideration than any of the foregoing. It is asserted by not a few, that among the educated classes the younger adults and those who are verging on maturity, are neither so well grown nor so strong as their seniors. On first hearing this assertion, we were inclined to class it as one of the many manifestations of the old tendency to exalt the past at the expense of the present. Calling to mind the facts that, as measured by ancient armour, modern men are proved to be larger than ancient men; and that the tables of mortality show no diminution, but rather an increase, in the duration of life, we paid little attention to what seemed a groundless belief. Detailed observation, however, has shaken our opinion. Omitting from the comparison the labouring classes, we have noticed a majority of cases in which the children do not reach the stature of their parents; and, in massiveness, making due allowance for difference of age, there seems a like inferiority. Medical men say that now-a-days people cannot bear nearly so much depletion as in times gone by. Premature baldness is far more common than it used to be. And an early decay of teeth occurs in the rising generation with startling frequency. In general vigour the contrast appears equally striking. Men of past generations, living riotously as they did, could bear more than men of the present generation, who live soberly, can bear. Though they drank hard, kept irregular hours, were regardless of fresh air, and thought little of cleanliness, our recent ancestors were capable of prolonged application without injury, even to a ripe old age: witness the annals of the bench and the bar. Yet we who think much about our bodily welfare; who eat with moderation, and do not drink to excess; who attend to ventilation, and use frequent ablutions; who make annual excursions, and have the benefit of greater medical knowledge;—we are continually breaking down under our work. Paying considerable attention to the laws of health, we seem to be weaker than our grandfathers who, in many respects, defied the laws of health. And, judging from the appearance and frequent ailments of the rising generation, they are likely to be even less robust than ourselves.

What is the meaning of this? Is it that past over-feeding, alike of adults and children, was less injurious than the under-feeding to which we have adverted as now so general? Is it that the deficient clothing which this delusive hardening-theory has encouraged, is to blame? Is it that the greater or less discouragement of juvenile sports, in deference to a false refinement is the cause? From our reasonings it may be inferred that each of these has probably had a share in producing the evil.[9] But there has been yet another detrimental influence at work, perhaps more potent than any of the others: we mean—excess of mental application.

On old and young, the pressure of modern life puts a still-increasing strain. In all businesses and professions, intenser competition taxes the energies and abilities of every adult; and, to fit the young to hold their places under this intenser competition, they are subject to severer discipline than heretofore. The damage is thus doubled. Fathers, who find themselves run hard by their multiplying competitors, and, while labouring under this disadvantage, have to maintain a more expensive style of living, are all the year round obliged to work early and late, taking little exercise and getting but short holidays. The constitutions shaken by this continued over-application, they bequeath to their children. And then these comparatively

---

[9] We are not certain that the propagation of subdued forms of constitutional disease through the agency of vaccination is not a part cause. Sundry facts in pathology suggest the inference, that when the system of a vaccinated child is excreting the vaccine virus by means of pustules, it will tend also to excrete through such pustules other morbific matters; especially if these morbific matters are of a kind ordinarily got rid of by the skin, as are some of the worst of them. Hence it is very possible—probable even—that a child with a constitutional taint, too slight to show itself in visible disease, may, through the medium of vitiated vaccine lymph taken from it, convey a like constitutional taint to other children, and these to others.

feeble children, predisposed to break down even under ordinary strains on their energies, are required to go through a *curriculum* much more extended than that prescribed for the unenfeebled children of past generations.

The disastrous consequences that might be anticipated, are everywhere visible. Go where you will, and before long there come under your notice cases of children or youths, of either sex, more or less injured by undue study. Here, to recover from a state of debility thus produced, a year's rustication has been found necessary. There you find a chronic congestion of the brain, that has already lasted many months, and threatens to last much longer. Now you hear of a fever that resulted from the over-excitement in some way brought on at school. And again, the instance is that of a youth who has already had once to desist from his studies, and who, since his return to them, is frequently taken out of his class in a fainting fit. We state facts—facts not sought for, but which have been thrust on our observation during the last two years; and that, too, within a very limited range. Nor have we by any means exhausted the list. Quite recently we had the opportunity of marking how the evil becomes hereditary: the case being that of a lady of robust parentage, whose system was so injured by the *régime* of a Scotch boarding-school, where she was under-fed and over-worked, that she invariably suffers from vertigo on rising in the morning; and whose children, inheriting this enfeebled brain, are several of them unable to bear even a moderate amount of study without headache or giddiness. At the present time we have daily under our eyes, a young lady whose system has been damaged for life by the college-course through which she has passed. Taxed as she was to such an extent that she had no energy left for exercise, she is, now that she has finished her education, a constant complainant. Appetite small and very capricious, mostly refusing meat; extremities perpetually cold, even when the weather is warm; a feebleness which forbids anything but the slowest walking, and that only for a short time; palpitation on going upstairs; greatly impaired vision—these, joined with checked growth and lax tissue, are among the results entailed. And to her case we may add that of her friend and fellow-student; who is similarly weak; who is liable to faint even under the excitement of a quiet party of friends; and who has at length been obliged by her medical attendant to desist from study entirely.

If injuries so conspicuous are thus frequent, how very general must be the smaller, and inconspicuous injuries! To one case where positive illness is traceable to over-application, there are probably at least half-a-dozen cases where the evil is unobtrusive and slowly accumulating—cases where there is frequent derangement of the functions, attributed to this or that special cause, or to constitutional delicacy; cases where there is retardation and premature arrest of bodily growth; cases where a latent tendency to consumption is brought out and established; cases where a predisposition is given to that now common cerebral disorder brought on by the labour of adult life. How commonly health is thus undermined, will be clear to all who, after noting the frequent ailments of hard-worked professional and mercantile men, will reflect on the much worse effects which undue application must produce on the undeveloped systems of children. The young can bear neither so much hardship, nor so much physical exertion, nor so much mental exertion, as the full grown. Judge, then, if the full grown manifestly suffer from the excessive mental exertion required of them, how great must be the damage which a mental exertion, often equally excessive, inflicts on the young!

Indeed, when we examine the merciless school drill frequently enforced, the wonder is, not that it does extreme injury, but that it can be borne at all. Take the instance given by Sir John Forbes, from personal knowledge; and which he asserts, after much inquiry, to be an average sample of the middle-class girls'-school system throughout England. Omitting detailed divisions of time, we quote the summary of the twenty-four hours.

In bed	9	hours	(the younger 10)
In school, at their studies and tasks	9	"	
In school, or in the house, the elder at optional studies or work, the younger at play	3½	"	(the younger 2½)
At meals	1½	"	
Exercise in the open air, in the shape of a formal walk, often with lesson-books in hand, and even this only when the weather is fine at the appointed time.	1	"	
	24		

And what are the results of this "astounding regimen," as Sir John Forbes terms it? Of course feebleness, pallor, want of spirits, general ill-health. But he describes something more. This utter disregard of physical welfare, out of extreme anxiety to cultivate the mind—this prolonged exercise of brain and deficient exercise of limbs,—he found to be habitually followed, not only by disordered functions but by malformation. He says:—"We lately visited, in a large town, a boarding-school containing forty girls; and we learnt, on close and accurate inquiry, that there was *not one* of the girl who had been at the school two years (and the majority had been as long) that was not more or less *crooked!*"[10]

It may be that since 1833, when this was written, some improvement has taken place. We hope it has. But that the system is still common—nay, that it is in some cases carried to a greater extreme than ever; we can personally testify. We recently went over a training-college for young men: one of those instituted of late years for the purpose of supplying schools with well-disciplined teachers. Here, under official supervision, where something better than the judgment of private school-mistresses might have been looked for, we found the daily routine to be as follows:—

At   6 o'clock the students are called,
"   7 to 8 studies,
"   8 to 9 scripture-reading, prayers, and breakfast,
"   9 to 12 studies,
"   12 to 1¼ leisure, nominally devoted to walking or other exercise, but often spent in study,

[10] *Cyclopædia of Practical Medicine*, vol. i. pp. 697, 698.

" 1¼ to 2 dinner, the meal commonly occupying twenty minutes,
" 2 to 5 studies,
" 5 to 6 tea and relaxation,
" 6 to 8½ studies,
" 8½ to 9½ private studies in preparing lessons for the next day,
" 10 to bed.

Thus, out of the twenty-four hours, eight are devoted to sleep; four and a quarter are occupied in dressing, prayers, meals, and the brief periods of rest accompanying them; ten and a half are given to study; and one and a quarter to exercise, which is optional and often avoided. Not only, however, are the ten-and-a-half hours of recognised study frequently increased to eleven-and-a-half by devoting to books the time set apart for exercise; but some of the students get up at four o'clock in the morning to prepare their lessons; and are actually encouraged by their teachers to do this! The course to be passed through in a given time is so extensive, and the teachers, whose credit is at stake in getting their pupils well through the examinations, are so urgent, that pupils are not uncommonly induced to spend twelve and thirteen hours a day in mental labour!

It needs no prophet to see that the bodily injury inflicted must be great. As we were told by one of the inmates, those who arrive with fresh complexions quickly become blanched. Illness is frequent: there are always some on the sick-list. Failure of appetite and indigestion are very common. Diarrhœa is a prevalent disorder: not uncommonly a third of the whole number of students suffering under it at the same time. Headache is generally complained of; and by some is borne almost daily for months. While a certain percentage break down entirely and go away.

That this should be the regimen of what is in some sort a model institution, established and superintended by the embodied enlightenment of the age, is a startling fact. That the severe examinations, joined with the short period assigned for preparation, should compel recourse to a system which inevitably undermines the health of all who pass through it, is proof, if not of cruelty, then of woeful ignorance.

The case is no doubt in a great degree exceptional—perhaps to be paralleled only in other institutions of the same class. But that cases so extreme should exist at all, goes far to show that the minds of the rising generation are greatly over-tasked. Expressing as they do the ideas of the educated community, the requirements of these training colleges, even in the absence of other evidence, would imply a prevailing tendency to an unduly urgent system of culture.

It seems strange that there should be so little consciousness of the dangers of over-education during youth, when there is so general a consciousness of the dangers of over-education during childhood. Most parents are partially aware of the evil consequences that follow infant-precocity. In every society may be heard reprobation of those who too early stimulate the minds of their little ones. And the dread of this early stimulation is great in proportion as there is adequate knowledge of the effects: witness the implied opinion of one of our most distinguished professors of physiology, who told us that he did not intend his little boy to learn any lessons until he was eight years old. But while to all it is a familiar truth that a forced development of intelligence in childhood, entails either physical feebleness, or ultimate stupidity, or early death; it appears not to be perceived that throughout youth the same truth holds. Yet it unquestionably does so. There is a given order in which, and a given rate at which, the faculties unfold. If the course of education conforms itself to that order and rate, well. If not—if the higher faculties are early taxed by presenting an order of knowledge more complex and abstract than can be readily assimilated; or if, by excess of culture, the intellect in general is developed to a degree beyond that which is natural to its age; the abnormal advantage gained will inevitably be accompanied by some equivalent, or more than equivalent, evil.

For Nature is a strict accountant; and if you demand of her in one direction more than she is prepared to lay out, she balances the account by making a deduction elsewhere. If you will let her follow her own course, taking care to supply, in right quantities and kinds, the raw materials of bodily and mental growth required at each age, she will eventually produce an individual more or less evenly developed. If, however, you insist on premature or undue growth of any one part, she will, with more or less protest, concede the point; but that she may do your extra work, she must leave some of her more important work undone. Let it never be forgotten that the amount of vital energy which the body at any moment possesses, is limited; and that, being limited, it is impossible to get from it more than a fixed quantity of results. In a child or youth the demands upon this vital energy are various and urgent. As before pointed out, the waste consequent on the day's bodily exercise has to be met; the wear of brain entailed by the day's study has to be made good; a certain additional growth of body has to be provided for; and also a certain additional growth of brain: to which must be added the amount of energy absorbed in digesting the large quantity of food required for meeting these many demands. Now, that to divert an excess of energy into any one of these channels is to abstract it from the others, is both manifest *à priori*, and proved *à posteriori*, by the experience of every one. Every one knows, for instance, that the digestion of a heavy meal makes such a demand on the system as to produce lassitude of mind and body, frequently ending in sleep. Every one knows, too, that excess of bodily exercise diminishes the power of thought—that the temporary prostration following any sudden exertion, or the fatigue produced by a thirty miles' walk, is accompanied by a disinclination to mental effort; that, after a month's pedestrian tour, the mental inertia is such that some days are required to overcome it; and that in peasants who spend their lives in muscular labour the activity of mind is very small. Again, it is a familiar truth that during those fits of rapid growth which sometimes occur in childhood, the great abstraction of energy is shown in an attendant prostration, bodily and mental. Once more, the facts that violent muscular exertion after eating, will stop digestion; and that children who are early put to hard labour become stunted; similarly exhibit the antagonism—similarly imply that excess of activity in one direction involves deficiency of it in other directions. Now, the law which is thus manifest in extreme cases, holds in all cases. These injurious abstractions of energy as certainly take place when the undue demands are slight and constant, as when they are great and sudden. Hence, if during youth the expenditure in mental labour exceeds that which Nature has provided for; the expenditure for other purposes falls below what it should have been; and evils of one kind or other are inevitably entailed. Let us briefly consider these evils.

Supposing the over-activity of brain to exceed the normal activity only in a moderate degree, there will be nothing more than some slight reaction on the development of the body: the stature falling a little below that which it would else have reached; or the bulk being less than it would have been; or the quality of tissue not being so good. One or more of these effects must necessarily occur. The extra quantity of blood supplied to the brain during mental exertion, and during the subsequent period in which the waste of cerebral substance is being made good, is blood that would else have been circulating through the limbs and viscera; and the growth or repair for which that blood would have supplied materials, is lost. The physical reaction being certain, the question is, whether the gain resulting from the extra culture is equivalent to the loss?—whether defect of bodily growth, or the want of that structural perfection which gives vigour and endurance, is compensated by the additional knowledge acquired?

When the excess of mental exertion is greater, there follow results far more serious; telling not only against bodily perfection, but against the perfection of the brain itself. It is a physiological law, first pointed out by M. Isidore St. Hilaire, and to which attention has been drawn by Mr. Lewes in his essay on "Dwarfs and Giants," that there is an antagonism between *growth* and *development*. By growth, as used in this antithetical sense, is to be understood *increase of size*; by development, *increase of structure*. And the law is, that great activity in either of these processes involves retardation or arrest of the other. A familiar example is furnished by the cases of the caterpillar and the chrysalis. In the caterpillar there is extremely rapid augmentation of bulk; but the structure is scarcely at all more complex when the caterpillar is full-grown than when it is small. In the chrysalis the bulk does not increase; on the contrary, weight is lost during this stage of the creature's life; but the elaboration of a more complex structure goes on with great activity. The antagonism, here so clear, is less traceable in higher creatures, because the two processes are carried on together. But we see it pretty well illustrated among ourselves when we contrast the sexes. A girl develops in body and mind rapidly, and ceases to grow comparatively early. A boy's bodily and mental development is slower, and his growth greater. At the age when the one is mature, finished, and having all faculties in full play, the other, whose vital energies have been more directed towards increase of size, is relatively incomplete in structure; and shows it in a comparative awkwardness, bodily and mental. Now this law is true of each separate part of the organism, as well as of the whole. The abnormally rapid advance of any organ in respect of structure, involves premature arrest of its growth; and this happens with the organ of the mind as certainly as with any other organ. The brain, which during early years is relatively large in mass but imperfect in structure, will, if required to perform its functions with undue activity, undergo a structural advance greater than is appropriate to its age; but the ultimate effect will be a falling short of the size and power that would else have been attained. And this is a part-cause—probably the chief cause—why precocious children, and youths who up to a certain time were carrying all before them, so often stop short and disappoint the high hopes of their parents.

But these results of over-education, disastrous as they are, are perhaps less disastrous than the effects produced on the health—the undermined constitution, the enfeebled energies, the morbid feelings. Recent discoveries in physiology have shown how immense is the influence of the brain over the functions of the body. Digestion, circulation, and through these all other organic processes, are profoundly affected by cerebral excitement. Whoever has seen repeated, as we have, the experiment first performed by Weber, showing the consequence of irritating the *vagus* nerve, which connects the brain with the viscera—whoever has seen the action of the heart suddenly arrested by irritating this nerve; slowly recommencing when the irritation is suspended; and again arrested the moment it is renewed; will have a vivid conception of the depressing influence which an over-wrought brain exercises on the body. The effects thus physiologically explained, are indeed exemplified in ordinary experience. There is no one but has felt the palpitation accompanying hope, fear, anger, joy—no one but has observed how laboured becomes the action of the heart when these feelings are violent. And though there are many who have never suffered that extreme emotional excitement which is followed by arrest of the heart's action and fainting; yet every one knows these to be cause and effect. It is a familiar fact, too, that disturbance of the stomach results from mental excitement exceeding a certain intensity. Loss of appetite is a common consequence alike of very pleasurable and very painful states of mind. When the event producing a pleasurable or painful state of mind occurs shortly after a meal, it not unfrequently happens either that the stomach rejects what has been eaten, or digests it with great difficulty and under protest. And as every one who taxes his brain much can testify, even purely intellectual action will, when excessive, produce analogous effects. Now the relation between brain and body which is so manifest in these extreme cases, holds equally in ordinary, less-marked cases. Just as these violent but temporary cerebral excitements produce violent but temporary disturbances of the viscera; so do the less violent but chronic cerebral excitements produce less violent but chronic visceral disturbances. This is not simply an inference:—it is a truth to which every medical man can bear witness; and it is one to which a long and sad experience enables us to give personal testimony. Various degrees and forms of bodily derangement, often taking years of enforced idleness to set partially right, result from this prolonged over-exertion of mind. Sometimes the heart is chiefly affected: habitual palpitations; a pulse much enfeebled; and very generally a diminution in the number of beats from seventy-two to sixty, or even fewer. Sometimes the conspicuous disorder is of the stomach: a dyspepsia which makes life a burden, and is amenable to no remedy but time. In many cases both heart and stomach are implicated. Mostly the sleep is short and broken. And very generally there is more or less mental depression.

Consider, then, how great must be the damage inflicted by undue mental excitement on children and youths. More or less of this constitutional disturbance will inevitably follow an exertion of brain beyond the normal amount; and when not so excessive as to produce absolute illness, is sure to entail a slowly accumulating degeneracy of *physique*. With a small and fastidious appetite, an imperfect digestion, and an enfeebled circulation, how can the developing body flourish? The due performance of every vital process depends on an adequate supply of good blood. Without enough good blood, no gland can secrete properly, no viscus can fully discharge its office. Without enough good blood, no nerve, muscle, membrane, or other tissue can be efficiently repaired. Without enough good blood, growth will neither be sound nor sufficient. Judge, then, how bad must be the consequences when to a growing body the weakened stomach supplies blood that is deficient in quantity and poor in quality; while the debilitated heart propels this poor and scanty blood with unnatural slowness.

And if, as all who investigate the matter must admit, physical degeneracy is a consequence of excessive study, how grave is the condemnation to be passed on this cramming-system above exemplified. It is a terrible mistake, from whatever point of view regarded. It is a mistake in so far as the mere acquirement of knowledge is concerned. For the mind, like the body, cannot assimilate beyond a certain rate; and if you ply it with facts faster than it can assimilate them, they are soon rejected again: instead of being built into the intellectual fabric, they fall out of recollection after the passing of the examination for which they were got up. It is a mistake, too, because it tends to make study distasteful. Either through the painful associations produced by ceaseless mental toil, or through the abnormal state of brain it leaves behind, it often generates an aversion to books; and, instead of that subsequent self-culture induced by rational education, there comes continued retrogression. It is a mistake, also, inasmuch as it assumes that the acquisition of knowledge is everything; and forgets that a much more important thing is the organisation of knowledge, for which time and spontaneous thinking are requisite. As Humboldt remarks respecting the progress of intelligence in general, that "the interpretation of Nature is obscured when the description languishes under too great an accumulation of insulated facts;" so, it may be remarked respecting the progress of individual intelligence, that the mind is over-burdened and hampered by an excess of ill-digested information. It is not the knowledge stored up as intellectual fat which is of value; but that which is turned into intellectual muscle. The mistake goes still deeper however. Even were the system good as producing intellectual efficiency, which it is not, it would still be bad, because, as we have shown, it is fatal to that vigour of *physique* needful to make intellectual training available in the struggle of life. Those who, in eagerness to cultivate their pupils' minds, are reckless of their bodies, do not remember that success in the world depends more on energy than on information; and that a policy which in cramming with information undermines energy, is self-defeating. The strong will and untiring activity due to abundant animal vigour, go far to compensate even great defects of education; and when joined with that quite adequate education which may be obtained without sacrificing health, they ensure an easy victory over competitors enfeebled by excessive study: prodigies of learning though they may be. A comparatively small and ill-made engine, worked at high pressure, will do more than a large and well-finished one worked at low-pressure. What folly is it, then, while finishing the engine, so to damage the boiler that it will not generate steam! Once more, the system is a mistake, as involving a false estimate of welfare in life. Even supposing it were a means to worldly success, instead of a means to worldly failure, yet, in the entailed ill-health, it would inflict a more than equivalent curse. What boots it to have attained wealth, if the wealth is accompanied by ceaseless ailments? What is the worth of distinction, if it has brought hypochondria with it? Surely no one needs telling that a good digestion, a bounding pulse, and high spirits, are elements of happiness which no external advantages can out-balance. Chronic bodily disorder casts a gloom over the brightest prospects; while the vivacity of strong health gilds even misfortune. We contend, then, that this over-education is vicious in every way—vicious, as giving knowledge that will soon be forgotten; vicious, as producing a disgust for knowledge; vicious, as neglecting that organisation of knowledge which is more important than its acquisition; vicious, as weakening or destroying that energy without which a trained intellect is useless; vicious, as entailing that ill-health for which even success would not compensate, and which makes failure doubly bitter. On women the effects of this forcing system are, if possible, even more injurious than on men. Being in great measure debarred from those vigorous and enjoyable exercises of body by which boys mitigate the evils of excessive study, girls feel these evils in their full intensity. Hence, the much smaller proportion of them who grow up well-made and healthy. In the pale, angular, flat-chested young ladies, so abundant in London drawing-rooms, we see the effect of merciless application, unrelieved by youthful sports; and this physical degeneracy hinders their welfare far more than their many accomplishments aid it. Mammas anxious to make their daughters attractive, could scarcely choose a course more fatal than this, which sacrifices the body to the mind. Either they disregard the tastes of the opposite sex, or else their conception of those tastes is erroneous. Men care little for erudition in women; but very much for physical beauty, good nature, and sound sense. How many conquests does the blue-stocking make through her extensive knowledge of history? What man ever fell in love with a woman because she understood Italian? Where is the Edwin who was brought to Angelina's feet by her German? But rosy cheeks and laughing eyes are great attractions. A finely rounded figure draws admiring glances. The liveliness and good humour that overflowing health produces, go a great way towards establishing attachments. Every one knows cases where bodily perfections, in the absence of all other recommendations, have incited a passion that carried all before it; but scarcely any one can point to a case where intellectual acquirements, apart from moral or physical attributes, have aroused such a feeling. The truth is that, out of the many elements uniting in various proportions to produce in a man's breast the complex emotion we call love, the strongest are those produced by physical attractions; the next in order of strength are those produced by moral attractions; the weakest are those produced by intellectual attractions; and even these are dependent less on acquired knowledge than on natural faculty—quickness, wit, insight. If any think the assertion a derogatory one, and inveigh against the masculine character for being thus swayed; we reply that they little know what they say when they thus call in question the Divine ordinations. Even were there no obvious meaning in the arrangement, we might be sure that some important end was subserved. But the meaning is quite obvious to those who examine. When we remember that one of Nature's ends, or rather her supreme end, is the welfare of posterity; further that, in so far as posterity are concerned, a cultivated intelligence based on a bad *physique* is of little worth, since its descendants will die out in a generation or two; and conversely that a good *physique*, however poor the accompanying mental endowments, is worth preserving, because, throughout future generations, the mental endowments may be indefinitely developed; we perceive how important is the balance of instincts above described. But, advantage apart, the instincts being thus balanced, it is folly to persist in a system which undermines a girl's constitution that it may overload her memory. Educate as highly as possible—the higher the better—providing no bodily injury is entailed (and we may remark, in passing, that a sufficiently high standard might be reached were the parrot-faculty cultivated less, and the human faculty more, and were the discipline extended over that now wasted period between leaving school and being married). But to educate in such manner, or to such extent, as to produce physical degeneracy, is to defeat the chief end for which the toil and cost and anxiety are submitted to. By subjecting their daughters to this high-pressure system, parents frequently ruin their prospects in life. Besides inflicting on them enfeebled health, with all its pains and disabilities and gloom; they not unfrequently doom them to celibacy.

The physical education of children is thus, in various ways, seriously faulty. It errs in deficient feeding; in deficient clothing; in deficient exercise (among girls at least); and in excessive mental application. Considering the regime as a whole, its tendency is too exacting: it asks too much and gives too little. In the extent to which it taxes the vital energies, it makes the juvenile life far more like the adult life than it should be. It overlooks the truth that, as in the foetus the entire vitality is expended in growth—as in the infant, the expenditure of vitality in growth is so great as to leave extremely little for either physical or mental action; so throughout childhood and youth, growth is the dominant requirement to which all others must be subordinated: a requirement which dictates the giving of much and the taking away of little—a requirement which, therefore, restricts the exertion of body and mind in proportion to the rapidity of growth—a requirement which permits the mental and physical activities to increase only as fast as the rate of growth diminishes.

The *rationale* of this high-pressure education is that it results from our passing phase of civilisation. In primitive times, when aggression and defence were the leading social activities, bodily vigour with its accompanying courage were the desiderata; and then education was almost wholly physical: mental cultivation was little cared for, and indeed, as in feudal ages, was often treated with contempt. But now that our state is relatively peaceful—now that muscular power is of use for little else than manual labour, while social success of nearly every kind depends very much on mental power; our education has become almost exclusively mental. Instead of respecting the body and ignoring the mind, we now respect the mind and ignore the body. Both these attitudes are wrong. We do not yet realise the truth that as, in this life of ours, the physical underlies the mental, the mental must not be developed at the expense of the physical. The ancient and modern conceptions must be combined.

Perhaps nothing will so much hasten the time when body and mind will both be adequately cared for, as a diffusion of the belief that the preservation of health is a *duty*. Few seem conscious that there is such a thing as physical morality. Men's habitual words and acts imply the idea that they are at liberty to treat their bodies as they please. Disorders entailed by disobedience to Nature's dictates, they regard simply as grievances: not as the effects of a conduct more or less flagitious. Though the evil consequences inflicted on their dependents, and on future generations, are often as great as those caused by crime; yet they do not think themselves in any degree criminal. It is true that, in the case of drunkenness, the viciousness of a bodily transgression is recognised; but none appear to infer that, if this bodily transgression is vicious, so too is every bodily transgression. The fact is, that all breaches of the laws of health are *physical sins*. When this is generally seen, then, and perhaps not till then, will the physical training of the young receive the attention it deserves.

PART II
ESSAYS ON KINDRED SUBJECTS

PROGRESS: ITS LAW AND CAUSE[11]

The current conception of Progress is somewhat shifting and indefinite. Sometimes it comprehends little more than simple growth—as of a nation in the number of its members and the extent of territory over which it has spread. Sometimes it has reference to quantity of material products—as when the advance of agriculture and manufactures is the topic. Sometimes the superior quality of these products is contemplated: and sometimes the new or improved appliances by which they are produced. When, again, we speak of moral or intellectual progress, we refer to the state of the individual or people exhibiting it; while, when the progress of Knowledge, of Science, of Art, is commented upon, we have in view certain abstract results of human thought and action. Not only, however, is the current conception of Progress more or less vague, but it is in great measure erroneous. It takes in not so much the reality of Progress as its accompaniments—not so much the substance as the shadow. That progress in intelligence seen during the growth of the child into the man, or the savage into the philosopher, is commonly regarded as consisting in the greater number of facts known and laws understood: whereas the actual progress consists in those internal modifications of which this increased knowledge is the expression. Social progress is supposed to consist in the produce of a greater quantity and variety of the articles required for satisfying men's wants; in the increasing security of person and property; in widening freedom of action: whereas, rightly understood, social progress consists in those changes of structure in the social organism which have entailed these consequences. The current conception is a teleological one. The phenomena are contemplated solely as bearing on human happiness. Only those changes are held to constitute progress which directly or indirectly tend to heighten human happiness. And they are thought to constitute progress simply *because* they tend to heighten human happiness. But rightly to understand progress, we must inquire what is the nature of these changes, considered apart from our interests. Ceasing, for example, to regard the successive geological modifications that have taken place in the Earth, as modifications that have gradually fitted it for the habitation of Man, and as *therefore* a geological progress, we must seek to determine the character common to the modifications—the law to which they all conform. And similarly in every other case. Leaving out of sight concomitants and beneficial consequences, let us ask what Progress is in itself.

In respect to that progress which individual organisms display in the course of their evolution, this question has been answered by the Germans. The investigations of Wolff, Goethe, and Von Baer, have established the truth that the series

---

[11] *Westminster Review*, April 1857.

of changes gone through during the development of a seed into a tree, or an ovum into an animal, constitute an advance from homogeneity of structure to heterogeneity of structure. In its primary stage, every germ consists of a substance that is uniform throughout, both in texture and chemical composition. The first step is the appearance of a difference between two parts of this substance; or, as the phenomenon is called in physiological language, a differentiation. Each of these differentiated divisions presently begins itself to exhibit some contrast of parts; and by and by these secondary differentiations become as definite as the original one. This process is continuously repeated—is simultaneously going on in all parts of the growing embryo; and by endless such differentiations there is finally produced that complex combination of tissues and organs constituting the adult animal or plant. This is the history of all organisms whatever. It is settled beyond dispute that organic progress consists in a change from the homogeneous to the heterogeneous.

Now, we propose in the first place to show, that this law of organic progress is the law of all progress. Whether it be in the development of the Earth, in the development of Life upon its surface, in the development of Society, of Government, of Manufactures, of Commerce, of Language, Literature, Science, Art, this same evolution of the simple into the complex, through successive differentiations, holds throughout. From the earliest traceable cosmical changes down to the latest results of civilisation, we shall find that the transformation of the homogeneous into the heterogeneous, is that in which Progress essentially consists.

With the view of showing that *if* the Nebular Hypothesis be true, the genesis of the solar system supplies one illustration of this law, let us assume that the matter of which the sun and planets consist was once in a diffused form; and that from the gravitation of its atoms there resulted a gradual concentration. By the hypothesis, the solar system in its nascent state existed as an indefinitely extended and nearly homogeneous medium—a medium almost homogeneous in density, in temperature, and in other physical attributes. The first advance towards consolidation resulted in a differentiation between the occupied space which the nebulous mass still filled, and the unoccupied space which it previously filled. There simultaneously resulted a contrast in density and a contrast in temperature, between the interior and the exterior of this mass. And at the same time there arose throughout it rotatory movements, whose velocities varied according to their distances from its centre. These differentiations increased in number and degree until there was the organised group of sun, planets, and satellites, which we now know—a group which represents numerous contrasts of structure and action among its members. There are the immense contrasts between the sun and planets, in bulk and in weight; as well as the subordinate contrasts between one planet and another, and between the planets and their satellites. There is the similarly marked contrast between the sun as almost stationary, and the planets as moving round him with great velocity; while there are the secondary contrasts between the velocities and periods of the several planets, and between their simple revolutions and the double ones of their satellites, which have to move round their primaries while moving round the sun. There is the yet further strong contrast between the sun and the planets in respect of temperature; and there is reason to suppose that the planets and satellites differ from each other in their proper heat, as well as in the heat they receive from the sun.

When we bear in mind that, in addition to these various contrasts, the planets and satellites also differ in respect to their distances from each other and their primary; in respect to the inclinations of their orbits, the inclinations of their axes, their times of rotation on their axes, their specific gravities, and their physical constitutions; we see what a high degree of heterogeneity the solar system exhibits, when compared with the almost complete homogeneity of the nebulous mass out of which it is supposed to have originated.

Passing from this hypothetical illustration, which must be taken for what it is worth, without prejudice to the general argument, let us descend to a more certain order of evidence. It is now generally agreed among geologists that the Earth was at first a mass of molten matter; and that it is still fluid and incandescent at the distance of a few miles beneath its surface. Originally, then, it was homogeneous in consistence, and, in virtue of the circulation that takes place in heated fluids, must have been comparatively homogeneous in temperature; and it must have been surrounded by an atmosphere consisting partly of the elements of air and water, and partly of those various other elements which assume a gaseous form at high temperatures. That slow cooling by radiation which is still going on at an inappreciable rate, and which, though originally far more rapid than now, necessarily required an immense time to produce any decided change, must ultimately have resulted in the solidification of the portion most able to part with its heat—namely, the surface. In the thin crust thus formed we have the first marked differentiation. A still further cooling, a consequent thickening of this crust, and an accompanying deposition of all solidifiable elements contained in the atmosphere, must finally have been followed by the condensation of the water previously existing as vapour. A second marked differentiation must thus have arisen: and as the condensation must have taken place on the coolest parts of the surface—namely, about the poles—there must thus have resulted the first geographical distinction of parts. To these illustrations of growing heterogeneity, which, though deduced from the known laws of matter, may be regarded as more or less hypothetical, Geology adds an extensive series that have been inductively established. Its investigations show that the Earth has been continually becoming more heterogeneous in virtue of the multiplication of the strata which form its crust; further, that it has been becoming more heterogeneous in respect of the composition of these strata, the latter of which, being made from the detritus of the older ones, are many of them rendered highly complex by the mixture of materials they contain; and that this heterogeneity has been vastly increased by the action of the Earth's still molten nucleus upon its envelope, whence have resulted not only a great variety of igneous rocks, but the tilting up of sedimentary strata at all angles, the formation of faults and metallic veins, the production of endless dislocations and irregularities. Yet again, geologists teach us that the Earth's surface has been growing more varied in elevation—that the most ancient mountain systems are the smallest, and the Andes and Himalayas the most modern; while in all probability there have been corresponding changes in the bed of the ocean. As a consequence of these ceaseless differentiations, we now find that no considerable portion of the Earth's exposed surface is like any other portion, either in contour, in geologic structure, or in chemical composition; and that in most parts it changes from mile to mile in all these characteristics.

Moreover, it must not be forgotten that there has been simultaneously going on a gradual differentiation of climates. As fast as the Earth cooled and its crust solidified, there arose appreciable differences in temperature between those parts of its surface most exposed to the sun and those less exposed. Gradually, as the cooling progressed, these differences became more pronounced; until there finally resulted those marked contrasts between regions of perpetual ice and snow, regions where winter and summer alternately reign for periods varying according to the latitude, and regions where summer follows summer with scarcely an appreciable variation. At the same time the successive elevations and subsidences of different portions of the Earth's crust, tending as they have done to the present irregular distribution of land and sea, have entailed various modifications of climate beyond those dependent on latitude; while a yet further series of such modifications have been produced by increasing differences of elevation in the land, which have in sundry places brought arctic, temperate, and tropical climates to within a few miles of each other. And the general result of these changes is, that not only has every extensive region its own meteorologic conditions, but that every locality in each region differs more or less from others in those conditions, as in its structure, its contour, its soil. Thus, between our existing Earth, the phenomena of whose varied crust neither geographers, geologists, mineralogists, nor meteorologists have yet enumerated, and the molten globe out of which it was evolved, the contrast in heterogeneity is sufficiently striking.

When from the Earth itself we turn to the plants and animals that have lived, or still live, upon its surface, we find ourselves in some difficulty from lack of facts. That every existing organism has been developed out of the simple into the complex, is indeed the first established truth of all; and that every organism that has existed was similarly developed, is an inference which no physiologist will hesitate to draw. But when we pass from individual forms of life to Life in general, and inquire whether the same law is seen in the *ensemble* of its manifestations,— whether modern plants and animals are of more heterogeneous structure than ancient ones, and whether the earth's present Flora and Fauna are more heterogeneous than the Flora and Fauna of the past,—we find the evidence so fragmentary, that every conclusion is open to dispute. Two-thirds of the Earth's surface being covered by water; a great part of the exposed land being inaccessible to, or untravelled by, the geologist; the greater part of the remainder having been scarcely more than glanced at; and even the most familiar portions, as England, having been so imperfectly explored that a new series of strata has been added within these four years,—it is manifestly impossible for us to say with any certainty what creatures have, and what have not, existed at any particular period. Considering the perishable nature of many of the lower organic forms, the metamorphosis of many sedimentary strata, and the gaps that occur among the rest, we shall see further reason for distrusting our deductions. On the one hand, the repeated discovery of vertebrate remains in strata previously supposed to contain none,—of reptiles where only fish were thought to exist,—of mammals where it was believed there were no creatures higher than reptiles,—renders it daily more manifest how small is the value of negative evidence.

On the other hand, the worthlessness of the assumption that we have discovered the earliest, or anything like the earliest, organic remains, is becoming equally clear. That the oldest known sedimentary rocks have been greatly changed by igneous action, and that still older ones have been totally transformed by it, is becoming undeniable. And the fact that sedimentary strata earlier than any we know, have been melted up, being admitted, it must also be admitted that we cannot say how far back in time this destruction of sedimentary strata has been going on. Thus it is manifest that the title, *Palæozoic*, as applied to the earliest known fossiliferous strata, involves a *petitio principii*; and that, for aught we know to the contrary, only the last few chapters of the Earth's biological history may have come down to us. On neither side, therefore, is the evidence conclusive. Nevertheless we cannot but think that, scanty as they are, the facts, taken altogether, tend to show both that the more heterogeneous organisms have been evolved in the later geologic periods, and that Life in general has been more heterogeneously manifested as time has advanced. Let us cite, in illustration, the one case of the *vertebrata*. The earliest known vertebrate remains are those of Fishes; and Fishes are the most homogeneous of the vertebrata. Later and more heterogeneous are Reptiles. Later still, and more heterogeneous still, are Mammals and Birds. If it be said, as it may fairly be said, that the Palæozoic deposits, not being estuary deposits, are not likely to contain the remains of terrestrial vertebrata, which may nevertheless have existed at that era, we reply that we are merely pointing to the leading facts, *such as they are.*

But to avoid any such criticism, let us take the mammalian subdivision only. The earliest known remains of mammals are those of small marsupials, which are the lowest of the mammalian type; while, conversely, the highest of the mammalian type—Man—is the most recent. The evidence that the vertebrate fauna, as a whole, has become more heterogeneous, is considerably stronger. To the argument that the vertebrate fauna of the Palæozoic period, consisting, so far as we know, entirely of Fishes, was less heterogeneous than the modern vertebrate fauna, which includes Reptiles, Birds, and Mammals, of multitudinous genera, it may be replied, as before, that estuary deposits of the Palæozoic period, could we find them, might contain other orders of vertebrata. But no such reply can be made to the argument that whereas the marine vertebrata of the Palæozoic period consisted entirely of cartilaginous fishes, the marine vertebrata of later periods include numerous genera of osseous fishes; and that, therefore, the later marine vertebrate faunas are more heterogeneous than the oldest known one. Nor, again, can any such reply be made to the fact that there are far more numerous orders and genera of mammalian remains in the tertiary formations than in the secondary formations. Did we wish merely to make out the best case, we might dwell upon the opinion of Dr. Carpenter, who says that "the general facts of Palæontology appear to sanction the belief, that *the same plan* may be traced out in what may be called *the general life of the globe*, as in *the individual life* of every one of the forms of organised being which now people it." Or we might quote, as decisive, the judgment of Professor Owen, who holds that the earlier examples of each group of creatures severally departed less widely from archetypal generality than the later ones—were severally less unlike the fundamental form common to the group as a whole; that is to say—constituted a less heterogeneous group of creatures; and who further upholds the doctrine of a biological progression. But in deference to an authority for whom we have the highest respect, who considers that the evidence at present obtained does not justify a verdict either way, we are content to leave the question open.

Whether an advance from the homogeneous to the heterogeneous is or is not displayed in the biological history of the globe, it is clearly enough displayed in the progress of the latest and most heterogeneous creature—Man. It is alike true that, during the period in which the Earth has been peopled, the human organism has grown more heterogeneous among the civilised divisions of the species; and that the species, as a whole, has been growing more heterogeneous in virtue of the multiplication of races and the differentiation of these races from each other.

In proof of the first of these positions, we may cite the fact that, in the relative development of the limbs, the civilised man departs more widely from the general type of the placental mammalia than do the lower human races. While often possessing well-developed body and arms, the Papuan has extremely small legs: thus reminding us of the quadrumana, in which there is no great contrast in size between the hind and fore limbs. But in the European, the greater length and massiveness of the legs has become very marked—the fore and hind limbs are relatively more heterogeneous. Again, the greater ratio which the cranial bones bear to the facial bones illustrates the same truth. Among the vertebrata in general, progress is marked by an increasing heterogeneity in the vertebral column, and more especially in the vertebræ constituting the skull: the higher forms being distinguished by the relatively larger size of the bones which cover the brain, and the relatively smaller size of those which form the jaw, etc. Now, this characteristic, which is stronger in Man than in any other creature, is stronger in the European than in the savage. Moreover, judging from the greater extent and variety of faculty he exhibits, we may infer that the civilised man has also a more complex or heterogeneous nervous system than the uncivilised man: and indeed the fact is in part visible in the increased ratio which his cerebrum bears to the subjacent ganglia.

If further elucidation be needed, we may find it in every nursery. The infant European has sundry marked points of resemblance to the lower human races; as in the flatness of the alæ of the nose, the depression of its bridge, the divergence and forward opening of the nostrils, the form of the lips, the absence of a frontal sinus, the width between the eyes, the smallness of the legs. Now, as the development process by which these traits are turned into those of the adult European, is a continuation of that change from the homogeneous to the heterogeneous displayed during the previous evolution of the embryo, which every physiologist will admit; it follows that the parallel developmental process by which the like traits of the barbarous races have been turned into those of the civilised races, has also been a continuation of the change from the homogeneous to the heterogeneous. The truth of the second position—that Mankind, as a whole, have become more heterogeneous—is so obvious as scarcely to need illustration. Every work on Ethnology, by its divisions and subdivisions of races, bears testimony to it. Even were we to admit the hypothesis that Mankind originated from several separate stocks, it would still remain true, that as, from each of these stocks, there have sprung many now widely different tribes, which are proved by philological evidence to have had a common origin, the race as a whole is far less homogeneous than it once was. Add to which, that we have, in the Anglo-Americans, an example of a new variety arising within these few generations; and that, if we may trust to the description of observers, we are likely soon to have another such example in Australia.

On passing from Humanity under its individual form, to Humanity as socially embodied, we find the general law still more variously exemplified. The change from the homogeneous to the heterogeneous is displayed equally in the progress of civilisation as a whole, and in the progress of every tribe or nation; and is still going on with increasing rapidity. As we see in existing barbarous tribes, society in its first and lowest form is a homogeneous aggregation of individuals having like powers and like functions: the only marked difference of function being that which accompanies difference of sex. Every man is warrior, hunter, fisherman, tool-maker, builder; every woman performs the same drudgeries; every family is self-sufficing, and save for purposes of aggression and defence, might as well live apart from the rest. Very early, however, in the process of social evolution, we find an incipient differentiation between the governing and the governed. Some kind of chieftainship seems coeval with the first advance from the state of separate wandering families to that of a nomadic tribe. The authority of the strongest makes itself felt among a body of savages as in a herd of animals, or a posse of schoolboys. At first, however, it is indefinite, uncertain; is shared by others of scarcely inferior power; and is unaccompanied by any difference in occupation or style of living: the first ruler kills his own game, makes his own weapons, builds his own hut, and economically considered, does not differ from others of his tribe. Gradually, as the tribe progresses, the contrast between the governing and the governed grows more decided. Supreme power becomes hereditary in one family; the head of that family, ceasing to provide for his own wants, is served by others; and he begins to assume the sole office of ruling.

At the same time there has been arising a co-ordinate species of government— that of Religion. As all ancient records and traditions prove, the earliest rulers are regarded as divine personages. The maxims and commands they uttered during their lives are held sacred after their deaths, and are enforced by their divinely-descended successors; who in their turns are promoted to the pantheon of the race, there to be worshipped and propitiated along with their predecessors: the most ancient of whom is the supreme god, and the rest subordinate gods. For a long time these connate forms of government—civil and religious—continue closely associated. For many generations the king continues to be the chief priest, and the priesthood to be members of the royal race. For many ages religious law continues to contain more or less of civil regulation, and civil law to possess more or less of religious sanction; and even among the most advanced nations these two controlling agencies are by no means completely differentiated from each other.

Having a common root with these, and gradually diverging from them, we find yet another controlling agency—that of Manners or ceremonial usages. All titles of honour are originally the names of the god-king; afterwards of God and the king; still later of persons of high rank; and finally come, some of them, to be used between man and man. All forms of complimentary address were at first the expressions of submission from prisoners to their conqueror, or from subjects to their ruler, either human or divine—expressions that were afterwards used to propitiate subordinate authorities, and slowly descended into ordinary intercourse. All modes of salutation were once obeisances made before the monarch and used in worship of him after his death. Presently others of the god-descended race were similarly saluted; and by degrees some of the salutations have become the due of all.[12] Thus, no sooner does the originally homogeneous social mass differentiate into the governed and the governing parts, than this last exhibits an incipient differentiation into religious and secular—Church and State; while at the same time there begins to be differentiated from both, that less definite species of government which rules our daily intercourse—a species of government which, as we may see in heralds' colleges, in books of the peerage, in masters of ceremonies, is not without a certain embodiment of its own. Each of these is itself subject to successive differentiations. In the course of ages, there arises, as among ourselves, a highly complex political organisation of monarch, ministers, lords and commons, with their subordinate administrative departments, courts of justice, revenue offices, etc., supplemented in the provinces by municipal governments, county governments, parish or union governments—all of them more or less elaborated. By its side there grows up a highly complex religious organisation, with its various grades of officials, from archbishops down to sextons, its colleges, convocations, ecclesiastical courts, etc.; to all which must be added the ever multiplying independent sects, each with its general and local authorities. And at the same time there is developed a highly complex aggregation of customs, manners, and temporary fashions, enforced by society at large, and serving to control those minor transactions between man and man which are not regulated by civil and religious law. Moreover it is to be observed that this ever increasing heterogeneity in the governmental appliances of each nation, has been accompanied by an increasing heterogeneity in the governmental appliances of different nations; all of which are more or less unlike in their political systems and legislation, in their creeds and religious institutions, in their customs and ceremonial usages.

Simultaneously there has been going on a second differentiation of a more familiar kind; that, namely, by which the mass of the community has been segregated into distinct classes and orders of workers. While the governing part has undergone the complex development above detailed, the governed part has undergone an equally complex development, which has resulted in that minute di-

---

[12] For detailed proof of these assertions see essay on "Manners and Fashion."

vision of labour characterising advanced nations. It is needless to trace out this progress from its first stages, up through the caste divisions of the East and the incorporated guilds of Europe, to the elaborate producing and distributing organisation existing among ourselves. Political economists have long since described the evolution which, beginning with a tribe whose members severally perform the same actions each for himself, ends with a civilised community whose members severally perform different actions for each other; and they have further pointed out the changes through which the solitary producer of any one commodity is transformed into a combination of producers who, united under a master, take separate parts in the manufacture of such commodity. But there are yet other and higher phases of this advance from the homogeneous to the heterogeneous in the industrial organisation of society.

Long after considerable progress has been made in the division of labour among different classes of workers, there is still little or no division of labour among the widely separated parts of the community; the nation continues comparatively homogeneous in the respect that in each district the same occupations are pursued. But when roads and other means of transit become numerous and good, the different districts begin to assume different functions, and to become mutually dependent. The calico manufacture locates itself in this county, the woollen-cloth manufacture in that; silks are produced here, lace there; stockings in one place, shoes in another; pottery, hardware, cutlery, come to have their special towns; and ultimately every locality becomes more or less distinguished from the rest by the leading occupation carried on in it. Nay, more, this subdivision of functions shows itself not only among the different parts of the same nation, but among different nations. That exchange of commodities which free-trade promises so greatly to increase, will ultimately have the effect of specialising, in a greater or less degree, the industry of each people. So that beginning with a barbarous tribe, almost if not quite homogeneous in the functions of its members, the progress has been, and still is, towards an economic aggregation of the whole human race; growing ever more heterogeneous in respect of the separate functions assumed by separate nations, the separate functions assumed by the local sections of each nation, the separate functions assumed by the many kinds of makers and traders in each town, and the separate functions assumed by the workers united in producing each commodity.

Not only is the law thus clearly exemplified in the evolution of the social organism, but it is exemplified with equal clearness in the evolution of all products of human thought and action, whether concrete or abstract, real or ideal. Let us take Language as our first illustration.

The lowest form of language is the exclamation, by which an entire idea is vaguely conveyed through a single sound; as among the lower animals. That human language ever consisted solely of exclamations, and so was strictly homogeneous in respect of its parts of speech, we have no evidence. But that language can be traced down to a form in which nouns and verbs are its only elements, is an established fact. In the gradual multiplication of parts of speech out of these primary ones—in the differentiation of verbs into active and passive, of nouns into abstract and concrete—in the rise of distinctions of mood, tense, person, of number and case—in the formation of auxiliary verbs, of adjectives, adverbs, pronouns, prepositions, articles—in the divergence of those orders, genera, species, and varieties of parts of speech by which civilised races express minute modifications of meaning—we see a change from the homogeneous to the heterogeneous. And it may be remarked, in passing, that it is more especially in virtue of having carried this subdivision of function to a greater extent and completeness, that the English language is superior to all others.

Another aspect under which we may trace the development of language is the differentiation of words of allied meanings. Philology early disclosed the truth that in all languages words may be grouped into families having a common ancestry. An aboriginal name applied indiscriminately to each of an extensive and ill-defined class of things or actions, presently undergoes modifications by which the chief divisions of the class are expressed. These several names springing from the primitive root, themselves become the parents of other names still further modified. And by the aid of those systematic modes which presently arise, of making derivations and forming compound terms expressing still smaller distinctions, there is finally developed a tribe of words so heterogeneous in sound and meaning, that to the uninitiated it seems incredible that they should have had a common origin. Meanwhile from other roots there are being evolved other such tribes, until there results a language of some sixty thousand or more unlike words, signifying as many unlike objects, qualities, acts.

Yet another way in which language in general advances from the homogeneous to the heterogeneous, is in the multiplication of languages. Whether as Max Müller and Bunsen think, all languages have grown from one stock, or whether, as some philologists say, they have grown from two or more stocks, it is clear that since large families of languages, as the Indo-European, are of one parentage, they have become distinct through a process of continuous divergence. The same diffusion over the Earth's surface which has led to the differentiation of the race, has simultaneously led to a differentiation of their speech: a truth which we see further illustrated in each nation by the peculiarities of dialect found in several districts. Thus the progress of Language conforms to the general law, alike in the evolution of languages, in the evolution of families of words, and in the evolution of parts of speech.

On passing from spoken to written language, we come upon several classes of facts, all having similar implications. Written language is connate with Painting and Sculpture; and at first all three are appendages of Architecture, and have a direct connection with the primary form of all Government—the theocratic. Merely noting by the way the fact that sundry wild races, as for example the Australians and the tribes of South Africa, are given to depicting personages and events upon the walls of caves, which are probably regarded as sacred places, let us pass to the case of the Egyptians. Among them, as also among the Assyrians, we find mural paintings used to decorate the temple of the god and the palace of the king (which were, indeed, originally identical); and as such they were governmental appliances in the same sense that state-pageants and religious feasts were. Further, they were governmental appliances in virtue of representing the worship of the god, the triumphs of the god-king, the submission of his subjects, and the punishment of the rebellious. And yet again they were governmental, as being the products of an art reverenced by the people as a sacred mystery. From the habitual use of this pictorial representations there naturally grew up the but slightly-modified practice of picture-writing—a practice which was found still extant among the Mexicans at the time they were discovered. By abbreviations analogous to those still going on in our own written and spoken language, the most familiar of these pictured figures were successively simplified; and ultimately there grew up a system of symbols, most of which had but a distant resemblance to the things for which they stood. The inference that the hieroglyphics of the Egyptians were thus produced, is confirmed by the fact that the picture-writing of the Mexicans was found to have given birth to a like family of ideographic forms; and among them, as among the Egyptians, these had been partially differentiated into the *kuriological* or imitative, and the *tropical* or symbolic: which were, however, used together in the same record. In Egypt, written language underwent a further differentiation: whence resulted the *hieratic* and the *epistolographic* or *enchorial*: both of which are derived from the original hieroglyphic. At the same time we find that for the expression of proper names which could not be otherwise conveyed, phonetic symbols were employed; and though it is alleged that the Egyptians never actually achieved complete alphabetic writing, yet it can scarcely be doubted that these phonetic symbols occasionally used in aid of their ideographic ones, were the germs out of which alphabetic writing grew. Once having become separate from hieroglyphics, alphabetic writing itself underwent numerous differentiations—multiplied alphabets were produced; between most of which, however, more or less connection can still be traced. And in each civilised nation there has now grown up, for the representation of one set of sounds, several sets of written signs used for distinct purposes. Finally, through a yet more important differentiation came printing; which, uniform in kind as it was at first, has since become multiform.

While written language was passing through its earlier stages of development, the mural decoration which formed its root was being differentiated into Painting and Sculpture. The gods, kings, men, and animals represented, were originally marked by indented outlines and coloured. In most cases these outlines were of such depth, and the object they circumscribed so far rounded and marked out in its leading parts, as to form a species of work intermediate between intaglio and bas-relief. In other cases we see an advance upon this: the raised spaces between the figures being chiselled off, and the figures themselves appropriately tinted, a painted bas-relief was produced. The restored Assyrian architecture at Sydenham exhibits this style of art carried to greater perfection—the persons and things represented, though still barbarously coloured, are carved out with more truth and in greater detail: and in the winged lions and bulls used for the angles of gateways, we may see a considerable advance towards a completely sculptured figure; which, nevertheless, is still coloured, and still forms part of the building. But while in Assyria the production of a statue proper seems to have been little, if at all, attempted, we may trace in Egyptian art the gradual separation of the sculptured figure from the wall. A walk through the collection in the British Museum will clearly show this; while it will at the same time afford an opportunity of observing the evident traces which the independent statues bear of their derivation from bas-relief: seeing that nearly all of them not only display that union of the limbs with the body which is the characteristic of bas-relief, but have the back of the statue united from head to foot with a block which stands in place of the original wall. Greece repeated the leading stages of this progress. As in Egypt and Assyria, these twin arts were at first united with each other and with their parent, Architecture, and were the aids of Religion and Government. On the friezes of Greek temples, we see coloured bas-reliefs representing sacrifices, battles, processions, games—all in some sort religious. On the pediments we see painted sculptures more or less united with the tympanum, and having for subjects the triumphs of gods or heroes. Even when we come to statues that are definitely separated from the buildings to which they pertain, we still find them coloured; and only in the later periods of Greek civilisation does the differentiation of sculpture from painting appear to have become complete.

In Christian art we may clearly trace a parallel re-genesis. All early paintings and sculptures throughout Europe were religious in subject—represented Christs, crucifixions, virgins, holy families, apostles, saints. They formed integral parts of church architecture, and were among the means of exciting worship; as in Roman Catholic countries they still are. Moreover, the early sculptures of Christ on the cross, of virgins, of saints, were coloured: and it needs but to call to mind the painted madonnas and crucifixes still abundant in continental churches and highways, to perceive the significant fact that painting and sculpture continue in closest connection with each other where they continue in closest connection with their parent. Even when Christian sculpture was pretty clearly differentiated from painting, it was still religious and governmental in its subjects—was used for tombs in churches and statues of kings: while, at the same time, painting, where not purely ecclesiastical, was applied to the decoration of palaces, and besides representing royal personages, was almost wholly devoted to sacred legends. Only in quite recent times have painting and sculpture become entirely secular arts. Only within these few centuries has painting been divided into historical, landscape, marine, architectural, genre, animal, still-life, etc., and sculpture grown heterogeneous in respect of the variety of real and ideal subjects with which it occupies itself.

Strange as it seems then, we find it no less true, that all forms of written language, of painting, and of sculpture, have a common root in the politico-religious decorations of ancient temples and palaces. Little resemblance as they now have, the bust that stands on the console, the landscape that hangs against the wall, and the copy of the *Times* lying upon the table, are remotely akin; not only in nature, but by extraction. The brazen face of the knocker which the postman has just lifted, is related not only to the woodcuts of the *Illustrated London News* which he is delivering, but to the characters of the *billet-doux* which accompanies it. Between the painted window, the prayer-book on which its light falls, and the adjacent monument, there is consanguinity. The effigies on our coins, the signs over shops, the figures that fill every ledger, the coats of arms outside the carriage panel, and the placards inside the omnibus, are, in common with dolls, blue-books, paper-hangings, lineally descended from the rude sculpture-paintings in which the Egyptians represented the triumphs and worship of their god-kings. Perhaps no example can be given which more vividly illustrates the multiplicity and heterogeneity of the products that in course of time may arise by successive differentiations from a common stock.

Before passing to other classes of facts, it should be observed that the evolution of the homogeneous into the heterogeneous is displayed not only in the separation of Painting and Sculpture from Architecture and from each other, and in the greater variety of subjects they embody, but it is further shown in the structure of each work. A modern picture or statue is of far more heterogeneous nature than an ancient one. An Egyptian sculpture-fresco represents all its figures as on one plane — that is, at the same distance from the eye; and so is less heterogeneous than a painting that represents them as at various distances from the eye. It exhibits all objects as exposed to the same degree of light; and so is less heterogeneous than a painting which exhibits different objects and different parts of each object as in different degrees of light. It uses scarcely any but the primary colours, and these in their full intensity; and so is less heterogeneous than a painting which, introducing the primary colours but sparingly, employs an endless variety of intermediate tints, each of heterogeneous composition, and differing from the rest not only in quality but in intensity. Moreover, we see in these earliest works a great uniformity of conception. The same arrangement of figures is perpetually reproduced — the same actions, attitudes, faces, dresses. In Egypt the modes of representation were so fixed that it was sacrilege to introduce a novelty; and indeed it could have been only in consequence of a fixed mode of representation that a system of hieroglyphics became possible. The Assyrian bas-reliefs display parallel characters. Deities, kings, attendants, winged figures and animals, are severally depicted in like positions, holding like implements, doing like things, and with like expression or non-expression of face. If a palm-grove is introduced, all the trees are of the same height, have the same number of leaves, and are equidistant. When water is imitated, each wave is a counterpart of the rest; and the fish, almost always of one kind, are evenly distributed over the surface. The beards of the kings, the gods, and the winged figures, are every where similar: as are the names of the lions, and equally so those of the horses. Hair is represented throughout by one form of curl. The king's beard is quite architecturally built up of compound tiers of uniform curls, alternating with twisted tiers placed in a transverse direction, and arranged with perfect regularity; and the terminal tufts of the bulls' tails are represented in exactly the same manner. Without tracing out analogous facts in early Christian art, in which, though less striking, they are still visible, the advance in heterogeneity will be sufficiently manifest on remembering that in the pictures of our own day the composition is endlessly varied; the attitudes, faces, expressions, unlike; the subordinate objects different in size, form, position, texture; and more or less of contrast even in the smallest details. Or, if we compare an Egyptian statue, seated bolt upright on a block with hands on knees, fingers outspread and parallel, eyes looking straight forward, and the two sides perfectly symmetrical in every particular, with a statue of the advanced Greek or the modern school, which is asymmetrical in respect of the position of the head, the body, the limbs, the arrangement of the hair, dress, appendages, and in its relations to neighbouring objects, we shall see the change from the homogeneous to the heterogeneous clearly manifested.

In the co-ordinate origin and gradual differentiation of Poetry, Music and Dancing, we have another series of illustrations. Rhythm in speech, rhythm in sound, and rhythm in motion, were in the beginning parts of the same thing, and have only in process of time become separate things. Among various existing barbarous tribes we find them still united. The dances of savages are accompanied by some kind of monotonous chant, the clapping of hands, the striking of rude instruments: there are measured movements, measured words, and measured tones; and the whole ceremony, usually having reference to war or sacrifice, is of governmental character. In the early records of the historic races we similarly find these three forms of metrical action united in religious festivals. In the Hebrew writings we read that the triumphal ode composed by Moses on the defeat of the Egyptians, was sung to an accompaniment of dancing and timbrels. The Israelites danced and sung "at the inauguration of the golden calf. And as it is generally agreed that this representation of the Deity was borrowed from the mysteries of Apis, it is probable that the dancing was copied from that of the Egyptians on those occasions." There was an annual dance in Shiloh on the sacred festival; and David danced before the ark. Again, in Greece the like relation is everywhere seen; the original type being there, as probably in other cases, a simultaneous chanting and mimetic representation of the life and adventures of the god. The Spartan dances were accompanied by hymns and songs; and in general the Greeks had "no festivals or religious assemblies but what were accompanied with songs and dances"—both of them being forms of worship used before altars. Among the Romans, too, there were sacred dances: the Salian and Lupercalian being named as of that kind. And even in Christian countries, as at Limoges, in comparatively recent times, the people have danced in the choir in honour of a saint. The incipient separation of these once united arts from each other and from religion, was early visible in Greece. Probably diverging from dances partly religious, partly warlike, as the Corybantian, came the war dances proper, of which there were various kinds; and from these resulted secular dances. Meanwhile Music and Poetry, though still united, came to have an existence separate from dancing. The aboriginal Greek poems, religious in subject, were not recited, but chanted; and though at first the chant of the poet was accompanied by the dance of the chorus, it ultimately grew into independence. Later still, when the poem had been differentiated into epic and lyric—when it became the custom to sing the lyric and recite the epic—poetry proper was born. As during the same period musical instruments were being multiplied, we may presume that music came to have an existence apart from words. And both of them were beginning to assume other forms besides the religious. Facts having like implications might be cited from the histories of later times and people: as the practices of our own early minstrels, who sang to the harp heroic narratives versified by themselves to music of their own composition: thus uniting the now separate offices of poet, composer, vocalist, and instrumentalist. But, without further illustration, the common origin and gradual differentiation of Dancing, Poetry, and Music will be sufficiently manifest.

The advance from the homogeneous to the heterogeneous is displayed not only in the separation of these arts from each other and from religion, but also in the multiplied differentiations which each of them afterwards undergoes. Not to dwell upon the numberless kinds of dancing that have, in course of time, come into use; and not to occupy space in detaining the progress of poetry, as seen in the development of the various forms of metre, of rhyme, and of general organisation; let us confine our attention to music as a type of the group. As argued by Dr. Burney, and as implied by the customs of still extant barbarous races, the first musical instruments were, without doubt, percussive—sticks, calabashes, tom-toms—and were used simply to mark the time of the dance; and in this constant repetition of the same sound, we see music in its most homogeneous form.

The Egyptians had a lyre with three strings. The early lyre of the Greeks had four, constituting their tetrachord. In course of some centuries lyres of seven and eight strings were employed. And, by the expiration of a thousand years, they had advanced to their "great system" of the double octave. Through all which changes there of course arose a greater heterogeneity of melody. Simultaneously there came into use the different modes—Dorian, Ionian, Phrygian, Æolian, and Lydian—answering to our keys; and of these there were ultimately fifteen. As yet, however, there was but little heterogeneity in the time of their music.

Instrumental music during this period being merely the accompaniment of vocal music, and vocal music being completely subordinated to words, the singer being also the poet, chanting his own compositions and making the lengths of his notes agree with the feet of his verses,—there unavoidably arose a tiresome uniformity of measure, which, as Dr. Burney says, "no resources of melody could disguise." Lacking the complex rhythm obtained by our equal bars and unequal notes the only rhythm was that produced by the quantity of the syllables and was of necessity comparatively monotonous. And further, it may be observed that the chant thus resulting, being like recitative, was much less clearly differentiated from ordinary speech than is our modern song.

Nevertheless, in virtue of the extended range of notes in use, the variety of modes, the occasional variations of time consequent on changes of metre, and the multiplication of instruments, music had, towards the close of Greek civilisation, attained to considerable heterogeneity—not indeed as compared with our music, but as compared with that which preceded it. As yet, however, there existed nothing but melody: harmony was unknown. It was not until Christian church-music had reached some development, that music in parts was evolved; and then it came into existence through a very unobtrusive differentiation. Difficult as it may be to conceive *à priori* how the advance from melody to harmony could take place without a sudden leap, it is none the less true that it did so. The circumstance which prepared the way for it was the employment of two choirs singing alternately the same air. Afterwards it became the practice—very possibly first suggested by a mistake—for the second choir to commence before the first had ceased; thus producing a fugue.

With the simple airs then in use, a partially harmonious fugue might not improbably thus result: and a very partially harmonious fugue satisfied the ears of that age, as we know from still preserved examples. The idea having once been given, the composing of airs productive of fugal harmony would naturally grow up; as in some way it *did* grow up out of this alternate choir-singing. And from the fugue to concerted music of two, three, four, and more parts, the transition was easy. Without pointing out in detail the increasing complexity that resulted from introducing notes of various lengths, from the multiplication of keys, from the use of accidentals, from varieties of time, and so forth, it needs but to contrast music as it is, with music as it was, to see how immense is the increase of heterogeneity. We see this if, looking at music in its *ensemble*, we enumerate its many different genera and species—if we consider the divisions into vocal, instrumental, and mixed; and their subdivisions into music for different voices and different instruments—if we observe the many forms of sacred music, from the simple hymn, the chant, the canon, motet, anthem, etc., up to the oratorio; and the still more numerous forms of secular music, from the ballad up to the serenata, from the instrumental solo up to the symphony.

Again, the same truth is seen on comparing any one sample of aboriginal music with a sample of modern music—even an ordinary song for the piano; which we find to be relatively highly heterogeneous, not only in respect of the varieties in the pitch and in the length of the notes, the number of different notes sounding at the same instant in company with the voice, and the variations of strength with which they are sounded and sung, but in respect of the changes of key, the changes of time, the changes of *timbre* of the voice, and the many other modifications of expression. While between the old monotonous dance-chant and a grand opera of our own day, with its endless orchestral complexities and vocal combinations, the contrast in heterogeneity is so extreme that it seems scarcely credible that the one should have been the ancestor of the other.

Were they needed, many further illustrations might be cited. Going back to the early time when the deeds of the god-king, chanted and mimetically represented in dances round his altar, were further narrated in picture-writings on the walls of temples and palaces, and so constituted a rude literature, we might trace the development of Literature through phases in which, as in the Hebrew Scriptures, it presents in one work theology, cosmogony, history, biography, civil law, ethics, poetry; through other phases in which, as in the Iliad, the religious, martial, historical, the epic, dramatic, and lyric elements are similarly commingled; down to its present heterogeneous development, in which its divisions and subdivisions are so numerous and varied as to defy complete classification. Or we might trace out the evolution of Science; beginning with the era in which it was not yet differentiated from Art, and was, in union with Art, the handmaid of Religion; passing through the era in which the sciences were so few and rudimentary, as to be simultaneously cultivated by the same philosophers; and ending with the era in which the genera and species are so numerous that few can enumerate them, and no one can adequately grasp even one genus. Or we might do the like with Architecture, with the Drama, with Dress.

But doubtless the reader is already weary of illustrations; and our promise has been amply fulfilled. We believe we have shown beyond question, that that which the German physiologists have found to be the law of organic development, is the law of all development. The advance from the simple to the complex, through a process of successive differentiations, is seen alike in the earliest changes of the Universe to which we can reason our way back; and in the earliest changes which we can inductively establish; it is seen in the geologic and climatic evolution of the Earth, and of every single organism on its surface; it is seen in the evolution of Humanity, whether contemplated in the civilised individual, or in the aggregation of races; it is seen in the evolution of Society in respect alike of its political, its religious, and its economical organisation; and it is seen in the evolution of all those endless concrete and abstract products of human activity which constitute the environment of our daily life. From the remotest past which Science can fathom, up to the novelties of yesterday, that in which Progress essentially consists, is the transformation of the homogeneous into the heterogeneous.

And now, from this uniformity of procedure, may we not infer some fundamental necessity whence it results? May we not rationally seek for some all-pervading principle which determines this all-pervading process of things? Does not the universality of the *law* imply a universal *cause*?

That we can fathom such cause, noumenally considered, is not to be supposed. To do this would be to solve that ultimate mystery which must ever transcend human intelligence. But it still may be possible for us to reduce the law of all Progress, above established, from the condition of an empirical generalisation, to the condition of a rational generalisation. Just as it was possible to interpret Kepler's laws as necessary consequences of the law of gravitation; so it may be possible to interpret this law of Progress, in its multiform manifestations, as the necessary consequence of some similarly universal principle. As gravitation was assignable as the *cause* of each of the groups of phenomena which Kepler formulated; so may some equally simple attribute of things be assignable as the cause of each of the groups of phenomena formulated in the foregoing pages. We may be able to affiliate all these varied and complex evolutions of the homogeneous into the heterogeneous, upon certain simple facts of immediate experience, which, in virtue of endless repetition, we regard as necessary.

The probability of a common cause, and the possibility of formulating it, being granted, it will be well, before going further, to consider what must be the general characteristics of such cause, and in what direction we ought to look for it. We can with certainty predict that it has a high degree of generality; seeing that it is common to such infinitely varied phenomena: just in proportion to the universality of its application must be the abstractness of its character. We need not expect to see in it an obvious solution of this or that form of Progress; because it equally refers to forms of Progress bearing little apparent resemblance to them: its association with multiform orders of facts, involves its dissociation from any particular order of facts. Being that which determines Progress of every kind — astronomic, geologic, organic, ethnologic, social, economic, artistic, etc. — it must be concerned with some fundamental attribute possessed in common by these; and must be expressible in terms of this fundamental attribute. The only obvious respect in which all kinds of Progress are alike, is, that they are modes of *change*; and hence, in some characteristic of changes in general, the desired solution will probably be found. We may suspect *à priori* that in some law of change lies the explanation of this universal transformation of the homogeneous into the heterogeneous.

Thus much premised, we pass at once to the statement of the law, which is this:—*Every active force produces more than one change—every cause produces more than one effect.*

Before this law can be duly comprehended, a few examples must be looked at. When one body is struck against another, that which we usually regard as the effect, is a change of position or motion in one or both bodies. But a moment's thought shows us that this is a careless and very incomplete view of the matter. Besides the visible mechanical result, sound is produced; or, to speak accurately, a vibration in one or both bodies, and in the surrounding air: and under some circumstances we call this the effect. Moreover, the air has not only been made to vibrate, but has had sundry currents caused in it by the transit of the bodies. Further, there is a disarrangement of the particles of the two bodies in the neighbourhood of their point of collision; amounting in some cases to a visible condensation. Yet more, this condensation is accompanied by the disengagement of heat. In some cases a spark—that is, light—results, from the incandescence of a portion struck off; and sometimes this incandescence is associated with chemical combination.

Thus, by the original mechanical force expended in the collision, at least five, and often more, different kinds of changes have been produced. Take, again, the lighting of a candle. Primarily this is a chemical change consequent on a rise of temperature. The process of combination having once been set going by extraneous heat, there is a continued formation of carbonic acid, water, etc.—in itself a result more complex than the extraneous heat that first caused it. But accompanying this process of combination there is a production of heat; there is a production of light; there is an ascending column of hot gases generated; there are currents established in the surrounding air. Moreover the decomposition of one force into many forces does not end here: each of the several changes produced becomes the parent of further changes. The carbonic acid given off will by and by combine with some base; or under the influence of sunshine give up its carbon to the leaf of a plant. The water will modify the hygrometric state of the air around; or, if the current of hot gases containing it come against a cold body, will be condensed: altering the temperature, and perhaps the chemical state, of the surface it covers. The heat given out melts the subjacent tallow, and expands whatever it warms. The light, falling on various substances, calls forth from them reactions by which it is modified; and so divers colours are produced. Similarly even with these secondary actions, which may be traced out into ever-multiplying ramifications, until they become too minute to be appreciated. And thus it is with all changes whatever. No case can be named in which an active force does not evolve forces of several kinds, and each of these, other groups of forces. Universally the effect is more complex than the cause.

Doubtless the reader already foresees the course of our argument. This multiplication of results, which is displayed in every event of to-day, has been going on from the beginning; and is true of the grandest phenomena of the universe as of the most insignificant. From the law that every active force produces more than one change, it is an inevitable corollary that through all time there has been an ever-growing complication of things. Starting with the ultimate fact that every cause produces more than one effect, we may readily see that throughout creation there must have gone on, and must still go on, a never-ceasing transformation of the homogeneous into the heterogeneous. But let us trace out this truth in detail.

Without committing ourselves to it as more than a speculation, though a highly probable one, let us again commence with the evolution of the solar system out of a nebulous medium.[13] From the mutual attraction of the atoms of a diffused mass whose form is unsymmetrical, there results not only condensation but rotation: gravitation simultaneously generates both the centripetal and the centrifugal forces. While the condensation and the rate of rotation are progressively increasing, the approach of the atoms necessarily generates a progressively increasing temperature. As this temperature rises, light begins to be evolved; and ultimately there results a revolving sphere of fluid matter radiating intense heat and light — a sun.

There are good reasons for believing that, in consequence of the high tangential velocity, and consequent centrifugal force, acquired by the outer parts of the condensing nebulous mass, there must be a periodical detachment of rotating rings; and that, from the breaking up of these nebulous rings, there must arise masses which in the course of their condensation repeat the actions of the parent mass, and so produce planets and their satellites — an inference strongly supported by the still extant rings of Saturn.

Should it hereafter be satisfactorily shown that planets and satellites were thus generated, a striking illustration will be afforded of the highly heterogeneous effects produced by the primary homogeneous cause; but it will serve our present purpose to point to the fact that from the mutual attraction of the particles of an irregular nebulous mass there result condensation, rotation, heat, and light.

It follows as a corollary from the Nebular Hypothesis, that the Earth must at first have been incandescent; and whether the Nebular Hypothesis be true or not, this original incandescence of the Earth is now inductively established — or, if not established, at least rendered so highly probable that it is a generally admitted geological doctrine. Let us look first at the astronomical attributes of this once molten globe. From its rotation there result the oblateness of its form, the alternations of day and night, and (under the influence of the moon) the tides, aqueous and atmospheric. From the inclination of its axis, there result the precession of the equinoxes and the many differences of the seasons, both simultaneous and successive, that pervade its surface. Thus the multiplication of effects is obvious. Several of the differentiations due to the gradual cooling of the Earth have been already noticed — as the formation of a crust, the solidification of sublimed elements, the precipitation of water, etc., — and we here again refer to them merely to point out

[13] The idea that the Nebular Hypothesis has been disproved because what were thought to be existing nebulæ have been resolved into clusters of stars is almost beneath notice. *A priori* it was highly improbable, if not impossible, that nebulous masses should still remain uncondensed, while others have been condensed millions of years ago.

that they are simultaneous effects of the one cause, diminishing heat.

Let us now, however, observe the multiplied changes afterwards arising from the continuance of this one cause. The cooling of the Earth involves its contraction. Hence the solid crust first formed is presently too large for the shrinking nucleus; and as it cannot support itself, inevitably follows the nucleus. But a spheroidal envelope cannot sink down into contact with a smaller internal spheroid, without disruption; it must run into wrinkles as the rind of an apple does when the bulk of its interior decreases from evaporation. As the cooling progresses and the envelope thickens, the ridges consequent on these contractions must become greater, rising ultimately into hills and mountains; and the later systems of mountains thus produced must not only be higher, as we find them to be, but they must be longer, as we also find them to be. Thus, leaving out of view other modifying forces, we see what immense heterogeneity of surface has arisen from the one cause, loss of heat—a heterogeneity which the telescope shows us to be paralleled on the face of the moon, where aqueous and atmospheric agencies have been absent.

But we have yet to notice another kind of heterogeneity of surface similarly and simultaneously caused. While the Earth's crust was still thin, the ridges produced by its contraction must not only have been small, but the spaces between these ridges must have rested with great evenness upon the subjacent liquid spheroid; and the water in those arctic and antarctic regions in which it first condensed, must have been evenly distributed. But as fast as the crust grew thicker and gained corresponding strength, the lines of fracture from time to time caused in it, must have occurred at greater distances apart; the intermediate surfaces must have followed the contracting nucleus with less uniformity; and there must have resulted larger areas of land and water. If any one, after wrapping up an orange in wet tissue paper, and observing not only how small are the wrinkles, but how evenly the intervening spaces lie upon the surface of the orange, will then wrap it up in thick cartridge-paper, and note both the greater height of the ridges and the much larger spaces throughout which the paper does not touch the orange, he will realise the fact, that as the Earth's solid envelope grew thicker, the areas of elevation and depression must have become greater. In place of islands more or less homogeneously scattered over an all-embracing sea, there must have gradually arisen heterogeneous arrangements of continent and ocean, such as we now know.

Once more, this double change in the extent and in the elevation of the lands, involved yet another species of heterogeneity, that of coast-line. A tolerably even surface raised out of the ocean, must have a simple, regular sea-margin; but a surface varied by table-lands and intersected by mountain-chains must, when raised out of the ocean, have an outline extremely irregular both in its leading features and in its details. Thus endless is the accumulation of geological and geographical results slowly brought about by this one cause—the contraction of the Earth.

When we pass from the agency which geologists term igneous, to aqueous and atmospheric agencies, we see the like ever growing complications of effects. The denuding actions of air and water have, from the beginning, been modifying every exposed surface; everywhere causing many different changes. Oxidation, heat, wind, frost, rain, glaciers, rivers, tides, waves, have been unceasingly producing disintegration; varying in kind and amount according to local circumstances. Acting upon a tract of granite, they here work scarcely an appreciable effect; there cause exfoliations of the surface, and a resulting heap of *débris* and boulders; and elsewhere, after decomposing the feldspar into a white clay, carry away this and the accompanying quartz and mica, and deposit them in separate beds, fluviatile and marine. When the exposed land consists of several unlike formations, sedimentary and igneous, the denudation produces changes proportionably more heterogeneous. The formations being disintegrable in different degrees, there follows an increased irregularity of surface. The areas drained by different rivers being differently constituted, these rivers carry down to the sea different combinations of ingredients; and so sundry new strata of distinct composition are formed.

And here indeed we may see very simply illustrated, the truth, which we shall presently have to trace out in more involved cases, that in proportion to the heterogeneity of the object or objects on which any force expends itself, is the heterogeneity of the results. A continent of complex structure, exposing many strata irregularly distributed, raised to various levels, tilted up at all angles, must, under the same denuding agencies, give origin to immensely multiplied results; each district must be differently modified; each river must carry down a different kind of detritus; each deposit must be differently distributed by the entangled currents, tidal and other, which wash the contorted shores; and this multiplication of results must manifestly be greatest where the complexity of the surface is greatest.

It is out of the question here to trace in detail the genesis of those endless complications described by Geology and Physical Geography: else we might show how the general truth, that every active force produces more than one change, is exemplified in the highly involved flow of the tides, in the ocean currents, in the winds, in the distribution of rain, in the distribution of heat, and so forth. But not to dwell upon these, let us, for the fuller elucidation of this truth in relation to the inorganic world, consider what would be the consequences of some extensive cosmical revolution—say the subsidence of Central America.

The immediate results of the disturbance would themselves be sufficiently complex. Besides the numberless dislocations of strata, the ejections of igneous matter, the propagation of earthquake vibrations thousands of miles around, the loud explosions, and the escape of gases; there would be the rush of the Atlantic and Pacific Oceans to supply the vacant space, the subsequent recoil of enormous waves, which would traverse both these oceans and produce myriads of changes along their shores, the corresponding atmospheric waves complicated by the currents surrounding each volcanic vent, and the electrical discharges with which such disturbances are accompanied. But these temporary effects would be insignificant compared with the permanent ones. The complex currents of the Atlantic and Pacific would be altered in direction and amount. The distribution of heat achieved by these ocean currents would be different from what it is. The arrangement of the isothermal lines, not even on the neighbouring continents, but even throughout Europe, would be changed. The tides would flow differently from what they do now. There would be more or less modification of the winds in their periods, strengths, directions, qualities. Rain would fall scarcely anywhere at the same times and in the same quantities as at present. In short, the meteorological conditions thousands of miles off, on all sides, would be more or less revolutionised.

Thus, without taking into account the infinitude of modifications which these changes of climate would produce upon the flora and fauna, both of land and sea, the reader will see the immense heterogeneity of the results wrought out by one force, when that force expends itself upon a previously complicated area; and he will readily draw the corollary that from the beginning the complication has advanced at an increasing rate.

Before going on to show how organic progress also depends upon the universal law that every force produces more than one change, we have to notice the manifestation of this law in yet another species of inorganic progress—namely, chemical. The same general causes that have wrought out the heterogeneity of the Earth, physically considered, have simultaneously wrought out its chemical heterogeneity. Without dwelling upon the general fact that the forces which have been increasing the variety and complexity of geological formations, have, at the same time, been bringing into contact elements not previously exposed to each other under conditions favourable to union, and so have been adding to the number of chemical compounds, let us pass to the more important complications that have resulted from the cooling of the Earth.

There is every reason to believe that at an extreme heat the elements cannot combine. Even under such heat as can be artificially produced, some very strong affinities yield, as for instance, that of oxygen for hydrogen; and the great majority of chemical compounds are decomposed at much lower temperatures. But without insisting upon the highly probable inference, that when the Earth was in its first state of incandescence there were no chemical combinations at all, it will suffice our purpose to point to the unquestionable fact that the compounds that can exist at the highest temperatures, and which must, therefore, have been the first that were formed as the Earth cooled, are those of the simplest constitutions. The protoxides—including under that head the alkalies, earths, etc.—are, as a class, the most stable compounds we know: most of them resisting decomposition by any heat we can generate. These, consisting severally of one atom of each component element, are combinations of the simplest order—are but one degree less homogeneous than the elements themselves. More heterogeneous than these, less stable, and therefore later in the Earth's history, are the deutoxides, tritoxides, peroxides, etc.; in which two, three, four, or more atoms of oxygen are united with one atom of metal or other element. Higher than these in heterogeneity are the hydrates; in which an oxide of hydrogen, united with an oxide of some other element, forms a substance whose atoms severally contain at least four ultimate atoms of three different kinds. Yet more heterogeneous and less stable still are the salts; which present us with compound atoms each made up of five, six, seven, eight, ten, twelve, or more atoms, of three, if not more, kinds. Then there are the hydrated salts, of a yet greater heterogeneity, which undergo partial decomposition at much lower temperatures. After them come the further-complicated supersalts and double salts, having a stability again decreased; and so throughout. Without entering into qualifications for which we lack space, we believe no chemist will deny it to be a general law of these inorganic combinations that, *other things equal*, the stability decreases as the complexity increases.

And then when we pass to the compounds of organic chemistry, we find this general law still further exemplified: we find much greater complexity and much less stability. An atom of albumen, for instance, consists of 482 ultimate atoms of five different kinds. Fibrine, still more intricate in constitution, contains in each atom, 298 atoms of carbon, 40 of nitrogen, 2 of sulphur, 228 of hydrogen, and 92 of oxygen—in all, 660 atoms; or, more strictly speaking—equivalents. And these two substances are so unstable as to decompose at quite ordinary temperatures; as that to which the outside of a joint of roast meat is exposed. Thus it is manifest that the present chemical heterogeneity of the Earth's surface has arisen by degrees, as the decrease of heat has permitted; and that it has shown itself in three forms—first, in the multiplication of chemical compounds; second, in the greater number of different elements contained in the more modern of these compounds: and third, in the higher and more varied multiples in which these more numerous elements combine.

To say that this advance in chemical heterogeneity is due to the one cause, diminution of the Earth's temperature, would be to say too much; for it is clear that aqueous and atmospheric agencies have been concerned; and, further, that the affinities of the elements themselves are implied. The cause has all along been a composite one: the cooling of the Earth having been simply the most general of the concurrent causes, or assemblage of conditions. And here, indeed, it may be remarked that in the several classes of facts already dealt with (excepting, perhaps, the first), and still more in those with which we shall presently deal, the causes are more or less compound; as indeed are nearly all causes with which we are acquainted. Scarcely any change can with logical accuracy be wholly ascribed to one agency, to the neglect of the permanent or temporary conditions under which only this agency produces the change. But as it does not materially affect our argument, we prefer, for simplicity's sake, to use throughout the popular mode of expression.

Perhaps it will be further objected, that to assign loss of heat as the cause of any changes, is to attribute these changes not to a force, but to the absence of a force. And this is true. Strictly speaking, the changes should be attributed to those forces which come into action when the antagonist force is withdrawn. But though there is an inaccuracy in saying that the freezing of water is due to the loss of its heat, no practical error arises from it; nor will a parallel laxity of expression vitiate our statements respecting the multiplication of effects. Indeed, the objection serves but to draw attention to the fact, that not only does the exertion of a force produce more than one change, but the withdrawal of a force produces more than one change. And this suggests that perhaps the most correct statement of our general principle would be its most abstract statement—every change is followed by more than one other change.

Returning to the thread of our exposition, we have next to trace out, in organic progress, this same all-pervading principle. And here, where the evolution of the homogeneous into the heterogeneous was first observed, the production of many changes by one cause is least easy to demonstrate. The development of a seed into a plant, or an ovum into an animal, is so gradual, while the forces which determine it are so involved, and at the same time so unobtrusive, that it is difficult to detect the multiplication of effects which is elsewhere so obvious. Nevertheless, guided by indirect evidence, we may pretty safely reach the conclusion that here too the law holds.

Observe, first, how numerous are the effects which any marked change works upon an adult organism — a human being, for instance. An alarming sound or sigh, besides the impressions on the organs of sense and the nerves, may produce a start, a scream, a distortion of the face, a trembling consequent upon a general muscular relaxation, a burst of perspiration, an excited action of the heart, a rush of blood to the brain, followed possibly by arrest of the heart's action and by syncope: and if the system be feeble, an indisposition with its long train of complicated symptoms may set in. Similarly in cases of disease. A minute portion of the small-pox virus introduced into the system, will, in a severe case, cause, during the first stage, rigors, heat of skin, accelerated pulse, furred tongue, loss of appetite, thirst, epigastric uneasiness, vomiting, headache, pains in the back and limbs, muscular weakness, convulsions, delirium, etc.; in the second stage, cutaneous eruption, itching, tingling, sore throat, swelled fauces, salivation, cough, hoarseness, dyspnœa, etc.; and in the third stage, œdematous inflammations, pneumonia, pleurisy, diarrhœa, inflammation of the brain, ophthalmia, erysipelas, etc.; each of which enumerated symptoms is itself more or less complex. Medicines, special foods, better air, might in like manner be instanced as producing multiplied results.

Now it needs only to consider that the many changes thus wrought by one force upon an adult organism, will be in part paralleled in an embryo organism, to understand how here also, the evolution of the homogeneous into the heterogeneous may be due to the production of many effects by one cause. The external heat and other agencies which determine the first complications of the germ, may, by acting upon these, superinduce further complications; upon these still higher and more numerous ones; and so on continually: each organ as it is developed serving, by its actions and reactions upon the rest, to initiate new complexities. The first pulsations of the fœtal heart must simultaneously aid the unfolding of every part. The growth of each tissue, by taking from the blood special proportions of elements, must modify the constitution of the blood; and so must modify the nutrition of all the other tissues. The heart's action, implying as it does a certain waste, necessitates an addition to the blood of effete matters, which must influence the rest of the system, and perhaps, as some think, cause the formation of excretory organs. The nervous connections established among the viscera must further multiply their mutual influences: and so continually.

Still stronger becomes the probability of this view when we call to mind the fact, that the same germ may be evolved into different forms according to circumstances. Thus, during its earlier stages, every embryo is sexless — becomes either male or female as the balance of forces acting upon it determines. Again, it is a well-established fact that the larva of a working-bee will develop into a queen-bee, if, before it is too late, its food be changed to that on which the larvæ of queen-bees are fed. Even more remarkable is the case of certain entozoa. The ovum of a tape-worm, getting into its natural habitat, the intestine, unfolds into the well-known form of its parent; but if carried, as it frequently is, into other parts of the system, it becomes a sac-like creature, called by naturalists the *Echinococcus*—a creature so extremely different from the tape-worm in aspect and structure, that only after careful investigations has it been proved to have the same origin. All which instances imply that each advance in embryonic complication results from the action of incident forces upon the complication previously existing.

Indeed, we may find *à priori* reason to think that the evolution proceeds after this manner. For since it is now known that no germ, animal or vegetable, contains the slightest rudiment, trace, or indication of the future organism—now that the microscope has shown us that the first process set up in every fertilised germ, is a process of repeated spontaneous fissions ending in the production of a mass of cells, not one of which exhibits any special character: there seems no alternative but to suppose that the partial organisation at any moment subsisting in a growing embryo, is transformed by the agencies acting upon it into the succeeding phase of organisation, and this into the next, until, through ever-increasing complexities, the ultimate form is reached. Thus, though the subtilty of the forces and the slowness of the results, prevent us from *directly* showing that the stages of increasing heterogeneity through which every embryo passes, severally arise from the production of many changes by one force, yet, *indirectly*, we have strong evidence that they do so.

We have marked how multitudinous are the effects which one cause may generate in an adult organism; that a like multiplication of effects must happen in the unfolding organism, we have observed in sundry illustrative cases; further, it has been pointed out that the ability which like germs have to originate unlike forms, implies that the successive transformations result from the new changes superinduced on previous changes; and we have seen that structureless as every germ originally is, the development of an organism out of it is otherwise incomprehensible. Not indeed that we can thus really explain the production of any plant or animal. We are still in the dark respecting those mysterious properties in virtue of which the germ, when subject to fit influences, undergoes the special changes that begin the series of transformations. All we aim to show, is, that given a germ possessing these mysterious properties, the evolution of an organism from it, probably depends upon that multiplication of effects which we have seen to be the cause of progress in general, so far as we have yet traced it.

When, leaving the development of single plants and animals, we pass to that of the Earth's flora and fauna, the course of our argument again becomes clear and simple. Though, as was admitted in the first part of this article, the fragmentary facts Palæontology has accumulated, do not clearly warrant us in saying that, in the lapse of geologic time, there have been evolved more heterogeneous organisms, and more heterogeneous assemblages of organisms, yet we shall now see that there *must* ever have been a tendency towards these results. We shall find that the production of many effects by one cause, which, as already shown, has been all along increasing the physical heterogeneity of the Earth, has further involved an increasing heterogeneity in its flora and fauna, individually and collectively. An illustration will make this clear.

Suppose that by a series of upheavals, occurring, as they are now known to do, at long intervals, the East Indian Archipelago were to be, step by step, raised into a continent, and a chain of mountains formed along the axis of elevation. By the first of these upheavals, the plants and animals inhabiting Borneo, Sumatra, New Guinea, and the rest, would be subjected to slightly modified sets of conditions. The climate in general would be altered in temperature, in humidity, and in its periodical variations; while the local differences would be multiplied. These modifications would affect, perhaps inappreciably, the entire flora and fauna of the region. The change of level would produce additional modifications: varying in different species, and also in different members of the same species, according to their distance from the axis of elevation. Plants, growing only on the sea-shore in special localities, might become extinct. Others, living only in swamps of a certain humidity, would, if they survived at all, probably undergo visible changes of appearance. While still greater alterations would occur in the plants gradually spreading over the lands newly raised above the sea. The animals and insects living on these modified plants, would themselves be in some degree modified by change of food, as well as by change of climate; and the modification would be more marked where, from the dwindling or disappearance of one kind of plant, an allied kind was eaten. In the lapse of the many generations arising before the next upheaval, the sensible or insensible alterations thus produced in each species would become organised—there would be a more or less complete adaptation to the new conditions. The next upheaval would superinduce further organic changes, implying wider divergences from the primary forms; and so repeatedly.

But now let it be observed that the revolution thus resulting would not be a substitution of a thousand more or less modified species for the thousand original species; but in place of the thousand original species there would arise several thousand species, or varieties, or changed forms. Each species being distributed over an area of some extent, and tending continually to colonise the new area exposed, its different members would be subject to different sets of changes. Plants and animals spreading towards the equator would not be affected in the same way with others spreading from it. Those spreading towards the new shores would undergo changes unlike the changes undergone by those spreading into the mountains. Thus, each original race of organisms, would become the root from which diverged several races differing more or less from it and from each other; and while some of these might subsequently disappear, probably more than one would survive in the next geologic period: the very dispersion itself increasing the chances of survival. Not only would there be certain modifications thus caused by change of physical conditions and food, but also in some cases other modifications caused by change of habit. The fauna of each island, peopling, step by step, the newly-raised tracts, would eventually come in contact with the faunas of other islands; and some members of these other faunas would be unlike any creatures before seen. Herbivores meeting with new beasts of prey, would, in some cases, be led into modes of defence or escape differing from those previously used; and simultaneously the beasts of prey would modify their modes of pursuit and attack. We know that when circumstances demand it, such changes of habit *do* take place in animals; and we know that if the new habits become the dominant ones, they must eventually in some degree alter the organisation.

Observe, now, however, a further consequence. There must arise not simply a tendency towards the differentiation of each race of organisms into several races; but also a tendency to the occasional production of a somewhat higher organism. Taken in the mass, these divergent varieties which have been caused by fresh physical conditions and habits of life, will exhibit changes quite indefinite in kind and degree; and changes that do not necessarily constitute an advance. Probably in most cases the modified type will be neither more nor less heterogeneous than the original one. In some cases the habits of life adopted being simpler than before, a less heterogeneous structure will result: there will be a retrogradation. But it *must* now and then occur, that some division of a species, falling into circumstances which give it rather more complex experiences, and demand actions somewhat more involved, will have certain of its organs further differentiated in proportionately small degrees, — will become slightly more heterogeneous.

Thus, in the natural course of things, there will from time to time arise an increased heterogeneity both of the Earth's flora and fauna, and of individual races included in them. Omitting detailed explanations, and allowing for the qualifications which cannot here be specified, we think it is clear that geological mutations have all along tended to complicate the forms of life, whether regarded separately or collectively. The same causes which have led to the evolution of the Earth's crust from the simple into the complex, have simultaneously led to a parallel evolution of the Life upon its surface. In this case, as in previous ones, we see that the transformation of the homogeneous into the heterogeneous is consequent upon the universal principle, that every active force produces more than one change.

The deduction here drawn from the established truths of geology and the general laws of life, gains immensely in weight on finding it to be in harmony with an induction drawn from direct experience. Just that divergence of many races from one race, which we inferred must have been continually occurring during geologic time, we know to have occurred during the pre-historic and historic periods, in man and domestic animals. And just that multiplication of effects which we concluded must have produced the first, we see has produced the last. Single causes, as famine, pressure of population, war, have periodically led to further dispersions of mankind and of dependent creatures: each such dispersion initiating new modifications, new varieties of type. Whether all the human races be or be not derived from one stock, philology makes it clear that whole groups of races now easily distinguishable from each other, were originally one race, — that the diffusion of one race into different climates and conditions of existence, has produced many modified forms of it.

Similarly with domestic animals. Though in some cases—as that of dogs— community of origin will perhaps be disputed, yet in other cases—as that of the sheep or the cattle of our own country—it will not be questioned that local differences of climate, food, and treatment, have transformed one original breed into numerous breeds now become so far distinct as to produce unstable hybrids. Moreover, through the complications of effects flowing from single causes, we here find, what we before inferred, not only an increase of general heterogeneity, but also of special heterogeneity. While of the divergent divisions and subdivisions of the human race, many have undergone changes not constituting an advance; while in some the type may have degraded; in others it has become decidedly more heterogeneous. The civilised European departs more widely from the vertebrate archetype than does the savage. Thus, both the law and the cause of progress, which, from lack of evidence, can be but hypothetically substantiated in respect of the earlier forms of life on our globe, can be actually substantiated in respect of the latest forms.

If the advance of Man towards greater heterogeneity is traceable to the production of many effects by one cause, still more clearly may the advance of Society towards greater heterogeneity be so explained. Consider the growth of an industrial organisation. When, as must occasionally happen, some individual of a tribe displays unusual aptitude for making an article of general use—a weapon, for instance—which was before made by each man for himself, there arises a tendency towards the differentiation of that individual into a maker of such weapon. His companions—warriors and hunters all of them,—severally feel the importance of having the best weapons that can be made; and are therefore certain to offer strong inducements to this skilled individual to make weapons for them. He, on the other hand, having not only an unusual faculty, but an unusual liking, for making such weapons (the talent and the desire for any occupation being commonly associated), is predisposed to fulfil these commissions on the offer of an adequate reward: especially as his love of distinction is also gratified. This first specialisation of function, once commenced, tends ever to become more decided. On the side of the weapon-maker continued practice gives increased skill—increased superiority to his products: on the side of his clients, cessation of practice entails decreased skill. Thus the influences that determine this division of labour grow stronger in both ways; and the incipient heterogeneity is, on the average of cases, likely to become permanent for that generation, if no longer.

Observe now, however, that this process not only differentiates the social mass into two parts, the one monopolising, or almost monopolising, the performance of a certain function, and the other having lost the habit, and in some measure the power, of performing that function; but it tends to imitate other differentiations. The advance we have described implies the introduction of barter,—the maker of weapons has, on each occasion, to be paid in such other articles as he agrees to take in exchange. But he will not habitually take in exchange one kind of article, but many kinds. He does not want mats only, or skins, or fishing gear, but he wants all these; and on each occasion will bargain for the particular things he most needs. What follows? If among the members of the tribe there exist any slight differences of skill in the manufacture of these various things, as there are almost sure to do, the weapon-maker will take from each one the thing which that one excels in making: he will exchange for mats with him whose mats are superior, and will bargain for the fishing gear of whoever has the best. But he who has bartered away his mats or his fishing gear, must make other mats or fishing gear for himself; and in so doing must, in some degree, further develop his aptitude. Thus it results that the small specialities of faculty possessed by various members of the tribe, will tend to grow more decided. If such transactions are from time to time repeated, these specialisations may become appreciable. And whether or not there ensue distinct differentiations of other individuals into makers of particular articles, it is clear that incipient differentiations take place throughout the tribe: the one original cause produces not only the first dual effect, but a number of secondary dual effects, like in kind, but minor in degree. This process, of which traces may be seen among groups of schoolboys, cannot well produce any lasting effects in an unsettled tribe; but where there grows up a fixed and multiplying community, these differentiations become permanent, and increase with each generation. A larger population, involving a greater demand for every commodity, intensifies the functional activity of each specialised person or class; and this renders the specialisation more definite where it already exists, and establishes it where it is nascent. By increasing the pressure on the means of subsistence, a larger population again augments these results; seeing that each person is forced more and more to confine himself to that which he can do best, and by which he can gain most. This industrial progress, by aiding future production, opens the way for a further growth of population, which reacts as before: in all which the multiplication of effects is manifest. Presently, under these same stimuli, new occupations arise. Competing workers, ever aiming to produce improved articles, occasionally discover better processes or raw materials. In weapons and cutting tools, the substitution of bronze for stone entails upon him who first makes it a great increase of demand—so great an increase that he presently finds all his time occupied in making the bronze for the articles he sells, and is obliged to depute the fashioning of these to others: and, eventually, the making of bronze, thus gradually differentiated from a pre-existing occupation, becomes an occupation by itself.

But now mark the ramified changes which follow this change. Bronze soon replaces stone, not only in the articles it was first used for, but in many others—in arms, tools, and utensils of various kinds; and so affects the manufacture of these things. Further, it affects the processes which these utensils subserve, and the resulting products—modifies buildings, carvings, dress, personal decorations. Yet again, it sets going sundry manufactures which were before impossible, from lack of a material fit for the requisite tools. And all these changes react on the people—increase their manipulative skill, their intelligence, their comfort,—refine their habits and tastes. Thus the evolution of a homogeneous society into a heterogeneous one, is clearly consequent on the general principle, that many effects are produced by one cause.

Our limits will not allow us to follow out this process in its higher complications: else might we show how the localisation of special industries in special parts of a kingdom, as well as the minute subdivision of labour in the making of each commodity, are similarly determined. Or, turning to a somewhat different order of illustrations, we might dwell on the multitudinous changes—material, intellectual, moral—caused by printing; or the further extensive series of changes wrought by gunpowder. But leaving the intermediate phases of social development, let us take a few illustrations from its most recent and its passing phases. To trace the effects of steam-power, in its manifold applications to mining, navigation, and manufactures of all kinds, would carry us into unmanageable detail. Let us confine ourselves to the latest embodiment of steam-power — the locomotive engine.

This, as the proximate cause of our railway system, has changed the face of the country, the course of trade, and the habits of the people. Consider, first, the complicated sets of changes that precede the making of every railway — the provisional arrangements, the meetings, the registration, the trial section, the parliamentary survey, the lithographed plans, the books of reference, the local deposits and notices, the application to Parliament, the passing Standing-Orders Committee, the first, second, and third readings: each of which brief heads indicates a multiplicity of transactions, and the development of sundry occupations — as those of engineers, surveyors, lithographers, parliamentary agents, share-brokers; and the creation of sundry others — as those of traffic-takers, reference-takers. Consider, next, the yet more marked changes implied in railway construction — the cuttings, embankings, tunnellings, diversions of roads; the building of bridges, and stations; the laying down of ballast, sleepers, and rails; the making of engines, tenders, carriages, and waggons: which processes, acting upon numerous trades, increase the importation of timber, the quarrying of stone, the manufacture of iron, the mining of coal, the burning of bricks: institute a variety of special manufactures weekly advertised in the *Railway Times*; and, finally, open the way to sundry new occupations, as those of drivers, stokers, cleaners, plate-layers, etc., etc. And then consider the changes, more numerous and involved still, which railways in action produce on the community at large. The organisation of every business is more or less modified: ease of communication makes it better to do directly what was before done by proxy; agencies are established where previously they would not have paid; goods are obtained from remote wholesale houses instead of near retail ones; and commodities are used which distance once rendered inaccessible. Again, the rapidity and small cost of carriage tend to specialise more than ever the industries of different districts — to confine each manufacture to the parts in which, from local advantages, it can be best carried on. Further, the diminished cost of carriage, facilitating distribution, equalises prices, and also, on the average, lowers prices: thus bringing divers articles within the means of those before unable to buy them, and so increasing their comforts and improving their habits. At the same time the practice of travelling is immensely extended. Classes who never before thought of it, take annual trips to the sea; visit their distant relations; make tours; and so we are benefited in body, feelings, and intellect. Moreover, the more prompt transmission of letters and of news produces further changes — makes the pulse of the nation faster. Yet more, there arises a wide dissemination of cheap literature through railway book-stalls, and of advertisements in railway carriages: both of them aiding ulterior progress.

And all the innumerable changes here briefly indicated are consequent on the invention of the locomotive engine. The social organism has been rendered more heterogeneous in virtue of the many new occupations introduced, and the many old ones further specialised; prices in every place have been altered; each trader has, more or less, modified his way of doing business; and almost every person has been affected in his actions, thoughts, emotions.

Illustrations to the same effect might be indefinitely accumulated. That every influence brought to bear upon society works multiplied effects; and that increase of heterogeneity is due to this multiplication of effects; may be seen in the history of every trade, every custom, every belief. But it is needless to give additional evidence of this. The only further fact demanding notice, is, that we here see still more clearly than ever, the truth before pointed out, that in proportion as the area on which any force expends itself becomes heterogeneous, the results are in a yet higher degree multiplied in number and kind. While among the primitive tribes to whom it was first known, caoutchouc caused but a few changes, among ourselves the changes have been so many and varied that the history of them occupies a volume.[14] Upon the small, homogeneous community inhabiting one of the Hebrides, the electric telegraph would produce, were it used, scarcely any results; but in England the results it produces are multitudinous. The comparatively simple organisation under which our ancestors lived five centuries ago, could have undergone but few modifications from an event like the recent one at Canton; but now the legislative decision respecting it sets up many hundreds of complex modifications, each of which will be the parent of numerous future ones.

Space permitting, we could willingly have pursued the argument in relation to all the subtler results of civilisation. As before, we showed that the law of Progress to which the organic and inorganic worlds conform, is also conformed to by Language, Sculpture, Music, etc.; so might we here show that the cause which we have hitherto found to determine Progress holds in these cases also. We might demonstrate in detail how, in Science, an advance of one division presently advances other divisions—how Astronomy has been immensely forwarded by discoveries in Optics, while other optical discoveries have initiated Microscopic Anatomy, and greatly aided the growth of Physiology—how Chemistry has indirectly increased our knowledge of Electricity, Magnetism, Biology, Geology—how Electricity has reacted on Chemistry and Magnetism, developed our views of Light and Heat, and disclosed sundry laws of nervous action.

In Literature the same truth might be exhibited in the manifold effects of the primitive mystery-play, not only as originating the modern drama, but as affecting through it other kinds of poetry and fiction; or in the still multiplying forms of periodical literature that have descended from the first newspaper, and which have severally acted and reacted on other forms of literature and on each other. The influence which a new school of Painting—as that of the pre-Raffaelites—exercises upon other schools; the hints which all kinds of pictorial art are deriving from Photography; the complex results of new critical doctrines, as those of Mr. Ruskin, might severally be dwelt upon as displaying the like multiplication of effects. But it would needlessly tax the reader's patience to pursue, in their many ramifications, these various changes: here become so involved and subtle as to be

---

[14] *Personal Narrative of the Origin of the Caoutchouc, or India-Rubber Manufacture in England.* By Thomas Hancock.

followed with some difficulty.

Without further evidence, we venture to think our case is made out. The imperfections of statement which brevity has necessitated, do not, we believe, militate against the propositions laid down. The qualifications here and there demanded would not, if made, affect the inferences. Though in one instance, where sufficient evidence is not attainable, we have been unable to show that the law of Progress applies; yet there is high probability that the same generalisation holds which holds throughout the rest of creation. Though, in tracing the genesis of Progress, we have frequently spoken of complex causes as if they were simple ones; it still remains true that such causes are far less complex than their results. Detailed criticisms cannot affect our main position. Endless facts go to show that every kind of progress is from the homogeneous to the heterogeneous; and that it is so because each change is followed by many changes. And it is significant that where the facts are most accessible and abundant, there are these truths most manifest.

However, to avoid committing ourselves to more than is yet proved, we must be content with saying that such are the law and the cause of all progress that is known to us. Should the Nebular Hypothesis ever be established, then it will become manifest that the Universe at large, like every organism, was once homogeneous; that as a whole, and in every detail, it has unceasingly advanced towards greater heterogeneity; and that its heterogeneity is still increasing. It will be seen that as in each event of to-day, so from the beginning, the decomposition of every expended force into several forces has been perpetually producing a higher complication; that the increase of heterogeneity so brought about is still going on, and must continue to go on; and that thus Progress is not an accident, not a thing within human control, but a beneficent necessity.

A few words must be added on the ontological bearings of our argument. Probably not a few will conclude that here is an attempted solution of the great questions with which Philosophy in all ages has perplexed itself. Let none thus deceive themselves. Only such as know not the scope and the limits of Science can fall into so grave an error. The foregoing generalisations apply, not to the genesis of things in themselves, but to their genesis as manifested to the human consciousness. After all that has been said, the ultimate mystery remains just as it was. The explanation of that which is explicable, does but bring out into greater clearness the inexplicableness of that which remains behind. However we may succeed in reducing the equation to its lowest terms, we are not thereby enabled to determine the unknown quantity: on the contrary, it only becomes more manifest that the unknown quantity can never be found.

Little as it seems to do so, fearless inquiry tends continually to give a firmer basis to all true Religion. The timid sectarian, alarmed at the progress of knowledge, obliged to abandon one by one the superstitions of his ancestors, and daily finding his cherished beliefs more and more shaken, secretly fears that all things may some day be explained; and has a corresponding dread of Science: thus evincing the profoundest of all infidelity—the fear lest the truth be bad. On the other hand, the sincere man of science, content to follow wherever the evidence leads him, becomes by each new inquiry more profoundly convinced that the Universe is an insoluble problem. Alike in the external and the internal worlds, he sees himself in the midst of perpetual changes, of which he can discover neither the beginning nor the end. If, tracing back the evolution of things, he allows himself to entertain the hypothesis that all matter once existed in a diffused form, he finds it utterly impossible to conceive how this came to be so; and equally, if he speculates on the future, he can assign no limit to the grand succession of phenomena ever unfolding themselves before him. On the other hand, if he looks inward, he perceives that both terminations of the thread of consciousness are beyond his grasp: he cannot remember when or how consciousness commenced, and he cannot examine the consciousness that at any moment exists; for only a state of consciousness that is already past can become the object of thought, and never one which is passing.

When, again, he turns from the succession of phenomena, external or internal, to their essential nature, he is equally at fault. Though he may succeed in resolving all properties of objects into manifestations of force, he is not thereby enabled to realise what force is; but finds, on the contrary, that the more he thinks about it, the more he is baffled. Similarly, though analysis of mental actions may finally bring him down to sensations as the original materials out of which all thought is woven, he is none the forwarder; for he cannot in the least comprehend sensation—cannot even conceive how sensation is possible. Inward and outward things he thus discovers to be alike inscrutable in their ultimate genesis and nature. He sees that the Materialist and Spiritualist controversy is a mere war of words; the disputants being equally absurd—each believing he understands that which it is impossible for any man to understand. In all directions his investigations eventually bring him face to face with the unknowable; and he ever more clearly perceives it to be the unknowable. He learns at once the greatness and the littleness of human intellect—its power in dealing with all that comes within the range of experience; its impotence in dealing with all that transcends experience. He feels, with a vividness which no others can, the utter incomprehensibleness of the simplest fact, considered in itself. He alone truly *sees* that absolute knowledge is impossible. He alone *knows* that under all things there lies an impenetrable mystery.

ON MANNERS AND FASHION[15]

Whoever has studied the physiognomy of political meetings, cannot fail to have remarked a connection between democratic opinions and peculiarities of costume. At a Chartist demonstration, a lecture on Socialism, or a *soirée* of the Friends of Italy, there will be seen many among the audience, and a still larger ratio among the speakers, who get themselves up in a style more or less unusual. One gentleman on the platform divides his hair down the centre, instead of on one side; another brushes it back off the forehead, in the fashion known as "bringing out the intellect;" a third has so long forsworn the scissors, that his locks sweep his shoulders. A considerable sprinkling of moustaches may be observed; here and there an imperial; and occasionally some courageous breaker of conventions exhibits a full-grown beard.[16] This nonconformity in hair is countenanced by various nonconformities in dress, shown by others of the assemblage. Bare necks, shirt-collars *à la* Byron, waistcoats cut Quaker fashion, wonderfully shaggy great coats, numerous oddities in form and colour, destroy the monotony usual in crowds. Even those exhibiting no conspicuous peculiarity, frequently indicate by something in the pattern or make-up of their clothes, that they pay small regard to what their tailors tell them about the prevailing taste. And when the gathering breaks up, the varieties of head-gear displayed—the number of caps, and the abundance of felt hats—suffice to prove that were the world at large like-minded, the black cylinders which tyrannise over us would soon be deposed.

The foreign correspondence of our daily press shows that this relationship between political discontent and the disregard of customs exists on the Continent also. Red republicanism has always been distinguished by its hirsuteness. The authorities of Prussia, Austria, and Italy, alike recognise certain forms of hat as indicative of disaffection, and fulminate against them accordingly. In some places the wearer of a blouse runs a risk of being classed among the *suspects*; and in others, he who would avoid the bureau of police, must beware how he goes out in any but the ordinary colours. Thus, democracy abroad, as at home, tends towards personal singularity.

Nor is this association of characteristics peculiar to modern times, or to reformers of the State. It has always existed; and it has been manifested as much in religious agitations as in political ones. Along with dissent from the chief established opinions and arrangements, there has ever been some dissent from the customary social practices. The Puritans, disapproving of the long curls of the Cavaliers, as of their principles, cut their own hair short, and so gained the name of

[15] *Westminster Review*, April 1854.
[16] This was written before moustaches and beards had become common.

"Roundheads." The marked religious nonconformity of the Quakers was accompanied by an equally-marked nonconformity of manners—in attire, in speech, in salutation. The early Moravians not only believed differently, but at the same time dressed differently, and lived differently, from their fellow Christians.

That the association between political independence and independence of personal conduct, is not a phenomenon of to-day only, we may see alike in the appearance of Franklin at the French court in plain clothes, and in the white hats worn by the last generation of radicals. Originality of nature is sure to show itself in more ways than one. The mention of George Fox's suit of leather, or Pestalozzi's school name, "Harry Oddity," will at once suggest the remembrance that men who have in great things diverged from the beaten track, have frequently done so in small things likewise. Minor illustrations of this truth may be gathered in almost every circle. We believe that whoever will number up his reforming and rationalist acquaintances, will find among them more than the usual proportion of those who in dress or behaviour exhibit some degree of what the world calls eccentricity.

If it be a fact that men of revolutionary aims in politics or religion, are commonly revolutionists in custom also, it is not less a fact that those whose office it is to uphold established arrangements in State and Church, are also those who most adhere to the social forms and observances bequeathed to us by past generations. Practices elsewhere extinct still linger about the headquarters of government. The monarch still gives assent to Acts of Parliament in the old French of the Normans; and Norman French terms are still used in law. Wigs, such as those we see depicted in old portraits, may yet be found on the heads of judges and barristers. The Beefeaters at the Tower wear the costume of Henry VIIth's bodyguard. The University dress of the present year varies but little from that worn soon after the Reformation. The claret-coloured coat, knee-breeches, lace shirt frills, ruffles, white silk stockings, and buckled shoes, which once formed the usual attire of a gentleman, still survive as the court-dress. And it need scarcely be said that at *levées* and drawing-rooms, the ceremonies are prescribed with an exactness, and enforced with a rigour, not elsewhere to be found.

Can we consider these two series of coincidences as accidental and unmeaning? Must we not rather conclude that some necessary relationship obtains between them? Are there not such things as a constitutional conservatism, and a constitutional tendency to change? Is there not a class which clings to the old in all things; and another class so in love with progress as often to mistake novelty for improvement? Do we not find some men ready to bow to established authority of whatever kind; while others demand of every such authority its reason, and reject it if it fails to justify itself? And must not the minds thus contrasted tend to become respectively conformist and nonconformist, not only in politics and religion, but in other things? Submission, whether to a government, to the dogmas of ecclesiastics, or to that code of behaviour which society at large has set up, is essentially of the same nature; and the sentiment which induces resistance to the despotism of rulers, civil or spiritual, likewise induces resistance to the despotism of the world's opinion. Look at them fundamentally, and all enactments, alike of the legislature, the consistory, and the saloon—all regulations, formal or virtual, have a common character: they are all limitations of men's freedom. "Do this—Refrain from that," are the blank formulas into which they may all be written: and in each case the understanding is that obedience will bring approbation here and paradise hereafter; while disobedience will entail imprisonment, or sending to Coventry, or eternal torments, as the case may be. And if restraints, however named, and through whatever apparatus of means exercised, are one in their action upon men, it must happen that those who are patient under one kind of restraint, are likely to be patient under another; and conversely, that those impatient of restraint in general, will, on the average, tend to show their impatience in all directions.

That Law, Religion, and Manners are thus related—that their respective kinds of operation come under one generalisation—that they have in certain contrasted characteristics of men a common support and a common danger—will, however, be most clearly seen on discovering that they have a common origin. Little as from present appearances we should suppose it, we shall yet find that at first, the control of religion, the control of laws and the control of manners, were all one control. However incredible it may now seem, we believe it to be demonstrable that the rules of etiquette, the provisions of the statute-book, and the commands of the decalogue, have grown from the same root. If we go far enough back into the ages of primeval Fetishism, it becomes manifest that originally Deity, Chief, and Master of the ceremonies were identical. To make good these positions, and to show their bearing on what is to follow, it will be necessary here to traverse ground that is in part somewhat beaten, and at first sight irrelevant to our topic. We will pass over it as quickly as consists with the exigencies of the argument.

That the earliest social aggregations were ruled solely by the will of the strong man, few dispute. That from the strong man proceeded not only Monarchy, but the conception of a God, few admit: much as Carlyle and others have said in evidence of it. If, however, those who are unable to believe this, will lay aside the ideas of God and man in which they have been educated, and study the aboriginal ideas of them, they will at least see some probability in the hypothesis. Let them remember that before experience had yet taught men to distinguish between the possible and the impossible; and while they were ready on the slightest suggestion to ascribe unknown powers to any object and make a fetish of it; their conceptions of humanity and its capacities were necessarily vague, and without specific limits. The man who by unusual strength, or cunning, achieved something that others had failed to achieve, or something which they did not understand, was considered by them as differing from themselves; and, as we see in the belief of some Polynesians that only their chiefs have souls, or in that of the ancient Peruvians that their nobles were divine by birth, the ascribed difference was apt to be not one of degree only, but one of kind.

Let them remember next, how gross were the notions of God, or rather of gods, prevalent during the same era and afterwards—how concretely gods were conceived as men of specific aspects dressed in specific ways—how their names were literally "the strong," "the destroyer," "the powerful one,"—how, according to the Scandinavian mythology, the "sacred duty of blood-revenge" was acted on

by the gods themselves,—and how they were not only human in their vindictiveness, their cruelty, and their quarrels with each other, but were supposed to have
amours on earth, and to consume the viands placed on their altars. Add to which,
that in various mythologies, Greek, Scandinavian, and others, the oldest beings
are giants; that according to a traditional genealogy the gods, demi-gods, and in
some cases men, are descended from these after the human fashion; and that while
in the East we hear of sons of God who saw the daughters of men that they were
fair, the Teutonic myths tell of unions between the sons of men and the daughters
of the gods.

Let them remember, too, that at first the idea of death differed widely from
that which we have; that there are still tribes who, on the decease of one of their
number, attempt to make the corpse stand, and put food into his mouth; that the
Peruvians had feasts at which the mummies of their dead Incas presided, when,
as Prescott says, they paid attention "to these insensible remains as if they were
instinct with life;" that among the Fejees it is believed that every enemy has to be
killed twice; that the Eastern Pagans give extension and figure to the soul, and
attribute to it all the same substances, both solid and liquid, of which our bodies
are composed; and that it is the custom among most barbarous races to bury food,
weapons, and trinkets along with the dead body, under the manifest belief that it
will presently need them.

Lastly, let them remember that the other world, as originally conceived, is
simply some distant part of this world—some Elysian fields, some happy hunt-
ing-ground, accessible even to the living, and to which, after death, men travel
in anticipation of a life analogous in general character to that which they led before. Then, co-ordinating these general facts—the ascription of unknown powers
to chiefs and medicine men; the belief in deities having human forms, passions,
and behaviour; the imperfect comprehension of death as distinguished from life;
and the proximity of the future abode to the present, both in position and character—let them reflect whether they do not almost unavoidably suggest the conclusion that the aboriginal god is the dead chief; the chief not dead in our sense,
but gone away carrying with him food and weapons to some rumoured region of
plenty, some promised land, whither he had long intended to lead his followers,
and whence he will presently return to fetch them.

This hypothesis once entertained, is seen to harmonise with all primitive ideas
and practices. The sons of the deified chief reigning after him, it necessarily happens that all early kings are held descendants of the gods; and the fact that alike
in Assyria, Egypt, among the Jews, Phœnicians, and ancient Britons, kings' names
were formed out of the names of the gods, is fully explained. The genesis of Poly-
theism out of Fetishism, by the successive migrations of the race of god-kings to
the other world—a genesis illustrated in the Greek mythology, alike by the precise
genealogy of the deities, and by the specifically asserted apotheosis of the later
ones—tends further to bear it out. It explains the fact that in the old creeds, as in
the still extant creed of the Otaheitans, every family has its guardian spirit, who
is supposed to be one of their departed relatives; and that they sacrifice to these
as minor gods—a practice still pursued by the Chinese and even by the Russians.

It is perfectly congruous with the Grecian myths concerning the wars of the Gods with the Titans and their final usurpation; and it similarly agrees with the fact that among the Teutonic gods proper was one Freir who came among them by adoption, "but was born among the *Vanes*, a somewhat mysterious *other* dynasty of gods, who had been conquered and superseded by the stronger and more warlike Odin dynasty." It harmonises, too, with the belief that there are different gods to different territories and nations, as there were different chiefs; that these gods contend for supremacy as chiefs do; and it gives meaning to the boast of neighbouring tribes—"Our god is greater than your god." It is confirmed by the notion universally current in early times, that the gods come from this other abode, in which they commonly live, and appear among men—speak to them, help them, punish them. And remembering this, it becomes manifest that the prayers put up by primitive peoples to their gods for aid in battle, are meant literally—that their gods are expected to come back from the other kingdom they are reigning over, and once more fight the old enemies they had before warred against so implacably; and it needs but to name the Iliad, to remind every one how thoroughly they believed the expectation fulfilled.

All government, then, being originally that of the strong man who has become a fetish by some manifestation of superiority, there arises, at his death—his supposed departure on a long projected expedition, in which he is accompanied by his slaves and concubines sacrificed at his tomb—their arises, then, the incipient division of religious from political control, of civil rule from spiritual. His son becomes deputed chief during his absence; his authority is cited as that by which his son acts; his vengeance is invoked on all who disobey his son; and his commands, as previously known or as asserted by his son, become the germ of a moral code; a fact we shall the more clearly perceive if we remember, that early moral codes inculcate mainly the virtues of the warrior, and the duty of exterminating some neighbouring tribe whose existence is an offence to the deity.

From this point onwards, these two kinds of authority, at first complicated together as those of principal and agent, become slowly more and more distinct. As experience accumulates, and ideas of causation grow more precise, kings lose their supernatural attributes; and, instead of God-king, become God-descended king, God-appointed king, the Lord's anointed, the vicegerent of heaven, ruler reigning by Divine right. The old theory, however, long clings to men in feeling, after it has disappeared in name; and "such divinity doth hedge a king," that even now, many, on first seeing one, feel a secret surprise at finding him an ordinary sample of humanity. The sacredness attaching to royalty attaches afterwards to its appended institutions—to legislatures, to laws. Legal and illegal are synonymous with right and wrong; the authority of Parliament is held unlimited; and a lingering faith in governmental power continually generates unfounded hopes from its enactments. Political scepticism, however, having destroyed the divine *prestige* of royalty, goes on ever increasing, and promises ultimately to reduce the State to a purely secular institution, whose regulations are limited in their sphere, and have no other authority than the general will. Meanwhile, the religious control has been little by little separating itself from the civil, both in its essence and in its forms.

While from the God-king of the savage have arisen in one direction, secular rulers who, age by age, have been losing the sacred attributes men ascribed to them; there has arisen in another direction, the conception of a deity, who, at first human in all things, has been gradually losing human materiality, human form, human passions, human modes of action: until now, anthropomorphism has become a reproach.

Along with this wide divergence in men's ideas of the divine and civil ruler has been taking place a corresponding divergence in the codes of conduct respectively proceeding from them. While the king was a deputy-god—a governor such as the Jews looked for in the Messiah—a governor considered, as the Czar still is, "our God upon Earth,"—it, of course, followed that his commands were the supreme rules. But as men ceased to believe in his supernatural origin and nature, his commands ceased to be the highest; and there arose a distinction between the regulations made by him, and the regulations handed down from the old god-kings, who were rendered ever more sacred by time and the accumulation of myths. Hence came respectively, Law and Morality: the one growing ever more concrete, the other more abstract; the authority of the one ever on the decrease, that of the other ever on the increase; originally the same, but now placed daily in more marked antagonism.

Simultaneously there has been going on a separation of the institutions administering these two codes of conduct. While they were yet one, of course Church and State were one: the king was arch-priest, not nominally, but really—alike the giver of new commands and the chief interpreter of the old commands; and the deputy-priests coming out of his family were thus simply expounders of the dictates of their ancestry: at first as recollected, and afterwards as ascertained by professed interviews with them. This union—which still existed practically during the middle ages, when the authority of kings was mixed up with the authority of the pope, when there were bishop-rulers having all the powers of feudal lords, and when priests punished by penances—has been, step by step, becoming less close. Though monarchs are still "defenders of the faith," and ecclesiastical chiefs, they are but nominally such. Though bishops still have civil power, it is not what they once had. Protestantism shook loose the bonds of union; Dissent has long been busy in organising a mechanism for the exercise of religious control, wholly independent of law; in America, a separate organisation for that purpose already exists; and if anything is to be hoped from the Anti-State-Church Association—or, as it has been newly named, "The Society for the Liberation of Religion from State Patronage and Control"—we shall presently have a separate organisation here also.

Thus alike in authority, in essence, and in form, political and spiritual rule have been ever more widely diverging from the same root. That increasing division of labour which marks the progress of society in other things, marks it also in this separation of government into civil and religious; and if we observe how the morality which forms the substance of religions in general, is beginning to be purified from the associated creeds, we may anticipate that this division will be ultimately carried much further.

Passing now to the third species of control—that of Manners—we shall find that this, too, while it had a common genesis with the others, has gradually come to have a distinct sphere and a special embodiment. Among early aggregations of men before yet social observances existed, the sole forms of courtesy known were the signs of submission to the strong man; as the sole law was his will, and the sole religion the awe of his supposed supernaturalness. Originally, ceremonies were modes of behaviour to the god-king. Our commonest titles have been derived from his names. And all salutations were primarily worship paid to him. Let us trace out these truths in detail, beginning with titles.

The fact already noticed, that the names of early kings among divers races are formed by the addition of certain syllables to the names of their gods—which certain syllables, like our *Mac* and *Fitz*, probably mean "son of," or "descended from"—at once gives meaning to the term *Father* as a divine title. And when we read, in Selden, that "the composition out of these names of Deities was not only proper to Kings: their Grandes and more honourable Subjects" (no doubt members of the royal race) "had sometimes the like;" we see how the term *Father*, properly used by these also, and by their multiplying descendants, came to be a title used by the people in general. And it is significant as bearing on this point, that among the most barbarous nation in Europe, where belief in the divine nature of the ruler still lingers, *Father* in this higher sense is still a regal distinction. When, again, we remember how the divinity at first ascribed to kings was not a complimentary fiction but a supposed fact; and how, further, under the Fetish philosophy the celestial bodies are believed to be personages who once lived among men; we see that the appellations of oriental rulers, "Brother to the Sun," etc., were probably once expressive of a genuine belief; and have simply, like many other things, continued in use after all meaning has gone out of them. We way infer, too, that the titles, God, Lord, Divinity, were given to primitive rulers literally—that the *nostra divinitas* applied to the Roman emperors, and the various sacred designations that have been borne by monarchs, down to the still extant phrase, "Our Lord the King," are the dead and dying forms of what were once living facts. From these names, God, Father, Lord, Divinity, originally belonging to the God-king, and afterwards to God and the king, the derivation of our commonest titles of respect is clearly traceable.

There is reason to think that these titles were originally proper names. Not only do we see among the Egyptians, where Pharaoh was synonymous with king, and among the Romans, where to be Cæsar meant to be Emperor, that the proper names of the greatest men were transferred to their successors, and so became class names; but in the Scandinavian mythology we may trace a human title of honour up to the proper name of a divine personage. In Anglo-Saxon *bealdor*, or *baldor*, means *Lord*; and Balder is the name of the favourite of Odin's sons—the gods who with him constitute the Teutonic Pantheon. How these names of honour became general is easily understood. The relatives of the primitive kings—the grandees described by Selden as having names formed on those of the gods, and shown by this to be members of the divine race—necessarily shared in the epithets, such as *Lord*, descriptive of superhuman relationships and nature. Their ever-multiplying offspring inheriting these, gradually rendered them comparatively common. And then they came to be applied to every man of power: partly from the fact that, in these early days when men conceived divinity simply as a stronger kind of humanity, great persons could be called by divine epithets with but little exaggeration; partly from the fact that the unusually potent were apt to be considered as unrecognised or illegitimate descendants of "the strong, the destroyer, the powerful one;" and partly, also, from compliment and the desire to propitiate.

Progressively as superstition diminished, this last became the sole cause. And if we remember that it is the nature of compliment, as we daily hear it, to attribute more than is due—that in the constantly widening application of "esquire," in the perpetual repetition of "your honour" by the fawning Irishman, and in the use of the name "gentleman" to any coalheaver or dustman by the lower classes of London, we have current examples of the depreciation of titles consequent on compliment—and that in barbarous times, when the wish to propitiate was stronger than now, this effect must have been greater; we shall see that there naturally arose an extensive misuse of all early distinctions. Hence the facts, that the Jews called Herod a god; that *Father*, in its higher sense, was a term used among them by servants to masters; that *Lord* was applicable to any person of worth and power. Hence, too, the fact that, in the later periods of the Roman Empire, every man saluted his neighbour as *Dominus* and *Rex*.

But it is in the titles of the middle ages, and in the growth of our modern ones out of them, that the process is most clearly seen. *Herr, Don, Signior, Seigneur, Sennor*, were all originally names of rulers—of feudal lords. By the complimentary use of these names to all who could, on any pretence, be supposed to merit them, and by successive degradations of them from each step in the descent to a still lower one, they have come to be common forms of address. At first the phrase in which a serf accosted his despotic chief, *mein herr* is now familiarly applied in Germany to ordinary people. The Spanish title *Don*, once proper to noblemen and gentlemen only, is now accorded to all classes. So, too, is it with *Signior* in Italy. *Seigneur* and *Monseigneur*, by contraction in *Sieur* and *Monsieur*, have produced the term of respect claimed by every Frenchman. And whether *Sire* be or be not a like contraction of *Signior*, it is clear that, as it was borne by sundry of the ancient feudal lords of France, who, as Selden says, "affected rather to bee stiled by the name of *Sire* than Baron, as *Le Sire de Montmorencie, Le Sire de Beauieu*, and the like," and as it has been commonly used to monarchs, our word *Sir*, which is derived from it, originally meant lord or king. Thus, too, is it with feminine titles. *Lady*, which, according to Horne Tooke, means *exalted*, and was at first given only to the few, is now given to all women of education. *Dame*, once an honourable name to which, in old books, we find the epithets of "high-born" and "stately" affixed, has now, by repeated widenings of its application, become relatively a term of contempt. And if we trace the compound of this, *ma Dame*, through its contractions—*Madam, ma'am, mam, mum*, we find that the "Yes'm" of Sally to her mistress is originally equivalent to "Yes, my exalted," or "Yes, your highness." Throughout, therefore, the genesis of words of honour has been the same. Just as with the Jews and with the Romans, has it been with the modern Europeans. Tracing these everyday names to their primitive significations of *lord* and *king*, and remembering that in aboriginal societies these were applied only to the gods and their descendants, we arrive at the conclusion that our familiar *Sir* and *Monsieur* are, in their primary and expanded meanings, terms of adoration.

Further to illustrate this gradual depreciation of titles and to confirm the inference drawn, it may be well to notice in passing, that the oldest of them have, as might be expected, been depreciated to the greatest extent. Thus, *Master*—a word proved by its derivation and by the similarity of the connate words in other languages (Fr., *maître* for *master*; Russ., *master*: Dan., *meester*; Ger., *meister*) to have been one of the earliest in use for expressing lordship—has now become applicable to children only, and under the modification of "Mister," to persons next above the labourer. Again, knighthood, the oldest kind of dignity, is also the lowest; and Knight Bachelor, which is the lowest order of knighthood, is more ancient than any other of the orders. Similarly, too, with the peerage, Baron is alike the earliest and least elevated of its divisions. This continual degradation of all names of honour has, from time to time, made it requisite to introduce new ones having that distinguishing effect which the originals had lost by generality of use; just as our habit of misapplying superlatives has, by gradually destroying their force, entailed the need for fresh ones. And if, within the last thousand years, this process has produced effects thus marked, we may readily conceive how, during previous thousands, the titles of gods and demi-gods came to be used to all persons exercising power; as they have since come to be used to persons of respectability.

If from names of honour we turn to phrases of honour, we find similar facts. The Oriental styles of address, applied to ordinary people—"I am your slave," "All I have is yours," "I am your sacrifice"—attribute to the individual spoken to the same greatness that *Monsieur* and *My Lord* do: they ascribe to him the character of an all-powerful ruler, so immeasurably superior to the speaker as to be his owner. So, likewise, with the Polish expressions of respect—"I throw myself under your feet," "I kiss your feet." In our now meaningless subscription to a formal letter—"Your most obedient servant,"—the same thing is visible. Nay, even in the familiar signature "Yours faithfully," the "yours," if interpreted as originally meant, is the expression of a slave to his master.

All these dead forms were once living embodiments of fact—were primarily the genuine indications of that submission to authority which they verbally assert; were afterwards naturally used by the weak and cowardly to propitiate those above them; gradually grew to be considered the due of such; and, by a continually wider misuse, have lost their meanings, as *Sir* and *Master* have done. That, like titles, they were in the beginning used only to the God-king, is indicated by the fact that, like titles, they were subsequently used in common to God and the king. Religious worship has ever largely consisted of professions of obedience, of being God's servants, of belonging to him to do what he will with. Like titles, therefore, these common phrases of honour had a devotional origin.

Perhaps, however, it is in the use of the word *you* as a singular pronoun that the popularising of what were once supreme distinctions is most markedly illustrated. This speaking of a single individual in the plural was originally an honour given only to the highest—was the reciprocal of the imperial "we" assumed by such. Yet now, by being applied to successively lower and lower classes, it has become all but universal. Only by one sect of Christians, and in a few secluded districts, is the primitive *thou* still used. And the *you*, in becoming common to all ranks, has simultaneously lost every vestige of the honour once attaching to it.

But the genesis of Manners out of forms of allegiance and worship is above all shown in men's modes of salutation. Note first the significance of the word. Among the Romans, the *salutatio* was a daily homage paid by clients and inferiors to superiors. This was alike the case with civilians and in the army. The very derivation of our word, therefore, is suggestive of submission. Passing to particular forms of obeisance (mark the word again), let us begin with the Eastern one of baring the feet. This was, primarily, a mark of reverence, alike to a god and a king. The act of Moses before the burning bush, and the practice of Mahometans, who are sworn on the Koran with their shoes off, exemplify the one employment of it; the custom of the Persians, who remove their shoes on entering the presence of their monarch, exemplifies the other. As usual, however, this homage, paid next to inferior rulers, has descended from grade to grade. In India, it is a common mark of respect; a polite man in Turkey always leaves his shoes at the door, while the lower orders of Turks never enter the presence of their superiors but in their stockings; and in Japan, this baring of the feet is an ordinary salutation of man to man.

Take another case. Selden, describing the ceremonies of the Romans, says:— "For whereas it was usual either to kiss the Images of their Gods, or adoring them, to stand somewhat off before them, solemnly moving the right hand to the lips, and then, casting it as if they had cast kisses, to turne the body on the same hand (which was the right forme of Adoration), it grew also by custom, first that the emperors, being next to Deities, and by some accounted as Deities, had the like done to them in acknowledgment of their Greatness." If, now, we call to mind the awkward salute of a village school-boy, made by putting his open hand up to his face and describing a semicircle with his forearm; and if we remember that the salute thus used as a form of reverence in country districts, is most likely a remnant of the feudal times; we shall see reason for thinking that our common wave of the hand to a friend across the street, represents what was primarily a devotional act.

Similarly have originated all forms of respect depending upon inclinations of the body. Entire prostration is the aboriginal sign of submission. The passage of Scripture, "Thou hast put all under his feet," and that other one, so suggestive in its anthropomorphism, "The Lord said unto my Lord, sit thou at my right hand, until I make thine enemies thy footstool," imply, what the Assyrian sculptures fully bear out, that it was the practice of the ancient god-kings of the East to trample upon the conquered. And when we bear in mind that there are existing savages who signify submission by placing the neck under the foot of the person submitted to, it becomes obvious that all prostration, especially when accompanied by kissing the foot, expressed a willingness to be trodden upon—was an attempt to mitigate wrath by saying, in signs, "Tread on me if you will." Remembering, further, that kissing the foot, as of the Pope and of a saint's statue, still continues in Europe to be a mark of extreme reverence; that prostration to feudal lords was once general; and that its disappearance must have taken place, not abruptly, but by gradual modification into something else; we have ground for deriving from these deepest of humiliations all inclinations of respect; especially as the transition is traceable. The reverence of a Russian serf, who bends his head to the ground, and the salaam of the Hindoo, are abridged prostrations; a bow is a short salaam; a nod is a short bow.

Should any hesitate to admit this conclusion, then perhaps, on being reminded that the lowest of these obeisances are common where the submission is most abject; that among ourselves the profundity of the bow marks the amount of respect; and lastly, that the bow is even now used devotionally in our churches—by Catholics to their altars, and by Protestants at the name of Christ—they will see sufficient evidence for thinking that this salutation also was originally worship.

The same may be said, too, of the curtsy, or courtesy, as it is otherwise written. Its derivation from *courtoisie*, courteousness, that is, behaviour like that at court, at once shows that it was primarily the reverence paid to a monarch. And if we call to mind that falling upon the knees, or upon one knee, has been a common obeisance of subjects to rulers; that in ancient manuscripts and tapestries, servants are depicted as assuming this attitude while offering the dishes to their masters at table; and that this same attitude is assumed towards our own queen at every presentation; we may infer, what the character of the curtsy itself suggests, that it is an abridged act of kneeling. As the word has been contracted from *courtoisie* into curtsy, so the motion has been contracted from a placing of the knee on the floor, to a lowering of the knee towards the floor. Moreover, when we compare the curtsy of a lady with the awkward one a peasant girl makes, which, if continued, would bring her down on both knees, we may see in this last a remnant of that greater reverence required of serfs. And when, from considering that simple kneeling of the West, still represented by the curtsy, we pass Eastward, and note the attitude of the Mahometan worshipper, who not only kneels but bows his head to the ground, we may infer that the curtsy also is an evanescent form of the aboriginal prostration.

In further evidence of this it may be remarked, that there has but recently disappeared from the salutations of men, an action having the same proximate derivation with the curtsy. That backward sweep of the foot with which the conventional stage-sailor accompanies his bow—a movement which prevailed generally in past generations, when "a bow and a scrape" went together, and which, within the memory of living persons, was made by boys to their schoolmaster with the effect of wearing a hole in the floor—is pretty clearly a preliminary to going on one knee. A motion so ungainly could never have been intentionally introduced; even if the artificial introduction of obeisances were possible. Hence we must regard it as the remnant of something antecedent: and that this something antecedent was humiliating may be inferred from the phrase, "scraping an acquaintance;" which, being used to denote the gaining of favour by obsequiousness, implies that the scrape was considered a mark of servility—that is, of *serf*-ility.

Consider, again, the uncovering of the head. Almost everywhere this has been a sign of reverence, alike in temples and before potentates; and it yet preserves among us some of its original meaning. Whether it rains, hails, or shines, you must keep your head bare while speaking to the monarch; and on no plea may you remain covered in a place of worship. As usual, however, this ceremony, at first a submission to gods and kings, has become in process of time a common civility. Once an acknowledgment of another's unlimited supremacy, the removal of the hat is now a salute accorded to very ordinary persons, and that uncovering, originally reserved for entrance into "the house of God," good manners now dictates on entrance into the house of a common labourer.

Standing, too, as a mark of respect, has undergone like extensions in its application. Shown, by the practice in our churches, to be intermediate between the humiliation signified by kneeling and the self-respect which sitting implies, and used at courts as a form of homage when more active demonstrations of it have been made, this posture is now employed in daily life to show consideration; as seen alike in the attitude of a servant before a master, and in that rising which politeness prescribes on the entrance of a visitor.

Many other threads of evidence might have been woven into our argument. As, for example, the significant fact, that if we trace back our still existing law of primogeniture—if we consider it as displayed by Scottish clans, in which not only ownership but government devolved from the beginning on the eldest son of the eldest—if we look further back, and observe that the old titles of lordship, *Signor, Seigneur, Sennor, Sire, Sieur,* all originally mean, senior, or elder—if we go Eastward, and find that *Sheick* has a like derivation, and that the Oriental names for priests, as *Pir,* for instance, are literally interpreted *old man*—if we note in Hebrew records how primeval is the ascribed superiority of the first-born, how great the authority of elders, and how sacred the memory of patriarchs—and if, then, we remember that among divine titles are "Ancient of Days," and "Father of Gods and men;"—we see how completely these facts harmonise with the hypothesis, that the aboriginal god is the first man sufficiently great to become a tradition, the earliest whose power and deeds made him remembered; that hence antiquity unavoidably became associated with superiority, and age with nearness in blood to "the powerful one;" that so there naturally arose that domination of the eldest which characterises all history, and that theory of human degeneracy which even yet survives.

We might further dwell on the facts, that *Lord* signifies high-born, or, as the same root gives a word meaning heaven, possibly heaven-born; that, before it became common, *Sir* or *Sire,* as well as *Father,* was the distinction of a priest; that *worship,* originally worth-ship—a term of respect that has been used commonly, as well as to magistrates—is also our term for the act of attributing greatness or worth to the Deity; so that to ascribe worth-ship to a man is to worship him. We might make much of the evidence that all early governments are more or less distinctly theocratic; and that among ancient Eastern nations even the commonest forms and customs appear to have been influenced by religion. We might enforce our argument respecting the derivation of ceremonies, by tracing out the aboriginal obeisance made by putting dust on the head, which probably symbolises putting the head in the dust: by affiliating the practice prevailing among certain tribes, of doing another honour by presenting him with a portion of hair torn from the head—an act which seems tantamount to saying, "I am your slave;" by investigating the Oriental custom of giving to a visitor any object he speaks of admiringly, which is pretty clearly a carrying out of the compliment, "All I have is yours."

Without enlarging, however, on these and many minor facts, we venture to think that the evidence already assigned is sufficient to justify our position. Had the proofs been few or of one kind, little faith could have been placed in the inference. But numerous as they are, alike in the case of titles, in that of complimentary phrases, and in that of salutes—similar and simultaneous, too, as the process of depreciation has been in all of these; the evidences become strong by mutual confirmation. And when we recollect, also, that not only have the results of this process been visible in various nations and in all times, but that they are occurring among ourselves at the present moment, and that the causes assigned for previous depreciations may be seen daily working out other ones—when we recollect this, it becomes scarcely possible to doubt that the process has been as alleged; and that our ordinary words, acts, and phrases of civility were originally acknowledgments of submission to another's omnipotence.

Thus the general doctrine, that all kinds of government exercised over men were at first one government—that the political, the religious, and the ceremonial forms of control are divergent branches of a general and once indivisible control— begins to look tenable. When, with the above facts fresh in mind, we read primitive records, and find that "there were giants in those days"—when we remember that in Eastern traditions Nimrod, among others, figures in all the characters of giant king, and divinity—when we turn to the sculptures exhumed by Mr. Layard, and contemplating in them the effigies of kings driving over enemies, trampling on prisoners, and adored by prostrate slaves, then observe how their actions correspond to the primitive names for the divinity, "the strong," "the destroyer," "the powerful one"—when we find that the earliest temples were also the residences of the kings—and when, lastly, we discover that among races of men still living there are current superstitions analogous to those which old records and old buildings indicate; we begin to realise the probability of the hypothesis that has been set forth.

Going back, in imagination, to the remote era when men's theories of things were yet unformed; and conceiving to ourselves the conquering chief as dimly figured in ancient myths, and poems, and ruins; we may see that all rules of conduct whatever spring from his will. Alike legislator and judge, all quarrels among his subjects are decided by him; and his words become the Law. Awe of him is the incipient Religion; and his maxims furnish its first precepts. Submission is made to him in the forms he prescribes; and these give birth to Manners. From the first, time develops political allegiance and the administration of justice; from the second, the worship of a being whose personality becomes ever more vague, and the inculcation of precepts ever more abstract; from the third, forms of honour and the rules of etiquette.

In conformity with the law of evolution of all organised bodies, that general functions are gradually separated into the special functions constituting them, there have grown up in the social organism for the better performance of the governmental office, an apparatus of law-courts, judges, and barristers; a national church, with its bishops and priests; and a system of caste, titles, and ceremonies, administered by society at large. By the first, overt aggressions are cognised and punished; by the second, the disposition to commit such aggressions is in some degree checked; by the third, those minor breaches of good conduct, which the others do not notice, are denounced and chastised. Law and Religion control behaviour in its essentials: Manners control it in its details. For regulating those daily actions which are too numerous and too unimportant to be officially directed, there comes into play this subtler set of restraints. And when we consider what these restraints are—when we analyse the words, and phrases, and salutes employed, we see that in origin as in effect, the system is a setting up of temporary governments between all men who come in contact, for the purpose of better managing the intercourse between them.

From the proposition, that these several kinds of government are essentially one, both in genesis and function, may be deduced several important corollaries, directly bearing on our special topic.

Let us first notice, that there is not only a common origin and office for all forms of rule, but a common necessity for them. The aboriginal man, coming fresh from the killing of bears and from lying in ambush for his enemy, has, by the necessities of his condition, a nature requiring to be curbed in its every impulse. Alike in war and in the chase, his daily discipline has been that of sacrificing other creatures to his own needs and passions. His character, bequeathed to him by ancestors who led similar lives, is moulded by this discipline—is fitted to this existence. The unlimited selfishness, the love of inflicting pain, the blood-thirstiness, thus kept active, he brings with him into the social state. These dispositions put him in constant danger of conflict with his equally savage neighbour. In small things as in great, in words as in deeds, he is aggressive; and is hourly liable to the aggressions of others like natured. Only, therefore, by the most rigorous control exercised over all actions, can the primitive unions of men be maintained. There must be a ruler strong, remorseless, and of indomitable will; there must be a creed terrible in its threats to the disobedient; and there must be the most servile submission of all inferiors to superiors. The law must be cruel; the religion must be stern; the ceremonies must be strict.

The co-ordinate necessity for these several kinds of restraint might be largely illustrated from history were there space. Suffice it to point out, that where the civil power has been weak, the multiplication of thieves, assassins, and banditti, has indicated the approach of social dissolution; that when, from the corruptness of its ministry, religion has lost its influence, as it did just before the Flagellants appeared, the State has been endangered; and that the disregard of established social observances has ever been an accompaniment of political revolutions. Whoever doubts the necessity for a government of manners proportionate in strength to the co-existing political and religious governments, will be convinced on calling to mind that until recently even elaborate codes of behaviour failed to keep gentlemen from quarrelling in the streets and fighting duels in taverns; and on remembering further, that even now people exhibit at the doors of a theatre, where there is no ceremonial law to rule them, a degree of aggressiveness which would produce confusion if carried into social intercourse.

As might be expected, we find that, having a common origin and like general functions, these several controlling agencies act during each era with similar degrees of vigour. Under the Chinese despotism, stringent and multitudinous in its edicts and harsh in the enforcement of them, and associated with which there is an equally stern domestic despotism exercised by the eldest surviving male of the family, there exists a system of observances alike complicated and rigid. There is a tribunal of ceremonies. Previous to presentation at court, ambassadors pass many days in practising the required forms. Social intercourse is cumbered by endless compliments and obeisances. Class distinctions are strongly marked by badges. The chief regret on losing an only son is, that there will be no one to perform the sepulchral rites. And if there wants a definite measure of the respect paid to social ordinances, we have it in the torture to which ladies submit in having their feet crushed. In India, and indeed throughout the East, there exists a like connection between the pitiless tyranny of rulers, the dread terrors of immemorial creeds, and the rigid restraint of unchangeable customs: the caste regulations continue still unalterable; the fashions of clothes and furniture have remained the same for ages; suttees are so ancient as to be mentioned by Strabo and Diodorus Siculus; justice is still administered at the palace-gates as of old; in short, "every usage is a precept of religion and a maxim of jurisprudence."

A similar relationship of phenomena was exhibited in Europe during the Middle Ages. While all its governments were autocratic, while feudalism held sway, while the Church was unshorn of its power, while the criminal code was full of horrors and the hell of the popular creed full of terrors, the rules of behaviour were both more numerous and more carefully conformed to than now. Differences of dress marked divisions of rank. Men were limited by law to a certain width of shoe-toes; and no one below a specified degree might wear a cloak less than so many inches long. The symbols on banners and shields were carefully attended to. Heraldry was an important branch of knowledge. Precedence was strictly insisted on. And those various salutes of which we now use the abridgments were gone through in full. Even during our own last century, with its corrupt House of Commons and little-curbed monarchs, we may mark a correspondence of social formalities. Gentlemen were still distinguished from lower classes by dress; people sacrificed themselves to inconvenient requirements—as powder, hooped petticoats, and towering head-dresses; and children addressed their parents as *Sir* and *Madam*.

A further corollary naturally following this last, and almost, indeed, forming part of it, is, that these several kinds of government decrease in stringency at the same rate. Simultaneously with the decline in the influence of priesthoods, and in the fear of eternal torments—simultaneously with the mitigation of political tyranny, the growth of popular power, and the amelioration of criminal codes; has taken place that diminution of formalities and that fading of distinctive marks, now so observable. Looking at home, we may note that there is less attention to precedence than there used to be. No one in our day ends an interview with the phrase "your humble servant." The employment of the word *Sir*, once general in social intercourse, is at present considered bad breeding; and on the occasions calling for them, it is held vulgar to use the words "Your Majesty," or "Your Royal Highness," more than once in a conversation. People no longer formally drink each other's healths; and even the taking wine with each other at dinner has ceased to be fashionable. The taking-off of hats between gentlemen has been gradually falling into disuse. Even when the hat is removed, it is no longer swept out at arm's length, but is simply lifted. Hence the remark made upon us by foreigners, that we take off our hats less than any other nation in Europe—a remark that should be coupled with the other, that we are the freest nation in Europe.

As already implied, this association of facts is not accidental. These titles of address and modes of salutation, bearing about them, as they all do, something of that servility which marks their origin, become distasteful in proportion as men become more independent themselves, and sympathise more with the independence of others. The feeling which makes the modern gentleman tell the labourer standing bareheaded before him to put on his hat—the feeling which gives us a dislike to those who cringe and fawn—the feeling which makes us alike assert our own dignity and respect that of others—the feeling which thus leads us more and more to discountenance all forms and names which confess inferiority and submission; is the same feeling which resists despotic power and inaugurates popular government, denies the authority of the Church and establishes the right of private judgment.

A fourth fact, akin to the foregoing, is, that these several kinds of government not only decline together, but corrupt together. By the same process that a Court of Chancery becomes a place not for the administration of justice, but for the withholding of it—by the same process that a national church, from being an agency for moral control, comes to be merely a thing of formulas and tithes and bishoprics—by this same process do titles and ceremonies that once had a meaning and a power become empty forms.

Coats of arms which served to distinguish men in battle, now figure on the carriage panels of retired grocers. Once a badge of high military rank, the shoulder-knot has become, on the modern footman, a mark of servitude. The name Banneret, which once marked a partially-created Baron—a Baron who had passed his military "little go"—is now, under the modification of Baronet, applicable to any one favoured by wealth or interest or party feeling. Knighthood has so far ceased to be an honour, that men now honour themselves by declining it. The military dignity *Escuyer* has, in the modern Esquire, become a wholly unmilitary affix. Not only do titles, and phrases, and salutes cease to fulfil their original functions, but the whole apparatus of social forms tends to become useless for its original purpose—the facilitation of social intercourse. Those most learned in ceremonies, and most precise in the observance of them, are not always the best behaved; as those deepest read in creeds and scriptures are not therefore the most religious; nor those who have the clearest notions of legality and illegality, the most honest. Just as lawyers are of all men the least noted for probity; as cathedral towns have a lower moral character than most others; so, if Swift is to be believed, courtiers are "the most insignificant race of people that the island can afford, and with the smallest tincture of good manners."

But perhaps it is in that class of social observances comprehended under the term Fashion, which we must here discuss parenthetically, that this process of corruption is seen with the greatest distinctness. As contrasted with Manners, which dictate our minor acts in relation to other persons, Fashion dictates our minor acts in relation to ourselves. While the one prescribes that part of our deportment which directly affects our neighbours; the other prescribes that part of our deportment which is primarily personal, and in which our neighbours are concerned only as spectators. Thus distinguished as they are, however, the two have a common source. For while, as we have shown, Manners originate by imitation of the behaviour pursued *towards* the great; Fashion originates by imitation *of* the behaviour of the great. While the one has its derivation in the titles, phrases, and salutes used *to* those in power; the other is derived from the habits and appearances exhibited *by* those in power.

The Carrib mother who squeezes her child's head into a shape like that of the chief; the young savage who makes marks on himself similar to the scars carried by the warriors of his tribe (which is probably the origin of tattooing); the Highlander who adopts the plaid worn by the head of his clan; the courtiers who affect greyness, or limp, or cover their necks, in imitation of their king; and the people who ape the courtiers; are alike acting under a kind of government connate with that of Manners, and, like it too, primarily beneficial. For notwithstanding the numberless absurdities into which this copyism has led the people, from nose-rings to ear-rings, from painted faces to beauty-spots, from shaven heads to powdered wigs, from filed teeth and stained nails to bell-girdles, peaked shoes, and breeches stuffed with bran,—it must yet be concluded, that as the strong men, the successful men, the men of will, intelligence, and originality, who have got to the top, are, on the average, more likely to show judgment in their habits and tastes than the mass, the imitation of such is advantageous.

By and by, however, Fashion, corrupting like these other forms of rule, almost wholly ceases to be an imitation of the best, and becomes an imitation of quite other than the best. As those who take orders are not those having a special fitness for the priestly office, but those who see their way to a living by it; as legislators and public functionaries do not become such by virtue of their political insight and power to rule, but by virtue of birth, acreage, and class influence; so, the self-elected clique who set the fashion, gain this prerogative, not by their force of nature, their intellect, their higher worth or better taste, but gain it solely by their unchecked assumption. Among the initiated are to be found neither the noblest in rank, the chief in power, the best cultured, the most refined, nor those of greatest genius, wit, or beauty; and their reunions, so far from being superior to others, are noted for their inanity. Yet, by the example of these sham great, and not by that of the truly great, does society at large now regulate its goings and comings, its hours, its dress, its small usages. As a natural consequence, these have generally little or none of that suitableness which the theory of fashion implies they should have. But instead of a continual progress towards greater elegance and convenience, which might be expected to occur did people copy the ways of the really best, or follow their own ideas of propriety, we have a reign of mere whim, of unreason, of change for the sake of change, of wanton oscillations from either extreme to the other—a reign of usages without meaning, times without fitness, dress without taste. And thus life *à la mode*, instead of being life conducted in the most rational manner, is life regulated by spendthrifts and idlers, milliners and tailors, dandies and silly women.

To these several corollaries—that the various orders of control exercised over men have a common origin and a common function, are called out by co-ordinate necessities and co-exist in like stringency, decline together and corrupt together—it now only remains to add that they become needless together. Consequent as all kinds of government are upon the unfitness of the aboriginal man for social life; and diminishing in coerciveness as they all do in proportion as this unfitness diminishes; they must one and all come to an end as humanity acquires complete adaptation to its new conditions. That discipline of circumstances which has already wrought out such great changes in us, must go on eventually to work out yet greater ones. That daily curbing of the lower nature and culture of the higher, which out of cannibals and devil worshippers has evolved philanthropists, lovers of peace, and haters of superstition, cannot fail to evolve out of these, men as much superior to them as they are to their progenitors. The causes that have produced past modifications are still in action; must continue in action as long as there exists any incongruity between man's desires and the requirements of the social state; and must eventually make him organically fit for the social state. As it is now needless to forbid man-eating and Fetishism, so will it ultimately become needless to forbid murder, theft, and the minor offences of our criminal code. When human nature has grown into conformity with the moral law, there will need no judges and statute-books; when it spontaneously takes the right course in all things, as in some things it does already, prospects of future reward or punishment will not be wanted as incentives; and when fit behaviour has become instinctive, there will need no code of ceremonies to say how behaviour shall be regulated.

Thus, then, may be recognised the meaning, the naturalness, the necessity of those various eccentricities of reformers which we set out by describing. They are not accidental; they are not mere personal caprices, as people are apt to suppose. On the contrary, they are inevitable results of the law of relationship above illustrated. That community of genesis, function, and decay which all forms of restraint exhibit, is simply the obverse of the fact at first pointed out, that they have in two sentiments of human nature a common preserver and a common destroyer. Awe of power originates and cherishes them all: love of freedom undermines and periodically weakens them all. The one defends despotism and asserts the supremacy of laws, adheres to old creeds and supports ecclesiastical authority, pays respect to titles and conserves forms; the other, putting rectitude above legality, achieves periodical instalments of political liberty, inaugurates Protestantism and works out its consequences, ignores the senseless dictates of Fashion and emancipates men from dead customs.

To the true reformer no institution is sacred, no belief above criticism. Everything shall conform itself to equity and reason; nothing shall be saved by its prestige. Conceding to each man liberty to pursue his own ends and satisfy his own tastes, he demands for himself like liberty; and consents to no restrictions on this, save those which other men's equal claims involve. No matter whether it be an ordinance of one man, or an ordinance of all men, if it trenches on his legitimate sphere of action, he denies its validity. The tyranny that would impose on him a particular style of dress and a set mode of behaviour, he resists equally with the tyranny that would limit his buyings and sellings, or dictate his creed. Whether the regulation be formally made by a legislature, or informally made by society at large—whether the penalty for disobedience be imprisonment, or frowns and social ostracism, he sees to be a question of no moment. He will utter his belief notwithstanding the threatened punishment; he will break conventions spite of the petty persecutions that will be visited on him. Show him that his actions are inimical to his fellow-men, and he will pause. Prove that he is disregarding their legitimate claims—that he is doing what in the nature of things must produce unhappiness; and he will alter his course. But until you do this—until you demonstrate that his proceedings are essentially inconvenient or inelegant, essentially irrational, unjust, or ungenerous, he will persevere.

Some, indeed, argue that his conduct *is* unjust and ungenerous. They say that he has no right to annoy other people by his whims; that the gentleman to whom his letter comes with no "Esq." appended to the address, and the lady whose evening party he enters with gloveless hands, are vexed at what they consider his want of respect, or want of breeding; that thus his eccentricities cannot be indulged save at the expense of his neighbours' feelings; and that hence his nonconformity is in plain terms selfishness.

He answers that this position, if logically developed, would deprive men of all liberty whatever. Each must conform all his acts to the public taste, and not his own. The public taste on every point having been once ascertained, men's habits must thenceforth remain for ever fixed; seeing that no man can adopt other habits without sinning against the public taste, and giving people disagreeable feelings. Consequently, be it an era of pig-tails or high-heeled shoes, of starched ruffs or trunk-hose, all must continue to wear pig-tails, high-heeled shoes, starched ruffs, or trunk-hose to the crack of doom.

If it be still urged that he is not justified in breaking through others' forms that he may establish his own, and so sacrificing the wishes of many to the wishes of one, he replies that all religious and political changes might be negatived on like grounds. He asks whether Luther's sayings and doings were not extremely offensive to the mass of his contemporaries; whether the resistance of Hampden was not disgusting to the time-servers around him; whether every reformer has not shocked men's prejudices, and given immense displeasure by the opinions he uttered. The affirmative answer he follows up by demanding what right the reformer has, then, to utter these opinions; whether he is not sacrificing the feelings of many to the feelings of one; and so proves that, to be consistent, his antagonists must condemn not only all nonconformity in actions, but all nonconformity in thoughts.

His antagonists rejoin that *his* position, too, may be pushed to an absurdity. They argue that if a man may offend by the disregard of some forms, he may as legitimately do so by the disregard of all; and they inquire—Why should he not go out to dinner in a dirty shirt, and with an unshorn chin? Why should he not spit on the drawing-room carpet, and stretch his heels up to the mantle-shelf?

The convention-breaker answers, that to ask this, implies a confounding of two widely-different classes of actions—the actions that are *essentially* displeasurable to those around, with the actions that are but *incidentally* displeasurable to them. He whose skin is so unclean as to offend the nostrils of his neighbours, or he who talks so loudly as to disturb a whole room, may be justly complained of, and rightly excluded by society from its assemblies. But he who presents himself in a surtout in place of a dress-coat, or in brown trousers instead of black, gives offence not to men's senses, or their innate tastes, but merely to their prejudices, their bigotry of convention. It cannot be said that his costume is less elegant or less intrinsically appropriate than the one prescribed; seeing that a few hours earlier in the day it is admired. It is the implied rebellion, therefore, that annoys. How little the cause of quarrel has to do with the dress itself, is seen in the fact that a century ago black clothes would have been thought preposterous for hours of recreation, and that a few years hence some now forbidden style may be nearer the requirements of Fashion than the present one. Thus the reformer explains that it is not against the natural restraints, but against the artificial ones, that he protests; and that manifestly the fire of sneers and angry glances which he has to bear, is poured upon him because he will not bow down to the idol which society has set up.

Should he be asked how we are to distinguish between conduct that is *absolutely* disagreeable to others, and conduct that is *relatively* so, he answers, that they will distinguish themselves if men will let them. Actions intrinsically repugnant will ever be frowned upon, and must ever remain as exceptional as now. Actions not intrinsically repugnant will establish themselves as proper. No relaxation of customs will introduce the practice of going to a party in muddy boots, and with unwashed hands; for the dislike of dirt would·continue were Fashion abolished to-morrow. That love of approbation which now makes people so solicitous to be *en règle* would still exist—would still make them careful of their personal appearance—would still induce them to seek admiration by making themselves ornamental—would still cause them to respect the natural laws of good behaviour, as they now do the artificial ones. The change would simply be from a repulsive monotony to a picturesque variety. And if there be any regulations respecting which it is uncertain whether they are based on reality or on convention, experiment will soon decide, if due scope be allowed.

When at length the controversy comes round, as controversies often do, to the point whence it started, and the "party of order" repeat their charge against the rebel, that he is sacrificing the feelings of others to the gratification of his own wilfulness, he replies once for all that they cheat themselves by misstatements. He accuses them of being so despotic, that, not content with being masters over their own ways and habits, they would be masters over his also; and grumble because he will not let them. He merely asks the same freedom which they exercise; they, however, propose to regulate his course as well as their own—to cut and clip his mode of life into agreement with their approved pattern; and then charge him with wilfulness and selfishness, because he does not quietly submit! He warns them that he shall resist, nevertheless; and that he shall do so, not only for the assertion of his own independence, but for their good. He tells them that they are slaves, and know it not; that they are shackled, and kiss their chains; that they have lived all their days in prison, and complain at the walls being broken down. He says he must persevere, however, with a view to his own release; and in spite of their present expostulations, he prophesies that when they have recovered from the fright which the prospect of freedom produces, they will thank him for aiding in their emancipation.

Unamiable as seems this find-fault mood, offensive as is this defiant attitude, we must beware of overlooking the truths enunciated, in dislike of the advocacy. It is an unfortunate hindrance to all innovation, that in virtue of their very function, the innovators stand in a position of antagonism; and the disagreeable manners, and sayings, and doings, which this antagonism generates, are commonly associated with the doctrines promulgated. Quite forgetting that whether the thing attacked be good or bad, the combative spirit is necessarily repulsive; and quite forgetting that the toleration of abuses seems amiable merely from its passivity; the mass of men contract a bias against advanced views, and in favour of stationary ones, from intercourse with their respective adherents. "Conservatism," as Emerson says, "is debonnair and social; reform is individual and imperious." And this remains true, however vicious the system conserved, however righteous the reform to be effected. Nay, the indignation of the purists is usually extreme in proportion as the evils to be got rid of are great. The more urgent the required change, the more intemperate is the vehemence of its promoters. Let no one, then, confound with the principles of this social nonconformity the acerbity and the disagreeable self-assertion of those who first display it.

The most plausible objection raised against resistance to conventions, is grounded on its impolicy, considered even from the progressist's point of view. It is urged by many of the more liberal and intelligent—usually those who have themselves shown some independence of behaviour in earlier days—that to rebel in these small matters is to destroy your own power of helping on reform in greater matters. "If you show yourself eccentric in manners or dress, the world," they say, "will not listen to you. You will be considered as crotchety, and impracticable. The opinions you express on important subjects, which might have been treated with respect had you conformed on minor points, will now inevitably be put down among your singularities; and thus, by dissenting in trifles, you disable yourself from spreading dissent in essentials."

Only noting, as we pass, that this is one of those anticipations which bring about their own fulfilment—that it is because most who disapprove these conventions do not show their disapproval, that the few who do show it look eccentric—and that did all act out their convictions, no such inference as the above would be drawn, and no such evil would result;—noting this as we pass, we go on to reply that these social restraints, and forms, and requirements, are not small evils, but among the greatest. Estimate their sum total, and we doubt whether they would not exceed most others. Could we add up the trouble, the cost, the jealousies, vexations, misunderstandings, the loss of time and the loss of pleasure, which these conventions entail—could we clearly realise the extent to which we are all daily hampered by them, daily enslaved by them; we should perhaps come to the conclusion that the tyranny of Mrs. Grundy is worse than any other tyranny we suffer under. Let us look at a few of its hurtful results; beginning with those of minor importance.

It produces extravagance. The desire to be *comme il faut*, which underlies all conformities, whether of manners, dress, or styles of entertainment, is the desire which makes many a spendthrift and many a bankrupt. To "keep up appearances," to have a house in an approved quarter furnished in the latest taste, to give expensive dinners and crowded *soirées*, is an ambition forming the natural outcome of the conformist spirit. It is needless to enlarge on these follies: they have been satirised by hosts of writers, and in every drawing-room. All that here concerns us, is to point out that the respect for social observances, which men think so praiseworthy, has the same root with this effort to be fashionable in mode of living; and that, other things equal, the last cannot be diminished without the first being diminished also. If, now, we consider all that this extravagance entails—if we count up the robbed tradesmen, the stinted governesses, the ill-educated children, the fleeced relatives, who have to suffer from it—if we mark the anxiety and the many moral delinquencies which its perpetrators involve themselves in; we shall see that this regard for conventions is not quite so innocent as it looks.

Again, it decreases the amount of social intercourse. Passing over the reckless, and those who make a great display on speculation with the occasional result of getting on in the world to the exclusion of much better men, we come to the far larger class who, being prudent and honest enough not to exceed their means, and yet having a strong wish to be "respectable," are obliged to limit their entertainments to the smallest possible number; and that each of these may be turned to the greatest advantage in meeting the claims upon their hospitality, are induced to issue their invitations with little or no regard to the comfort or mutual fitness of their guests. A few inconveniently-large assemblies, made up of people mostly strange to each other or but distantly acquainted, and having scarcely any tastes in common, are made to serve in place of many small parties of friends intimate enough to have some bond of thought and sympathy. Thus the quantity of intercourse is diminished, and the quality deteriorated. Because it is the custom to make costly preparations and provide costly refreshments; and because it entails both less expense and less trouble to do this for many persons on a few occasions than for few persons on many occasions; the reunions of our less wealthy classes are rendered alike infrequent and tedious.

Let it be further observed, that the existing formalities of social intercourse drive away many who most need its refining influence: and drive them into injurious habits and associations. Not a few men, and not the least sensible men either, give up in disgust this going out to stately dinners, and stiff evening-parties;

and instead, seek society in clubs, and cigar-divans, and taverns. "I'm sick of this standing about in drawing-rooms, talking nonsense, and trying to look happy," will answer one of them when taxed with his desertion. "Why should I any longer waste time and money, and temper? Once I was ready enough to rush home from the office to dress; I sported embroidered shirts, submitted to tight boots, and cared nothing for tailors' and haberdashers' bills. I know better now. My patience lasted a good while; for though I found each night pass stupidly, I always hoped the next would make amends. But I'm undeceived. Cab-hire and kid gloves cost more than any evening party pays for; or rather—it is worth the cost of them to avoid the party. No, no; I'll no more of it. Why should I pay five shillings a time for the privilege of being bored?"

If, now, we consider that this very common mood tends towards billiard-rooms, towards long sittings over cigars and brandy-and-water, towards Evans's and the Coal Hole, towards every place where amusement may be had; it becomes a question whether these precise observances which hamper our set meetings, have not to answer for much of the prevalent dissoluteness. Men must have excitements of some kind or other; and if debarred from higher ones will fall back upon lower. It is not that those who thus take to irregular habits are essentially those of low tastes. Often it is quite the reverse. Among half a dozen intimate friends, abandoning formalities and sitting at ease round the fire, none will enter with greater enjoyment into the highest kind of social intercourse—the genuine communion of thought and feeling; and if the circle includes women of intelligence and refinement, so much the greater is their pleasure. It is because they will no longer be choked with the mere dry husks of conversation which society offers them, that they fly its assemblies, and seek those with whom they may have discourse that is at least real, though unpolished. The men who thus long for substantial mental sympathy, and will go where they can get it, are often, indeed, much better at the core than the men who are content with the inanities of gloved and scented party-goers—men who feel no need to come morally nearer to their fellow creatures than they can come while standing, tea-cup in hand, answering trifles with trifles; and who, by feeling no such need, prove themselves shallow-thoughted and cold-hearted.

It is true, that some who shun drawing-rooms do so from inability to bear the restraints prescribed by a genuine refinement, and that they would be greatly improved by being kept under these restraints. But it is not less true that, by adding to the legitimate restraints, which are based on convenience and a regard for others, a host of factitious restraints based only on convention, the refining discipline, which would else have been borne with benefit, is rendered unbearable, and so misses its end. Excess of government invariably defeats itself by driving away those to be governed. And if over all who desert its entertainments in disgust either at their emptiness or their formality, society thus loses its salutary influence—if such not only fail to receive that moral culture which the company of ladies, when rationally regulated, would give them, but, in default of other relaxation, are driven into habits and companionships which often end in gambling and drunkenness; must we not say that here, too, is an evil not to be passed over as insignificant?

Then consider what a blighting effect these multitudinous preparations and ceremonies have upon the pleasures they profess to subserve. Who, on calling to mind the occasions of his highest social enjoyments, does not find them to have been wholly informal, perhaps impromptu? How delightful a picnic of friends, who forget all observances save those dictated by good nature! How pleasant the little unpretended gatherings of book-societies, and the like; or those purely accidental meetings of a few people well known to each other! Then, indeed, we may see that "a man sharpeneth the countenance of his friend." Cheeks flush, and eyes sparkle. The witty grow brilliant, and even the dull are excited into saying good things. There is an overflow of topics; and the right thought, and the right words to put it in, spring up unsought. Grave alternates with gay: now serious converse, and now jokes, anecdotes, and playful raillery. Every one's best nature is shown, every one's best feelings are in pleasurable activity; and, for the time, life seems well worth having.

Go now and dress for some half-past eight dinner, or some ten o'clock "at home;" and present yourself in spotless attire, with every hair arranged to perfection. How great the difference! The enjoyment seems in the inverse ratio of the preparation. These figures, got up with such finish and precision, appear but half alive. They have frozen each other by their primness; and your faculties feel the numbing effects of the atmosphere the moment you enter it. All those thoughts, so nimble and so apt awhile since, have disappeared—have suddenly acquired a preternatural power of eluding you. If you venture a remark to your neighbour, there comes a trite rejoinder, and there it ends. No subject you can hit upon outlives half a dozen sentences. Nothing that is said excites any real interest in you; and you feel that all you say is listened to with apathy. By some strange magic, things that usually give pleasure seem to have lost all charm.

You have a taste for art. Weary of frivolous talk, you turn to the table, and find that the book of engravings and the portfolio of photographs are as flat as the conversation. You are fond of music. Yet the singing, good as it is, you hear with utter indifference; and say "Thank you" with a sense of being a profound hypocrite. Wholly at ease though you could be, for your own part, you find that your sympathies will not let you. You see young gentlemen feeling whether their ties are properly adjusted, looking vacantly round, and considering what they shall do next. You see ladies sitting disconsolately, waiting for some one to speak to them, and wishing they had the wherewith to occupy their fingers. You see the hostess standing about the doorway, keeping a factitious smile on her face, and racking her brain to find the requisite nothings with which to greet her guests as they enter. You see numberless traits of weariness and embarrassment; and, if you have any fellow-feeling, these cannot fail to produce a feeling of discomfort. The disorder is catching; and do what you will you cannot resist the general infection. You struggle against it; you make spasmodic efforts to be lively; but none of your sallies or your good stories do more than raise a simper or a forced laugh: intellect and feeling are alike asphyxiated. And when, at length, yielding to your disgust, you rush away, how great is the relief when you get into the fresh air, and see the stars! How you "Thank God, that's over!" and half resolve to avoid all such boredom for the future!

What, now, is the secret of this perpetual miscarriage and disappointment? Does not the fault lie with all these needless adjuncts—these elaborate dressings, these set forms, these expensive preparations, these many devices and arrangements that imply trouble and raise expectation? Who that has lived thirty years in the world has not discovered that Pleasure is coy; and must not be too directly pursued, but must be caught unawares? An air from a street-piano, heard while at work, will often gratify more than the choicest music played at a concert by the most accomplished musicians. A single good picture seen in a dealer's window, may give keener enjoyment than a whole exhibition gone through with catalogue and pencil. By the time we have got ready our elaborate apparatus by which to secure happiness, the happiness is gone. It is too subtle to be contained in these receivers, garnished with compliments, and fenced round with etiquette. The more we multiply and complicate appliances, the more certain are we to drive it away.

The reason is patent enough. These higher emotions to which social intercourse ministers, are of extremely complex nature; they consequently depend for their production upon very numerous conditions; the more numerous the conditions, the greater the liability that one or other of them will be disturbed, and the emotions consequently prevented. It takes a considerable misfortune to destroy appetite; but cordial sympathy with those around may be extinguished by a look or a word. Hence it follows, that the more multiplied the *unnecessary* requirements with which social intercourse is surrounded, the less likely are its pleasures to be achieved. It is difficult enough to fulfil continuously all the *essentials* to a pleasurable communion with others: how much more difficult, then, must it be continuously to fulfil a host of *non-essentials* also! It is, indeed, impossible. The attempt inevitably ends in the sacrifice of the first to the last—the essentials to the non-essentials. What chance is there of getting any genuine response from the lady who is thinking of your stupidity in taking her in to dinner on the wrong arm? How are you likely to have agreeable converse with the gentleman who is fuming internally because he is not placed next to the hostess? Formalities, familiar as they may become, necessarily occupy attention—necessarily multiply the occasions for mistake, misunderstanding, and jealousy, on the part of one or other—necessarily distract all minds from the thoughts and feelings that should occupy them—necessarily, therefore, subvert those conditions under which only any sterling intercourse is to be had.

And this indeed is the fatal mischief which these conventions entail—a mischief to which every other is secondary. They destroy those highest of our pleasures which they profess to subserve. All institutions are alike in this, that however useful, and needful even, they originally were, they not only in the end cease to be so, but become detrimental. While humanity is growing, they continue fixed; daily get more mechanical and unvital; and by and by tend to strangle what they before preserved. It is not simply that they become corrupt and fail to act: they become obstructions. Old forms of government finally grow so oppressive, that they must be thrown off even at the risk of reigns of terror. Old creeds end in being dead formulas, which no longer aid but distort and arrest the general mind; while the State-churches administering them, come to be instruments for subsidising conservatism and repressing progress. Old schemes of education, incarnated in public schools and colleges, continue filling the heads of new generations with what has become relatively useless knowledge, and, by consequence, excluding knowledge which is useful. Not an organisation of any kind—political, religious, literary, philanthropic—but what, by its ever-multiplying regulations, its accumulating wealth, its yearly addition of officers, and the creeping into it of patronage and party feeling, eventually loses its original spirit, and sinks into a mere lifeless mechanism, worked with a view to private ends—a mechanism which not merely fails of its first purpose, but is a positive hindrance to it.

Thus is it, too, with social usages. We read of the Chinese that they have "ponderous ceremonies transmitted from time immemorial," which make social intercourse a burden. The court forms prescribed by monarchs for their own exaltation, have, in all times and places, ended in consuming the comfort of their lives. And so the artificial observances of the dining-room and saloon, in proportion as they are many and strict, extinguish that agreeable communion which they were originally intended to secure. The dislike with which people commonly speak of society that is "formal," and "stiff," and "ceremonious," implies the general recognition of this fact; and this recognition, logically developed, involves that all usages of behaviour which are not based on natural requirements, are injurious. That these conventions defeat their own ends is no new assertion. Swift, criticising the manners of his day, says—"Wise men are often more uneasy at the over-civility of these refiners than they could possibly be in the conversation of peasants and mechanics."

But it is not only in these details that the self-defeating action of our arrangements is traceable: it is traceable in the very substance and nature of them. Our social intercourse, as commonly managed, is a mere semblance of the reality sought. What is it that we want? Some sympathetic converse with our fellow-creatures: some converse that shall not be mere dead words, but the vehicle of living thoughts and feelings—converse in which the eyes and the face shall speak, and the tones of the voice be full of meaning—converse which shall make us feel no longer alone, but shall draw us closer to another, and double our own emotions by adding another's to them. Who is there that has not, from time to time, felt how cold and flat is all this talk about politics and science, and the new books and the new men, and how a genuine utterance of fellow-feeling outweighs the whole of it? Mark the words of Bacon:—"For a crowd is not a company, and faces are but a gallery of pictures, and talk but a tinkling cymbal, where there is no love."

If this be true, then it is only after acquaintance has grown into intimacy, and intimacy has ripened into friendship, that the real communion which men need becomes possible. A rationally-formed circle must consist almost wholly of those on terms of familiarity and regard, with but one or two strangers. What folly, then, underlies the whole system of our grand dinners, our "at homes," our evening parties—assemblages made up of many who never met before, many others who just bow to each other, many others who though familiar feel mutual indifference, with just a few real friends lost in the general mass! You need but look round at the artificial expressions of face, to see at once how it is. All have their disguises on; and how can there be sympathy between masks? No wonder that in private every one exclaims against the stupidity of these gatherings. No wonder that hostesses get them up rather because they must than because they wish. No wonder that the invited go less from the expectation of pleasure than from fear of giving offence. The whole thing is a gigantic mistake—an organised disappointment.

And then note, lastly, that in this case, as in all others, when an organisation has become effete and inoperative for its legitimate purpose, it is employed for quite other ones—quite opposite ones. What is the usual plea put in for giving and attending these tedious assemblies? "I admit that they are stupid and frivolous enough," replies every man to your criticisms; "but then, you know, one must keep up one's connections." And could you get from his wife a sincere answer, it would be—"Like you, I am sick of these frivolities; but then, we must get our daughters married." The one knows that there is a profession to push, a practice to gain, a business to extend: or parliamentary influence, or county patronage, or votes, or office, to be got: position, berths, favours, profit. The other's thoughts run upon husbands and settlements, wives and dowries. Worthless for their ostensible purpose of daily bringing human beings into pleasurable relations with each other, these cumbrous appliances of our social intercourse are now perseveringly kept in action with a view to the pecuniary and matrimonial results which they indirectly produce.

Who then shall say that the reform of our system of observances is unimportant? When we see how this system induces fashionable extravagance, with its entailed bankruptcy and ruin—when we mark how greatly it limits the amount of social intercourse among the less wealthy classes—when we find that many who most need to be disciplined by mixing with the refined are driven away by it, and led into dangerous and often fatal courses—when we count up the many minor evils it inflicts, the extra work which its costliness entails on all professional and mercantile men, the damage to public taste in dress and decoration by the setting up of its absurdities as standards for imitation, the injury to health indicated in the faces of its devotees at the close of the London season, the mortality of milliners and the like, which its sudden exigencies yearly involve;—and when to all these we add its fatal sin, that it blights, withers up, and kills, that high enjoyment it professedly ministers to—that enjoyment which is a chief end of our hard struggling in life to obtain—shall we not conclude that to reform our system of etiquette and fashion, is an aim yielding to few in urgency?

There needs, then, a protestantism in social usages. Forms that have ceased to facilitate and have become obstructive—whether political, religious, or other—have ever to be swept away; and eventually are so swept away in all cases. Signs are not wanting that some change is at hand. A host of satirists, led on by Thackeray, have been for years engaged in bringing our sham-festivities, and our fashionable follies, into contempt; and in their candid moods, most men laugh at the frivolities with which they and the world in general are deluded. Ridicule has always been a revolutionary agent. That which is habitually assailed with sneers and sarcasms cannot long survive. Institutions that have lost their roots in men's respect and faith are doomed; and the day of their dissolution is not far off. The time is approaching, then, when our system of social observances must pass through some crisis, out of which it will come purified and comparatively simple.

How this crisis will be brought about, no one can with any certainty say. Whether by the continuance and increase of individual protests, or whether by the union of many persons for the practice and propagation of some better system, the future alone can decide. The influence of dissentients acting without co-operation, seems, under the present state of things, inadequate. Standing severally alone, and having no well-defined views; frowned on by conformists, and expostulated with even by those who secretly sympathise with them; subject to petty persecutions, and unable to trace any benefit produced by their example; they are apt, one by one, to give up their attempts as hopeless. The young convention-breaker eventually finds that he pays too heavily for his nonconformity. Hating, for example, everything that bears about it any remnant of servility, he determines, in the ardour of his independence, that he will uncover to no one. But what he means simply as a general protest, he finds that ladies interpret into a personal disrespect. Though he sees that, from the days of chivalry downwards, these marks of supreme consideration paid to the other sex have been but a hypocritical counterpart to the actual subjection in which men have held them—a pretended submission to compensate for a real domination; and though he sees that when the true dignity of women is recognised, the mock dignities given to them will be abolished; yet he does not like to be thus misunderstood, and so hesitates in his practice.

In other cases, again, his courage fails him. Such of his unconventionalities as can be attributed only to eccentricity, he has no qualms about: for, on the whole, he feels rather complimented than otherwise in being considered a disregarder of public opinion. But when they are liable to be put down to ignorance, to ill-breeding, or to poverty, he becomes a coward. However clearly the recent innovation of eating some kinds of fish with knife and fork proves the fork-and-bread practice to have had little but caprice for its basis, yet he dares not wholly ignore that practice while fashion partially maintains it. Though he thinks that a silk handkerchief is quite as appropriate for drawing-room use as a white cambric one, he is not altogether at ease in acting out his opinion. Then, too, he begins to perceive that his resistance to prescription brings round disadvantageous results which he had not calculated upon. He had expected that it would save him from a great deal of social intercourse of a frivolous kind—that it would offend the fools, but not the sensible people; and so would serve as a self-acting test by which those worth knowing would be separated from those not worth knowing. But the fools prove to be so greatly in the majority that, by offending them, he closes against himself nearly all the avenues though which the sensible people are to be reached. Thus he finds, that his nonconformity is frequently misinterpreted; that there are but few directions in which he dares to carry it consistently out; that the annoyances and disadvantages which it brings upon him are greater than he anticipated; and that the chances of his doing any good are very remote. Hence he gradually loses resolution, and lapses, step by step, into the ordinary routine of observances.

Abortive as individual protests thus generally turn out, it may possibly be that nothing effectual will be done until there arises some organised resistance to this invisible despotism, by which our modes and habits are dictated. It may happen, that the government of Manners and Fashion will be rendered less tyrannical, as the political and religious governments have been, by some antagonistic union. Alike in Church and State, men's first emancipations from excess of restriction were achieved by numbers, bound together by a common creed or a common political faith. What remained undone while there were but individual schismatics or rebels, was effected when there came to be many acting in concert. It is tolerably clear that these earliest instalments of freedom could not have been obtained in any other way; for so long as the feeling of personal independence was weak and the rule strong, there could never have been a sufficient number of separate dissentients to produce the desired results. Only in these later times, during which the secular and spiritual controls have been growing less coercive, and the tendency towards individual liberty greater, has it become possible for smaller and smaller sects and parties to fight against established creeds and laws; until now men may safely stand even alone in their antagonism.

The failure of individual nonconformity to customs, as above illustrated, suggests that an analogous series of changes may have to be gone through in this case also. It is true that the *lex non scripta* differs from the *lex scripta* in this, that, being unwritten, it is more readily altered; and that it has, from time to time, been quietly ameliorated. Nevertheless, we shall find that the analogy holds substantially good. For in this case, as in the others, the essential revolution is not the substituting of any one set of restraints for any other, but the limiting or abolishing the authority which prescribes restraints. Just as the fundamental change inaugurated by the Reformation was not a superseding of one creed by another, but an ignoring of the arbiter who before dictated creeds—just as the fundamental change which Democracy long ago commenced, was not from this particular law to that, but from the despotism of one to the freedom of all; so, the parallel change yet to be wrought out in this supplementary government of which we are treating, is not the replacing of absurd usages by sensible ones, but the dethronement of that secret, irresponsible power which now imposes our usages, and the assertion of the right of all individuals to choose their own usages. In rules of living, a West-end clique is our Pope; and we are all papists, with but a mere sprinkling of heretics. On all who decisively rebel, comes down the penalty of excommunication, with its long catalogue of disagreeable and, indeed, serious consequences.

The liberty of the subject asserted in our constitution, and ever on the increase, has yet to be wrested from this subtler tyranny. The right of private judgment, which our ancestors wrung from the church, remains to be claimed from this dictator of our habits. Or, as before said, to free us from these idolatries and superstitious conformities, there has still to come a protestanism in social usages. Parallel, therefore, as is the change to be wrought out, it seems not improbable that it may be wrought out in an analogous way. That influence which solitary dissentients fail to gain, and that perseverance which they lack, may come into existence when they unite. That persecution which the world now visits upon them from mistaking their nonconformity for ignorance or disrespect, may diminish when it is seen to result from principle. The penalty which exclusion now entails may disappear when they become numerous enough to form visiting circles of their own. And when a successful stand has been made, and the brunt of the opposition has passed, that large amount of secret dislike to our observances which now pervades society, may manifest itself with sufficient power to effect the desired emancipation.

Whether such will be the process, time alone can decide. That community of origin, growth, supremacy, and decadence, which we have found among all kinds of government, suggests a community in modes of change also. On the other hand, Nature often performs substantially similar operations, in ways apparently different. Hence these details can never be foretold.

Meanwhile, let us glance at the conclusions that have been reached. On the one side, government, originally one, and afterwards subdivided for the better fulfilment of its function, must be considered as having ever been, in all its branches—political, religious, and ceremonial—beneficial; and, indeed, absolutely necessary. On the other side, government, under all its forms, must be regarded as subserving a temporary office, made needful by the unfitness of aboriginal humanity for social life; and the successive diminutions of its coerciveness in State, in Church, and in Custom, must be looked upon as steps towards its final disappearance. To complete the conception, there requires to be borne in mind the third fact, that the genesis, the maintenance, and the decline of all governments, however named, are alike brought about by the humanity to be controlled: from which may be drawn the inference that, on the average, restrictions of every kind cannot last much longer than they are wanted, and cannot be destroyed much faster than they ought to be.

Society, in all its developments, undergoes the process of exuviation. These old forms which it successively throws off, have all been once vitally united with it—have severally served as the protective envelopes within which a higher humanity was being evolved. They are cast aside only when they become hindrances—only when some inner and better envelope has been formed; and they bequeath to us all that there was in them good. The periodical abolitions of tyrannical laws have left the administration of justice not only uninjured, but purified. Dead and buried creeds have not carried with them the essential morality they contained, which still exists, uncontaminated by the sloughs of superstition. And all that there is of justice and kindness and beauty, embodied in our cumbrous forms of etiquette, will live perennially when the forms themselves have been forgotten.

ON THE GENESIS OF SCIENCE[17]

There has ever prevailed among men a vague notion that scientific knowledge differs in nature from ordinary knowledge. By the Greeks, with whom Mathematics—literally *things learnt*—was alone considered as knowledge proper, the distinction must have been strongly felt; and it has ever since maintained itself in the general mind. Though, considering the contrast between the achievements of science and those of daily unmethodic thinking, it is not surprising that such a distinction has been assumed; yet it needs but to rise a little above the common point of view, to see that no such distinction can really exist: or that at best, it is but a superficial distinction. The same faculties are employed in both cases; and in both cases their mode of operation is fundamentally the same.

If we say that science is organised knowledge, we are met by the truth that all knowledge is organised in a greater or less degree—that the commonest actions of the household and the field presuppose facts colligated, inferences drawn, results expected; and that the general success of these actions proves the data by which they were guided to have been correctly put together. If, again, we say that science is prevision—is a seeing beforehand—is a knowing in what times, places, combinations, or sequences, specified phenomena will be found; we are yet obliged to confess that the definition includes much that is utterly foreign to science in its ordinary acceptation. For example, a child's knowledge of an apple. This, as far as it goes, consists in previsions. When a child sees a certain form and colours, it knows that if it puts out its hand it will have certain impressions of resistance, and roundness, and smoothness; and if it bites, a certain taste. And manifestly its general acquaintance with surrounding objects is of like nature—is made up of facts concerning them, so grouped as that any part of a group being perceived, the existence of the other facts included in it is foreseen.

If, once more, we say that science is *exact* prevision, we still fail to establish the supposed difference. Not only do we find that much of what we call science is not exact, and that some of it, as physiology, can never become exact; but we find further, that many of the previsions constituting the common stock alike of wise and ignorant, *are* exact. That an unsupported body will fall; that a lighted candle will go out when immersed in water; that ice will melt when thrown on the fire— these, and many like predictions relating to the familiar properties of things have as high a degree of accuracy as predictions are capable of. It is true that the results predicated are of a very general character; but it is none the less true that they are rigorously correct as far as they go: and this is all that is requisite to fulfil the definition. There is perfect accordance between the anticipated phenomena and the

[17] *British Quarterly Review*, July 1854.

actual ones; and no more than this can be said of the highest achievements of the sciences specially characterised as exact.

Seeing thus that the assumed distinction between scientific knowledge and common knowledge is not logically justifiable; and yet feeling, as we must, that however impossible it may be to draw a line between them, the two are not practically identical; there arises the question—What is the relationship that exists between them? A partial answer to this question may be drawn from the illustrations just given. On reconsidering them, it will be observed that those portions of ordinary knowledge which are identical in character with scientific knowledge, comprehend only such combinations of phenomena as are directly cognisable by the senses, and are of simple, invariable nature. That the smoke from a fire which she is lighting will ascend, and that the fire will presently boil water, are previsions which the servant-girl makes equally well with the most learned physicist; they are equally certain, equally exact with his; but they are previsions concerning phenomena in constant and direct relation—phenomena that follow visibly and immediately after their antecedents—phenomena of which the causation is neither remote nor obscure—phenomena which may be predicted by the simplest possible act of reasoning.

If, now, we pass to the previsions constituting what is commonly known as science—that an eclipse of the moon will happen at a specified time; and when a barometer is taken to the top of a mountain of known height, the mercurial column will descend a stated number of inches; that the poles of a galvanic battery immersed in water will give off, the one an inflammable and the other an inflaming gas, in definite ratio—we perceive that the relations involved are not of a kind habitually presented to our senses; that they depend, some of them, upon special combinations of causes; and that in some of them the connection between antecedents and consequents is established only by an elaborate series of inferences. The broad distinction, therefore, between the two orders of knowledge, is not in their nature, but in their remoteness from perception.

If we regard the cases in their most general aspect, we see that the labourer, who, on hearing certain notes in the adjacent hedge, can describe the particular form and colours of the bird making them; and the astronomer, who, having calculated a transit of Venus, can delineate the black spot entering on the sun's disc, as it will appear through the telescope, at a specified hour; do essentially the same thing. Each knows that on fulfilling the requisite conditions, he shall have a preconceived impression—that after a definite series of actions will come a group of sensations of a foreknown kind. The difference, then, is not in the fundamental character of the mental acts; or in the correctness of the previsions accomplished by them; but in the complexity of the processes required to achieve the previsions. Much of our commonest knowledge is, as far as it goes, rigorously precise. Science does not increase this precision; cannot transcend it. What then does it do? It reduces other knowledge to the same degree of precision. That certainty which direct perception gives us respecting coexistences and sequences of the simplest and most accessible kind, science gives us respecting coexistences and sequences, complex in their dependencies or inaccessible to immediate observation. In brief, regarded from this point of view, science may be called *an extension of the perceptions by means of reasoning.*

On further considering the matter, however, it will perhaps be felt that this definition does not express the whole fact—that inseparable as science may be from common knowledge, and completely as we may fill up the gap between the simplest previsions of the child and the most recondite ones of the natural philosopher, by interposing a series of previsions in which the complexity of reasoning involved is greater and greater, there is yet a difference between the two beyond that which is here described. And this is true. But the difference is still not such as enables us to draw the assumed line of demarcation. It is a difference not between common knowledge and scientific knowledge; but between the successive phases of science itself, or knowledge itself—whichever we choose to call it. In its earlier phases science attains only to *certainty* of foreknowledge; in its later phases it further attains to *completeness.* We begin by discovering *a* relation: we end by discovering *the* relation. Our first achievement is to foretell the *kind* of phenomenon which will occur under specific conditions: our last achievement is to foretell not only the kind but the *amount.* Or, to reduce the proposition to its most definite form—undeveloped science is *qualitative* prevision: developed science is *quantitative* prevision.

This will at once be perceived to express the remaining distinction between the lower and the higher stages of positive knowledge. The prediction that a piece of lead will take more force to lift it than a piece of wood of equal size, exhibits certainty, but not completeness, of foresight. The kind of effect in which the one body will exceed the other is foreseen; but not the amount by which it will exceed. There is qualitative prevision only. On the other hand, the prediction that at a stated time two particular planets will be in conjunction; that by means of a lever having arms in a given ratio, a known force will raise just so many pounds; that to decompose a specified quantity of sulphate of iron by carbonate of soda will require so many grains—these predictions exhibit foreknowledge, not only of the nature of the effects to be produced, but of the magnitude, either of the effects themselves, of the agencies producing them, or of the distance in time or space at which they will be produced. There is not only qualitative but quantitative prevision.

And this is the unexpressed difference which leads us to consider certain orders of knowledge as especially scientific when contrasted with knowledge in general. Are the phenomena *measurable?* is the test which we unconsciously employ. Space is measurable: hence Geometry. Force and space are measureable: hence Statics. Time, force, and space are measureable: hence Dynamics. The invention of the barometer enabled men to extend the principles of mechanics to the atmosphere; and Aerostatics existed. When a thermometer was devised there arose a science of heat, which was before impossible. Such of our sensations as we have not yet found modes of measuring do not originate sciences. We have no science of smells; nor have we one of tastes. We have a science of the relations of sounds differing in pitch, because we have discovered a way to measure them; but we have no science of sounds in respect to their loudness or their *timbre,* because we have got no measures of loudness and *timbre.*

Obviously it is this reduction of the sensible phenomena it represents, to relations of magnitude, which gives to any division of knowledge its especially scientific character. Originally men's knowledge of weights and forces was in the same condition as their knowledge of smells and tastes is now—a knowledge not extending beyond that given by the unaided sensations; and it remained so until weighing instruments and dynamometers were invented. Before there were hour-glasses and clepsydras, most phenomena could be estimated as to their durations and intervals, with no greater precision than degrees of hardness can be estimated by the fingers. Until a thermometric scale was contrived, men's judgments respecting relative amounts of heat stood on the same footing with their present judgments respecting relative amounts of sound. And as in these initial stages, with no aids to observation, only the roughest comparisons of cases could be made, and only the most marked differences perceived; it is obvious that only the most simple laws of dependence could be ascertained—only those laws which, being uncomplicated with others, and not disturbed in their manifestations, required no niceties of observation to disentangle them. Whence it appears not only that in proportion as knowledge becomes quantitative do its previsions become complete as well as certain, but that until its assumption of a quantitative character it is necessarily confined to the most elementary relations.

Moreover it is to be remarked that while, on the one hand, we can discover the laws of the greater proportion of phenomena only by investigating them quantitatively; on the other hand we can extend the range of our quantitative previsions only as fast as we detect the laws of the results we predict. For clearly the ability to specify the magnitude of a result inaccessible to direct measurement, implies knowledge of its mode of dependence on something which can be measured—implies that we know the particular fact dealt with to be an instance of some more general fact. Thus the extent to which our quantitative previsions have been carried in any direction, indicates the depth to which our knowledge reaches in that direction. And here, as another aspect of the same fact, we may further observe that as we pass from qualitative to quantitative prevision, we pass from inductive science to deductive science. Science while purely inductive is purely qualitative: when inaccurately quantitative it usually consists of part induction, part deduction: and it becomes accurately quantitative only when wholly deductive. We do not mean that the deductive and the quantitative are coextensive; for there is manifestly much deduction that is qualitative only. We mean that all quantitative prevision is reached deductively; and that induction can achieve only qualitative prevision.

Still, however, it must not be supposed that these distinctions enable us to separate ordinary knowledge from science, much as they seem to do so. While they show in what consists the broad contrast between the extreme forms of the two, they yet lead us to recognise their essential identity; and once more prove the difference to be one of degree only. For, on the one hand, the commonest positive knowledge is to some extent quantitative; seeing that the amount of the foreseen result is known within certain wide limits. And, on the other hand, the highest quantitative prevision does not reach the exact truth, but only a very near approximation to it. Without clocks the savage knows that the day is longer in the summer than in the winter; without scales he knows that stone is heavier than flesh: that is, he can foresee respecting certain results that their amounts will exceed these, and be less than those—he knows *about* what they will be. And, with his most delicate instruments and most elaborate calculations, all that the man of science can do, is to reduce the difference between the foreseen and the actual results to an unimportant quantity.

Moreover, it must be borne in mind not only that all the sciences are qualitative in their first stages,—not only that some of them, as Chemistry, have but recently reached the quantitative stage—but that the most advanced sciences have attained to their present power of determining quantities not present to the senses, or not directly measurable, by a slow process of improvement extending through thousands of years. So that science and the knowledge of the uncultured are alike in the nature of their previsions, widely as they differ in range; they possess a common imperfection, though this is immensely greater in the last than in the first; and the transition from the one to the other has been through a series of steps by which the imperfection has been rendered continually less, and the range continually wider.

These facts, that science and the positive knowledge of the uncultured cannot be separated in nature, and that the one is but a perfected and extended form of the other, must necessarily underlie the whole theory of science, its progress, and the relations of its parts to each other. There must be serious incompleteness in any history of the sciences, which, leaving out of view the first steps of their genesis, commences with them only when they assume definite forms. There must be grave defects, if not a general untruth, in a philosophy of the sciences considered in their interdependence and development, which neglects the inquiry how they came to be distinct sciences, and how they were severally evolved out of the chaos of primitive ideas.

Not only a direct consideration of the matter, but all analogy, goes to show that in the earlier and simpler stages must be sought the key to all subsequent intricacies. The time was when the anatomy and physiology of the human being were studied by themselves—when the adult man was analysed and the relations of parts and of functions investigated, without reference either to the relations exhibited in the embryo or to the homologous relations existing in other creatures. Now, however, it has become manifest that no true conceptions, no true generalisations, are possible under such conditions. Anatomists and physiologists now find that the real natures of organs and tissues can be ascertained only by tracing their early evolution; and that the affinities between existing genera can be satisfactorily made out only by examining the fossil genera to which they are allied. Well, is it not clear that the like must be true concerning all things that undergo development? Is not science a growth? Has not science, too, its embryology? And must not the neglect of its embryology lead to a misunderstanding of the principles of its evolution and of its existing organisation?

There are *à priori* reasons, therefore, for doubting the truth of all philosophies of the sciences which tacitly proceed upon the common notion that scientific knowledge and ordinary knowledge are separate; instead of commencing, as they should, by affiliating the one upon the other, and showing how it gradually came to be distinguishable from the other. We may expect to find their generalisations essentially artificial; and we shall not be deceived. Some illustrations of this may here be fitly introduced, by way of preliminary to a brief sketch of the genesis of science from the point of view indicated. And we cannot more readily find such illustrations than by glancing at a few of the various *classifications* of the sciences that have from time to time been proposed. To consider all of them would take too much space: we must content ourselves with some of the latest.

Commencing with those which may be soonest disposed of, let us notice first the arrangement propounded by Oken. An abstract of it runs thus:—

> Part I.   MATHESIS.—*Pneumatogeny*: Primary Art, Primary Consciousness, God, Primary Rest, Time, Polarity, Motion, Man, Space, Point. Line, Surface, Globe, Rotation.—*Hylogeny*: Gravity, Matter, Ether, Heavenly Bodies, Light, Heat, Fire.

(He explains that MATHESIS is the doctrine of the whole; *Pneumatogeny* being the doctrine of immaterial totalities, and *Hylogeny* that of material totalities.)

> Part II.   ONTOLOGY.—*Cosmogeny*: Rest, Centre, Motion, Line, Planets, Form, Planetary System, Comets.—*Stöchiogeny*: Condensation, Simple Matter, Elements, Air, Water, Earth—*Stöchiology*: Functions of the Elements, etc., etc.—*Kingdoms of Nature*: Individuals.

(He says in explanation that "ONTOLOGY teaches us the phenomena of matter. The first of these are the heavenly bodies comprehended by *Cosmogeny*. These divide into elements—*Stöchiogeny*. The earth element divides into minerals—*Mineralogy*. These unite into one collective body—*Geogeny*. The whole in singulars is the living, or *Organic*, which again divides into plants and animals. *Biology*, therefore, divides into *Organogeny, Phytosophy, Zoosophy*.")

>   FIRST KINGDOM.—MINERALS. *Mineralogy, Geology*.

> Part III.   BIOLOGY.—*Organosophy, Phytogeny, Phyto-physiology, Phytology, Zoogeny, Physiology, Zoology, Psychology*.

A glance over this confused scheme shows that it is an attempt to classify knowledge, not after the order in which it has been, or may be, built up in the human consciousness; but after an assumed order of creation. It is a pseudo-scientific cosmogony, akin to those which men have enunciated from the earliest times downwards; and only a little more respectable. As such it will not be thought worthy of much consideration by those who, like ourselves, hold that experience is the sole origin of knowledge. Otherwise, it might have been needful to dwell on the incongruities of the arrangements—to ask how motion can be treated of before space? how there can be rotation without matter to rotate? how polarity can be dealt with without involving points and lines? But it will serve our present purpose just to point out a few of the extreme absurdities resulting from the doctrine which Oken seems to hold in common with Hegel, that "to philosophise on Nature is to re-think the great thought of Creation." Here is a sample:—

"Mathematics is the universal science; so also is Physio-philosophy, although it is only a part, or rather but a condition of the universe; both are one, or mutually congruent.

"Mathematics is, however, a science of mere forms without substance. Physio-philosophy is, therefore, *mathematics endowed with substance.*"

From the English point of view it is sufficiently amusing to find such a dogma not only gravely stated, but stated as an unquestionable truth. Here we see the experiences of quantitative relations which men have gathered from surrounding bodies and generalised (experiences which had been scarcely at all generalised at the beginning of the historic period)—we find these generalised experiences, these intellectual abstractions, elevated into concrete actualities, projected back into Nature, and considered as the internal framework of things—the skeleton by which matter is sustained. But this new form of the old realism is by no means the most startling of the physio-philosophic principles. We presently read that,

"The highest mathematical idea, or the fundamental principle of all mathematics is the zero = 0."....

"Zero is in itself nothing. Mathematics is based upon nothing, and, *consequently*, arises out of nothing.

"Out of nothing, *therefore*, it is possible for something to arise; for mathematics, consisting of propositions, is something, in relation to 0."

By such "consequentlys" and "therefores" it is, that men philosophise when they "re-think the great thought of Creation." By dogmas that pretend to be reasons, nothing is made to generate mathematics; and by clothing mathematics with matter, we have the universe! If now we deny, as we *do* deny, that the highest mathematical idea is the zero;—if, on the other hand, we assert, as we *do* assert, that the fundamental idea underlying all mathematics, is that of equality; the whole of Oken's cosmogony disappears. And here, indeed, we may see illustrated, the distinctive peculiarity of the German method of procedure in these matters— the bastard *à priori* method, as it may be termed. The legitimate *à priori* method sets out with propositions of which the negation is inconceivable; the *à priori* method as illegitimately applied, sets out either with propositions of which the negation is *not* inconceivable, or with propositions like Oken's, of which the *affirmation* is inconceivable.

It is needless to proceed further with the analysis; else might we detail the steps by which Oken arrives at the conclusions that "the planets are coagulated colours, for they are coagulated light; that the sphere is the expanded nothing;" that gravity is "a weighty nothing, a heavy essence, striving towards a centre;" that "the earth is the identical, water the indifferent, air the different; or the first the centre, the second the radius, the last the periphery of the general globe or of fire." To comment on them would be nearly as absurd as are the propositions themselves. Let us pass on to another of the German systems of knowledge—that of Hegel.

The simple fact that Hegel puts Jacob Bœhme on a par with Bacon, suffices alone to show that his standpoint is far remote from the one usually regarded as scientific: so far remote, indeed, that it is not easy to find any common basis on which to found a criticism. Those who hold that the mind is moulded into conformity with surrounding things by the agency of surrounding things, are necessarily at a loss how to deal with those, who, like Schelling and Hegel, assert that surrounding things are solidified mind—that Nature is "petrified intelligence." However, let us briefly glance at Hegel's classification. He divides philosophy into three parts:—

> 1.   *Logic*, or the science of the idea in itself, the pure idea.
>
> 2.   *The Philosophy of Nature*, or the science of the idea considered under its other form—of the idea as Nature.
>
> 3.   *The Philosophy of the Mind*, or the science of the idea in its return to itself.

Of these, the second is divided into the natural sciences, commonly so called; so that in its more detailed form the series runs thus:—Logic, Mechanics, Physics, Organic Physics, Psychology.

Now, if we believe with Hegel, first, that thought is the true essence of man; second, that thought is the essence of the world; and that, therefore, there is nothing but thought; his classification, beginning with the science of pure thought, may be acceptable. But otherwise, it is an obvious objection to his arrangement, that thought implies things thought of—that there can be no logical forms without the substance of experience—that the science of ideas and the science of things must have a simultaneous origin. Hegel, however, anticipates this objection, and, in his obstinate idealism, replies, that the contrary is true; that all contained in the forms, to become something, requires to be thought: and that logical forms are the foundations of all things.

It is not surprising that, starting from such premises, and reasoning after this fashion, Hegel finds his way to strange conclusions. Out of *space* and *time* he proceeds to build up *motion, matter, repulsion, attraction, weight*, and *inertia*. He then goes on to logically evolve the solar system. In doing this he widely diverges from the Newtonian theory; reaches by syllogism the conviction that the planets are the most perfect celestial bodies; and, not being able to bring the stars within his theory, says that they are mere formal existences and not living matter, and that as compared with the solar system they are as little admirable as a cutaneous eruption or a swarm of flies.[18]

Results so outrageous might be left as self-disproved, were it not that speculators of this class are not alarmed by any amount of incongruity with established beliefs. The only efficient mode of treating systems like this of Hegel, is to show that they are self-destructive—that by their first steps they ignore that authority on

---

[18] It is somewhat curious that the author of *The Plurality of Worlds*, with quite other aims, should have persuaded himself into similar conclusions.

which all their subsequent steps depend. If Hegel professes, as he manifestly does, to develop his scheme by reasoning—if he presents successive inferences as *necessarily following* from certain premises; he implies the postulate that a belief which necessarily follows after certain antecedents is a true belief: and, did an opponent reply to one of his inferences, that, though it was impossible to think the opposite, yet the opposite was true, he would consider the reply irrational. The procedure, however, which he would thus condemn as destructive of all thinking whatever, is just the procedure exhibited in the enunciation of his own first principles.

Mankind find themselves unable to conceive that there can be thought without things thought of. Hegel, however, asserts that there *can* be thought without things thought of. That ultimate test of a true proposition—the inability of the human mind to conceive the negation of it—which in all other cases he considers valid, he considers invalid where it suits his convenience to do so; and yet at the same time denies the right of an opponent to follow his example. If it is competent for him to posit dogmas, which are the direct negations of what human consciousness recognises; then is it also competent for his antagonists to stop him at every step in his argument by saying, that though the particular inference he is drawing seems to his mind, and to all minds, necessarily to follow from the premises, yet it is not true, but the contrary inference is true. Or, to state the dilemma in another form:—If he sets out with inconceivable propositions, then may he with equal propriety make all his succeeding propositions inconceivable ones—may at every step throughout his reasoning draw exactly the opposite conclusion to that which seems involved.

Hegel's mode of procedure being thus essentially suicidal, the Hegelian classification which depends upon it falls to the ground. Let us consider next that of M. Comte.

As all his readers must admit, M. Comte presents us with a scheme of the sciences which, unlike the foregoing ones, demands respectful consideration. Widely as we differ from him, we cheerfully bear witness to the largeness of his views, the clearness of his reasoning, and the value of his speculations as contributing to intellectual progress. Did we believe a serial arrangement of the sciences to be possible, that of M. Comte would certainly be the one we should adopt. His fundamental propositions are thoroughly intelligible; and if not true, have a great semblance of truth. His successive steps are logically co-ordinated; and he supports his conclusions by a considerable amount of evidence—evidence which, so long as it is not critically examined, or not met by counter evidence, seems to substantiate his positions. But it only needs to assume that antagonistic attitude which *ought* to be assumed towards new doctrines, in the belief that, if true, they will prosper by conquering objectors—it needs but to test his leading doctrines either by other facts than those he cites, or by his own facts differently applied, to at once show that they will not stand. We will proceed thus to deal with the general principle on which he bases his hierarchy of the sciences.

In the second chapter of his *Cours de Philosophic Positive*, M. Comte says:—"Our problem is, then, to find the one *rational* order, amongst a host of possible systems." ... "This order is determined by the degree of simplicity, or, what comes to the same thing, of generality of their phenomena." And the arrangement he deduces runs thus: *Mathematics, Astronomy, Physics, Chemistry, Physiology, Social Physics*. This he asserts to be "the true *filiation* of the sciences." He asserts further, that the principle of progression from a greater to a less degree of generality, "which gives this order to the whole body of science, arranges the parts of each science." And, finally, he asserts that the gradations thus established *à priori* among the sciences, and the parts of each science, "is in essential conformity with the order which has spontaneously taken place among the branches of natural philosophy;" or, in other words—corresponds with the order of historic development.

Let us compare these assertions with the facts. That there may be perfect fairness, let us make no choice, but take as the field for our comparison, the succeeding section treating of the first science—Mathematics; and let us use none but M. Comte's own facts, and his own admissions. Confining ourselves to this one science, of course our comparisons must be between its several parts. M. Comte says, that the parts of each science must be arranged in the order of their decreasing generality; and that this order of decreasing generality agrees with the order of historical development. Our inquiry must be, then, whether the history of mathematics confirms this statement.

Carrying out his principle, M. Comte divides Mathematics into "Abstract Mathematics, or the Calculus (taking the word in its most extended sense) and Concrete Mathematics, which is composed of General Geometry and of Rational Mechanics." The subject-matter of the first of these is *number*; the subject-matter of the second includes *space, time, motion, force*. The one possesses the highest possible degree of generality; for all things whatever admit of enumeration. The others are less general; seeing that there are endless phenomena that are not cognisable either by general geometry or rational mechanics. In conformity with the alleged law, therefore, the evolution of the calculus must throughout have preceded the evolution of the concrete sub-sciences. Now somewhat awkwardly for him, the first remark M. Comte makes bearing upon this point is, that "from an historical point of view, mathematical analysis *appears to have risen out of* the contemplation of geometrical and mechanical facts." True, he goes on to say that, "it is not the less independent of these sciences logically speaking;" for that "analytical ideas are, above all others, universal, abstract, and simple; and geometrical conceptions are necessarily founded on them."

We will not take advantage of this last passage to charge M. Comte with teaching, after the fashion of Hegel, that there can be thought without things thought of. We are content simply to compare the two assertions, that analysis arose out of the contemplation of geometrical and mechanical facts, and that geometrical conceptions are founded upon analytical ones. Literally interpreted they exactly cancel each other. Interpreted, however, in a liberal sense, they imply, what we believe to be demonstrable, that the two had *a simultaneous origin*. The passage is either nonsense, or it is an admission that abstract and concrete mathematics are coeval. Thus, at the very first step, the alleged congruity between the order of generality and the order of evolution does not hold good.

But may it not be that though abstract and concrete mathematics took their rise at the same time, the one afterwards developed more rapidly than the other; and has ever since remained in advance of it? No: and again we call M. Comte himself as witness. Fortunately for his argument he has said nothing respecting the early stages of the concrete and abstract divisions after their divergence from a common root; otherwise the advent of Algebra long after the Greek geometry had reached a high development, would have been an inconvenient fact for him to deal with. But passing over this, and limiting ourselves to his own statements, we find, at the opening of the next chapter, the admission, that "the historical development of the abstract portion of mathematical science has, since the time of Descartes, been for the most part *determined* by that of the concrete." Further on we read respecting algebraic functions that "most functions were concrete in their origin—even those which are at present the most purely abstract; and the ancients discovered only through geometrical definitions elementary algebraic properties of functions to which a numerical value was not attached till long afterwards, rendering abstract to us what was concrete to the old geometers." How do these statements tally with his doctrine? Again, having divided the calculus into algebraic and arithmetical, M. Comte admits, as perforce he must, that the algebraic is more general than the arithmetical; yet he will not say that algebra preceded arithmetic in point of time. And again, having divided the calculus of functions into the calculus of direct functions (common algebra) and the calculus of indirect functions (transcendental analysis), he is obliged to speak of this last as possessing a higher generality than the first; yet it is far more modern. Indeed, by implication, M. Comte himself confesses this incongruity; for he says:—"It might seem that the transcendental analysis ought to be studied before the ordinary, as it provides the equations which the other has to resolve; but though the transcendental *is logically independent of the ordinary*, it is best to follow the usual method of study, taking the ordinary first." In all these cases, then, as well as at the close of the section where he predicts that mathematicians will in time "create procedures of *a wider generality*", M. Comte makes admissions that are diametrically opposed to the alleged law.

In the succeeding chapters treating of the concrete department of mathematics, we find similar contradictions M. Comte himself names the geometry of the ancients *special* geometry, and that of moderns the *general* geometry. He admits that while "the ancients studied geometry with reference to the bodies under notice, or specially; the moderns study it with reference to the *phenomena* to be considered, or generally." He admits that while "the ancients extracted all they could out of one line or surface before passing to another," "the moderns, since Descartes, employ themselves on questions which relate to any figure whatever." These facts are the reverse of what, according to his theory, they should be. So, too, in mechanics. Before dividing it into statics and dynamics, M. Comte treats of the three laws of *motion*, and is obliged to do so; for statics, the more *general* of the two divisions, though it does not involve motion, is impossible as a science until the laws of motion are ascertained. Yet the laws of motion pertain to dynamics, the more *special* of the divisions. Further on he points out that after Archimedes, who discovered the law of equilibrium of the lever, statics made no progress until the establishment of dynamics enabled us to seek "the conditions of equilibrium through the laws of the composition of forces." And he adds—"At this day *this is the method univer-*

sally employed. At the first glance it does not appear the most rational—dynamics being more complicated than statics, and precedence being natural to the simpler. It would, in fact, be more philosophical to refer dynamics to statics, as has since been done." Sundry discoveries are afterwards detailed, showing how completely the development of statics has been achieved by considering its problems dynamically; and before the close of the section M. Comte remarks that "before hydrostatics could be comprehended under statics, it was necessary that the abstract theory of equilibrium should be made so general as to apply directly to fluids as well as solids. This was accomplished when Lagrange supplied, as the basis of the whole of rational mechanics, the single principle of virtual velocities." In which statement we have two facts directly at variance: with M. Comte's doctrine; first, that the simpler science, statics, reached its present development only by the aid of the principle of virtual velocities, which belongs to the more complex science, dynamics; and that this "single principle" underlying all rational mechanics—this *most general form* which includes alike the relations of statical, hydro-statical, and dynamical forces—was reached so late as the time of Lagrange.

Thus it is *not* true that the historical succession of the divisions of mathematics has corresponded with the order of decreasing generality. It is *not* true that abstract mathematics was evolved antecedently to, and independently of concrete mathematics. It is *not* true that of the subdivisions of abstract mathematics, the more general came before the more special. And it is *not* true that concrete mathematics, in either of its two sections, began with the most abstract and advanced to the less abstract truths.

It may be well to mention, parenthetically, that in defending his alleged law of progression from the general to the special, M. Comte somewhere comments upon the two meanings of the word *general*, and the resulting liability to confusion. Without now discussing whether the asserted distinction can be maintained in other cases, it is manifest that it does not exist here. In sundry of the instances above quoted, the endeavours made by M. Comte himself to disguise, or to explain away, the precedence of the special over the general, clearly indicate that the generality spoken of is of the kind meant by his formula. And it needs but a brief consideration of the matter to show that, even did he attempt it, he could not distinguish this generality, which, as above proved, frequently comes last, from the generality which he says always comes first. For what is the nature of that mental process by which objects, dimensions, weights, times, and the rest, are found capable of having their relations expressed numerically? It is the formation of certain abstract conceptions of unity, duality and multiplicity, which are applicable to all things alike. It is the invention of general symbols serving to express the numerical relations of entities, whatever be their special characters. And what is the nature of the mental process by which numbers are found capable of having their relations expressed algebraically? It is just the same. It is the formation of certain abstract conceptions of numerical functions which are the same whatever be the magnitudes of the numbers. It is the invention of general symbols serving to express the relations between numbers, as numbers express the relations between things. And transcendental analysis stands to algebra in the same position that algebra stands in to arithmetic.

To briefly illustrate their respective powers—arithmetic can express in one formula the value of a *particular* tangent to a *particular* curve; algebra can express in one formula the values of *all* tangents to a *particular* curve; transcendental analysis can express in one formula the values of *all* tangents to *all* curves. Just as arithmetic deals with the common properties of lines, areas, bulks, forces, periods; so does algebra deal with the common properties of the numbers which arithmetic presents; so does transcendental analysis deal with the common properties of the equations exhibited by algebra. Thus, the generality of the higher branches of the calculus, when compared with the lower, is the same kind of generality as that of the lower branches when compared with geometry or mechanics. And on examination it will be found that the like relation exists in the various other cases above given.

Having shown that M. Comte's alleged law of progression does not hold among the several parts of the same science, let us see how it agrees with the facts when applied to separate sciences. "Astronomy," says M. Comte, at the opening of Book III., "was a positive science, in its geometrical aspect, from the earliest days of the school of Alexandria; but Physics, which we are now to consider, had no positive character at all till Galileo made his great discoveries on the fall of heavy bodies." On this, our comment is simply that it is a misrepresentation based upon an arbitrary misuse of words—a mere verbal artifice. By choosing to exclude from terrestrial physics those laws of magnitude, motion, and position, which he includes in celestial physics, M. Comte makes it appear that the one owes nothing to the other. Not only is this altogether unwarrantable, but it is radically inconsistent with his own scheme of divisions. At the outset he says—and as the point is important we quote from the original—"Pour la *physique inorganique* nous voyons d'abord, en nous conformant toujours a l'ordre de généralité et de dépendance des phénomènes, qu'elle doit être partagée en deux sections distinctes, suivant qu'elle considère les phénomènes généraux de l'univers, ou, en particulier, ceux que présentent les corps terrestres. D'où la physique céleste, ou l'astronomie, soit géométrique, soit mechanique; et la physique terrestre."

Here then we have *inorganic physics* clearly divided into *celestial physics* and *terrestrial physics*—the phenomena presented by the universe, and the phenomena presented by earthly bodies. If now celestial bodies and terrestrial bodies exhibit sundry leading phenomena in common, as they do, how can the generalisation of these common phenomena be considered as pertaining to the one class rather than to the other? If inorganic physics includes geometry (which M. Comte has made it do by comprehending *geometrical* astronomy in its sub-section—celestial physics); and if its sub-section—terrestrial physics, treats of things having geometrical properties; how can the laws of geometrical relations be excluded from terrestrial physics? Clearly if celestial physics includes the geometry of objects in the heavens, terrestrial physics includes the geometry of objects on the earth. And if terrestrial physics includes terrestrial geometry, while celestial physics includes celestial geometry, then the geometrical part of terrestrial physics precedes the geometrical part of celestial physics; seeing that geometry gained its first ideas from surrounding objects. Until men had learnt geometrical relations from bodies on the earth, it was impossible for them to understand the geometrical relations of bodies in the heavens.

So, too, with celestial mechanics, which had terrestrial mechanics for its parent. The very conception of *force*, which underlies the whole of mechanical astronomy, is borrowed from our earthly experiences; and the leading laws of mechanical action as exhibited in scales, levers, projectiles, etc., had to be ascertained before the dynamics of the solar system could be entered upon. What were the laws made use of by Newton in working out his grand discovery? The law of falling bodies disclosed by Galileo; that of the composition of forces also disclosed by Galileo; and that of centrifugal force found out by Huyghens—all of them generalisations of terrestrial physics. Yet, with facts like these before him, M. Comte places astronomy before physics in order of evolution! He does not compare the geometrical parts of the two together, and the mechanical parts of the two together; for this would by no means suit his hypothesis. But he compares the geometrical part of the one with the mechanical part of the other, and so gives a semblance of truth to his position. He is led away by a verbal delusion. Had he confined his attention to the things and disregarded the words, he would have seen that before mankind scientifically co-ordinated *any one class of phenomena* displayed in the heavens, they had previously co-ordinated *a parallel class of phenomena* displayed upon the surface of the earth.

Were it needful we could fill a score pages with the incongruities of M. Comte's scheme. But the foregoing samples will suffice. So far is his law of evolution of the sciences from being tenable, that, by following his example, and arbitrarily ignoring one class of facts, it would be possible to present, with great plausibility, just the opposite generalisation to that which he enunciates. While he asserts that the rational order of the sciences, like the order of their historic development, "is determined by the degree of simplicity, or, what comes to the same thing, of generality of their phenomena;" it might contrariwise be asserted, that, commencing with the complex and the special, mankind have progressed step by step to a knowledge of greater simplicity and wider generality. So much evidence is there of this as to have drawn from Whewell, in his *History of the Inductive Sciences*, the general remark that "the reader has already seen repeatedly in the course of this history, complex and derivative principles presenting themselves to men's minds before simple and elementary ones."

Even from M. Comte's own work, numerous facts, admissions, and arguments, might be picked out, tending to show this. We have already quoted his words in proof that both abstract and concrete mathematics have progressed towards a higher degree of generality, and that he looks forward to a higher generality still. Just to strengthen this adverse hypothesis, let us take a further instance. From the *particular* case of the scales, the law of equilibrium of which was familiar to the earliest nations known, Archimedes advanced to the more *general* case of the unequal lever with unequal weights; the law of equilibrium of which *includes* that of the scales. By the help of Galileo's discovery concerning the composition of forces, D'Alembert "established, for the first time, the equations of equilibrium of *any* system of forces applied to the different points of a solid body"—equations which include all cases of levers and an infinity of cases besides. Clearly this is progress towards a higher generality—towards a knowledge more independent of special circumstances—towards a study of phenomena "the most disengaged from the incidents of particular cases;" which is M. Comte's definition of "the most simple phenomena." Does it not indeed follow from the familiarly admitted fact, that mental advance is from the concrete to the abstract, from the particular to the general, that the universal and therefore most simple truths are the last to be discovered? Is not the government of the solar system by a force varying inversely as the square of the distance, a simpler conception than any that preceded it? Should we ever succeed in reducing all orders of phenomena to some single law—say of atomic action, as M. Comte suggests—must not that law answer to his test of being *independent* of all others, and therefore most simple? And would not such a law generalise the phenomena of gravity, cohesion, atomic affinity, and electric repulsion, just as the laws of number generalise the quantitative phenomena of space, time, and force?

The possibility of saying so much in support of an hypothesis the very reverse of M. Comte's, at once proves that his generalisation is only a half-truth. The fact is, that neither proposition is correct by itself; and the actuality is expressed only by putting the two together. The progress of science is duplex: it is at once from the special to the general, and from the general to the special: it is analytical and synthetical at the same time.

M. Comte himself observes that the evolution of science has been accomplished by the division of labour; but he quite misstates the mode in which this division of labour has operated. As he describes it, it has simply been an arrangement of phenomena into classes, and the study of each class by itself. He does not recognise the constant effect of progress in each class upon *all* other classes; but only on the class succeeding it in his hierarchical scale. Or if he occasionally admits collateral influences and intercommunications, he does it so grudgingly, and so quickly puts the admissions out of sight and forgets them, as to leave the impression that, with but trifling exceptions, the sciences aid each other only in the order of their alleged succession. The fact is, however, that the division of labour in science, like the division of labour in society, and like the "physiological division of labour" in individual organisms, has been not only a specialisation of functions, but a continuous helping of each division by all the others, and of all by each. Every particular class of inquirers has, as it were, secreted its own particular order of truths from the general mass of material which observation accumulates; and all other classes of inquirers have made use of these truths as fast as they were elaborated, with the effect of enabling them the better to elaborate each its own order of truths.

It was thus in sundry of the cases we have quoted as at variance with M. Comte's doctrine. It was thus with the application of Huyghens's optical discovery to astronomical observation by Galileo. It was thus with the application of the isochronism of the pendulum to the making of instruments for measuring intervals, astronomical and other. It was thus when the discovery that the refraction and dispersion of light did not follow the same law of variation, affected both astronomy and physiology by giving us achromatic telescopes and microscopes. It was thus when Bradley's discovery of the aberration of light enabled him to make the first step towards ascertaining the motions of the stars. It was thus when Cavendish's torsion-balance experiment determined the specific gravity of the earth, and so gave a datum for calculating the specific gravities of the sun and planets. It was thus when tables of atmospheric refraction enabled observers to write down the real places of the heavenly bodies instead of their apparent places. It was thus when the discovery of the different expansibilities of metals by heat, gave us the means of correcting our chronometrical measurements of astronomical periods. It was thus when the lines of the prismatic spectrum were used to distinguish the heavenly bodies that are of like nature with the sun from those which are not. It was thus when, as recently, an electro-telegraphic instrument was invented for the more accurate registration of meridional transits. It was thus when the difference in the rates of a clock at the equator, and nearer the poles, gave data for calculating the oblateness of the earth, and accounting for the precession of the equinoxes. It was thus—but it is needless to continue.

Here, within our own limited knowledge of its history, we have named ten additional cases in which the single science of astronomy has owed its advance to sciences coming *after* it in M. Comte's series. Not only its secondary steps, but its greatest revolutions have been thus determined. Kepler could not have discovered his celebrated laws had it not been for Tycho Brahe's accurate observations; and it was only after some progress in physical and chemical science that the improved instruments with which those observations were made, became possible. The heliocentric theory of the solar system had to wait until the invention of the telescope before it could be finally established. Nay, even the grand discovery of all—the law of gravitation—depended for its proof upon an operation of physical science, the measurement of a degree on the Earth's surface. So completely indeed did it thus depend, that Newton *had actually abandoned his hypothesis* because the length of a degree, as then stated, brought out wrong results; and it was only after Picart's more exact measurement was published, that he returned to his calculations and proved his great generalisation. Now this constant intercommunion, which, for brevity's sake, we have illustrated in the case of one science only, has been taking place with all the sciences. Throughout the whole course of their evolution there has been a continuous *consensus* of the sciences—a *consensus* exhibiting a general correspondence with the *consensus* of faculties in each phase of mental development; the one being an objective registry of the subjective state of the other.

From our present point of view, then, it becomes obvious that the conception of a *serial* arrangement of the sciences is a vicious one. It is not simply that the schemes we have examined are untenable; but it is that the sciences cannot be rightly placed in any linear order whatever. It is not simply that, as M. Comte admits, a classification "will always involve something, if not arbitrary, at least artificial;" it is not, as he would have us believe, that, neglecting minor imperfections a classification may be substantially true; but it is that any grouping of the sciences in a succession gives a radically erroneous idea of their genesis and their dependencies. There is no "one *rational* order among a host of possible systems." There is no "true *filiation* of the sciences." The whole hypothesis is fundamentally false. Indeed, it needs but a glance at its origin to see at once how baseless it is. Why a *series*? What reason have we to suppose that the sciences admit of a *linear* arrangement? Where is our warrant for assuming that there is some *succession* in which they can be placed? There is no reason; no warrant. Whence then has arisen the supposition? To use M. Comte's own phraseology, we should say, it is a metaphysical conception. It adds another to the cases constantly occurring, of the human mind being made the measure of Nature. We are obliged to think in sequence; it is the law of our minds that we must consider subjects separately, one after another: *therefore* Nature must be serial—*therefore* the sciences must be classifiable in a succession. See here the birth of the notion, and the sole evidence of its truth. Men have been obliged when arranging in books their schemes of education and systems of knowledge, to choose *some* order or other. And from inquiring what is the best order, have naturally fallen into the belief that there is an order which truly represents the facts—have persevered in seeking such an order; quite overlooking the previous question whether it is likely that Nature has consulted the convenience of book-making.

For German philosophers, who hold that Nature is "petrified intelligence," and that logical forms are the foundations of all things, it is a consistent hypothesis that as thought is serial, Nature is serial; but that M. Comte, who is so bitter an opponent of all anthropomorphism, even in its most evanescent shapes, should have committed the mistake of imposing upon the external world an arrangement which so obviously springs from a limitation of the human consciousness, is somewhat strange. And it is the more strange when we call to mind how, at the outset, M. Comte remarks that in the beginning *"toutes les sciences sont cultivées simultanément par les mêmes esprits;"* that this is *"inevitable et même indispensable;"* and how he further remarks that the different sciences are *"comme les diverses branches d'un tronc unique."* Were it not accounted for by the distorting influence of a cherished hypothesis, it would be scarcely possible to understand how, after recognising truths like these, M. Comte should have persisted in attempting to construct *"une échelle encyclopédique."*

The metaphor which M. Comte has here so inconsistently used to express the relations of the sciences—branches of one trunk—is an approximation to the truth, though not the truth itself. It suggests the facts that the sciences had a common origin; that they have been developing simultaneously; and that they have been from time to time dividing and subdividing. But it does not suggest the yet more important fact, that the divisions and subdivisions thus arising do not remain separate, but now and again reunite in direct and indirect ways. They inosculate; they severally send off and receive connecting growths; and the intercommunion has been ever becoming more frequent, more intricate, more widely ramified. There has all along been higher specialisation, that there might be a larger generalisation; and a deeper analysis, that there might be a better synthesis. Each larger generalisation has lifted sundry specialisations still higher; and each better synthesis has prepared the way for still deeper analysis.

And here we may fitly enter upon the task awhile since indicated—a sketch of the Genesis of Science, regarded as a gradual outgrowth from common knowledge—an extension of the perceptions by the aid of the reason. We propose to treat it as a psychological process historically displayed; tracing at the same time the advance from qualitative to quantitative prevision; the progress from concrete facts to abstract facts, and the application of such abstract facts to the analysis of new orders of concrete facts; the simultaneous advance in generalisation and specialisation; the continually increasing subdivision and reunion of the sciences; and their constantly improving *consensus*.

To trace out scientific evolution from its deepest roots would, of course, involve a complete analysis of the mind. For as science is a development of that common knowledge acquired by the unaided senses and uncultured reason, so is that common knowledge itself gradually built up out of the simplest perceptions. We must, therefore, begin somewhere abruptly; and the most appropriate stage to take for our point of departure will be the adult mind of the savage.

Commencing thus, without a proper preliminary analysis, we are naturally somewhat at a loss how to present, in a satisfactory manner, those fundamental processes of thought out of which science ultimately originates. Perhaps our argument may be best initiated by the proposition, that all intelligent action whatever depends upon the discerning of distinctions among surrounding things. The condition under which only it is possible for any creature to obtain food and avoid danger is, that it shall be differently affected by different objects—that it shall be led to act in one way by one object, and in another way by another. In the lower orders of creatures this condition is fulfilled by means of an apparatus which acts automatically. In the higher orders the actions are partly automatic, partly conscious. And in man they are almost wholly conscious.

Throughout, however, there must necessarily exist a certain classification of things according to their properties—a classification which is either organically registered in the system, as in the inferior creation, or is formed by experience, as in ourselves. And it may be further remarked, that the extent to which this classification is carried, roughly indicates the height of intelligence—that while the lowest organisms are able to do little more than discriminate organic from inorganic matter; while the generality of animals carry their classifications no further than to a limited number of plants or creatures serving for food, a limited number of beasts of prey, and a limited number of places and materials; the most degraded of the human race possess a knowledge of the distinctive natures of a great variety of substances, plants, animals, tools, persons, etc., not only as classes but as individuals.

What now is the mental process by which classification is effected? Manifestly it is a recognition of the *likeness* or *unlikeness* of things, either in respect of their sizes, colours, forms, weights, textures, tastes, etc., or in respect of their modes of action. By some special mark, sound, or motion, the savage identifies a certain four-legged creature he sees, as one that is good for food, and to be caught in a particular way; or as one that is dangerous; and acts accordingly. He has classed together all the creatures that are *alike* in this particular. And manifestly in choosing the wood out of which to form his bow, the plant with which to poison his arrows, the bone from which to make his fish-hooks, he identifies them through their chief sensible properties as belonging to the general classes, wood, plant, and bone, but distinguishes them as belonging to sub-classes by virtue of certain properties in which they are *unlike* the rest of the general classes they belong to; and so forms genera and species.

And here it becomes manifest that not only is classification carried on by grouping together in the mind things that are *like*; but that classes and sub-classes are formed and arranged according to the *degrees of unlikeness*. Things widely contrasted are alone distinguished in the lower stages of mental evolution; as may be any day observed in an infant. And gradually as the powers of discrimination increase, the widely contrasted classes at first distinguished, come to be each divided into sub-classes, differing from each other less than the classes differ; and these sub-classes are again divided after the same manner. By the continuance of which process, things are gradually arranged into groups, the members of which are less and less *unlike*; ending, finally, in groups whose members differ only as individuals, and not specifically. And thus there tends ultimately to arise the notion of *complete likeness*. For, manifestly, it is impossible that groups should continue to be subdivided in virtue of smaller and smaller differences, without there being a simultaneous approximation to the notion of *no difference*.

Let us next notice that the recognition of likeness and unlikeness, which underlies classification, and out of which continued classification evolves the idea of complete likeness—let us next notice that it also underlies the process of *naming*, and by consequence *language*. For all language consists, at the beginning, of symbols which are as *like* to the things symbolised as it is practicable to make them. The language of signs is a means of conveying ideas by mimicking the actions or peculiarities of the things referred to. Verbal language is also, at the beginning, a mode of suggesting objects or acts by imitating the sounds which the objects make, or with which the acts are accompanied. Originally these two languages were used simultaneously. It needs but to watch the gesticulations with which the savage accompanies his speech—to see a Bushman or a Kaffir dramatising before an audience his mode of catching game—or to note the extreme paucity of words in all primitive vocabularies; to infer that at first, attitudes, gestures, and sounds, were all combined to produce as good a *likeness* as possible, of the things, animals, persons, or events described; and that as the sounds came to be understood by themselves the gestures fell into disuse: leaving traces, however, in the manners of the more excitable civilised races. But be this as it may, it suffices simply to observe, how many of the words current among barbarous peoples are like the sounds appertaining to the things signified; how many of our own oldest and simplest words have the same peculiarity; how children tend to invent imitative words; and how the sign-language spontaneously formed by deaf mutes is invariably based upon imitative actions—to at once see that the nation of *likeness* is that from which the nomenclature of objects takes its rise.

Were there space we might go on to point out how this law of life is traceable, not only in the origin but in the development of language; how in primitive tongues the plural is made by a duplication of the singular, which is a multiplication of the word to make it *like* the multiplicity of the things; how the use of metaphor—that prolific source of new words—is a suggesting of ideas that are *like* the ideas to be conveyed in some respect or other; and how, in the copious use of simile, fable, and allegory among uncivilised races, we see that complex conceptions, which there is yet no direct language for, are rendered, by presenting known conceptions more or less *like* them.

This view is further confirmed, and the predominance of this notion of likeness in primitive times further illustrated, by the fact that our system of presenting ideas to the eye originated after the same fashion. Writing and printing have descended from picture-language. The earliest mode of permanently registering a fact was by depicting it on a wall; that is—by exhibiting something as *like* to the thing to be remembered as it could be made. Gradually as the practice grew habitual and extensive, the most frequently repeated forms became fixed, and presently abbreviated; and, passing through the hieroglyphic and ideographic phases, the symbols lost all apparent relations to the things signified: just as the majority of our spoken words have done.

Observe again, that the same thing is true respecting the genesis of reasoning. The *likeness* that is perceived to exist between cases, is the essence of all early reasoning and of much of our present reasoning. The savage, having by experience discovered a relation between a certain object and a certain act, infers that the *like* relation will be found in future cases. And the expressions we constantly use in our arguments—"*analogy* implies," "the cases are not *parallel*," "by *parity* of reasoning," "there is no *similarity*,"—show how constantly the idea of likeness underlies our ratiocinative processes.

Still more clearly will this be seen on recognising the fact that there is a certain parallelism between reasoning and classification; that the two have a common root; and that neither can go on without the other. For on the one hand, it is a familiar truth that the attributing to a body in consequence of some of its properties, all those other properties in virtue of which it is referred to a particular class, is an act of inference. And, on the other hand, the forming of a generalisation is the putting together in one class all those cases which present like relations; while the drawing a deduction is essentially the perception that a particular case belongs to a certain class of cases previously generalised. So that as classification is a grouping together of *like things*; reasoning is a grouping together of *like relations* among things. Add to which, that while the perfection gradually achieved in classification consists in the formation of groups of *objects* which are *completely alike*; the perfection gradually achieved in reasoning consists in the formation of groups of *cases* which are *completely alike*.

Once more we may contemplate this dominant idea of likeness as exhibited in art. All art, civilised as well as savage, consists almost wholly in the making of objects *like* other objects; either as found in Nature, or as produced by previous art. If we trace back the varied art-products now existing, we find that at each stage the divergence from previous patterns is but small when compared with the agreement; and in the earliest art the persistency of imitation is yet more conspicuous. The old forms and ornaments and symbols were held sacred, and perpetually copied. Indeed, the strong imitative tendency notoriously displayed by the lowest human races, ensures among them a constant reproducing of likeness of things, forms, signs, sounds, actions, and whatever else is imitable; and we may even suspect that this aboriginal peculiarity is in some way connected with the culture and development of this general conception, which we have found so deep and widespread in its applications.

And now let us go on to consider how, by a further unfolding of this same fundamental notion, there is a gradual formation of the first germs of science. This idea of likeness which underlies classification, nomenclature, language spoken and written, reasoning, and art; and which plays so important a part because all acts of intelligence are made possible only by distinguishing among surrounding things, or grouping them into like and unlike;—this idea we shall find to be the one of which science is the especial product. Already during the stage we have been describing, there has existed *qualitative* prevision in respect to the commoner phenomena with which savage life is familiar; and we have now to inquire how the elements of *quantitative* prevision are evolved. We shall find that they originate by the perfecting of this same idea of likeness; that they have their rise in that conception of *complete likeness* which, as we have seen, necessarily results from the continued process of classification.

For when the process of classification has been carried as far as it is possible for the uncivilised to carry it—when the animal kingdom has been grouped not merely into quadrupeds, birds, fishes, and insects, but each of these divided into kinds—when there come to be sub-classes, in each of which the members differ only as individuals, and not specifically; it is clear that there must occur a frequent observation of objects which differ so little as to be indistinguishable. Among several creatures which the savage has killed and carried home, it must often happen that some one, which he wished to identify, is so exactly like another that he cannot tell which is which. Thus, then, there originates the notion of *equality*. The things which among ourselves are called *equal*—whether lines, angles, weights, temperatures, sounds or colours—are things which produce in us sensations that cannot be distinguished from each other. It is true we now apply the word *equal* chiefly to the separate phenomena which objects exhibit, and not to groups of phenomena; but this limitation of the idea has evidently arisen by subsequent analysis. And that the notion of equality did thus originate, will, we think, become obvious on remembering that as there were no artificial objects from which it could have been abstracted, it must have been abstracted from natural objects; and that the various families of the animal kingdom chiefly furnish those natural objects which display the requisite exactitude of likeness.

The same order of experiences out of which this general idea of equality is evolved, gives birth at the same time to a more complex idea of equality; or, rather, the process just described generates an idea of equality which further experience separates into two ideas—*equality of things* and *equality of relations*. While organic, and more especially animal forms, occasionally exhibit this perfection of likeness out of which the notion of simple equality arises, they more frequently exhibit only that kind of likeness which we call *similarity*; and which is really compound equality. For the similarity of two creatures of the same species but of different sizes, is of the same nature as the similarity of two geometrical figures. In either case, any two parts of the one bear the same ratio to one another as the homologous parts of the other. Given in any species, the proportions found to exist among the bones, and we may, and zoologists do, predict from any one, the dimensions of the rest; just as, when knowing the proportions subsisting among the parts of a geometrical figure, we may, from the length of one, calculate the others. And if, in the case of similar geometrical figures, the similarity can be established only by proving exactness of proportion among the homologous parts; if we express this relation between two parts in the one, and the corresponding parts in the other, by the formula A is to B as *a* is to *b*; if we otherwise write this, A to B = *a* to *b*; if, consequently, the fact we prove is that the relation of A to B *equals* the relation of *a* to *b*; then it is manifest that the fundamental conception of similarity is *equality of relations.*

With this explanation we shall be understood when we say that the notion of equality of relations is the basis of all exact reasoning. Already it has been shown that reasoning in general is a recognition of *likeness* of relations; and here we further find that while the notion of likeness of things ultimately evolves the idea of simple equality, the notion of likeness of relations evolves the idea of equality of relations: of which the one is the concrete germ of exact science, while the other is its abstract germ.

Those who cannot understand how the recognition of similarity in creatures of the same kind can have any alliance with reasoning, will get over the difficulty on remembering that the phenomena among which equality of relations is thus perceived, are phenomena of the same order and are present to the senses at the same time; while those among which developed reason perceives relations, are generally neither of the same order, nor simultaneously present. And if further, they will call to mind how Cuvier and Owen, from a single part of a creature, as a tooth, construct the rest by a process of reasoning based on this equality of relations, they will see that the two things are intimately connected, remote as they at first seem. But we anticipate. What it concerns us here to observe is, that from familiarity with organic forms there simultaneously arose the ideas of *simple equality,* and *equality of relations.*

At the same time, too, and out of the same mental processes, came the first distinct ideas of *number.* In the earliest stages, the presentation of several like objects produced merely an indefinite conception of multiplicity; as it still does among Australians, and Bushmen, and Damaras, when the number presented exceeds three or four. With such a fact before us we may safely infer that the first clear numerical conception was that of duality as contrasted with unity. And this notion of duality must necessarily have grown up side by side with those of likeness and equality; seeing that it is impossible to recognise the likeness of two things without also perceiving that there are two. From the very beginning the conception of number must have been as it is still, associated with the likeness or equality of the things numbered. If we analyse it, we find that simple enumeration is a registration of repeated impressions of any kind. That these may be capable of enumeration it is needful that they be more or less alike; and before any *absolutely true* numerical results can be reached, it is requisite that the units be *absolutely equal*. The only way in which we can establish a numerical relationship between things that do not yield us like impressions, is to divide them into parts that *do* yield us like impressions. Two unlike magnitudes of extension, force, time, weight, or what not, can have their relative amounts estimated only by means of some small unit that is contained many times in both; and even if we finally write down the greater one as a unit and the other as a fraction of it, we state, in the denominator of the fraction, the number of parts into which the unit must be divided to be comparable with the fraction.

It is, indeed, true, that by an evidently modern process of abstraction, we occasionally apply numbers to unequal units, as the furniture at a sale or the various animals on a farm, simply as so many separate entities; but no true result can be brought out by calculation with units of this order. And, indeed, it is the distinctive peculiarity of the calculus in general, that it proceeds on the hypothesis of that absolute equality of its abstract units, which no real units possess; and that the exactness of its results holds only in virtue of this hypothesis. The first ideas of number must necessarily then have been derived from like or equal magnitudes as seen chiefly in organic objects; and as the like magnitudes most frequently observed magnitudes of extension, it follows that geometry and arithmetic had a simultaneous origin.

Not only are the first distinct ideas of number co-ordinate with ideas of likeness and equality, but the first efforts at numeration displayed the same relationship. On reading the accounts of various savage tribes, we find that the method of counting by the fingers, still followed by many children, is the aboriginal method. Neglecting the several cases in which the ability to enumerate does not reach even to the number of fingers on one hand, there are many cases in which it does not extend beyond ten—the limit of the simple finger notation. The fact that in so many instances, remote, and seemingly unrelated nations, have adopted *ten* as their basic number; together with the fact that in the remaining instances the basic number is either *five* (the fingers of one hand) or *twenty* (the fingers and toes); almost of themselves show that the fingers were the original units of numeration. The still surviving use of the word *digit*, as the general name for a figure in arithmetic, is significant; and it is even said that our word *ten* (Sax. *tyn*; Dutch, *tien*; German, *zehn*) means in its primitive expanded form *two hands*. So that originally, to say there were ten things, was to say there were two hands of them.

From all which evidence it is tolerably clear that the earliest mode of conveying the idea of any number of things, was by holding up as many fingers as there were things; that is—using a symbol which was *equal*, in respect of multiplicity, to the group symbolised. For which inference there is, indeed, strong confirmation in the recent statement that our own soldiers are even now spontaneously adopting this device in their dealings with the Turks. And here it should be remarked that in this recombination of the notion of equality with that of multiplicity, by which the first steps in numeration are effected, we may see one of the earliest of those inosculations between the diverging branches of science, which are afterwards of perpetual occurrence.

Indeed, as this observation suggests, it will be well, before tracing the mode in which exact science finally emerges from the merely approximate judgments of the senses, and showing the non-serial evolution of its divisions, to note the non-serial character of those preliminary processes of which all after development is a continuation. On reconsidering them it will be seen that not only are they divergent growths from a common root, not only are they simultaneous in their progress; but that they are mutual aids; and that none can advance without the rest. That completeness of classification for which the unfolding of the perceptions paves the way, is impossible without a corresponding progress in language, by which greater varieties of objects are thinkable and expressible. On the one hand it is impossible to carry classification far without names by which to designate the classes; and on the other hand it is impossible to make language faster than things are classified.

Again, the multiplication of classes and the consequent narrowing of each class, itself involves a greater likeness among the things classed together; and the consequent approach towards the notion of complete likeness itself allows classification to be carried higher. Moreover, classification necessarily advances *pari passu* with rationality—the classification of *things* with the classification of *relations*. For things that belong to the same class are, by implication, things of which the properties and modes of behaviour—the co-existences and sequences—are more or less the same; and the recognition of this sameness of co-existences and sequences is reasoning. Whence it follows that the advance of classification is necessarily proportionate to the advance of generalisations. Yet further, the notion of *likeness*, both in things and relations, simultaneously evolves by one process of culture the ideas of *equality* of things and *equality* of relations; which are the respective bases of exact concrete reasoning and exact abstract reasoning—Mathematics and Logic. And once more, this idea of equality, in the very process of being formed, necessarily gives origin to two series of relations—those of magnitude and those of number: from which arise geometry and the calculus. Thus the process throughout is one of perpetual subdivision and perpetual intercommunication of the divisions. From the very first there has been that *consensus* of different kinds of knowledge, answering to the *consensus* of the intellectual faculties, which, as already said, must exist among the sciences.

Let us now go on to observe how, out of the notions of *equality* and *number*, as arrived at in the manner described, there gradually arose the elements of quantitative prevision.

Equality, once having come to be definitely conceived, was readily applicable to other phenomena than those of magnitude. Being predicable of all things producing indistinguishable impressions, there naturally grew up ideas of equality in weights, sounds, colours, etc.; and indeed it can scarcely be doubted that the occasional experience of equal weights, sounds, and colours, had a share in developing the abstract conception of equality—that the ideas of equality in size, relations, forces, resistances, and sensible properties in general, were evolved during the same period. But however this may be, it is clear that as fast as the notion of equality gained definiteness, so fast did that lowest kind of quantitative prevision which is achieved without any instrumental aid, become possible.

The ability to estimate, however roughly, the amount of a foreseen result, implies the conception that it will be *equal to* a certain imagined quantity; and the correctness of the estimate will manifestly depend upon the accuracy at which the perceptions of sensible equality have arrived. A savage with a piece of stone in his hand, and another piece lying before him of greater bulk of the same kind (a fact which he infers from the *equality* of the two in colour and texture) knows about what effort he must put forth to raise this other piece; and he judges accurately in proportion to the accuracy with which he perceives that the one is twice, three times, four times, etc., as large as the other; that is—in proportion to the precision of his ideas of equality and number. And here let us not omit to notice that even in these vaguest of quantitative previsions, the conception of *equality of relations* is also involved. For it is only in virtue of an undefined perception that the relation between bulk and weight in the one stone is *equal* to the relation between bulk and weight in the other, that even the roughest approximation can be made.

But how came the transition from those uncertain perceptions of equality which the unaided senses give, to the certain ones with which science deals? It came by placing the things compared in juxtaposition. Equality being predicated of things which give us indistinguishable impressions, and no accurate comparison of impressions being possible unless they occur in immediate succession, it results that exactness of equality is ascertainable in proportion to the closeness of the compared things. Hence the fact that when we wish to judge of two shades of colour whether they are alike or not, we place them side by side; hence the fact that we cannot, with any precision, say which of two allied sounds is the louder, or the higher in pitch, unless we hear the one immediately after the other; hence the fact that to estimate the ratio of weights, we take one in each hand, that we may compare their pressures by rapidly alternating in thought from the one to the other; hence the fact, that in a piece of music we can continue to make equal beats when the first beat has been given, but cannot ensure commencing with the same length of beat on a future occasion; and hence, lastly, the fact, that of all magnitudes, those of *linear extension* are those of which the equality is most accurately ascertainable, and those to which by consequence all others have to be reduced. For it is the peculiarity of linear extension that it alone allows its magnitudes to be placed in *absolute* juxtaposition, or, rather, in coincident position; it alone can test the equality of two magnitudes by observing whether they will coalesce, as two equal mathematical lines do, when placed between the same points; it alone can test *equality* by trying whether it will become *identity*. Hence, then, the fact, that all exact science is reducible, by an ultimate analysis, to results measured in equal units of linear extension.

Still it remains to be noticed in what manner this determination of equality by comparison of linear magnitudes originated. Once more may we perceive that surrounding natural objects supplied the needful lessons. From the beginning there must have been a constant experience of like things placed side by side—men standing and walking together; animals from the same herd; fish from the same shoal. And the ceaseless repetition of these experiences could not fail to suggest the observation, that the nearer together any objects were, the more visible became any inequality between them. Hence the obvious device of putting in apposition things of which it was desired to ascertain the relative magnitudes. Hence the idea of *measure*. And here we suddenly come upon a group of facts which afford a solid basis to the remainder of our argument; while they also furnish strong evidence in support of the foregoing speculations. Those who look sceptically on this attempted rehabilitation of the earliest epochs of mental development, and who more especially think that the derivation of so many primary notions from organic forms is somewhat strained, will perhaps see more probability in the several hypotheses that have been ventured, on discovering that all measures of *extension* and *force* originated from the lengths and weights of organic bodies; and all measures of *time* from the periodic phenomena of either organic or inorganic bodies.

Thus, among linear measures, the cubit of the Hebrews was the *length of the forearm* from the elbow to the end of the middle finger; and the smaller scriptural dimensions are expressed in *hand-breadths* and *spans*. The Egyptian cubit, which was similarly derived, was divided into digits, which were *finger-breadths*; and each finger-breadth was more definitely expressed as being equal to four *grains of barley* placed breadthwise. Other ancient measures were the orgyia or *stretch of the arms*, the *pace*, and the *palm*. So persistent has been the use of these natural units of length in the East, that even now some of the Arabs mete out cloth by the forearm. So, too, is it with European measures. The *foot* prevails as a dimension throughout Europe, and has done since the time of the Romans, by whom, also, it was used: its lengths in different places varying not much more than men's feet vary. The heights of horses are still expressed in *hands*. The inch is the length of the terminal joint of *the thumb*; as is clearly shown in France, where *pouce* means both thumb and inch. Then we have the inch divided into three *barley-corns*.

So completely, indeed, have these organic dimensions served as the substrata of all mensuration, that it is only by means of them that we can form any estimate of some of the ancient distances. For example, the length of a degree on the Earth's surface, as determined by the Arabian astronomers shortly after the death of Haroun-al-Raschid, was fifty-six of their miles. We know nothing of their mile further than that it was 4000 cubits; and whether these were sacred cubits or common cubits, would remain doubtful, but that the length of the cubit is given as twenty-seven inches, and each inch defined as the thickness of six barley-grains. Thus one of the earliest measurements of a degree comes down to us in barley-grains. Not only did organic lengths furnish those approximate measures which satisfied men's needs in ruder ages, but they furnished also the standard measures required in later times. One instance occurs in our own history. To remedy the irregularities then prevailing, Henry I. commanded that the ulna, or ancient ell, which answers to the modern yard, should be made of the exact length of *his own arm*.

Measures of weight again had a like derivation. Seeds seem commonly to have supplied the unit. The original of the carat used for weighing in India is *a small bean*. Our own systems, both troy and avoirdupois, are derived primarily from wheat-corns. Our smallest weight, the grain, is *a grain of wheat*. This is not a speculation; it is an historically registered fact. Henry III. enacted that an ounce should be the weight of 640 dry grains of wheat from the middle of the ear. And as all the other weights are multiples or sub-multiples of this, it follows that the grain of wheat is the basis of our scale. So natural is it to use organic bodies as weights, before artificial weights have been established, or where they are not to be had, that in some of the remoter parts of Ireland the people are said to be in the habit, even now, of putting a man into the scales to serve as a measure for heavy commodities.

Similarly with time. Astronomical periodicity, and the periodicity of animal and vegetable life, are simultaneously used in the first stages of progress for estimating epochs. The simplest unit of time, the day, nature supplies ready made. The next simplest period, the mooneth or month, is also thrust upon men's notice by the conspicuous changes constituting a lunation. For larger divisions than these, the phenomena of the seasons, and the chief events from time to time occurring, have been used by early and uncivilised races. Among the Egyptians the rising of the Nile served as a mark. The New Zealanders were found to begin their year from the reappearance of the Pleiades above the sea. One of the uses ascribed to birds, by the Greeks, was to indicate the seasons by their migrations. Barrow describes the aboriginal Hottentot as denoting periods by the number of moons before or after the ripening of one of his chief articles of food. He further states that the Kaffir chronology is kept by the moon, and is registered by notches on sticks—the death of a favourite chief, or the gaining of a victory, serving for a new era. By which last fact, we are at once reminded that in early history, events are commonly recorded as occurring in certain reigns, and in certain years of certain reigns: a proceeding which practically made a king's reign a measure of duration.

And, as further illustrating the tendency to divide time by natural phenomena and natural events, it may be noticed that even by our own peasantry the definite divisions of months and years are but little used; and that they habitually refer to occurrences as "before sheep-shearing," or "after harvest," or "about the time when the squire died." It is manifest, therefore, that the more or less equal periods perceived in Nature gave the first units of measure for time; as did Nature's more or less equal lengths and weights give the first units of measure for space and force.

It remains only to observe, as further illustrating the evolution of quantitative ideas after this manner, that measures of value were similarly derived. Barter, in one form or other, is found among all but the very lowest human races. It is obviously based upon the notion of *equality of worth*. And as it gradually merges into trade by the introduction of some kind of currency, we find that the *measures of worth*, constituting this currency, are organic bodies; in some cases *cowries*, in others *cocoa-nuts*, in others *cattle*, in others *pigs*; among the American Indians peltry or *skins*, and in Iceland *dried fish*.

Notions of exact equality and of measure having been reached, there came to be definite ideas of relative magnitudes as being multiples one of another; whence the practice of measurement by direct apposition of a measure. The determination of linear extensions by this process can scarcely be called science, though it is a step towards it; but the determination of lengths of time by an analogous process may be considered as one of the earliest samples of quantitative prevision. For when it is first ascertained that the moon completes the cycle of her changes in about thirty days—a fact known to most uncivilised tribes that can count beyond the number of their fingers—it is manifest that it becomes possible to say in what number of days any specified phase of the moon will recur; and it is also manifest that this prevision is effected by an opposition of two times, after the same manner that linear space is measured by the opposition of two lines. For to express the moon's period in days, is to say how many of these units of measure are contained in the period to be measured—is to ascertain the distance between two points in time by means of a *scale of days*, just as we ascertain the distance between two points in space by a scale of feet or inches: and in each case the scale coincides with the thing measured—mentally in the one; visibly in the other. So that in this simplest, and perhaps earliest case of quantitative prevision, the phenomena are not only thrust daily upon men's notice, but Nature is, as it were, perpetually repeating that process of measurement by observing which the prevision is effected. And thus there may be significance in the remark which some have made, that alike in Hebrew, Greek, and Latin, there is an affinity between the word meaning moon, and that meaning measure.

This fact, that in very early stages of social progress it is known that the moon goes through her changes in about thirty days, and that in about twelve moons the seasons return—this fact that chronological astronomy assumes a certain scientific character even before geometry does; while it is partly due to the circumstance that the astronomical divisions, day, month, and year, are ready made for us, is partly due to the further circumstances that agricultural and other operations were at first regulated astronomically, and that from the supposed divine nature of the heavenly bodies their motions determined the periodical religious festivals. As instances of the one we have the observation of the Egyptians, that the rising of the Nile corresponded with the heliacal rising of Sirius; the directions given by Hesiod for reaping and ploughing, according to the positions of the Pleiades; and his maxim that "fifty days after the turning of the sun is a seasonable time for beginning a voyage." As instances of the other, we have the naming of the days after the sun, moon, and planets; the early attempts among Eastern nations to regulate the calendar so that the gods might not be offended by the displacement of their sacrifices; and the fixing of the great annual festival of the Peruvians by the position of the sun. In all which facts we see that, at first, science was simply an appliance of religion and industry.

After the discoveries that a lunation occupies nearly thirty days, and that some twelve lunations occupy a year—discoveries of which there is no historical account, but which may be inferred as the earliest, from the fact that existing uncivilised races have made them—we come to the first known astronomical records, which are those of eclipses. The Chaldeans were able to predict these. "This they did, probably," says Dr. Whewell in his useful history, from which most of the materials we are about to use will be drawn, "by means of their cycle of 223 months, or about eighteen years; for at the end of this time, the eclipses of the moon begin to return, at the same intervals and in the same order as at the beginning." Now this method of calculating eclipses by means of a recurring cycle,—the *Saros* as they called it—is a more complex case of prevision by means of coincidence of measures. For by what observations must the Chaldeans have discovered this cycle? Obviously, as Delambre infers, by inspecting their registers; by comparing the successive intervals; by finding that some of the intervals were alike; by seeing that these equal intervals were eighteen years apart; by discovering that *all* the intervals that were eighteen years apart were equal; by ascertaining that the intervals formed a series which repeated itself, so that if one of the cycles of intervals were superposed on another the divisions would fit. This once perceived, and it manifestly became possible to use the cycle as a scale of time by which to measure out future periods. Seeing thus that the process of so predicting eclipses is in essence the same as that of predicting the moon's monthly changes, by observing the number of days after which they repeat—seeing that the two differ only in the extent and irregularity of the intervals, it is not difficult to understand how such an amount of knowledge should so early have been reached. And we shall be less surprised, on remembering that the only things involved in these previsions were *time* and *number*; and that the time was in a manner self-numbered.

Still, the ability to predict events recurring only after so long a period as eighteen years, implies a considerable advance in civilisation—a considerable development of general knowledge; and we have now to inquire what progress in other sciences accompanied, and was necessary to, these astronomical previsions. In the first place, there must clearly have been a tolerably efficient system of calculation. Mere finger-counting, mere head-reckoning, even with the aid of a regular decimal notation, could not have sufficed for numbering the days in a year; much less the years, months, and days between eclipses. Consequently there must have been a mode of registering numbers; probably even a system of numerals. The earliest numerical records, if we may judge by the practices of the less civilised races now existing, were probably kept by notches cut on sticks, or strokes marked on walls; much as public-house scores are kept now. And there seems reason to believe that the first numerals used were simply groups of straight strokes, as some of the still-extant Roman ones are; leading us to suspect that these groups of strokes were used to represent groups of fingers, as the groups of fingers had been used to represent groups of objects—a supposition quite in conformity with the aboriginal system of picture writing and its subsequent modifications. Be this so or not, however, it is manifest that before the Chaldeans discovered their *Saros*, there must have been both a set of written symbols serving for an extensive numeration, and a familiarity with the simpler rules of arithmetic.

Not only must abstract mathematics have made some progress, but concrete mathematics also. It is scarcely possible that the buildings belonging to this era should have been laid out and erected without any knowledge of geometry. At any rate, there must have existed that elementary geometry which deals with direct measurement—with the apposition of lines; and it seems that only after the discovery of those simple proceedings, by which right angles are drawn, and relative positions fixed, could so regular an architecture be executed. In the case of the other division of concrete mathematics—mechanics, we have definite evidence of progress. We know that the lever and the inclined plane were employed during this period: implying that there was a qualitative prevision of their effects, though not a quantitative one. But we know more. We read of weights in the earliest records; and we find weights in ruins of the highest antiquity. Weights imply scales, of which we have also mention; and scales involve the primary theorem of mechanics in its least complicated form—involve not a qualitative but a quantitative prevision of mechanical effects. And here we may notice how mechanics, in common with the other exact sciences, took its rise from the simplest application of the idea of *equality*. For the mechanical proposition which the scales involve, is, that if a lever with *equal* arms, have *equal* weights suspended from them, the weights will remain at *equal* altitudes. And we may further notice how, in this first step of rational mechanics, we see illustrated that truth awhile since referred to, that as magnitudes of linear extension are the only ones of which the equality is exactly ascertainable, the equalities of other magnitudes have at the outset to be determined by means of them. For the equality of the weights which balance each other in scales, wholly depends upon the equality of the arms: we can know that the weights are equal only by proving that the arms are equal. And when by this means we have obtained a system of weights,—a set of equal units of force, then does a science of mechanics become possible. Whence, indeed, it follows, that rational mechanics could not possibly have any other starting-point than the scales.

Let us further remember, that during this same period there was a limited knowledge of chemistry. The many arts which we know to have been carried on must have been impossible without a generalised experience of the modes in which certain bodies affect each other under special conditions. In metallurgy, which was extensively practised, this is abundantly illustrated. And we even have evidence that in some cases the knowledge possessed was, in a sense, quantitative. For, as we find by analysis that the hard alloy of which the Egyptians made their cutting tools, was composed of copper and tin in fixed proportions, there must have been an established prevision that such an alloy was to be obtained only by mixing them in these proportions. It is true, this was but a simple empirical generalisation; but so was the generalisation respecting the recurrence of eclipses; so are the first generalisations of every science.

Respecting the simultaneous advance of the sciences during this early epoch, it only remains to remark that even the most complex of them must have made some progress—perhaps even a greater relative progress than any of the rest. For under what conditions only were the foregoing developments possible? There first required an established and organised social system. A long continued registry of eclipses; the building of palaces; the use of scales; the practice of metallurgy—alike imply a fixed and populous nation. The existence of such a nation not only presupposes laws, and some administration of justice, which we know existed, but it presupposes successful laws—laws conforming in some degree to the conditions of social stability—laws enacted because it was seen that the actions forbidden by them were dangerous to the State. We do not by any means say that all, or even the greater part, of the laws were of this nature; but we do say, that the fundamental ones were. It cannot be denied that the laws affecting life and property were such. It cannot be denied that, however little these were enforced between class and class, they were to a considerable extent enforced between members of the same class. It can scarcely be questioned, that the administration of them between members of the same class was seen by rulers to be necessary for keeping their subjects together. And knowing, as we do, that, other things equal, nations prosper in proportion to the justness of their arrangements, we may fairly infer that the very cause of the advance of these earliest nations out of aboriginal barbarism was the greater recognition among them of the claims to life and property.

But supposition aside, it is clear that the habitual recognition of these claims in their laws implied some prevision of social phenomena. Even thus early there was a certain amount of social science. Nay, it may even be shown that there was a vague recognition of that fundamental principle on which all the true social science is based—the equal rights of all to the free exercise of their faculties. That same idea of *equality* which, as we have seen, underlies all other science, underlies also morals and sociology. The conception of justice, which is the primary one in morals; and the administration of justice, which is the vital condition of social existence; are impossible without the recognition of a certain likeness in men's claims in virtue of their common humanity. *Equity* literally means *equalness*; and if it be admitted that there were even the vaguest ideas of equity in these primitive eras, it must be admitted that there was some appreciation of the equalness of men's liberties to pursue the objects of life—some appreciation, therefore, of the essential principle of national equilibrium.

Thus in this initial stage of the positive sciences, before geometry had yet done more than evolve a few empirical rules—before mechanics had passed beyond its first theorem—before astronomy had advanced from its merely chronological phase into the geometrical; the most involved of the sciences had reached a certain degree of development—a development without which no progress in other sciences was possible.

Only noting as we pass, how, thus early, we may see that the progress of exact science was not only towards an increasing number of previsions, but towards previsions more accurately quantitative—how, in astronomy, the recurring period of the moon's motions was by and by more correctly ascertained to be nineteen years, or two hundred and thirty-five lunations; how Callipus further corrected this Metonic cycle, by leaving out a day at the end of every seventy-six years; and how these successive advances implied a longer continued registry of observations, and the co-ordination of a greater number of facts—let us go on to inquire how geometrical astronomy took its rise.

The first astronomical instrument was the gnomon. This was not only early in use in the East, but it was found also among the Mexicans; the sole astronomical observations of the Peruvians were made by it; and we read that 1100 B.C., the Chinese found that, at a certain place, the length of the sun's shadow, at the summer solstice, was to the height of the gnomon as one and a half to eight. Here again it is observable, not only that the instrument is found ready made, but that Nature is perpetually performing the process of measurement. Any fixed, erect object—a column, a dead palm, a pole, the angle of a building—serves for a gnomon; and it needs but to notice the changing position of the shadow it daily throws to make the first step in geometrical astronomy. How small this first step was, may be seen in the fact that the only things ascertained at the outset were the periods of the summer and winter solstices, which corresponded with the least and greatest lengths of the mid-shadow; and to fix which, it was needful merely to mark the point to which each day's shadow reached.

And now let it not be overlooked that in the observing at what time during the next year this extreme limit of the shadow was again reached, and in the inference that the sun had then arrived at the same turning point in his annual course, we have one of the simplest instances of that combined use of *equal magnitudes* and *equal relations*, by which all exact science, all quantitative prevision, is reached. For the relation observed was between the length of the sun's shadow and his position in the heavens; and the inference drawn was that when, next year, the extremity of his shadow came to the same point, he occupied the same place. That is, the ideas involved were, the equality of the shadows, and the equality of the relations between shadow and sun in successive years. As in the case of the scales, the equality of relations here recognised is of the simplest order. It is not as those habitually dealt with in the higher kinds of scientific reasoning, which answer to the general type—the relation between two and three equals the relation between six and nine; but it follows the type—the relation between two and three, equals the relation between two and three; it is a case of not simply *equal* relations, but *coinciding* relations. And here, indeed, we may see beautifully illustrated how the idea of equal relations takes its rise after the same manner that that of equal magnitude does. As already shown, the idea of equal magnitudes arose from the observed coincidence of two lengths placed together; and in this case we have not only two coincident lengths of shadows, but two coincident relations between sun and shadows.

From the use of the gnomon there naturally grew up the conception of angular measurements; and with the advance of geometrical conceptions there came the hemisphere of Berosus, the equinoctial armil, the solstitial armil, and the quadrant of Ptolemy—all of them employing shadows as indices of the sun's position, but in combination with angular divisions. It is obviously out of the question for us here to trace these details of progress. It must suffice to remark that in all of them we may see that notion of equality of relations of a more complex kind, which is best illustrated in the astrolabe, an instrument which consisted "of circular rims, movable one within the other, or about poles, and contained circles which were to be brought into the position of the ecliptic, and of a plane passing through the sun and the poles of the ecliptic"—an instrument, therefore, which represented, as by a model, the relative positions of certain imaginary lines and planes in the heavens; which was adjusted by putting these representative lines and planes into parallelism and coincidence with the celestial ones; and which depended for its use upon the perception that the relations between these representative lines and planes were *equal* to the relations between those represented.

Were there space, we might go on to point out how the conception of the heavens as a revolving hollow sphere, the discovery of the globular form of the earth, the explanation of the moon's phases, and indeed all the successive steps taken, involved this same mental process. But we must content ourselves with referring to the theory of eccentrics and epicycles, as a further marked illustration of it. As first suggested, and as proved by Hipparchus to afford an explanation of the leading irregularities in the celestial motions, this theory involved the perception that the progressions, retrogressions, and variations of velocity seen in the heavenly bodies, might be reconciled with their assumed uniform movement in circles, by supposing that the earth was not in the centre of their orbits; or by supposing that they revolved in circles whose centres revolved round the earth; or by both. The discovery that this would account for the appearances, was the discovery that in certain geometrical diagrams the relations were such, that the uniform motion of a point would, when looked at from a particular position, present analogous irregularities; and the calculations of Hipparchus involved the belief that the relations subsisting among these geometrical curves were *equal* to the relations subsisting among the celestial orbits.

Leaving here these details of astronomical progress, and the philosophy of it, let us observe how the relatively concrete science of geometrical astronomy, having been thus far helped forward by the development of geometry in general, reacted upon geometry, caused it also to advance, and was again assisted by it. Hipparchus, before making his solar and lunar tables, had to discover rules for calculating the relations between the sides and angles of triangles—*trigonometry* a subdivision of pure mathematics. Further, the reduction of the doctrine of the sphere to the quantitative form needed for astronomical purposes, required the formation of a *spherical trigonometry*, which was also achieved by Hipparchus. Thus both plane and spherical trigonometry, which are parts of the highly abstract and simple science of extension, remained undeveloped until the less abstract and more complex science of the celestial motions had need of them. The fact admitted by M. Comte, that since Descartes the progress of the abstract division of mathematics has been determined by that of the concrete division, is paralleled by the still more significant fact that even thus early the progress of mathematics was determined by that of astronomy.

And here, indeed, we may see exemplified the truth, which the subsequent history of science frequently illustrates, that before any more abstract division makes a further advance, some more concrete division must suggest the necessity for that advance—must present the new order of questions to be solved. Before astronomy presented Hipparchus with the problem of solar tables, there was nothing to raise the question of the relations between lines and angles; the subject-matter of trigonometry had not been conceived. And as there must be subject-matter before there can be investigation, it follows that the progress of the concrete divisions is as necessary to that of the abstract, as the progress of the abstract to that of the concrete.

Just incidentally noticing the circumstance that the epoch we are describing witnessed the evolution of algebra, a comparatively abstract division of mathematics, by the union of its less abstract divisions, geometry and arithmetic—a fact proved by the earliest extant samples of algebra, which are half algebraic, half geometric—we go on to observe that during the era in which mathematics and astronomy were thus advancing, rational mechanics made its second step; and something was done towards giving a quantitative form to hydrostatics, optics, and harmonics. In each case we shall see, as before, how the idea of equality underlies all quantitative prevision; and in what simple forms this idea is first applied.

As already shown, the first theorem established in mechanics was, that equal weights suspended from a lever with equal arms would remain in equilibrium. Archimedes discovered that a lever with unequal arms was in equilibrium when one weight was to its arm as the other arm to its weight; that is — when the numerical relation between one weight and its arm was *equal* to the numerical relation between the other arm and its weight.

The first advance made in hydrostatics, which we also owe to Archimedes, was the discovery that fluids press *equally* in all directions; and from this followed the solution of the problem of floating bodies: namely, that they are in equilibrium when the upward and downward pressures are *equal*.

In optics, again, the Greeks found that the angle of incidence is *equal* to the angle of reflection; and their knowledge reached no further than to such simple deductions from this as their geometry sufficed for. In harmonics they ascertained the fact that three strings of *equal* lengths would yield the octave, fifth and fourth, when strained by weights having certain definite ratios; and they did not progress much beyond this. In the one of which cases we see geometry used in elucidation of the laws of light; and in the other, geometry and arithmetic made to measure the phenomena of sound.

Did space permit, it would be desirable here to describe the state of the less advanced sciences — to point out how, while a few had thus reached the first stages of quantitative prevision, the rest were progressing in qualitative prevision — how some small generalisations were made respecting evaporation, and heat, and electricity, and magnetism, which, empirical as they were, did not in that respect differ from the first generalisations of every science — how the Greek physicians had made advances in physiology and pathology, which, considering the great imperfection of our present knowledge, are by no means to be despised — how zoology had been so far systematised by Aristotle, as, to some extent, enabled him from the presence of certain organs to predict the presence of others — how in Aristotle's *Politics* there is some progress towards a scientific conception of social phenomena, and sundry previsions respecting them — and how in the state of the Greek societies, as well as in the writings of Greek philosophers, we may recognise not only an increasing clearness in that conception of equity on which the social science is based, but also some appreciation of the fact that social stability depends upon the maintenance of equitable regulations. We might dwell at length upon the causes which retarded the development of some of the sciences, as, for example, chemistry; showing that relative complexity had nothing to do with it — that the oxidation of a piece of iron is a simpler phenomenon than the recurrence of eclipses, and the discovery of carbonic acid less difficult than that of the precession of the equinoxes — but that the relatively slow advance of chemical knowledge was due, partly to the fact that its phenomena were not daily thrust on men's notice as those of astronomy were; partly to the fact that Nature does not habitually supply the means, and suggest the modes of investigation, as in the sciences dealing with time, extension, and force; and partly to the fact that the great majority of the materials with which chemistry deals, instead of being ready to hand, are made known only by the arts in their slow growth; and partly to the fact that even when known, their chemical properties are not self-exhibited, but have to be sought out by experiment.

Merely indicating all these considerations, however, let us go on to contemplate the progress and mutual influence of the sciences in modern days; only parenthetically noticing how, on the revival of the scientific spirit, the successive stages achieved exhibit the dominance of the same law hitherto traced—how the primary idea in dynamics, a uniform force, was defined by Galileo to be a force which generates *equal* velocities in *equal* successive times—how the uniform action of gravity was first experimentally determined by showing that the time elapsing before a body thrown up, stopped, was *equal* to the time it took to fall—how the first fact in compound motion which Galileo ascertained was, that a body projected horizontally will have a uniform motion onwards and a uniformly accelerated motion downwards; that is, will describe *equal* horizontal spaces in *equal* times, compounded with *equal* vertical increments in *equal* times—how his discovery respecting the pendulum was, that its oscillations occupy *equal* intervals of time whatever their length—how the principle of virtual velocities which he established is, that in any machine the weights that balance each other are reciprocally as their virtual velocities; that is, the relation of one set of weights to their velocities *equals* the relation of the other set of velocities to their weights; and how thus his achievements consisted in showing the equalities of certain magnitudes and relations, whose equalities had not been previously recognised.

When mechanics had reached the point to which Galileo brought it—when the simple laws of force had been disentangled from the friction and atmospheric resistance by which all their earthly manifestations are disguised—when progressing knowledge of *physics* had given a due insight into these disturbing causes—when, by an effort of abstraction, it was perceived that all motion would be uniform and rectilinear unless interfered with by external forces—and when the various consequences of this perception had been worked out; then it became possible, by the union of geometry and mechanics, to initiate physical astronomy. Geometry and mechanics having diverged from a common root in men's sensible experiences; having, with occasional inosculations, been separately developed, the one partly in connection with astronomy, the other solely by analysing terrestrial movements; now join in the investigations of Newton to create a true theory of the celestial motions. And here, also, we have to notice the important fact that, in the very process of being brought jointly to bear upon astronomical problems, they are themselves raised to a higher phase of development. For it was in dealing with the questions raised by celestial dynamics that the then incipient infinitesimal calculus was unfolded by Newton and his continental successors; and it was from inquiries into the mechanics of the solar system that the general theorems of mechanics contained in the *Principia*,—many of them of purely terrestrial application—took their rise. Thus, as in the case of Hipparchus, the presentation of a new order of concrete facts to be analysed, led to the discovery of new abstract facts;

and these abstract facts having been laid hold of, gave means of access to endless groups of concrete facts before incapable of quantitative treatment.

Meanwhile, physics had been carrying further that progress without which, as just shown, rational mechanics could not be disentangled. In hydrostatics, Stevinus had extended and applied the discovery of Archimedes. Torricelli had proved atmospheric pressure, "by showing that this pressure sustained different liquids at heights inversely proportional to their densities;" and Pascal "established the necessary diminution of this pressure at increasing heights in the atmosphere:" discoveries which in part reduced this branch of science to a quantitative form. Something had been done by Daniel Bernouilli towards the dynamics of fluids. The thermometer had been invented; and a number of small generalisations reached by it. Huyghens and Newton had made considerable progress in optics; Newton had approximately calculated the rate of transmission of sound; and the continental mathematicians had succeeded in determining some of the laws of sonorous vibrations. Magnetism and electricity had been considerably advanced by Gilbert. Chemistry had got as far as the mutual neutralisation of acids and alkalies. And Leonardo da Vinci had advanced in geology to the conception of the deposition of marine strata as the origin of fossils. Our present purpose does not require that we should give particulars. All that it here concerns us to do is to illustrate the *consensus* subsisting in this stage of growth, and afterwards. Let us look at a few cases.

The theoretic law of the velocity of sound enunciated by Newton on purely mechanical considerations, was found wrong by one-sixth. The error remained unaccounted for until the time of Laplace, who, suspecting that the heat disengaged by the compression of the undulating strata of the air, gave additional elasticity, and so produced the difference, made the needful calculations and found he was right. Thus acoustics was arrested until thermology overtook and aided it. When Boyle and Marriot had discovered the relation between the density of gases and the pressures they are subject to; and when it thus became possible to calculate the rate of decreasing density in the upper parts of the atmosphere, it also became possible to make approximate tables of the atmospheric refraction of light. Thus optics, and with it astronomy, advanced with barology. After the discovery of atmospheric pressure had led to the invention of the air-pump by Otto Guericke; and after it had become known that evaporation increases in rapidity as atmospheric pressure decreases; it became possible for Leslie, by evaporation in a vacuum, to produce the greatest cold known; and so to extend our knowledge of thermology by showing that there is no zero within reach of our researches. When Fourier had determined the laws of conduction of heat, and when the Earth's temperature had been found to increase below the surface one degree in every forty yards, there were data for inferring the past condition of our globe; the vast period it has taken to cool down to its present state; and the immense age of the solar system—a purely astronomical consideration.

Chemistry having advanced sufficiently to supply the needful materials, and a physiological experiment having furnished the requisite hint, there came the discovery of galvanic electricity. Galvanism reacting on chemistry disclosed the metallic bases of the alkalies, and inaugurated the electro-chemical theory; in the hands of Oersted and Ampère it led to the laws of magnetic action; and by its aid Faraday has detected significant facts relative to the constitution of light. Brewster's discoveries respecting double refraction and dipolarisation proved the essential truth of the classification of crystalline forms according to the number of axes, by showing that the molecular constitution depends upon the axes. In these and in numerous other cases, the mutual influence of the sciences has been quite independent of any supposed hierarchical order. Often, too, their inter-actions are more complex than as thus instanced—involve more sciences than two. One illustration of this must suffice. We quote it in full from the *History of the Inductive Sciences*. In book xi., chap, ii., on "The Progress of the Electrical Theory," Dr. Whewell writes:—

> "Thus at that period, mathematics was behind experiment, and a problem was proposed, in which theoretical results were wanted for comparison with observation, but could not be accurately obtained; as was the case in astronomy also, till the time of the approximate solution of the problem of three bodies, and the consequent formation of the tables of the moon and planets, on the theory of universal gravitation. After some time, electrical theory was relieved from this reproach, mainly in consequence of the progress which astronomy had occasioned in pure mathematics. About 1801 there appeared in the *Bulletin des Sciences*, an exact solution of the problem of the distribution of electric fluid on a spheroid, obtained by Biot, by the application of the peculiar methods which Laplace had invented for the problem of the figure of the planets. And, in 1811, M. Poisson applied Laplace's artifices to the case of two spheres acting upon one another in contact, a case to which many of Coulomb's experiments were referrible; and the agreement of the results of theory and observation, thus extricated from Coulomb's numbers obtained above forty years previously, was very striking and convincing."

Not only do the sciences affect each other after this direct manner, but they affect each other indirectly. Where there is no dependence, there is yet analogy—*equality of relations*; and the discovery of the relations subsisting among one set of phenomena, constantly suggests a search for the same relations among another set. Thus the established fact that the force of gravitation varies inversely as the square of the distance, being recognised as a necessary characteristic of all influences proceeding from a centre, raised the suspicion that heat and light follow the same law; which proved to be the case—a suspicion and a confirmation which were repeated in respect to the electric and magnetic forces. Thus again the discovery of the polarisation of light led to experiments which ended in the discovery of the polarisation of heat—a discovery that could never have been made without the antecedent one. Thus, too, the known refrangibility of light and heat lately produced the inquiry whether sound also is not refrangible; which on trial it turns out to be.

In some cases, indeed, it is only by the aid of conceptions derived from one class of phenomena that hypotheses respecting other classes can be formed. The theory, at one time favoured, that evaporation is a solution of water in air, was an assumption that the relation between water and air is *like* the relation between salt and water; and could never have been conceived if the relation between salt and water had not been previously known. Similarly the received theory of evaporation—that it is a diffusion of the particles of the evaporating fluid in virtue of their atomic repulsion—could not have been entertained without a foregoing experience of magnetic and electric repulsions. So complete in recent days has become this *consensus* among the sciences, caused either by the natural entanglement of their phenomena, or by analogies in the relations of their phenomena, that scarcely any considerable discovery concerning one order of facts now takes place, without very shortly leading to discoveries concerning other orders.

To produce a tolerably complete conception of this process of scientific evolution, it would be needful to go back to the beginning, and trace in detail the growth of classifications and nomenclatures; and to show how, as subsidiary to science, they have acted upon it, and it has reacted upon them. We can only now remark that, on the one hand, classifications and nomenclatures have aided science by continually subdividing the subject-matter of research, and giving fixity and diffusion to the truths disclosed; and that on the other hand, they have caught from it that increasing quantitativeness, and that progress from considerations touching single phenomena to considerations touching the relations among many phenomena, which we have been describing.

Of this last influence a few illustrations must be given. In chemistry it is seen in the facts, that the dividing of matter into the four elements was ostensibly based upon the single property of weight; that the first truly chemical division into acid and alkaline bodies, grouped together bodies which had not simply one property in common, but in which one property was constantly related to many others; and that the classification now current, places together in groups *supporters of combustion, metallic and non-metallic bases, acids, salts*, etc., bodies which are often quite unlike in sensible qualities, but which are like in the majority of their *relations* to other bodies. In mineralogy again, the first classifications were based upon differences in aspect, texture, and other physical attributes. Berzelius made two attempts at a classification based solely on chemical constitution. That now current, recognises as far as possible the *relations* between physical and chemical characters. In botany the earliest classes formed were *trees, shrubs*, and *herbs*: magnitude being the basis of distinction. Dioscorides divided vegetables into *aromatic, alimentary, medicinal*, and *vinous*: a division of chemical character. Cæsalpinus classified them by the seeds, and seed-vessels, which he preferred because of the *relations* found to subsist between the character of the fructification and the general character of the other parts.

While the "natural system" since developed, carrying out the doctrine of Linnæus, that "natural orders must be formed by attention not to one or two, but to *all* the parts of plants," bases its divisions on like peculiarities which are found to be *constantly related* to the greatest number of other like peculiarities. And similarly in zoology, the successive classifications, from having been originally determined by external and often subordinate characters not indicative of the essential nature, have been gradually more and more determined by those internal and fundamental differences, which have uniform *relations* to the greatest number of other differences. Nor shall we be surprised at this analogy between the modes of progress of positive science and classification, when we bear in mind that both proceed by making generalisations; that both enable us to make previsions differing only in their precision; and that while the one deals with equal properties and relations, the other deals with properties and relations that approximate towards equality in variable degrees.

Without further argument, it will, we think, be sufficiently clear that the sciences are none of them separately evolved—are none of them independent either logically or historically; but that all of them have, in a greater or less degree, required aid and reciprocated it. Indeed, it needs but to throw aside these, and contemplate the mixed character of surrounding phenomena, to at once see that these notions of division and succession in the kinds of knowledge are none of them actually true, but are simple scientific fictions: good, if regarded merely as aids to study; bad, if regarded as representing realities in Nature. Consider them critically, and no facts whatever are presented to our senses uncombined with other facts—no facts whatever but are in some degree disguised by accompanying facts: disguised in such a manner that all must be partially understood before any one can be understood. If it be said, as by M. Comte, that gravitating force should be treated of before other forces, seeing that all things are subject to it, it may on like grounds be said that heat should be first dealt with; seeing that thermal forces are everywhere in action; that the ability of any portion of matter to manifest visible gravitative phenomena depends on its state of aggregation, which is determined by heat; that only by the aid of thermology can we explain those apparent exceptions to the gravitating tendency which are presented by steam and smoke, and so establish its universality, and that, indeed, the very existence of the solar system in a solid form is just as much a question of heat as it is one of gravitation.

Take other cases:—All phenomena recognised by the eyes, through which only are the data of exact science ascertainable, are complicated with optical phenomena; and cannot be exhaustively known until optical principles are known. The burning of a candle cannot be explained without involving chemistry, mechanics, thermology. Every wind that blows is determined by influences partly solar, partly lunar, partly hygrometric; and implies considerations of fluid equilibrium and physical geography. The direction, dip, and variations of the magnetic needle, are facts half terrestrial, half celestial—are caused by earthly forces which have cycles of change corresponding with astronomical periods. The flowing of the gulf-stream and the annual migration of icebergs towards the equator, depending as they do on the balancing of the centripetal and centrifugal forces acting on the ocean, involve in their explanation the Earth's rotation and spheroidal form, the laws of hydrostatics, the relative densities of cold and warm water, and the doctrines of evaporation. It is no doubt true, as M. Comte says, that "our position in the solar system, and the motions, form, size, equilibrium of the mass of our world among the planets, must be known before we can understand the phenomena going on at its surface." But, fatally for his hypothesis, it is also true that we must understand a great part of the phenomena going on at its surface before we can know its position, etc., in the solar system. It is not simply that, as we have already shown, those geometrical and mechanical principles by which celestial appearances are explained, were first generalised from terrestrial experiences; but it is that the very obtainment of correct data, on which to base astronomical generalisations, implies advanced terrestrial physics.

Until after optics had made considerable advance, the Copernican system remained but a speculation. A single modern observation on a star has to undergo a careful analysis by the combined aid of various sciences—has to *be digested by the organism of the sciences*; which have severally to assimilate their respective parts of the observation, before the essential fact it contains is available for the further development of astronomy. It has to be corrected not only for nutation of the earth's axis and for precession of the equinoxes, but for aberration and for refraction; and the formation of the tables by which refraction is calculated, presupposes knowledge of the law of decreasing density in the upper atmospheric strata; of the law of decreasing temperature, and the influence of this on the density; and of hygrometric laws as also affecting density. So that, to get materials for further advance, astronomy requires not only the indirect aid of the sciences which have presided over the making of its improved instruments, but the direct aid of an advanced optics, of barology, of thermology, of hygrometry; and if we remember that these delicate observations are in some cases registered electrically, and that they are further corrected for the "personal equation"—the time elapsing between seeing and registering, which varies with different observers—we may even add electricity and psychology. If, then, so apparently simple a thing as ascertaining the position of a star is complicated with so many phenomena, it is clear that this notion of the independence of the sciences, or certain of them, will not hold.

Whether objectively independent or not, they cannot be subjectively so—they cannot have independence as presented to our consciousness; and this is the only kind of independence with which we are concerned. And here, before leaving these illustrations, and especially this last one, let us not omit to notice how clearly they exhibit that increasingly active *consensus* of the sciences which characterises their advancing development. Besides finding that in these later times a discovery in one science commonly causes progress in others; besides finding that a great part of the questions with which modern science deals are so mixed as to require the co-operation of many sciences for their solution; we find in this last case that, to make a single good observation in the purest of the natural sciences, requires the combined assistance of half a dozen other sciences.

Perhaps the clearest comprehension of the interconnected growth of the sciences may be obtained by contemplating that of the arts, to which it is strictly analogous, and with which it is inseparably bound up. Most intelligent persons must have been, at one time or other, struck with the vast array of antecedents pre-supposed by one of our processes of manufacture. Let him trace the production of a printed cotton, and consider all that is implied by it. There are the many successive improvements through which the power-looms reached their present perfection;

there is the steam-engine that drives them, having its long history from Papin downwards; there are the lathes in which its cylinder was bored, and the string of ancestral lathes from which those lathes proceeded; there is the steam-hammer under which its crank shaft was welded; there are the puddling-furnaces, the blast-furnaces, the coal-mines and the iron-mines needful for producing the raw material; there are the slowly improved appliances by which the factory was built, and lighted, and ventilated; there are the printing engine, and the die house, and the colour laboratory with its stock of materials from all parts of the world, implying cochineal-culture, logwood-cutting, indigo-growing; there are the implements used by the producers of cotton, the gins by which it is cleaned, the elaborate machines by which it is spun: there are the vessels in which cotton is imported, with the building-slips, the rope-yards, the sail-cloth factories, the anchor-forges, needful for making them; and besides all these directly necessary antecedents, each of them involving many others, there are the institutions which have developed the requisite intelligence, the printing and publishing arrangements which have spread the necessary information, the social organisation which has rendered possible such a complex co-operation of agencies.

Further analysis would show that the many arts thus concerned in the economical production of a child's frock, have each of them been brought to its present efficiency by slow steps which the other arts have aided; and that from the beginning this reciprocity has been ever on the increase. It needs but on the one hand to consider how utterly impossible it is for the savage, even with ore and coal ready, to produce so simple a thing as an iron hatchet; and then to consider, on the other hand, that it would have been impracticable among ourselves, even a century ago, to raise the tubes of the Britannia bridge from lack of the hydraulic press; to at once see how mutually dependent are the arts, and how all must advance that each may advance. Well, the sciences are involved with each other in just the same manner. They are, in fact, inextricably woven into the same complex web of the arts; and are only conventionally independent of it. Originally the two were one. How to fix the religious festivals; when to sow: how to weigh commodities; and in what manner to measure ground; were the purely practical questions out of which arose astronomy, mechanics, geometry. Since then there has been a perpetual inosculation of the sciences and the arts. Science has been supplying art with truer generalisations and more completely quantitative previsions. Art has been supplying science with better materials and more perfect instruments. And all along the interdependence has been growing closer, not only between art and science, but among the arts themselves, and among the sciences themselves.

How completely the analogy holds throughout, becomes yet clearer when we recognise the fact that *the sciences are arts to each other*. If, as occurs in almost every case, the fact to be analysed by any science, has first to be prepared—to be disentangled from disturbing facts by the afore discovered methods of other sciences; the other sciences so used, stand in the position of arts. If, in solving a dynamical problem, a parallelogram is drawn, of which the sides and diagonal represent forces, and by putting magnitudes of extension for magnitudes of force a measurable relation is established between quantities not else to be dealt with; it may be fairly said that geometry plays towards mechanics much the same part that the fire of the founder plays towards the metal he is going to cast. If, in analysing the phenomena of the coloured rings surrounding the point of contact between two lenses, a Newton ascertains by calculation the amount of certain interposed spaces, far too minute for actual measurement; he employs the science of number for essentially the same purpose as that for which the watchmaker employs tools. If, before writing down his observation on a star, the astronomer has to separate from it all the errors resulting from atmospheric and optical laws, it is manifest that the refraction-tables, and logarithm-books, and formulæ, which he successively uses, serve him much as retorts, and filters, and cupels serve the assayer who wishes to separate the pure gold from all accompanying ingredients.

So close, indeed, is the relationship, that it is impossible to say where science begins and art ends. All the instruments of the natural philosopher are the products of art; the adjusting one of them for use is an art; there is art in making an observation with one of them; it requires art properly to treat the facts ascertained; nay, even the employing established generalisations to open the way to new generalisations, may be considered as art. In each of these cases previously organised knowledge becomes the implement by which new knowledge is got at: and whether that previously organised knowledge is embodied in a tangible apparatus or in a formula, matters not in so far as its essential relation to the new knowledge is concerned. If, as no one will deny, art is applied knowledge, then such portion of a scientific investigation as consists of applied knowledge is art. So that we may even say that as soon as any prevision in science passes out of its originally passive state, and is employed for reaching other previsions, it passes from theory into practice—becomes science in action—becomes art. And when we thus see how purely conventional is the ordinary distinction, how impossible it is to make any real separation—when we see not only that science and art were originally one; that the arts have perpetually assisted each other; that there has been a constant reciprocation of aid between the sciences and arts; but that the sciences act as arts to each other, and that the established part of each science becomes an art to the growing part—when we recognise the closeness of these associations, we shall the more clearly perceive that as the connection of the arts with each other has been ever becoming more intimate; as the help given by sciences to arts and by arts to sciences, has been age by age increasing; so the interdependence of the sciences themselves has been ever growing greater, their mutual relations more involved, their *consensus* more active.

In here ending our sketch of the Genesis of Science, we are conscious of having done the subject but scant justice. Two difficulties have stood in our way: one, the having to touch on so many points in such small space; the other, the necessity of treating in serial arrangement a process which is not serial—a difficulty which must ever attend all attempts to delineate processes of development, whatever their special nature. Add to which, that to present in anything like completeness and proportion, even the outlines of so vast and complex a history, demands years of study. Nevertheless, we believe that the evidence which has been assigned suffices to substantiate the leading propositions with which we set out. Inquiry into the first stages of science confirms the conclusion which we drew from the analysis of science as now existing, that it is not distinct from common knowledge, but an outgrowth from it—an extension of the perception by means of the reason.

That which we further found by analysis to form the more specific characteristic of scientific previsions, as contrasted with the previsions of uncultured intelligence—their quantitativeness—we also see to have been the characteristic alike in the initial steps in science, and of all the steps succeeding them. The facts and admissions cited in disproof of the assertion that the sciences follow one another, both logically and historically, in the order of their decreasing generality, have been enforced by the sundry instances we have met with, in which the more general or abstract sciences have been advanced only at the instigation of the more special or concrete—instances serving to show that a more general science as much owes its progress to the presentation of new problems by a more special science, as the more special science owes its progress to the solutions which the more general science is thus led to attempt—instances therefore illustrating the position that scientific advance is as much from the special to the general as from the general to the special.

Quite in harmony with this position we find to be the admissions that the sciences are as branches of one trunk, and that they were at first cultivated simultaneously; and this harmony becomes the more marked on finding, as we have done, not only that the sciences have a common root, but that science in general has a common root with language, classification, reasoning, art; that throughout civilisation these have advanced together, acting and reacting upon each other just as the separate sciences have done; and that thus the development of intelligence in all its divisions and subdivisions has conformed to this same law which we have shown that the sciences conform to. From all which we may perceive that the sciences can with no greater propriety be arranged in a succession, than language, classification, reasoning, art, and science, can be arranged in a succession; that, however needful a succession may be for the convenience of books and catalogues, it must be recognised merely as a convention; and that so far from its being the function of a philosophy of the sciences to establish a hierarchy, it is its function to show that the linear arrangements required for literary purposes, have none of them any basis either in Nature or History.

There is one further remark we must not omit—a remark touching the importance of the question that has been discussed. Unfortunately it commonly happens that topics of this abstract nature are slighted as of no practical moment; and, we doubt not, that many will think it of very little consequence what theory respecting the genesis of science may be entertained. But the value of truths is often great, in proportion as their generality is wide. Remote as they seem from practical application, the highest generalisations are not unfrequently the most potent in their effects, in virtue of their influence on all those subordinate generalisations which regulate practice. And it must be so here. Whenever established, a correct theory of the historical development of the sciences must have an immense effect upon education; and, through education, upon civilisation. Greatly as we differ from him in other respects, we agree with M. Comte in the belief that, rightly conducted, the education of the individual must have a certain correspondence with the evolution of the race.

No one can contemplate the facts we have cited in illustration of the early stages of science, without recognising the *necessity* of the processes through which those stages were reached—a necessity which, in respect to the leading truths, may likewise be traced in all after stages. This necessity, originating in the very nature of the phenomena to be analysed and the faculties to be employed, more or less fully applies to the mind of the child as to that of the savage. We say more or less fully, because the correspondence is not special but general only. Were the *environment* the same in both cases, the correspondence would be complete. But though the surrounding material out of which science is to be organised, is, in many cases, the same to the juvenile mind and the aboriginal mind, it is not so throughout; as, for instance, in the case of chemistry, the phenomena of which are accessible to the one, but were inaccessible to the other. Hence, in proportion as the environment differs, the course of evolution must differ. After admitting sundry exceptions, however, there remains a substantial parallelism; and, if so, it becomes of great moment to ascertain what really has been the process of scientific evolution. The establishment of an erroneous theory must be disastrous in its educational results; while the establishments of a true one must eventually be fertile in school-reforms and consequent social benefits.

ON THE PHYSIOLOGY OF LAUGHTER[19]

Why do we smile when a child puts on a man's hat? or what induces us to laugh on reading that the corpulent Gibbon was unable to rise from his knees after making a tender declaration? The usual reply to such questions is, that laughter results from a perception of incongruity. Even were there not on this reply the obvious criticism that laughter often occurs from extreme pleasure or from mere vivacity, there would still remain the real problem—How comes a sense of the incongruous to be followed by these peculiar bodily actions? Some have alleged that laughter is due to the pleasure of a relative self-elevation, which we feel on seeing the humiliation of others. But this theory, whatever portion of truth it may contain, is, in the first place, open to the fatal objection, that there are various humiliations to others which produce in us anything but laughter; and, in the second place, it does not apply to the many instances in which no one's dignity is implicated: as when we laugh at a good pun. Moreover, like the other, it is merely a generalisation of certain conditions to laughter; and not an explanation of the odd movements which occur under these conditions. Why, when greatly delighted, or impressed with certain unexpected contrasts of ideas, should there be a contraction of particular facial muscles, and particular muscles of the chest and abdomen? Such answer to this question as may be possible can be rendered only by physiology.

Every child has made the attempt to hold the foot still while it is tickled, and has failed; and probably there is scarcely any one who has not vainly tried to avoid winking, when a hand has been suddenly passed before the eyes. These examples of muscular movements which occur independently of the will, or in spite of it, illustrate what physiologists call reflex-action; as likewise do sneezing and coughing. To this class of cases, in which involuntary motions are accompanied by sensations, has to be added another class of cases, in which involuntary motions are unaccompanied by sensations:—instance the pulsations of the heart; the contractions of the stomach during digestion. Further, the great mass of seemingly-voluntary acts in such creatures as insects, worms, molluscs, are considered by physiologists to be as purely automatic as is the dilatation or closure of the iris under variations in quantity of light; and similarly exemplify the law, that an impression on the end of an afferent nerve is conveyed to some ganglionic centre, and is thence usually reflected along an efferent nerve to one or more muscles which it causes to contract.

In a modified form this principle holds with voluntary acts. Nervous excitation always *tends* to beget muscular motion; and when it rises to a certain in-

[19] *Macmillan's Magazine*, March 1860.

tensity, always does beget it. Not only in reflex actions, whether with or without sensation, do we see that special nerves, when raised to a state of tension, discharge themselves on special muscles with which they are indirectly connected; but those external actions through which we read the feelings of others, show us that under any considerable tension, the nervous system in general discharges itself on the muscular system in general: either with or without the guidance of the will. The shivering produced by cold, implies irregular muscular contractions, which, though at first only partly involuntary, become, when the cold is extreme, almost wholly involuntary. When you have severely burnt your finger, it is very difficult to preserve a dignified composure: contortion of face, or movement of limb, is pretty sure to follow. If a man receives good news with neither change of feature nor bodily motion, it is inferred that he is not much pleased, or that he has extraordinary self-control—either inference implying that joy almost universally produces contraction of the muscles; and so, alters the expression, or attitude, or both. And when we hear of the feats of strength which men have performed when their lives were at stake—when we read how, in the energy of despair, even paralytic patients have regained for a time the use of their limbs, we see still more clearly the relations between nervous and muscular excitements. It becomes manifest both that emotions and sensations tend to generate bodily movements and that the movements are vehement in proportion as the emotions or sensations are intense.[20]

This, however, is not the sole direction in which nervous excitement expends itself. Viscera as well as muscles may receive the discharge. That the heart and blood-vessels (which, indeed, being all contractile, may in a restricted sense be classed with the muscular system) are quickly affected by pleasures and pains, we have daily proved to us. Every sensation of any acuteness accelerates the pulse; and how sensitive the heart is to emotions, is testified by the familiar expressions which use heart and feeling as convertible terms. Similarly with the digestive organs. Without detailing the various ways in which these may be influenced by our mental states, it suffices to mention the marked benefits derived by dyspeptics, as well as other invalids, from cheerful society, welcome news, change of scene, to show how pleasurable feeling stimulates the viscera in general into greater activity.

There is still another direction in which any excited portion of the nervous system may discharge itself; and a direction in which it usually does discharge itself when the excitement is not strong. It may pass on the stimulus to some other portion of the nervous system. This is what occurs in quiet thinking and feeling. The successive states which constitute consciousness, result from this. Sensations excite ideas and emotions; these in their turns arouse other ideas and emotions; and so, continuously. That is to say, the tension existing in particular nerves, or groups of nerves, when they yield us certain sensations, ideas, or emotions, generates an equivalent tension in some other nerves, or groups of nerves, with which there is a connection: the flow of energy passing on, the one idea or feeling dies in producing the next.

---

[20] For numerous illustrations see essay on "The Origin and Function of Music."

Thus, then, while we are totally unable to comprehend how the excitement of certain nerves should generate feeling—while, in the production of consciousness by physical agents acting on physical structure, we come to an absolute mystery never to be solved; it is yet quite possible for us to know by observation what are the successive forms which this absolute mystery may take. We see that there are three channels along which nerves in a state of tension may discharge themselves; or rather, I should say, three classes of channels. They may pass on the excitement to other nerves that have no direct connections with the bodily members, and may so cause other feelings and ideas; or they may pass on the excitement to one or more motor nerves, and so cause muscular contractions; or they may pass on the excitement to nerves which supply the viscera, and may so stimulate one or more of these.

For simplicity's sake, I have described these as alternative routes, one or other of which any current of nerve-force must take; thereby, as it may be thought, implying that such current will be exclusively confined to some one of them. But this is by no means the case. Rarely, if ever, does it happen that a state of nervous tension, present to consciousness as a feeling, expends itself in one direction only. Very generally it may be observed to expend itself in two; and it is probable that the discharge is never absolutely absent from any one of the three. There is, however, variety in the *proportions* in which the discharge is divided among these different channels under different circumstances. In a man whose fear impels him to run, the mental tension generated is only in part transformed into a muscular stimulus: there is a surplus which causes a rapid current of ideas. An agreeable state of feeling produced, say by praise, is not wholly used up in arousing the succeeding phase of the feeling, and the new ideas appropriate to it; but a certain portion overflows into the visceral nervous system, increasing the action of the heart, and probably facilitating digestion. And here we come upon a class of considerations and facts which open the way to a solution of our special problem.

For starting with the unquestionable truth, that at any moment the existing quantity of liberated nerve-force, which in an inscrutable way produces in us the state we call feeling, *must* expend itself in some direction—*must* generate an equivalent manifestation of force somewhere—it clearly follows that, if of the several channels it may take, one is wholly or partially closed, more must be taken by the others; or that if two are closed, the discharge along the remaining one must be more intense; and that, conversely, should anything determine an unusual efflux in one direction, there will be a diminished efflux in other directions.

Daily experience illustrates these conclusions. It is commonly remarked, that the suppression of external signs of feeling, makes feeling more intense. The deepest grief is silent grief. Why? Because the nervous excitement not discharged in muscular action, discharges itself in other nervous excitements—arouses more numerous and more remote associations of melancholy ideas, and so increases the mass of feelings. People who conceal their anger are habitually found to be more revengeful than those who explode in loud speech and vehement action. Why? Because, as before, the emotion is reflected back, accumulates, and intensifies. Similarly, men who, as proved by their powers of representation, have the keenest appreciation of the comic, are usually able to do and say the most ludicrous things with perfect gravity.

On the other hand, all are familiar with the truth that bodily activity deadens emotion. Under great irritation we get relief by walking about rapidly. Extreme effort in the bootless attempt to achieve a desired end greatly diminishes the intensity of the desire. Those who are forced to exert themselves after misfortunes, do not suffer nearly so much as those who remain quiescent. If any one wishes to check intellectual excitement, he cannot choose a more efficient method than running till he is exhausted. Moreover, these cases, in which the production of feeling and thought is hindered by determining the nervous energy towards bodily movements, have their counterparts in the cases in which bodily movements are hindered by extra absorption of nervous energy in sudden thoughts and feelings. If, when walking along, there flashes on you an idea that creates great surprise, hope, or alarm, you stop; or if sitting cross-legged, swinging your pendent foot, the movement is at once arrested. From the viscera, too, intense mental action abstracts energy. Joy, disappointment, anxiety, or any moral perturbation rising to a great height, will destroy appetite; or if food has been taken, will arrest digestion; and even a purely intellectual activity, when extreme, will do the like.

Facts, then, fully bear out these *à priori* inferences, that the nervous excitement at any moment present to consciousness as feeling, must expend itself in some way or other; that of the three classes of channels open to it, it must take one, two, or more, according to circumstances; that the closure or obstruction of one, must increase the discharge through the others; and conversely, that if to answer some demand, the efflux of nervous energy in one direction is unusually great, there must be a corresponding decrease of the efflux in other directions. Setting out from these premises, let us now see what interpretation is to be put on the phenomena of laughter.

That laughter is a display of muscular excitement, and so illustrates the general law that feeling passing a certain pitch habitually vents itself in bodily action, scarcely needs pointing out. It perhaps needs pointing out, however, that strong feeling of almost any kind produces this result. It is not a sense of the ludicrous, only, which does it; nor are the various forms of joyous emotion the sole additional causes. We have, besides, the sardonic laughter and the hysterical laughter, which result from mental distress; to which must be added certain sensations, as tickling, and, according to Mr. Bain, cold, and some kinds of acute pain.

Strong feeling, mental or physical, being, then, the general cause of laughter, we have to note that the muscular actions constituting it are distinguished from most others by this, that they are purposeless. In general, bodily motions that are prompted by feelings are directed to special ends; as when we try to escape a danger, or struggle to secure a gratification. But the movements of chest and limbs which we make when laughing have no object. And now remark that these quasi-convulsive contractions of the muscles, having no object, but being results of an uncontrolled discharge of energy, we may see whence arise their special characters—how it happens that certain classes of muscles are affected first, and then certain other classes. For an overflow of nerve-force, undirected by any motive, will manifestly take first the most habitual routes; and if these do not suffice, will next overflow into the less habitual ones. Well, it is through the organs of speech that feeling passes into movement with the greatest frequency. The jaws, tongue, and lips are used not only to express strong irritation or gratification; but that very moderate flow of mental energy which accompanies ordinary conversation, finds its chief vent through this channel. Hence it happens that certain muscles round the mouth, small and easy to move, are the first to contract under pleasurable emotion. The class of muscles which, next after those of articulation, are most constantly set in action (or extra action, we should say) by feelings of all kinds, are those of respiration. Under pleasurable or painful sensations we breathe more rapidly: possibly as a consequence of the increased demand for oxygenated blood. The sensations that accompany exertion also bring on hard-breathing; which here more evidently responds to the physiological needs. And emotions, too, agreeable and disagreeable, both, at first, excite respiration; though the last subsequently depress it. That is to say, of the bodily muscles, the respiratory are more constantly implicated than any others in those various acts which our feelings impel us to; and, hence, when there occurs an undirected discharge of nervous energy into the muscular system, it happens that, if the quantity be considerable, it convulses not only certain of the articulatory and vocal muscles, but also those which expel air from the lungs.

Should the feeling to be expended be still greater in amount—too great to find vent in these classes of muscles—another class comes into play. The upper limbs are set in motion. Children frequently clap their hands in glee; by some adults the hands are rubbed together; and others, under still greater intensity of delight, slap their knees and sway their bodies backwards and forwards. Last of all, when the other channels for the escape of the surplus nerve-force have been filled to overflowing, a yet further and less-used group of muscles is spasmodically affected: the head is thrown back and the spine bent inwards—there is a slight degree of what medical men call opisthotonos. Thus, then, without contending that the phenomena of laughter in all their details are to be so accounted for, we see that in their *ensemble* they conform to these general principles:—that feeling excites to muscular action; that when the muscular action is unguided by a purpose, the muscles first affected are those which feeling most habitually stimulates; and that as the feeling to be expended increases in quantity, it excites an increasing number of muscles, in a succession determined by the relative frequency with which they respond to the regulated dictates of feeling.

There still, however, remains the question with which we set out. The explanation here given applies only to the laughter produced by acute pleasure or pain: it does not apply to the laughter that follows certain perceptions of incongruity. It is an insufficient explanation that, in these cases, laughter is a result of the pleasure we take in escaping from the restraint of grave feelings. That this is a part-cause is true. Doubtless very often, as Mr. Bain says, "it is the coerced form of seriousness and solemnity without the reality that gives us that stiff position from which a contact with triviality or vulgarity relieves us, to our uproarious delight." And in so far as mirth is caused by the gush of agreeable feeling that follows the cessation of mental strain, it further illustrates the general principle above set forth. But no explanation is thus afforded of the mirth which ensues when the short silence between the *andante* and *allegro* in one of Beethoven's symphonies, is broken by a loud sneeze. In this, and hosts of like cases, the mental tension is not coerced but spontaneous—not disagreeable but agreeable; and the coming impressions to which the attention is directed, promise a gratification that few, if any, desire to escape. Hence, when the unlucky sneeze occurs, it cannot be that the laughter of the audience is due simply to the release from an irksome attitude of mind: some other cause must be sought.

This cause we shall arrive at by carrying our analysis a step further. We have but to consider the quantity of feeling that exists under such circumstances, and then to ask what are the conditions that determine the direction of its discharge, to at once reach a solution. Take a case. You are sitting in a theatre, absorbed in the progress of an interesting drama. Some climax has been reached which has aroused your sympathies—say, a reconciliation between the hero and heroine, after long and painful misunderstanding. The feelings excited by this scene are not of a kind from which you seek relief; but are, on the contrary, a grateful relief from the painful feelings with which you have witnessed the previous estrangement. Moreover, the sentiments these fictitious personages have for the moment inspired you with, are not such as would lead you to rejoice in any indignity offered to them; but rather, such as would make you resent the indignity. And now, while you are contemplating the reconciliation with a pleasurable sympathy, there appears from behind the scenes a tame kid, which, having stared round at the audience, walks up to the lovers and sniffs at them. You cannot help joining in the roar which greets this *contretemps*. Inexplicable as is this irresistible burst on the hypothesis of a pleasure in escaping from mental restraint; or on the hypothesis of a pleasure from relative increase of self-importance, when witnessing the humiliation of others; it is readily explicable if we consider what, in such a case, must become of the feeling that existed at the moment the incongruity arose. A large mass of emotion had been produced; or, to speak in physiological language, a large portion of the nervous system was in a state of tension. There was also great expectation with respect to the further evolution of the scene—a quantity of vague, nascent thought and emotion, into which the existing quantity of thought and emotion was about to pass.

Had there been no interruption, the body of new ideas and feelings next excited would have sufficed to absorb the whole of the liberated nervous energy. But now, this large amount of nervous energy, instead of being allowed to expend itself in producing an equivalent amount of the new thoughts and emotions which were nascent, is suddenly checked in its flow. The channels along which the discharge was about to take place are closed. The new channel opened—that afforded by the appearance and proceedings of the kid—is a small one; the ideas and feelings suggested are not numerous and massive enough to carry off the nervous energy to be expended. The excess must therefore discharge itself in some other direction; and in the way already explained, there results an efflux through the motor nerves to various classes of the muscles, producing the half-convulsive actions we term laughter.

This explanation is in harmony with the fact, that when, among several persons who witness the same ludicrous occurrence, there are some who do not laugh; it is because there has arisen in them an emotion not participated in by the rest, and which is sufficiently massive to absorb all the nascent excitement. Among the spectators of an awkward tumble, those who preserve their gravity are those in whom there is excited a degree of sympathy with the sufferer, sufficiently great to serve as an outlet for the feeling which the occurrence had turned out of its previous course. Sometimes anger carries off the arrested current; and so prevents laughter. An instance of this was lately furnished me by a friend who had been witnessing the feats at Franconi's. A tremendous leap had just been made by an acrobat over a number of horses. The clown, seemingly envious of this success, made ostentatious preparations for doing the like; and then, taking the preliminary run with immense energy, stopped short on reaching the first horse, and pretended to wipe some dust from its haunches. In the majority of the spectators, merriment was excited; but in my friend, wound up by the expectation of the coming leap to a state of great nervous tension, the effect of the baulk was to produce indignation. Experience thus proves what the theory implies: namely, that the discharge of arrested feelings into the muscular system, takes place only in the absence of other adequate channels—does not take place if there arise other feelings equal in amount to those arrested.

Evidence still more conclusive is at hand. If we contrast the incongruities which produce laughter with those which do not, we at once see that in the non-ludicrous ones the unexpected state of feeling aroused, though wholly different in kind, is not less in quantity or intensity. Among incongruities that may excite anything but a laugh, Mr. Bain instances—"A decrepit man under a heavy burden, five loaves and two fishes among a multitude, and all unfitness and gross disproportion; an instrument out of tune, a fly in ointment, snow in May, Archimedes studying geometry in a siege, and all discordant things; a wolf in sheep's clothing, a breach of bargain, and falsehood in general; the multitude taking the law in their own hands, and everything of the nature of disorder; a corpse at a feast, parental cruelty, filial ingratitude, and whatever is unnatural; the entire catalogue of the vanities given by Solomon, are all incongruous, but they cause feelings of pain, anger, sadness, loathing, rather than mirth." Now in these cases, where the totally unlike state of consciousness suddenly produced is not inferior in mass to the preceding one, the conditions to laughter are not fulfilled. As above shown, laughter naturally results only when consciousness is unawares transferred from great things to small—only when there is what we call a *descending* incongruity.

And now observe, finally, the fact, alike inferable *à priori* and illustrated in experience, that an *ascending* incongruity not only fails to cause laughter, but works on the muscular system an effect of exactly the reverse kind. When after something very insignificant there arises without anticipation something very great, the emotion we call wonder results; and this emotion is accompanied not by an excitement of the muscles, but by a relaxation of them. In children and country people, that falling of the jaw which occurs on witnessing something that is imposing and unexpected exemplifies this effect. Persons who have been wonder-struck at the production of very striking results by a seemingly inadequate cause, are frequently described as unconsciously dropping the things they held in their hands. Such are just the effects to be anticipated. After an average state of consciousness, absorbing but a small quantity of nervous energy, is aroused without the slightest notice, a strong emotion of awe, terror, or admiration, joined with the astonishment due to an apparent want of adequate causation. This new state of consciousness demands far more nervous energy than that which it has suddenly replaced; and this increased absorption of nervous energy in mental changes involves a temporary diminution of the outflow in other directions: whence the pendent jaw and the relaxing grasp.

One further observation is worth making. Among the several sets of channels into which surplus feeling might be discharged, was named the nervous system of the viscera. The sudden overflow of an arrested mental excitement, which, as we have seen, results from a descending incongruity, must doubtless stimulate not only the muscular system, as we see it does, but also the internal organs; the heart and stomach must come in for a share of the discharge. And thus there seems to be a good physiological basis for the popular notion that mirth-creating excitement facilitates digestion.

Though in doing so I go beyond the boundaries of the immediate topic, I may fitly point out that the method of inquiry here followed, is one which enables us to understand various phenomena besides those of laughter. To show the importance of pursuing it, I will indicate the explanation it furnishes of another familiar class of facts.

All know how generally a large amount of emotion disturbs the action of the intellect, and interferes with the power of expression. A speech delivered with great facility to tables and chairs, is by no means so easily delivered to an audience. Every schoolboy can testify that his trepidation, when standing before a master, has often disabled him from repeating a lesson which he had duly learnt. In explanation of this we commonly say that the attention is distracted—that the proper train of ideas is broken by the intrusion of ideas that are irrelevant. But the question is, in what manner does unusual emotion produce this effect; and we are here supplied with a tolerably obvious answer. The repetition of a lesson, or set speech previously thought out, implies the flow of a very moderate amount of nervous excitement through a comparatively narrow channel. The thing to be done is simply to call up in succession certain previously-arranged ideas—a process in which no great amount of mental energy is expended. Hence, when there is a large quantity of emotion, which must be discharged in some direction or other; and when, as usually happens, the restricted series of intellectual actions to be gone through, does not suffice to carry it off; there result discharges along other channels besides the one prescribed: there are aroused various ideas foreign to the train of thought to be pursued; and these tend to exclude from consciousness those which should occupy it.

And now observe the meaning of those bodily actions spontaneously set up under these circumstances. The school-boy saying his lesson commonly has his fingers actively engaged—perhaps in twisting about a broken pen, or perhaps squeezing the angle of his jacket; and if told to keep his hands still, he soon again falls into the same or a similar trick. Many anecdotes are current of public speakers having incurable automatic actions of this class: barristers who perpetually wound and unwound pieces of tape; members of parliament ever putting on and taking off their spectacles. So long as such movements are unconscious, they facilitate the mental actions. At least this seems a fair inference from the fact that confusion frequently results from putting a stop to them: witness the case narrated by Sir Walter Scott of his school-fellow, who became unable to say his lesson after the removal of the waistcoat-button that he habitually fingered while in class. But why do they facilitate the mental actions? Clearly because they draw off a portion of the surplus nervous excitement. If, as above explained, the quantity of mental energy generated is greater than can find vent along the narrow channel of thought that is open to it; and if, in consequence, it is apt to produce confusion by rushing into other channels of thought; then by allowing it an exit through the motor nerves into the muscular system, the pressure is diminished, and irrelevant ideas are less likely to intrude on consciousness.

This further illustration will, I think, justify the position that something may be achieved by pursuing in other cases this method of psychological inquiry. A complete explanation of the phenomena, requires us to trace out *all* the consequences of any given state of consciousness; and we cannot do this without studying the effects, bodily and mental, as varying in quantity at each other's expense. We should probably learn much if we in every case asked—Where is all the nervous energy gone?

ON THE ORIGIN AND FUNCTION OF MU-SIC[21]

When Carlo, standing, chained to his kennel, sees his master in the distance, a slight motion of the tail indicates his but faint hope that he is about to be let out. A much more decided wagging of the tail, passing by and by into lateral undulations of the body, follows his master's nearer approach. When hands are laid on his collar, and he knows that he is really to have an outing, his jumping and wriggling are such that it is by no means easy to loose his fastenings. And when he finds himself actually free, his joy expends itself in bounds, in pirouettes, and in scourings hither and thither at the top of his speed. Puss, too, by erecting her tail, and by every time raising her back to meet the caressing hand of her mistress, similarly expresses her gratification by certain muscular actions; as likewise do the parrot by awkward dancing on his perch, and the canary by hopping and fluttering about his cage with unwonted rapidity. Under emotions of an opposite kind, animals equally display muscular excitement. The enraged lion lashes his sides with his tail, knits his brows, protrudes his claws. The cat sets up her back; the dog retracts his upper lip; the horse throws back his ears. And in the struggles of creatures in pain, we see that the like relation holds between excitement of the muscles and excitement of the nerves of sensation.

In ourselves, distinguished from lower creatures as we are by feelings alike more powerful and more varied, parallel facts are at once more conspicuous and more numerous. We may conveniently look at them in groups. We shall find that pleasurable sensations and painful sensations, pleasurable emotions and painful emotions, all tend to produce active demonstrations in proportion to their intensity.

In children, and even in adults who are not restrained by regard for appearances, a highly agreeable taste is followed by a smacking of the lips. An infant will laugh and bound in its nurse's arms at the sight of a brilliant colour or the hearing of a new sound. People are apt to beat time with head or feet to music which particularly pleases them. In a sensitive person an agreeable perfume will produce a smile; and smiles will be seen on the faces of a crowd gazing at some splendid burst of fireworks Even the pleasant sensation of warmth felt on getting to the fireside out of a winter's storm, will similarly express itself in the face.

Painful sensations, being mostly far more intense than pleasurable ones, cause muscular actions of a much more decided kind. A sudden twinge produces a convulsive start of the whole body. A pain less violent, but continuous, is accompa-

[21] *Fraser's Magazine*, October 1857.

nied by a knitting of the brows, a setting of the teeth or biting of the lip, and a contraction of the features generally. Under a persistent pain of a severer kind, other muscular actions are added: the body is swayed to and fro; the hands clench anything they can lay hold of; and should the agony rise still higher, the sufferer rolls about on the floor almost convulsed.

Though more varied, the natural language of the pleasurable emotions comes within the same generalisation. A smile, which is the commonest expression of gratified feeling, is a contraction of certain facial muscles; and when the smile broadens into a laugh, we see a more violent and more general muscular excitement produced by an intenser gratification. Rubbing together of the hands, and that other motion which Dickens somewhere describes as "washing with impalpable soap in invisible water," have like implications. Children may often be seen to "jump for joy." Even in adults of excitable temperament, an action approaching to it is sometimes witnessed. And dancing has all the world through been regarded as natural to an elevated state of mind. Many of the special emotions show themselves in special muscular actions. The gratification resulting from success, raises the head and gives firmness to the gait. A hearty grasp of the hand is currently taken as indicative of friendship. Under a gush of affection the mother clasps her child to her breast, feeling as though she could squeeze it to death. And so in sundry other cases. Even in that brightening of the eye with which good news is received we may trace the same truth; for this appearance of greater brilliancy is due to an extra contraction of the muscle which raises the eyelid, and so allows more light to fall upon, and be reflected from, the wet surface of the eyeball.

The bodily indications of painful emotions are equally numerous, and still more vehement. Discontent is shown by raised eyebrows and wrinkled forehead; disgust by a curl of the lip; offence by a pout. The impatient man beats a tattoo with his fingers on the table, swings his pendent leg with increasing rapidity, gives needless pokings to the fire, and presently paces with hasty strides about the room. In great grief there is wringing of the hands, and even tearing of the hair. An angry child stamps, or rolls on its back and kicks its heels in the air; and in manhood, anger, first showing itself in frowns, in distended nostrils, in compressed lips, goes on to produce grinding of the teeth, clenching of the fingers, blows of the fist on the table, and perhaps ends in a violent attack on the offending person, or in throwing about and breaking the furniture. From that pursing of the mouth indicative of slight displeasure, up to the frantic struggles of the maniac, we shall find that mental irritation tends to vent itself in bodily activity.

All feelings, then—sensations or emotions, pleasurable or painful—have this common characteristic, that they are muscular stimuli. Not forgetting the few apparently exceptional cases in which emotions exceeding a certain intensity produce prostration, we may set it down as a general law that, alike in man and animals, there is a direct connection between feeling and motion; the last growing more vehement as the first grows more intense. Were it allowable here to treat the matter scientifically, we might trace this general law down to the principle known among physiologists as that of *reflex action*.[22] Without doing this, however, the

[22] Those who seek information on this point may find it in an interesting tract by Mr.

above numerous instances justify the generalisation, that mental excitement of all kinds ends in excitement of the muscles; and that the two preserve a more or less constant ratio to each other.

"But what has all this to do with *The Origin and Function of Music*?" asks the reader. Very much, as we shall presently see. All music is originally vocal. All vocal sounds are produced by the agency of certain muscles. These muscles, in common with those of the body at large, are excited to contraction by pleasurable and painful feelings. And therefore it is that feelings demonstrate themselves in sounds as well as in movements. Therefore it is that Carlo barks as well as leaps when he is let out—that puss purrs as well as erects her tail—that the canary chirps as well as flutters. Therefore it is that the angry lion roars while he lashes his sides, and the dog growls while he retracts his lip. Therefore it is that the maimed animal not only struggles, but howls. And it is from this cause that in human beings bodily suffering expresses itself not only in contortions, but in shrieks and groans—that in anger, and fear, and grief, the gesticulations are accompanied by shouts and screams—that delightful sensations are followed by exclamations—and that we hear screams of joy and shouts of exultation.

We have here, then, a principle underlying all vocal phenomena; including those of vocal music, and by consequence those of music in general. The muscles that move the chest, larynx, and vocal chords, contracting like other muscles in proportion to the intensity of the feelings; every different contraction of these muscles involving, as it does, a different adjustment of the vocal organs; every different adjustment of the vocal organs causing a change in the sound emitted;—it follows that variations of voice are the physiological results of variations of feeling; it follows that each inflection or modulation is the natural outcome of some passing emotion or sensation; and it follows that the explanation of all kinds of vocal expression must be sought in this general relation between mental and muscular excitements. Let us, then, see whether we cannot thus account for the chief peculiarities in the utterance of the feelings: grouping these peculiarities under the heads of *loudness, quality, or timbre, pitch, intervals,* and *rate of variation.*

Between the lungs and the organs of voice there is much the same relation as between the bellows of an organ and its pipes. And as the loudness of the sound given out by an organ-pipe increases with the strength of the blast from the bellows; so, other things equal, the loudness of a vocal sound increases with the strength of the blast from the lungs. But the expulsion of air from the lungs is effected by certain muscles of the chest and abdomen. The force with which these muscles contract, is proportionate to the intensity of the feeling experienced. Hence, *à priori,* loud sounds will be the habitual results of strong feelings. That they are so we have daily proof. The pain which, if moderate, can be borne silently, causes outcries if it becomes extreme. While a slight vexation makes a child whimper, a fit of passion calls forth a howl that disturbs the neighbourhood. When the voices in an adjacent room become unusually audible, we infer anger, or surprise, or joy. Loudness of applause is significant of great approbation; and with uproarious mirth we associate the idea of high enjoyment. Commencing with the silence

Alexander Bain, on *Animal Instinct and Intelligence.*

of apathy, we find that the utterances grow louder as the sensations or emotions, whether pleasurable or painful, grow stronger.

That different *qualities* of voice accompany different mental states, and that under states of excitement the tones are more sonorous than usual, is another general fact admitting of a parallel explanation. The sounds of common conversation have but little resonance; those of strong feeling have much more. Under rising ill temper the voice acquires a metallic ring. In accordance with her constant mood, the ordinary speech of a virago has a piercing quality quite opposite to that softness indicative of placidity. A ringing laugh marks an especially joyous temperament. Grief unburdening itself uses tones approaching in *timbre* to those of chanting: and in his most pathetic passages an eloquent speaker similarly falls into tones more vibratory than those common to him. Now any one may readily convince himself that resonant vocal sounds can be produced only by a certain muscular effort additional to that ordinarily needed. If after uttering a word in his speaking voice, the reader, without changing the pitch or the loudness, will *sing* this word, he will perceive that before he can sing it, he has to alter the adjustment of the vocal organs; to do which a certain force must be used; and by putting his fingers on that external prominence marking the top of the larynx, he will have further evidence that to produce a sonorous tone the organs must be drawn out of their usual position. Thus, then, the fact that the tones of excited feeling are more vibratory than those of common conversation is another instance of the connection between mental excitement and muscular excitement. The speaking voice, the recitative voice, and the singing voice, severally exemplify one general principle.

That the *pitch* of the voice varies according to the action of the vocal muscles scarcely needs saying. All know that the middle notes, in which they converse, are made without any appreciable effort; and all know that to make either very high or very low notes requires a considerable effort. In either ascending or descending from the pitch of ordinary speech, we are conscious of an increasing muscular strain, which, at both extremes of the register, becomes positively painful. Hence it follows from our general principle, that while indifference or calmness will use the medium tones, the tones used during excitement will be either above or below them; and will rise higher and higher, or fall lower and lower, as the feelings grow stronger. This physiological deduction we also find to be in harmony with familiar facts. The habitual sufferer utters his complaints in a voice raised considerably above the natural key; and agonising pain vents itself in either shrieks or groans—in very high or very low notes. Beginning at his talking pitch, the cry of the disappointed urchin grows more shrill as it grows louder. The "Oh!" of astonishment or delight, begins several notes below the middle voice, and descends still lower. Anger expresses itself in high tones, or else in "curses not loud but *deep*." Deep tones, too, are always used in uttering strong reproaches. Such an exclamation as "Beware!" if made dramatically—that is, if made with a show of feeling—must be many notes lower than ordinary. Further, we have groans of disapprobation, groans of horror, groans of remorse. And extreme joy and fear are alike accompanied by shrill outcries.

Nearly allied to the subject of pitch, is that of *intervals*; and the explanation of them carries our argument a step further. While calm speech is comparatively monotonous, emotion makes use of fifths, octaves, and even wider intervals. Listen to any one narrating or repeating something in which he has no interest, and his voice will not wander more than two or three notes above or below his medium note, and that by small steps; but when he comes to some exciting event he will be heard not only to use the higher and lower notes of his register, but to go from one to the other by larger leaps. Being unable in print to imitate these traits of feeling, we feel some difficulty in fully realising them to the reader. But we may suggest a few remembrances which will perhaps call to mind a sufficiency of others. If two men living in the same place, and frequently seeing one another, meet, say at a public assembly, any phrase with which one may be heard to accost the other—as "Hallo, are you here?"—will have an ordinary intonation. But if one of them, after long absence, has unexpectedly returned, the expression of surprise with which his friend may greet him—"Hallo! how came you here?"—will be uttered in much more strongly contrasted tones. The two syllables of the word "Hallo" will be, the one much higher and the other much lower than before; and the rest of the sentence will similarly ascend and descend by longer steps.

Again, if, supposing her to be in an adjoining room, the mistress of the house calls "Mary," the two syllables of the name will be spoken in an ascending interval of a third. If Mary does not reply, the call will be repeated probably in a descending fifth; implying the slightest shade of annoyance at Mary's inattention. Should Mary still make no answer, the increasing annoyance will show itself by the use of a descending octave on the next repetition of the call. And supposing the silence to continue, the lady, if not of a very even temper, will show her irritation at Mary's seemingly intentional negligence by finally calling her in tones still more widely contrasted—the first syllable being higher and the last lower than before.

Now, these and analogous facts, which the reader will readily accumulate, clearly conform to the law laid down. For to make large intervals requires more muscular action than to make small ones. But not only is the *extent* of vocal intervals thus explicable as due to the relation between nervous and muscular excitement, but also in some degree their *direction*, as ascending or descending. The middle notes being those which demand no appreciable effort of muscular adjustment; and the effort becoming greater as we either ascend or descend; it follows that a departure from the middle notes in either direction will mark increasing emotion; while a return towards the middle notes will mark decreasing emotion. Hence it happens that an enthusiastic person uttering such a sentence as—"It was the most splendid sight I ever saw!" will ascend to the first syllable of the word "splendid," and thence will descend: the word "splendid" marking the climax of the feeling produced by the recollection. Hence, again, it happens that, under some extreme vexation produced by another's stupidity, an irascible man, exclaiming—"What a confounded fool the fellow is!" will begin somewhat below his middle voice, and descending to the word "fool," which he will utter in one of his deepest notes, will then ascend again. And it may be remarked, that the word "fool" will not only be deeper and louder than the rest, but will also have more emphasis of articulation—another mode in which muscular excitement is shown.

There is some danger, however, in giving instances like this; seeing that as the mode of rendering will vary according to the intensity of the feeling which the reader feigns to himself, the right cadence may not be hit upon. With single words there is less difficulty. Thus the "Indeed!" with which a surprising fact is received, mostly begins on the middle note of the voice, and rises with the second syllable; or, if disapprobation as well as astonishment is felt, the first syllable will be below the middle note, and the second lower still. Conversely, the word "Alas!" which marks not the rise of a paroxysm of grief, but its decline, is uttered in a cadence descending towards the middle note; or, if the first syllable is in the lower part of the register, the second ascends towards the middle note. In the "Heigh-ho!" expressive of mental and muscular prostration, we may see the same truth; and if the cadence appropriate to it be inverted, the absurdity of the effect clearly shows how the meaning of intervals is dependent on the principle we have been illustrating.

The remaining characteristic of emotional speech which we have to notice is that of *variability of pitch*. It is scarcely possible here to convey adequate ideas of this more complex manifestation. We must be content with simply indicating some occasions on which it may be observed. On a meeting of friends, for instance—as when there arrives a party of much-wished-for-visitors—the voices of all will be heard to undergo changes of pitch not only greater but much more numerous than usual. If a speaker at a public meeting is interrupted by some squabble among those he is addressing, his comparatively level tones will be in marked contrast with the rapidly changing one of the disputants. And among children, whose feelings are less under control than those of adults, this peculiarity is still more decided. During a scene of complaint and recrimination between two excitable little girls, the voices may be heard to run up and down the gamut several times in each sentence. In such cases we once more recognise the same law: for muscular excitement is shown not only in strength of contraction but also in the rapidity with which different muscular adjustments succeed each other.

Thus we find all the leading vocal phenomena to have a physiological basis. They are so many manifestations of the general law that feeling is a stimulus to muscular action—a law conformed to throughout the whole economy, not of man only, but of every sensitive creature—a law, therefore, which lies deep in the nature of animal organisation. The expressiveness of these various modifications of voice is therefore innate. Each of us, from babyhood upwards, has been spontaneously making them, when under the various sensations and emotions by which they are produced. Having been conscious of each feeling at the same time that we heard ourselves make the consequent sound, we have acquired an established association of ideas between such sound and the feeling which caused it. When the like sound is made by another, we ascribe the like feeling to him; and by a further consequence we not only ascribe to him that feeling, but have a certain degree of it aroused in ourselves: for to become conscious of the feeling which another is experiencing, is to have that feeling awakened in our own consciousness, which is the same thing as experiencing the feeling. Thus these various modifications of voice become not only a language through which we understand the emotions of others, but also the means of exciting our sympathy with such emotions.

Have we not here, then, adequate data for a theory of music? These vocal peculiarities which indicate excited feeling *are those which especially distinguish song from ordinary speech*. Every one of the alterations of voice which we have found to be a physiological result of pain or pleasure, *is carried to its greatest extreme in vocal music*. For instance, we saw that, in virtue of the general relation between mental and muscular excitement, one characteristic of passionate utterance is *loudness*. Well, its comparative loudness is one of the distinctive marks of song as contrasted with the speech of daily life; and further, the *forte* passages of an air are those intended to represent the climax of its emotion. We next saw that the tones in which emotion expresses itself are, in conformity with this same law, of a more sonorous *timbre* than those of calm conversation. Here, too, song displays a still higher degree of the peculiarity; for the singing tone is the most resonant we can make. Again, it was shown that, from a like cause, mental excitement vents itself in the higher and lower notes of the register; using the middle notes but seldom. And it scarcely needs saying that vocal music is still more distinguished by its comparative neglect of the notes in which we talk, and its habitual use of those above or below them and, moreover, that its most passionate effects are commonly produced at the two extremities of its scale, but especially the upper one.

A yet further trait of strong feeling, similarly accounted for, was the employment of larger intervals than are employed in common converse. This trait, also, every ballad and *aria* carries to an extent beyond that heard in the spontaneous utterances of emotion: add to which, that the direction of these intervals, which, as diverging from or converging towards the medium tones, we found to be physiologically expressive of increasing or decreasing emotion, may be observed to have in music like meanings. Once more, it was pointed out that not only extreme but also rapid variations of pitch are characteristic of mental excitement; and once more we see in the quick changes of every melody, that song carries the characteristic as far, if not farther. Thus, in respect alike of *loudness, timbre, pitch, intervals*, and *rate of variation*, song employs and exaggerates the natural language of the emotions;—it arises from a systematic combination of those vocal peculiarities which are the physiological effects of acute pleasure and pain.

Besides these chief characteristics of song as distinguished from common speech, there are sundry minor ones similarly explicable as due to the relation between mental and muscular excitement; and before proceeding further these should be briefly noticed. Thus, certain passions, and perhaps all passions when pushed to an extreme, produce (probably through their influence over the action of the heart) an effect the reverse of that which has been described: they cause a physical prostration, one symptom of which is a general relaxation of the muscles, and a consequent trembling. We have the trembling of anger, of fear, of hope, of joy; and the vocal muscles being implicated with the rest, the voice too becomes tremulous. Now, in singing, this tremulousness of voice is very effectively used by some vocalists in highly pathetic passages; sometimes, indeed, because of its effectiveness, too much used by them—as by Tamberlik, for instance.

Again, there is a mode of musical execution known as the *staccato*, appropriate to energetic passages—to passages expressive of exhilaration, of resolution, of confidence. The action of the vocal muscles which produces this staccato style is analogous to the muscular action which produces the sharp decisive, energetic movements of body indicating these states of mind; and therefore it is that the staccato style has the meaning we ascribe to it. Conversely, slurred intervals are expressive of gentler and less active feelings; and are so because they imply the smaller muscular vivacity due to a lower mental energy. The difference of effect resulting from difference of *time* in music is also attributable to the same law. Already it has been pointed out that the more frequent changes of pitch which ordinarily result from passion are imitated and developed in song; and here we have to add, that the various rates of such changes, appropriate to the different styles of music, are further traits having the same derivation. The slowest movements, *largo* and *adagio*, are used where such depressing emotions as grief, or such unexciting emotions as reverence, are to be portrayed; while the more rapid movements, *andante*, *allegro*, *presto*, represent successively increasing degrees of mental vivacity; and do this because they imply that muscular activity which flows from this mental vivacity. Even the *rhythm*, which forms a remaining distinction between song and speech, may not improbably have a kindred cause. Why the actions excited by strong feeling should tend to become rhythmical is not very obvious; but that they do so there are divers evidences. There is the swaying of the body to and fro under pain or grief, of the leg under impatience or agitation. Dancing, too, is a rhythmical action natural to elevated emotion. That under excitement speech acquires a certain rhythm, we may occasionally perceive in the highest efforts of an orator. In poetry, which is a form of speech used for the better expression of emotional ideas, we have this rhythmical tendency developed. And when we bear in mind that dancing, poetry, and music are connate—are originally constituent parts of the same thing, it becomes clear that the measured movement common to them all implies a rhythmical action of the whole system, the vocal apparatus included; and that so the rhythm of music is a more subtle and complex result of this relation between mental and muscular excitement.

But it is time to end this analysis, which possibly we have already carried too far. It is not to be supposed that the more special peculiarities of musical expression are to be definitely explained. Though probably they may all in some way conform to the principle that has been worked out, it is obviously impracticable to trace that principle in its more ramified applications. Nor is it needful to our argument that it should be so traced. The foregoing facts sufficiently prove that what we regard as the distinctive traits of song, are simply the traits of emotional speech intensified and systematised. In respect of its general characteristics, we think it has been made clear that vocal music, and by consequence all music, is an idealisation of the natural language of passion.

As far as it goes, the scanty evidence furnished by history confirms this conclusion. Note first the fact (not properly an historical one, but fitly grouped with such) that the dance-chants of savage tribes are very monotonous; and in virtue of their monotony are much more nearly allied to ordinary speech than are the songs of civilised races. Joining with this the fact that there are still extant among boatmen and others in the East, ancient chants of a like monotonous character, we may infer that vocal music originally diverged from emotional speech in a gradual, unobtrusive manner; and this is the inference to which our argument points. Further evidence to the same effect is supplied by Greek history. The early poems of the Greeks—which, be it remembered, were sacred legends embodied in that rhythmical, metaphorical language which strong feeling excites—were not recited, but chanted: the tones and the cadences were made musical by the same influences which made the speech poetical.

By those who have investigated the matter, this chanting is believed to have been not what we call singing, but nearly allied to our recitative (far simpler indeed, if we may judge from the fact that the early Greek lyre, which had but *four* strings, was played in *unison* with the voice, which was therefore confined to four notes), and as such, much less remote from common speech than our own singing is. For recitative, or musical recitation, is in all respects intermediate between speech and song. Its average effects are not so *loud* as those of song. Its tones are less sonorous in *timbre* than those of song. Commonly it diverges to a smaller extent from the middle notes—uses notes neither so high nor so low in *pitch*. The *intervals* habitual to it are neither so wide nor so varied. Its *rate of variation* is not so rapid. And at the same time that its primary *rhythm* is less decided, it has none of that secondary rhythm produced by recurrence of the same or parallel musical phrases, which is one of the marked characteristics of song. Thus, then, we may not only infer, from the evidence furnished by existing barbarous tribes, that the vocal music of pre-historic times was emotional speech very slightly exalted; but we see that the earliest vocal music of which we have any account differed much less from emotional speech than does the vocal music of our days.

That recitative—beyond which, by the way, the Chinese and Hindoos seem never to have advanced—grew naturally out of the modulations and cadences of strong feeling, we have indeed still current evidence. There are even now to be met with occasions on which strong feeling vents itself in this form. Whoever has been present when a meeting of Quakers was addressed by one of their preachers (whose practice it is to speak only under the influence of religious emotion), must have been struck by the quite unusual tones, like those of a subdued chant, in which the address was made. It is clear, too, that the intoning used in some churches is representative of this same mental state; and has been adopted on account of the instinctively felt congruity between it and the contrition, supplication, or reverence verbally expressed.

And if, as we have good reason to believe, recitative arose by degrees out of emotional speech, it becomes manifest that by a continuance of the same process song has arisen out of recitative. Just as, from the orations and legends of savages, expressed in the metaphorical, allegorical style natural to them, there sprung epic poetry, out of which lyric poetry was afterwards developed; so, from the exalted tones and cadences in which such orations and legends were delivered, came the chant or recitative music, from whence lyrical music has since grown up. And there has not only thus been a simultaneous and parallel genesis, but there is also a parallelism of results. For lyrical poetry differs from epic poetry, just as lyrical music differs from recitative: each still further intensifies the natural language of the emotions. Lyrical poetry is more metaphorical, more hyperbolic, more elliptical, and adds the rhythm of lines to the rhythm of feet; just as lyrical music is louder, more sonorous, more extreme in its intervals, and adds the rhythm of phrases to the rhythm of bars. And the known fact that out of epic poetry the stronger passions developed lyrical poetry as their appropriate vehicle, strengthens the inference that they similarly developed lyrical music out of recitative.

Nor indeed are we without evidences of the transition. It needs but to listen to an opera to hear the leading gradations. Between the comparatively level recitative of ordinary dialogue, the more varied recitative with wider intervals and higher tones used in exciting scenes, the still more musical recitative which preludes an air, and the air itself, the successive steps are but small; and the fact that among airs themselves gradations of like nature may be traced, further confirms the conclusion that the highest form of vocal music was arrived at by degrees.

Moreover, we have some clue to the influences which have induced this development; and may roughly conceive the process of it. As the tones, intervals, and cadences of strong emotion were the elements out of which song was elaborated, so we may expect to find that still stronger emotion produced the elaboration: and we have evidence implying this. Instances in abundance may be cited, showing that musical composers are men of extremely acute sensibilities. The Life of Mozart depicts him as one of intensely active affections and highly impressionable temperament. Various anecdotes represent Beethoven as very susceptible and very passionate. Mendelssohn is described by those who knew him to have been full of fine feeling. And the almost incredible sensitiveness of Chopin has been illustrated in the memoirs of George Sand. An unusually emotional nature being thus the general characteristic of musical composers, we have in it just the agency required for the development of recitative and song. Intenser feeling producing intenser manifestations, any cause of excitement will call forth from such a nature tones and changes of voice more marked than those called forth from an ordinary nature—will generate just those exaggerations which we have found to distinguish the lower vocal music from emotional speech, and the higher vocal music from the lower. Thus it becomes credible that the four-toned recitative of the early Greek poets (like all poets, nearly allied to composers in the comparative intensity of their feelings), was really nothing more than the slightly exaggerated emotional speech natural to them, which grew by frequent use into an organised form. And it is readily conceivable that the accumulated agency of subsequent poet-musicians, inheriting and adding to the products of those who went before them, sufficed, in the course of the ten centuries which we know it took, to develop this four-toned recitative into a vocal music having a range of two octaves.

Not only may we so understand how more sonorous tones, greater extremes of pitch, and wider intervals, were gradually introduced; but also how there arose a greater variety and complexity of musical expression. For this same passionate, enthusiastic temperament, which naturally leads the musical composer to express the feelings possessed by others as well as himself, in extremer intervals and more marked cadences than they would use, also leads him to give musical utterance to feelings which they either do not experience, or experience in but slight degrees.

In virtue of this general susceptibility which distinguishes him, he regards with emotion, events, scenes, conduct, character, which produce upon most men no appreciable effect. The emotions so generated, compounded as they are of the simpler emotions, are not expressible by intervals and cadences natural to these, but by combinations of such intervals and cadences: whence arise more involved musical phrases, conveying more complex, subtle, and unusual feelings. And thus we may in some measure understand how it happens that music not only so strongly excites our more familiar feelings, but also produces feelings we never had before—arouses dormant sentiments of which we had not conceived the possibility and do not know the meaning; or, as Richter says—tells us of things we have not seen and shall not see.

Indirect evidences of several kinds remain to be briefly pointed out. One of them is the difficulty, not to say impossibility, of otherwise accounting for the expressiveness of music. Whence comes it that special combinations of notes should have special effects upon our emotions?—that one should give us a feeling of exhilaration, another of melancholy, another of affection, another of reverence? Is it that these special combinations have intrinsic meanings apart from the human constitution?—that a certain number of aerial waves per second, followed by a certain other number, in the nature of things signify grief, while in the reverse order they signify joy; and similarly with all other intervals, phrases, and cadences? Few will be so irrational as to think this. Is it, then, that the meanings of these special combinations are conventional only?—that we learn their implications, as we do those of words, by observing how others understand them? This is an hypothesis not only devoid of evidence, but directly opposed to the experience of every one. How, then, are musical effects to be explained? If the theory above set forth be accepted, the difficulty disappears. If music, taking for its raw material the various modifications of voice which are the physiological results of excited feelings, intensifies, combines, and complicates them—if it exaggerates the loudness, the resonance, the pitch, the intervals, and the variability, which, in virtue of an organic law, are the characteristics of passionate speech—if, by carrying out these further, more consistently, more unitedly, and more sustainedly, it produces an idealised language of emotion; then its power over us becomes comprehensible. But in the absence of this theory, the expressiveness of music appears to be inexplicable.

Again, the preference we feel for certain qualities of sound presents a like difficulty, admitting only of a like solution. It is generally agreed that the tones of the human voice are more pleasing than any others. Grant that music takes its rise from the modulations of the human voice under emotion, and it becomes a natural consequence that the tones of that voice should appeal to our feelings more than any others; and so should be considered more beautiful than any others. But deny that music has this origin, and the only alternative is the untenable position that the vibrations proceeding from a vocalist's throat are, objectively considered, of a higher order than those from a horn or a violin. Similarly with harsh and soft sounds. If the conclusiveness of the foregoing reasonings be not admitted, it must be supposed that the vibrations causing the last are intrinsically better than those causing the first; and that, in virtue of some pre-established harmony, the higher feelings and natures produce the one, and the lower the other. But if the foregoing reasonings be valid, it follows, as a matter of course, that we shall like the sounds that habitually accompany agreeable feelings, and dislike those that habitually accompany disagreeable feelings.

Once more, the question—How is the expressiveness of music to be otherwise accounted for? may be supplemented by the question—How is the genesis of music to be otherwise accounted for? That music is a product of civilisation is manifest; for though savages have their dance-chants, these are of a kind scarcely to be dignified by the title musical: at most, they supply but the vaguest rudiment of music, properly so called. And if music has been by slow steps developed in the course of civilisation, it must have been developed out of something. If, then, its origin is not that above alleged, what is its origin?

Thus we find that the negative evidence confirms the positive, and that, taken together, they furnish strong proof. We have seen that there is a physiological relation, common to man and all animals, between feeling and muscular action; that as vocal sounds are produced by muscular action, there is a consequent physiological relation between feeling and vocal sounds; that all the modifications of voice expressive of feeling are the direct results of this physiological relation; that music, adopting all these modifications, intensifies them more and more as it ascends to its higher and higher forms, and becomes music simply in virtue of thus intensifying them; that, from the ancient epic poet chanting his verses, down to the modern musical composer, men of unusually strong feelings prone to express them in extreme forms, have been naturally the agents of these successive intensifications; and that so there has little by little arisen a wide divergence between this idealised language of emotion and its natural language: to which direct evidence we have just added the indirect—that on no other tenable hypothesis can either the expressiveness or the genesis of music be explained.

And now, what is the *function* of music? Has music any effect beyond the immediate pleasure it produces? Analogy suggests that it has. The enjoyments of a good dinner do not end with themselves, but minister to bodily well-being. Though people do not marry with a view to maintain the race, yet the passions which impel them to marry secure its maintenance. Parental affection is a feeling which, while it conduces to parental happiness, ensures the nurture of offspring. Men love to accumulate property, often without thought of the benefits it produces; but in pursuing the pleasure of acquisition they indirectly open the way to other pleasures. The wish for public approval impels all of us to do many things which we should otherwise not do,—to undertake great labours, face great dangers, and habitually rule ourselves in a way that smooths social intercourse: that is, in gratifying our love of approbation we subserve divers ulterior purposes. And, generally, our nature is such that in fulfilling each desire, we in some way facilitate the fulfilment of the rest. But the love of music seems to exist for its own sake. The delights of melody and harmony do not obviously minister to the welfare either of the individual or of society. May we not suspect, however, that this exception is apparent only? Is it not a rational inquiry—What are the indirect benefits which accrue from music, in addition to the direct pleasure it gives?

But that it would take us too far out of our track, we should prelude this inquiry by illustrating at some length a certain general law of progress;—the law that alike in occupations, sciences, arts, the divisions that had a common root, but by continual divergence have become distinct, and are now being separately developed, are not truly independent, but severally act and react on each other to their mutual advancement. Merely hinting thus much, however, by way of showing that there are many analogies to justify us, we go on to express the opinion that there exists a relationship of this kind between music and speech.

All speech is compounded of two elements, the words and the tones in which they are uttered—the signs of ideas and the signs of feelings. While certain articulations express the thought, certain vocal sounds express the more or less of pain or pleasure which the thought gives. Using the word *cadence* in an unusually extended sense, as comprehending all modifications of voice, we may say that *cadence is the commentary of the emotions upon the propositions of the intellect*. The duality of spoken language, though not formally recognised, is recognised in practice by every one; and every one knows that very often more weight attaches to the tones than to the words. Daily experience supplies cases in which the same sentence of disapproval will be understood as meaning little or meaning much, according to the inflections of voice which accompany it; and daily experience supplies still more striking cases in which words and tones are in direct contradiction—the first expressing consent, while the last express reluctance; and the last being believed rather than the first.

These two distinct but interwoven elements of speech have been undergoing a simultaneous development. We know that in the course of civilisation words have been multiplied, new parts of speech have been introduced, sentences have grown more varied and complex; and we may fairly infer that during the same time new modifications of voice have come into use, fresh intervals have been adopted, and cadences have become more elaborate. For while, on the one hand, it is absurd to suppose that, along with the undeveloped verbal forms of barbarism, there existed a developed system of vocal inflections; it is, on the other hand, necessary to suppose that, along with the higher and more numerous verbal forms needed to convey the multiplied and complicated ideas of civilised life, there have grown up those more involved changes of voice which express the feelings proper to such ideas. If intellectual language is a growth, so also, without doubt, is emotional language a growth.

Now, the hypothesis which we have hinted above, is, that beyond the direct pleasure which it gives, music has the indirect effect of developing this language of the emotions. Having its root, as we have endeavoured to show, in those tones, intervals, and cadences of speech which express feeling—arising by the combination and intensifying of these, and coming finally to have an embodiment of its own—music has all along been reacting upon speech, and increasing its power of rendering emotion. The use in recitative and song of inflections more expressive than ordinary ones, must from the beginning have tended to develop the ordinary ones. Familiarity with the more varied combinations of tones that occur in vocal music can scarcely have failed to give greater variety of combination to the tones in which we utter our impressions and desires. The complex musical phrases by which composers have conveyed complex emotions, may rationally be supposed to have influenced us in making those involved cadences of conversation by which we convey our subtler thoughts and feelings.

That the cultivation of music has no effect on the mind, few will be absurd enough to contend. And if it has an effect, what more natural effect is there than this of developing our perception of the meanings of inflections, qualities, and modulations of voice; and giving us a correspondingly increased power of using them? Just as mathematics, taking its start from the phenomena of physics and astronomy, and presently coming to be a separate science, has since reacted on physics and astronomy to their immense advancement—just as chemistry, first arising out of the processes of metallurgy and the industrial arts, and gradually growing into an independent study, has now become an aid to all kinds of production—just as physiology, originating out of medicine and once subordinate to it, but latterly pursued for its own sake, is in our day coming to be the science on which the progress of medicine depends;—so, music, having its root in emotional language, and gradually evolved from it, has ever been reacting upon and further advancing it. Whoever will examine the facts will find this hypothesis to be in harmony with the method of civilisation everywhere displayed.

It will scarcely be expected that much direct evidence in support of this conclusion can be given. The facts are of a kind which it is difficult to measure, and of which we have no records. Some suggestive traits, however, may be noted. May we not say, for instance, that the Italians, among whom modern music was earliest cultivated, and who have more especially practised and excelled in melody (the division of music with which our argument is chiefly concerned)—may we not say that these Italians speak in more varied and expressive inflections and cadences than any other nation? On the other hand, may we not say that, confined almost exclusively as they have hitherto been to their national airs, which have a marked family likeness, and therefore accustomed to but a limited range of musical expression, the Scotch are unusually monotonous in the intervals and modulations of their speech? And again, do we not find among different classes of the same nation, differences that have like implications? The gentleman and the clown stand in a very decided contrast with respect to variety of intonation. Listen to the conversation of a servant-girl, and then to that of a refined, accomplished lady, and the more delicate and complex changes of voice used by the latter will be conspicuous. Now, without going so far as to say that out of all the differences of culture to which the upper and lower classes are subjected, difference of musical culture is that to which alone this difference of speech is ascribable, yet we may fairly say that there seems a much more obvious connection of cause and effect between these than between any others. Thus, while the inductive evidence to which we can appeal is but scanty and vague, yet what there is favours our position.

Probably most will think that the function here assigned to music is one of very little moment. But further reflection may lead them to a contrary conviction. In its bearings upon human happiness, we believe that this emotional language which musical culture develops and refines is only second in importance to the language of the intellect; perhaps not even second to it. For these modifications of voice produced by feelings are the means of exciting like feelings in others. Joined with gestures and expressions of face, they give life to the otherwise dead words in which the intellect utters its ideas; and so enable the hearer not only to *understand* the state of mind they accompany, but to *partake* of that state. In short, they are the chief media of *sympathy*. And if we consider how much both our general welfare and our immediate pleasures depend upon sympathy, we shall recognise the importance of whatever makes this sympathy greater. If we bear in mind that by their fellow-feeling men are led to behave justly, kindly, and considerately to each other—that the difference between the cruelty of the barbarous and the humanity of the civilised, results from the increase of fellow-feeling; if we bear in mind that this faculty which makes us sharers in the joys and sorrows of others, is the basis of all the higher affections—that in friendship, love, and all domestic pleasures, it is an essential element; if we bear in mind how much our direct gratifications are intensified by sympathy,—how, at the theatre, the concert, the picture gallery, we lose half our enjoyment if we have no one to enjoy with us; if, in short, we bear in mind that for all happiness beyond what the unfriended recluse can have, we are indebted to this same sympathy;—we shall see that the agencies which communicate it can scarcely be overrated in value.

The tendency of civilisation is more and more to repress the antagonistic elements of our characters and to develop the social ones—to curb our purely selfish desires and exercise our unselfish ones—to replace private gratifications by gratifications resulting from, or involving, the happiness of others. And while, by this adaptation to the social state, the sympathetic side of our nature is being unfolded, there is simultaneously growing up a language of sympathetic intercourse—a language through which we communicate to others the happiness we feel, and are made sharers in their happiness.

This double process, of which the effects are already sufficiently appreciable, must go on to an extent of which we can as yet have no adequate conception. The habitual concealment of our feelings diminishing, as it must, in proportion as our feelings become such as do not demand concealment, we may conclude that the exhibition of them will become much more vivid than we now dare allow it to be; and this implies a more expressive emotional language. At the same time, feelings of a higher and more complex kind, as yet experienced only by the cultivated few, will become general; and there will be a corresponding development of the emotional language into more involved forms. Just as there has silently grown up a language of ideas, which, rude as it at first was, now enables us to convey with precision the most subtle and complicated thoughts; so, there is still silently growing up a language of feelings, which, notwithstanding its present imperfection, we may expect will ultimately enable men vividly and completely to impress on each other all the emotions which they experience from moment to moment.

Thus if, as we have endeavoured to show, it is the function of music to facilitate the development of this emotional language, we may regard music as an aid to the achievement of that higher happiness which it indistinctly shadows forth. Those vague feelings of unexperienced felicity which music arouses—those indefinite impressions of an unknown ideal life which it calls up, may be considered as a prophecy, to the fulfilment of which music is itself partly instrumental. The strange capacity which we have for being so affected by melody and harmony may be taken to imply both that it is within the possibilities of our nature to realise those intenser delights they dimly suggest, and that they are in some way concerned in the realisation of them. On this supposition the power and the meaning of music become comprehensible; but otherwise they are a mystery.

We will only add, that if the probability of these corollaries be admitted, then music must take rank as he highest of the fine arts—as the one which, more than any other, ministers to human welfare. And thus, even leaving out of view the immediate gratifications it is hourly giving, we cannot too much applaud that progress of musical culture which is becoming one of the characteristics of our age.

Lector House believes that a society develops through a two-fold approach of continuous learning and adaptation, which is derived from the study of classic literary works spread across the historic timeline of literature records. Therefore, we aim at reviving, repairing and redeveloping all those inaccessible or damaged but historically as well as culturally important literature across subjects so that the future generations may have an opportunity to study and learn from past works to embark upon a journey of creating a better future.

This book is a result of an effort made by Lector House towards making a contribution to the preservation and repair of original ancient works which might hold historical significance to the approach of continuous learning across subjects.

HAPPY READING & LEARNING!

LECTOR HOUSE LLP
E-MAIL: lectorpublishing@gmail.com

www.ingramcontent.com/pod-product-compliance
Lightning Source LLC
LaVergne TN
LVHW090004200726
843493LV00004B/757